BUSINESS COMMUNICATION

BUSINESS
COMMUNICATION

A PROBLEM-SOLVING
APPROACH

FOURTH EDITION

Roy W. Poe
Rosemary T. Fruehling

Sponsoring Editor: **Mark B. Moscowitz**
Editing Supervisor: **Nicola von Schreiber**
Design and Art Supervisor: **Meri Shardin**
Production Supervisor: **Mirabel Flores**

Interior Design: **PLK Graphics Inc.**
Cover Design: **Renee Kilbride Edelman**
Technical Studio: **Burmar Technical Corp.**

Library of Congress Cataloging-in-Publication Data
Poe, Roy W.
    Business communication: a problem-solving approach/Roy W. Poe,
Rosemary T. Fruehling—4th ed.
      p. cm.
    Includes index.
    ISBN 1-56118-317-2
    1. Commercial correspondence. 2. Business writing 3. Business
communication. I. Fruehling, Rosemary T. II. Title
HF5721.P6 1989
651.7'4—dc 19   88-21080
                                  CIP

Business Communication: A Problem-Solving Approach
Fourth Edition

CONTENTS

Preface   vii

PART ONE   WRITING BUSINESS LETTERS   1

Chapter 1: What an Effective Business Letter Is—and Is Not   4

Chapter 2: Building Goodwill Through Business Letters   14

Chapter 3: Writing Person to Person   29

Chapter 4: Making Your Letters Easy and Interesting to Read   42

Chapter 5: Making Your Letters Persuasive   59

Chapter 6: Request Letters   82
Case 1: Requesting Free Materials   82
Case 2: Requesting Product Information   86
Case 3: Requesting an Appointment   89
Case 4: Requesting a Routine Favor   93
Case 5: Requesting a Special Favor   97
Case 6: Requesting the Services of a Speaker   101

Chapter 7: Response Letters   106
Case 1: Responding Favorably to a Product Inquiry   106
Case 2: Explaining a Pricing Policy to a Prospective Buyer   110
Case 3: Responding to "Problem" Letters   114
Case 4: Responding With a Gentle "No"   120

Chapter 8: Transmittal and Confirmation Letters   125
Case 1: Transmittal Letters   125
Case 2: Confirmation Letters   130

Chapter 9: Sales and Sales-Promotion Letters   136
Case 1: Writing a Sales Letter   136
Case 2: Following Up an Inquiry   144
Case 3: Welcoming a New Customer   147
Case 4: Winning Back Former Customers   151

Chapter 10: Customer-to-Supplier Letters   156
Case 1: Placing Orders With Suppliers   156
Case 2: Thanking a Supplier for a Special Favor   159
Case 3: Customer Not Given an Expected Discount   162
Case 4: Customer Dissatisfied With Merchandise   165
Case 5: Customer Complains About a Delay in Shipment   169

Chapter 11: Supplier-to-Customer Letters   173
Case 1: Thanking a Customer for an Order   173
Case 2: Customer Takes an Unearned Discount   178
Case 3: Customer Returns Unsalable Merchandise   181
Case 4: Granting and Refusing Credit to Customers   186
Case 5: Collecting Money Due From a Customer   190

Chapter 12: Administrative Communications   197
Case 1: Responding in the Executive's Absence   197
Case 2: Using Discretion in Writing for an Executive   203
Case 3: Referring Communications to Others   206
Case 4: Writing on Behalf of and for the Executive   211

Chapter 13: Public Relations Letters   215
Case 1: Thanking a Correspondent for Favorable Comments   215
Case 2: Apologizing for Inconveniences   218
Case 3: Saying "No" to a Request That Cannot Be Granted   221
Case 4: Handling Requests to Make a Donation or Purchase Advertising   224
Case 5: Responding to a Request That Violates Company Policy   230
Case 6: Responding to a Critic   235

Chapter 14: Human Resources Communications   241
Case 1: Responding to Job Applications   241
Case 2: Confirming a Job Offer   249
Case 3: Letters of Congratulation and Appreciation to Employees   254
Case 4: Congratulating a Coworker on a Promotion   258
Case 5: Writing Letters of Sympathy   262
Case 6: Writing a Reference Letter   265

Chapter 15: Employment Communications   271
Case 1: Assessing and Conveying Your Qualifications   271
Case 2: Writing the Application Letter   283
Case 3: Thanking the Interviewer   290
Case 4: Accepting a Job Offer   293
Case 5: Resigning From a Position—Better Opportunity   298
Case 6: Resigning From a Position—Dissatisfaction   301

PART TWO WRITING EFFECTIVE MEMORANDUMS   307

Chapter 16: Everyday Memorandums   312
Case 1: Writing a Transmittal Memorandum   312
Case 2: Writing a Request Memorandum   314
Case 3: Writing a Confirmation Memorandum   318
Case 4: Writing an Informational Memorandum   320

PART THREE WRITING EFFECTIVE BUSINESS REPORTS   327

Chapter 17: Basic Guidelines for Writing Reports   329

Chapter 18: Memorandums as Reports   342
Case 1: Writing a Periodic Memorandum Report   342
Case 2: Reporting the Results of an Informal Study   346
Case 3: Presenting Ideas and Suggestions by Memorandum   351
Case 4: Reporting the Minutes of Meetings   356

Chapter 19: Writing Formally Structured Reports   366
Case Problem: Writing a Research Report   366

Chapter 20: Writing at the Computer   377

Index   401

PREFACE

The problem-solving approach to the teaching of business communication was pioneered by the authors in 1973. Since that time other books have featured a variation of this method, although we naturally feel that none has succeeded so well, an opinion that is supported by a loyal audience of teachers in various colleges and universities throughout the United States and abroad.

MAJOR CONCEPTS

Business Communication, Fourth Edition embraces eight major concepts.

1. *Business communications are highly individualistic and cannot be written to formula.* There is no magic formula for writing a good letter, memorandum, or report. Individual writers approach a communication situation differently, and each produces a unique communication, depending on how they feel about their job and the information to be communicated, their relationship to the reader, and the attitudes and policies of the organization they represent.

2. *To produce effective communications, students should be involved as deeply as possible in each writing situation.* It is extremely important that students really care about the results of their communications. This is very difficult to bring about when assignments are presented as abstract situations in which students feel only a bystander role. To implement this involvement, the authors ask students to imagine themselves in various positions—assistant office manager, sales training supervisor, administrative assistant, director of publicity, and so on—thus approaching each communication problem as a participant rather than as an onlooker. Each case is constructed around a role-playing situation; this is effectively demonstrated in the "Your Job" and Supplementary Projects at the end of each chapter or case.

3. *Examples of letters and reports are most effective when related to situations with which students are familiar.* In the typical textbook, students are shown primarily "good" examples of communications—and always in situations unrelated to the student's experience. In *Business Communication, Fourth Edition*, students have a direct involvement in the case problems, and the examples are possible solutions to these problems; the examples offer one or more "wrong" solutions, with analyses, and one or more recommended solutions, again with analyses. This device, the authors believe, is much superior to narrative presentation of "rules" followed by an abstract illustration of the rules.

4. *Most of the challenging communications faced by the writer on the job are those that require choosing between alternatives—which may be only unpleasant or less than cheerful alternatives.* Many students have been taught that every communication must be friendly, tactful, positive, and goodwill-engendering. Although this is true for many letters and memorandums, as a generalization it is idealistic. Writers face many problems that arise out of human error, misunderstandings, and carelessness, and students should be prepared to deal with them. Thus numerous situations are given in which the student,

as a writer-entrepreneur, must say no, apologize for mistakes of fellow employees, reprimand recalcitrant customers and suppliers, and take the hard line when there is no recourse.

5. *Students should be given the opportunity to read a great many business letters on various subjects before starting to write.* Few students have been exposed to typical communications that flow in and out of all business and government offices, so in the opening chapters this opportunity is offered. Here we describe the role of communications in business and the "rules" that determine their effectiveness before students actually start to write letters. By reading and analyzing successful letters at the outset, students are, we think, better prepared to understand the presentation of practical writing projects that follow in later chapters.

6. *Since the typical employee writes as many as if not more memorandums than letters, memorandums should be given thorough coverage in a business communication course. Business Communication, Fourth Edition,* introduces the memorandum briefly early and later devotes two complete chapters to the topic—Everyday Memorandums (Chapter 16) and Memorandums as Reports (Chapter 18).

7. *Human relations should be a constant theme in a business communication course.* Good writing is largely the application of effective human and sound management principles to communication situations. The qualities that are common to outstanding managers and executives are also present in good communicators. Fundamental is a feeling for the individual—daily practice of the old axiom, "Do unto others...." This principle has always been stressed in this program and is continued in the Fourth Edition.

8. *Some students enter the business communication course somewhat rusty in the matter of English style and usage, and this topic should be presented early in the course and reviewed frequently.* Proper and concise word usage is a must in effective communications. It has become increasingly important in this rapidly emerging electronic age, where one improper usage can cause endless errors and often create ill will. To emphasize word usage, we include specific coverage on avoiding "businessese," "computerese," "federalese," clichés, euphemisms, slang, exaggeration, jargon, and other faults that can destroy effectiveness. In addition, starting with the cases in Chapter 6, Style Checkup exercises require students to apply the principles of style learned previously in their education to their newly developed skills as business writers.

SOME FEATURES OF THE FOURTH EDITION

Following are some of the major features of the new edition.

- Chapters 1 through 4 have been substantially rewritten. Although the objectives and general treatment of the fundamentals have been retained, the material has been "spiced up," thus adding more excitement for the learner.
- Two new chapters have been added to the Fourth Edition: Customer-to-Supplier Letters (Chapter 10) and Supplier-to-Customer Letters (Chapter 11). We think of these chapters as the *core* of business communications, since many if not most business letters are written by customers to suppliers and suppliers to customers.
- Another important chapter that has been added is Public Relations Letters (Chapter 13). Some of these communications appeared in earlier editions; however, for the sake of emphasis we have given them an "umbrella" all their own.
- A change in nomenclature should be noted. The old Personnel Communications chapter has been retitled Human Resources Communications (Chapter 14) and the term "human resources" is used instead of "personnel." This reflects the modern tendency for business firms to classify their employees as human resources rather than as personnel, to give workers more dignity.

- Although the memorandum form of business communications is introduced early in the Fourth Edition, full treatment of these very important letters is given in two chapters toward the end of the book (Chapters 16 and 18).
- Another new chapter is Writing at the Computer (Chapter 20). Writing at the computer is becoming more common as word processing equipment finds its way into more offices. In this chapter we present the advantages of using the computer for composition, along with the techniques employed to produce more meaningful communications.

THE WORKBOOK

The *Workbook for Business Communication, Fourth Edition,* is carefully integrated, chapter by chapter and case by case, with the textbook and provides supplementary practice in writing letters, memorandums, and reports. The workbook emphasizes analyzing communications, editing and revising weak communications, and restructuring and simplifying garbled and incoherent messages. In many instances, letterheads and inter-office forms are provided. A special feature of the workbook is a section for each case entitled English Usage Revisited. These drills provide practice in dealing with over 90 common problems in punctuation, capitalization, sentence structure, possessives, word usage, spelling, and grammar.

INSTRUCTOR'S MANUAL AND KEY

The *Instructor's Manual and Key* contains purpose and teaching suggestions and the key to both the textbook and workbook. It also includes for review purposes English usage tests on punctuation, capitalization, sentence structure, possessives, word usage, spelling, and grammar. The key to these tests is included in the Manual.

ACKNOWLEDGMENTS

The authors wish to thank the dozens of educators and businesspeople interviewed for this course. Special gratitude is extended to the following educators who gave unselfishly of their time and experience to review and critique the course in detail: Barbara Ann Henry, Barclay College, Sacramento, California; Sonja H. Litton, King's College, Charlotte, North Carolina; Mary Jane Malizioso, Trocaire College, Buffalo, New York; Anne M. O'Brien, Castle Junior College, Windham, New Hampshire; Gertrude A. Siptroth, Criss College, Anaheim, California; and Suzanne R. Varisco, Fisher College, Boston, Massachusetts.

Roy W. Poe
Rosemary T. Fruehling

PART ONE

WRITING BUSINESS LETTERS

Letters are sometimes referred to as substitutes for personal visits. Most people find it impossible to meet and talk with everyone with whom they want to communicate—whether friends or relatives who live in a distant town, fellow employees just three doors or floors away, or customers, clients, and suppliers who are scattered everywhere. And the telephone is not always a satisfactory means of communication. Thus all of us must depend on letters to represent us.

This fact alone makes letters a powerful medium of communication in all walks of life. But even if we could handle all our business and social communications on a face-to-face basis, we would still need to prepare written messages. One reason is that we often need a permanent record of what was said, to whom, by whom, and on what date. Equally if not more important is that written communications can often do a far better job than spoken communications. We'll demonstrate that last statement many, many times throughout this book.

THE ROLE OF LETTERS IN BUSINESS

What do we mean when we use the term *letter*? Of course, you know that it is a written message from one individual or organization to another individual or organization. However, there are really two types of letters used in business:

1. Those addressed to people outside one's own organization. (In this book, when we speak of *business letters* or simply *letters*, we are referring to this type.)
2. Those addressed to people within one's own organization. (These may be thought of as interoffice letters, although they are usually called *memorandums* or simply *memos*.)

The distinction between letters that are sent to outsiders and those sent to fellow employees is arbitrary, since the content, language, and tone are quite similar. In many instances, the only real difference is in format (setup), as you will see later.

Businesses use written communications in dozens of different ways. Six of the most important uses of both *business letters* and *memorandums* are to:

- Ask for and supply information and services.
- Confirm agreements made and decisions reached.
- Transmit important documents and other materials.
- Obtain and grant special favors.
- Establish and maintain a favorable image (picture) of the organization.
- Promote effective personnel relations.

Business letters, however, have four additional uses, unique to themselves, which are to:

- Promote the sale of merchandise or services.
- Arrange for the purchase or sale of goods and services on both cash and credit bases.
- Collect money due from customers and clients who purchase on credit.
- Develop and maintain good relations with customers, clients, suppliers, and the public at large.

BUSINESS COMMUNICATIONS IN YOUR FUTURE

There are many reasons why you should know how to write effective business communications. In the first place, your value to the organization you work for will be greatly enhanced, which often means more rapid progress up the promotion ladder. Competent writers are not as plentiful as you might imagine, and those who write well stand out like a beacon.

Second, those who can compose effective business letters make new friends and keep old ones for the organization, thereby increasing sales and profits, which all businesses need for survival.

Third, good writers can save a great deal of time, effort, and money for an organization. Millions of dollars are wasted each year by people who write windy and garbled messages that exhaust and befuddle their readers.

Finally, your rating as an employee—which hinges greatly on your skill in working harmoniously with the people around you—shoots up dramatically when you master the art of writing sensible, tactful, and finely honed memorandums.

How Much Writing?

How heavy will your writing responsibilities be? The answer to that question depends, of course, on what your job is. If you are a supervisor or manager with a number of people reporting to you, or if you have the responsibility for building and maintaining effective customer and public relations, your writing duties are apt to be quite heavy. Too, the types of communications you produce will depend largely on your position and field of work. Customer-service people are likely to spend most of their working day writing letters to customers. Many of them produce very few memos. On the other hand, an accountant or data processing manager usually writes only a few business letters but composes large quantities of memos. For others—say, marketing, human resources, or purchasing managers—the number of letters written is often about the same as the number of memos.

Does It Really Matter?

You might think that the job you are aiming at will require very little writing ability, and you could be right. But remember that a great many people accept positions quite far removed from their college major. Even if they enter the field in which they were specifically trained, there's no guarantee that they will stay in it. They may discover that the work isn't their cup of tea after all, or perhaps they will receive opportunities outside their field that are just too attractive to pass up. And don't forget that really good people get promoted. For example, more and more men and women who were trained to be accountants are being selected for high executive positions that embrace all facets of business management, including that of company president. In the rarefied atmosphere of the executive suite, writing skill is an absolute must!

CHAPTER 1

WHAT AN EFFECTIVE BUSINESS LETTER IS—AND IS NOT

What makes a letter effective? One definition might be:

A letter is *effective* when it achieves the writer's purpose.

For example, assume that you wrote a letter to a customer to collect money that is overdue. Then, as a result of your letter, the customer sent in the payment. Your letter would be considered effective because it achieved its goal.

Often, however, a letter has more than one goal. When writing to collect an overdue payment from a customer, you have an obvious *primary goal:* to get the customer to pay quickly. At the same time, you also have this *secondary goal:* to retain the customer's goodwill and future business. In this case, receiving the customer's payment is only one way to judge the effectiveness of the letter. Receiving the customer's *continued business* is another way to evaluate the success of the letter.

As you see, then, the *reader's reaction* determines whether the letter is truly effective. The reader's reaction to the letter, not the writer's opinion of the letter, is the final judge. Therefore, writing effective letters depends strongly on your ability to establish a positive personal relationship with each reader.

To develop a positive personal relationship, focus on the reader's need for individual attention. Remember that you are always writing to a person, not to a machine. Treat and address that person with understanding and friendliness, and talk with your reader in a professional manner. How do you show that you are understanding, friendly, and professional? By choosing words, building sentences, and constructing paragraphs that are suited to each reader and to each situation.

With this information, we can now update our definition as follows:

A letter is effective when the reader reacts positively to the writer's goals.

This text presents a special system for writing letters that relies on your own ability to develop a positive personal relationship with each reader. As you will see later in this chapter, there are *no* "magic formulas" for doing so!

WHY FORMULAS DON'T WORK

Imagine following a script to talk with a friend or a business acquaintance: "First say this, next say that, then say...." Will such a script express your feelings in all cases? Will it reflect the unique relationship you have with each individual person? No matter how well written the script may be, it will not be helpful in all cases.

Formulas are perfect for computing compound interest and figuring tax payments, and recipes are great for duplicating gourmet dishes. However, formulas and recipes cannot be used to control or predict your personal relationships. Repeating a canned script simply does not allow you to show that you are understanding, friendly, and professional.

Of course, the "writing formulas" presented in many texts certainly do have some merit. Consider, for example, these often-quoted steps in writing formulas:

1. State the purpose of your letter immediately.
2. Make the first paragraph as short as possible.
3. Be brief—say no more than is necessary.
4. End the letter quickly—don't waste the reader's time.

For many letter writing situations, following these steps will surely present a sound letter. For example:

```
Dear Ms. Hargrove:

Thank you for returning the signed leasing agree-
ment for the Danville Square warehouse.

The building is now ready for occupancy, and you
may begin using it whenever you wish.

                    Yours very cordially,


Ladies and Gentlemen:

Please send me complete information about your
group insurance plan, which was advertised in the
June issue of Fortune.

                    Sincerely yours,
```

While the four-step formula works well in these two cases, not every letter writing situation is so simple. In most situations the formula will be inappropriate because it does not take into consideration:

1. Your individual style in expressing yourself.
2. Your relationship with each reader.
3. Each unique situation.
4. Your specific objective(s).

Your Individual Style

You express your individual style and your personal tastes naturally in many of the things you do, and you should also do so in your letter writing. For instance, in Case Example 1 on page 6, note how five different people responded to the same request in their own individual styles.

Case Example 1
Responding to a Request

Situation   Cosmotron Computers Inc. manufactures and distributes a complete line of personal computers and computer peripherals. Whenever the company receives a request for information about its products, it is naturally eager to reply with a personal letter (plus a product brochure and a list of authorized Cosmotron dealers). Note how five different Cosmotron staff members responded to the same request for information.

A

Dear Ms. Brooke:

I'm pleased to send you a brochure describing the complete line of Cosmotron computers, along with a list of authorized Cosmotron dealers in your area.

Thank you for your interest in our products.

                        Sincerely yours,

B

Dear Ms. Brooke:

A brochure describing Cosmotron computers is enclosed, together with a list of Cosmotron dealers in your area. It is a pleasure to send these materials to you. Please let me know if you should need any further information.

                        Sincerely yours,

C

Dear Ms. Brooke:

Enclosed is a brochure describing the complete line of Cosmotron computers, as well as a list of the authorized dealers in your area. Thank you for requesting this information.

If you have any questions or need any other information on our products, please call me toll free at 1-800-555-7500.

                        Sincerely yours,

D

Dear Ms. Brooke:

Here are the materials you requested--a brochure describing the complete line of Cosmotron com-

puters and a list of authorized Cosmotron dealers
in your area.

If you should need any further information on
Cosmotron products, please be sure to contact me.

Sincerely yours,

E Dear Ms. Brooke:

We are very pleased to send you the enclosed brochure, which describes all the computers that
Cosmotron offers. Also enclosed is a list of all
the authorized Cosmotron dealers in your area.

Thank you for requesting this information.

Sincerely,

Analysis Let's analyze these five letters to determine which is "best."

1. Is each letter courteous and accurate? Yes, each letter responds to Ms. Brooke's specific request courteously and accurately. Each letter does the job very well.
2. Is each letter written in the same style? No, each letter has its own unique style, a style that reflects the individual writer in each case. Thus you see that good writers are not cast from a single mold. Each writer has a unique style for expressing his or her own personality.

The Writer-Reader Relationship

The content and the tone of a letter is often influenced by the relationship that exists between the writer and the reader, as shown in Case Example 2.

Case Example 2
Requesting Sample Materials
Offered by a Speaker

Situation Assume that you recently attended a convention sponsored by the American Management Society. At one session, "Effective Time-Management Techniques," the speaker discussed a set of videocassettes her company has developed on the topic and offered to send a sample videocassette to anyone who wrote to her. When you returned to your office, you wrote the following letter.

Dear Ms. Havermeyer:

I enjoyed your presentation at the AMS convention

in San Diego last week. I was especially interested in the videocassette program that your company has developed, "Effective Time-Management
Techniques."

Would you please send me the sample videocassette
you mentioned, as well as any descriptive materials that may also be of interest. I would be
very grateful.

> Very sincerely yours,

Your friend Maria Hernandez also wrote for the sample videocassette, but
because she and Ms. Havermeyer are good friends (they went to the same college
and were graduated in the same year), Maria's letter reflects a very different
writer-reader relationship, as you will see below:

Dear Louise:

What a pleasant surprise to see you in San Diego!
I thoroughly enjoyed your presentation on "Effective Time-Management Techniques"--obviously,
so did everyone else in the audience.

As I mentioned, Lou, I'm now the assistant marketing manager for Phoenix Industries, and I've
been searching for new training programs on time
management. The videocassette program you described in your presentation sounds ideally
suited to our needs, and I'm really eager to
learn more about the program. Please send me the
sample videocassette you mentioned and any materials that describe the program.

Remember that you promised you would visit Chicago within the next few weeks. When you do
visit, be sure to leave at least one evening free
for dinner. Then we'll have time to share
"news" about old friends.

Warmest regards.

> Cordially,

Analysis Each letter accomplishes its goal: to request the materials that the
speaker offered. Yet each letter is different—as it should be, of course. Each
letter reflects a unique writer-reader relationship.

1. The first letter appropriately reflects a new, formal business relationship.

2. Maria's letter reflects her relationship with a close friend and former classmate.

No formula for requesting sample materials from a speaker could possibly reflect both relationships!

The Specific Situation

Just as writer-reader relationships differ, so, too, do writing *situations*—another reason why formulas do not work.

Case Example 3
Thanking Two Speakers

Situation   You recently invited speakers to address employees in your company on various management techniques. Now you are ready to send all the speakers checks in appreciation of their efforts, along with personal thank you letters, of course. To Dr. Victoria Tennent, whose presentation was outstanding, you write:

```
Dear Dr. Tennent:

All the employees who attended this year's Man-
agers' Forum are still talking about your superb
speech. Managers at all levels unanimously re-
port that they learned much from your informative
and enjoyable presentation.

Thank you, Dr. Tennent, for sharing your insights
into "Handling Interpersonal Problems" and for
contributing to the success of this year's meet-
ing. As I promised, I have enclosed a modest
honorarium to show our appreciation.

We certainly hope that we will have the privilege
of hearing you again at future Managers' Forums
here at Cornwall Manufacturing. Thank you very
much for being with us.

                         Cordially yours,
```

Another speaker on the same program, Mr. Bartholomew Llewellyn, agreed to substitute at the last minute for someone who canceled suddenly. To Mr. Llewellyn, whose performance was less than satisfactory, you write:

```
Dear Mr. Llewellyn:

We appreciate your taking time from your busy
```

schedule to speak at our annual Managers' Forum--
especially on such short notice.

Mr. Llewellyn, we have enclosed a check for $200
in payment of your services as one of our guest
speakers. The five-day seminar ended yesterday,
and we think that it was quite successful. Thank
you for participating in this meeting.

Cordially yours,

Analysis Both letters are courteous, as they should be, of course, and both letters are sincere. Yet your thank you letters to these two speakers are different because each speaker presents a different situation.

1. The tone of the letter to Dr. Tennent is enthusiastic, reflecting her excellent presentation.
2. The letter to Mr. Llewellyn cannot reflect the same kind of enthusiasm without deliberately lying. The letter to Mr. Llewellyn neither compliments him nor insults him.

Your Specific Objective

Each letter you write has a specific objective, and that objective has an important bearing on both the content and the tone of the letter. The letters in Case Example 4 illustrate this point.

Case Example 4
Reminding Customers of Balances Due

Situation You are the supervisor of the Credit Department for Edison Electronics, a wholesaler of appliances, computers, and electronic equipment. You must write to two different customers to collect money that is overdue.

The first customer is Gladys Eckerly, the owner of and manager of Eckerly's Discount Palace. Mrs Eckerly is a valuable customer. She has been purchasing merchandise on credit from your company for ten years. However, she often needs to be reminded—sometimes three or four times—before she pays the balance of her account. You have sent her two reminders about the $6,420 balance that is currently outstanding; now you decide to write another:

Dear Mrs. Eckerly:

Perhaps you've been so busy that you have forgot-
ten to send us your check for $6,420, the balance
due on your account. I'm getting ready to prepare a schedule of delinquent accounts for our
controller, and I'd really hate to see your name
on the list. (I know that you would, too.) Early

receipt of your check will assure the immediate
removal of your name. <u>Please</u> send your check--
<u>today</u>.

I hope you're having a great summer season!

Sincerely,

Another appliance dealer, Lawrence J. Silver, of Silver's Appliance Warehouse,
applied for and received credit privileges just four months ago. He then purchased
merchandise totaling $5,700 in value, and he has not yet made any payments
toward this outstanding balance. In fact, Mr. Silver has not responded to any of
your three reminders. (The last one was rather blunt.) You want to collect the
money due, and you want to avoid suing him. You write:

Dear Mr. Silver:

When you ordered merchandise from us four months
ago, we delivered the entire order quickly, as
you requested. Now, however, four months later,
you have not made any payment toward the outstanding balance of $5,700. Moreover, you haven't
even responded to my three written reminders or
to the telephone messages I have left you!

Frankly, Mr. Silver, I am greatly puzzled by your
indifference to this obligation. Also, I am
rather concerned about the possible consequences
to your credit rating. Are <u>you</u> equally concerned?

My next step will be rather obvious--and rather
unpleasant. Please avoid that next step by sending us your check by July 21.

Very truly yours,

Analyses   Both letters—the one to Gladys Eckerly and the one to Lawrence
Silver—reflect your specific goals:

1. Your specific objectives in writing to Mrs. Eckerly are to (a) persuade her to
   pay the outstanding balance quickly and (b) retain her goodwill, her friendship,
   and her business.
2. Your objective in writing to Mr. Silver is simply *to collect the balance due
   amount*. Establishing goodwill is not a realistic goal at this point!

Guidelines for Effective Letters

As you see from all the examples given so far, each letter you write is expressly
tailored to suit (1) a *particular* reader, (2) a *specific* situation, and (3) a
certain objective. Although no cut-and-dry formula or recipe will fit your needs
every time, there are, indeed, general guidelines that will help you achieve
success in your letters.

Effective letters are usually:

1. Goodwill builders.
2. Personalized—that is, directed *from* you *to* one specific person.
3. Easy and interesting to read.
4. Persuasive in tone and helpful to the reader.

Guidelines for achieving these objectives will be discussed in detail in the next four chapters.

PROJECTS

1. Read the letter on the next page, and then answer the questions below.
   a. What, in your opinion, is the reader-writer relationship?
   b. What is the writer's objective in sending the letter?
   c. What do you think Driscoll's reaction will be to the letter?
2. You are a sales correspondent for Gourmet Foods. Recently you received a letter from Mrs. Millie Lundquist telling you how much she has enjoyed the booklet *Creative Canapes,* which she received after responding to a coupon advertisement your company placed in *Family Circle* magazine in behalf of a new product, Ham Flakes. Mrs. Lundquist merely wanted you to know that Ham Flakes is an excellent product and that the recipes sent her have been very popular with her guests.

   Write three responses to Mrs. Lundquist, each somewhat different from the others but all brief, friendly, and appreciative. (The purpose of this project is to emphasize that there is more than one method of writing an effective letter.)
3. You work for a large firm that manufactures hardware. State your objective and describe the tone (reader-writer relationship) in each response you would send.
   a. On his first order for 24 hacksaw blades, an important new customer complains that he was sent 12-inch blades instead of the 10-inch blades he ordered. You consult the original order and find that the customer did indeed request 12-inch blades.
   b. A first-time customer writes complaining that the spray nozzles of eight cans of Satin-Shine spray paint are defective. The customer asks for replacements and offers to return the defective cans. (You have received similar complaints from other customers.)
   c. An old and valued dealer whom you know personally writes that the statement he received of his account is in error. He was not given credit for merchandise that he returned, although he was sent a credit memorandum showing the amount credited. The dealer is entirely right; your accounts receivable clerk called up the customer's account on the computer and saw that he had made an error.
   d. Inez Lubeck wrote that a dealer (a customer of yours) from whom she bought a Trident riding mower is unethical because he refused to accept for refund a mower that she claims does a poor job of cutting grass. You telephone

**HEALTH CARE
SYSTEMS INC.**
1600 CLINTON ROAD
ATLANTA, GEORGIA 30333

September 14, 19--

Dear Kathy:

It was a real pleasure to read in <u>Insurance News</u> and in the
local papers that you were elected president of the Women
in Insurance Association at that organization's annual convention.

You do honor not only to Atlanta but also to the entire
profession of insurance, and I congratulate you on this
recognition of your ability.

We at Health Care Systems Inc. are happy to be associated
with you and the other fine people at National Insurance,
and we hope that we can continue to be of service to you.

Cordially yours,

P. R. Alvarez

P. R. Alvarez

Ms. Kathleen Driscoll
First Vice President
National Insurance Company
100 Peachtree, NW
Atlanta, Georgia 30303

the dealer and learn that the mower, sold to Lubeck about six months ago,
has been damaged—the blade is twisted, and other parts show evidence of
considerable abuse.

e. You receive a request for a donation from the Statesville Youth Symphony.
(Statesville is the home of one of your dealers.) You must decline the request.

f. The owner of Harrell's Building Center, a store that opened about a week
ago, writes to tell you about the great success of the grand opening of the
store and to thank your company for providing materials and other assistance.

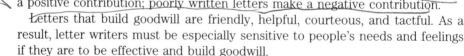

CHAPTER 2

BUILDING GOODWILL THROUGH BUSINESS LETTERS

Goodwill is an elusive term. Generally speaking, it means "a favorable public image; the prestige a company has acquired in the eyes of the public." For example, if people consider the company that sells Presto tools a good company, an honorable company, a fair company, then people will be favorably disposed toward buying Presto products.

As a result, goodwill is greatly advanced by a company's reputation for:

- Manufacturing high-quality products.
- Selling at fair prices.
- Offering a generous returns policy.
- Advocating honesty with its customers, employees, and suppliers.
- Fostering public safety and employee safety.
- Following an equal employment opportunity policy.
- Supporting local community activities.
- Donating money to worthy charities.

Of course, the opposite is also true. A company's goodwill is negative if it has a reputation for low-quality products, unfair prices, and so on. Executives know that a poor public image will eventually be translated into poor sales and low profits. Understandably, then, large companies spend millions of dollars daily in an effort to establish and maintain good *public relations*, another name for goodwill. To win the goodwill of the public is always an important goal for any organization. Without friends and supporters—without goodwill—nonprofit organizations, too, will suffer.

Although we can easily understand what goodwill *means*, it is difficult to quantify goodwill, and it is equally difficult to predict how to gain goodwill. Once again, no formulas can ensure success. However, executives agree that business letters certainly do contribute to a company's public relations: Good letters make a positive contribution; poorly written letters make a negative contribution.

Letters that build goodwill are friendly, helpful, courteous, and tactful. As a result, letter writers must be especially sensitive to people's needs and feelings if they are to be effective and build goodwill.

As you read the sample letters below, be sure to observe how these four qualities are built into each letter and how they contribute to the organization's goodwill.

BUILDING GOODWILL WHEN WRITING "YES"

Whenever you are in a position to say "yes" to someone's request, you have a relatively easy task! Yet if the response is not friendly, helpful, courteous, and tactful, even a "yes" may fail to build goodwill.

Case Example 1
Responding to a Request for Information

Situation   Walter B. Fitch, executive vice president of Dickson Pharmacies, wrote to Rachel D'Amato (the marketing manager for Ultra Business Systems) for information about installing CENTRODEX, a computerized record-keeping system, in each of the 12 drugstores in the Dickson chain. Here is the response that a new administrative assistant drafted for Ms. D'Amato's signature:

Dear Mr. Fitch:

Thank you for requesting information about CENTRODEX, the latest, most comprehensive record-keeping system for pharmacies.

Please read the enclosed booklet that explains the CENTRODEX system and describes its features.

Again, thank you for your interest in our products.

Analysis

1. This letter is certainly friendly and courteous.
2. However, the letter is really not very *helpful*. Remember that the product here will probably sell for more than $40,000. For that price, a simple "thank you—here's a brochure" just isn't helpful enough!

Realizing that her assistant's draft was not helpful enough, Ms. D'Amato rewrote the letter as shown on page 16.

Analysis   This is certainly a better response:

1. Rachel's letter is friendly, courteous, and tactful.
2. Rachel's letter is also exceptionally *helpful.* She, too, sends Mr. Fitch materials on CENTRODEX. But she also goes out of her way to arrange for the local Ultra representative to (a) contact Mr. Fitch after he has had an opportunity to review the materials and (b) set up a convenient time for Mr. Fitch to see a CENTRODEX operation in action. She even gives him a toll-free number to call if he should have any questions. Her degree of helpfulness matches the potential importance of this particular sale.
3. Rachel ends her letter with a courteous thank you.

ULTRA BUSINESS SYSTEMS, INC.

One Hanover Building • Chicago Heights, Illinois 60411• 800/555/2500

August 2, 19--

Mr. Walter B. Fitch
Executive Vice President
Dickson Pharmacies Inc.
2350 Michigan Avenue
Chicago, IL 60616

Dear Mr. Fitch:

How pleased we are to learn of your interest in CENTRODEX,
the lastest and most comprehensive computerized recordkeeping
system of its kind. The enclosed materials, which include
an illustrated booklet, should provide you with complete
information about this unique system.

After you've had an opportunity to review these materials,
Mr. Fitch, more than likely you'd like to see the system in
action. Therefore, I'm asking Sandra Gable, our Iowa representative, to call you to arrange a visit at your convenience to a CENTRODEX operation in the greater Chicago
area. You should hear from Sandra within the next ten days
or so.

In the meantime, if you should need any information, please
feel free to call us at 1-800-555-2500.

Thank you for writing to us.

Sincerely,

Rachel D'Amato

Rachel D'Amato
Marketing Manager

jst
Enclosures
cc: Sandra Gable

Case Example 2
Apologizing for an Error

Situation Through a "computer error" of some sort, First State & Loan incorrectly rejected payment on a customer's check. The customer, Mrs. Frances Quimby, was understandably irate when she called the bank to explain what had happened.

A few weeks ago, she had mailed a $100 donation to her alma mater, Waterston College. This morning she received a polite letter from the college's Alumnae Committee telling her that her check had been returned unpaid. Mrs. Quimby was especially embarrassed because the letter was signed by a former classmate who heads the Alumnae Committee. The response Mrs. Quimby received is on page 18.

Analysis Ms. Poole's letter makes every effort to build goodwill in this negative situation.

1. She is friendly (but not too friendly) in her tone.
2. Ms. Poole tactfully explains precisely how the error occurred.
3. Ms. Poole is helpful: She tries to alleviate Mrs. Quimby's embarrassment by calling the Alumnae Committee and by sending a copy of the letter to the head of the committee. Another way that Ms. Poole is helpful is by showing that she is understanding. She explains that she, too, would be embarrassed under the same circumstances.
4. Ms. Poole shows courtesy by taking the time to write a very personal explanation; her letter does not use an "I'm sorry" formula. Also, she thanks Mrs. Quimby for informing the bank of the error.

Case Example 3
Acknowledging a Compliment and a Suggestion

Situation Professor A. J. Andrews wrote a complimentary letter to Somerset Oil Inc. about a public-service television program that the company sponsors. Andrea Sarto, an assistant manager in the Public Relations Department, replied to Professor Andrews as shown on page 19.

Analysis Andrea's letter is a strong goodwill-building letter:

1. She expresses genuine appreciation to Professor Andrews for both writing to Somerset Oil and praising the television series.
2. Andrea compliments Professor Andrews for his excellent suggestion and explains how the company plans to follow that suggestion.
3. She closes the letter with a hearty expression of appreciation.

Case Example 4
Thanking a Customer for Support

Situation Megabytes, a wholesaler of computers and computer accessories, opened for business only one year ago. Competition has been extremely tough throughout the year. The owner of Megabytes, Katherine Isolda, knows that she

FIRST STATE & LOAN
10 Plaza Square Philadelphia, PA 19141 215-555-2500

September 1, 19--

Mrs. Frances Quimby
130 Marcus Avenue
Langhorne, PA 19047

Dear Mrs. Quimby:

I am very sorry for the unfortunate error we made. Please
accept my sincere apologies.

When you called to tell me that your check had been incorrectly returned unpaid, I was naturally very concerned.
When you explained that the check was a donation to your
alma mater, I felt doubly concerned. I immediately thought
of how I would feel if the same thing happened to me! I
suddenly felt the full impact of the embarrassment you must
have felt.

Of course, I quickly found out how we had made this error.
I discovered that one of our new clerks had incorrectly
keyed in 789 instead of 798 (the last three digits of your
account). Because making keyboarding errors is human and
unavoidable, we proofread all our work twice in an effort to
correct every error. I am sorry that we missed this one.

In an effort to clear up this matter, Mrs. Quimby, after we
spoke this morning, I called the Alumnae Committee, spoke
with Mrs. Dorothy Dixon, and explained our error. Mrs.
Dixon was very understanding indeed. I am sending her a
copy of this letter.

We hope that you will excuse our oversight, and we thank you
for bringing this matter to our attention.

                    Sincerely,

                    Eunice Poole

                    Eunice A. Poole
                    Senior Vice President

APK
cc: Mrs. Dorothy Dixon

succeeded in part because of the support she received from a number of retail stores, and she wants to express her appreciation to these loyal customers, as shown on page 20.

Analysis Katherine's letter is very effective for building goodwill among her customers.

1. Her appreciation is certainly genuine, and her letter conveys that feeling.
2. Katherine tactfully underscores that she (a) understands her customers' needs and (b) values her customers' comments.

SOMERSET OIL INC.
Somerset Center
Norman, Oklahoma 73069
405-555-6500

May 3, 19--

Professor A. J. Andrews
Chairperson, Sociology Department
Hillsdale College
Lincoln, Nebraska 68504

Dear Professor Andrews:

How thoughtful you were to write us in praise of our new
television series, America in Transition. Naturally, I'm
delighted to hear that you have enjoyed these programs--
especially that you found them "provocative and stimulating." We must, of course, share the credit with our producers.

Your suggestion that we include programs on the arts is very
appropriate. Together with our producers, we have developed
six new shows devoted to music, painting, photography,
theater, dance, and cinematography. Beginning with "Music
in America," these new shows will be aired on six consecutive Thursdays starting on October 9 at nine o'clock (EST).

Professor Andrews, we certainly hope that you find these new
shows equally entertaining and informative. In any case, we
thank you for writing to us. Letters like yours always
boost our spirits!

Very cordially yours,

Andrea Sarto

Andrea Sarto
Assistant Manager
Public Relations

LRS

---

3. She is helpful because she lets Bob know that he can depend on her and her
staff in the future for quality products, low prices, advertising support, and
so on.

Just as top executives always try to build goodwill among customers and the
general public, they also take advantage of opportunities to build goodwill among
employees. Although memos are the usual format for messages written within a

**DISTRIBUTORS OF
COMPUTERS and COMPUTER PERIPHERALS**
Napa, California 94558 415-555-1750

January 24, 19--

Mr. Robert Denman
President
Novato Computer Center
450 Lake Avenue
Novato, CA 94947

Dear Bob:

In the year since I opened Megabytes, I learned several important business lessons. One is that the loyal support of
key customers--like you, Bob--is the real key to success.
Thank you for your support!

Getting through this first year was certainly a challenge.
Several competitors, as you know, opened and closed in just
a few months! Megabytes survived the first year not only
because we offered high-quality products and very low prices
but because we listened attentively to our customers. We
intend to continue to listen attentively in the future--
especially to loyal supporters like you.

Of course, we also intend to continue to offer high-quality
products and "pencil-sharpened" prices! In addition, we've
got a few ideas for providing you with faster service, more
joint-advertising ventures, and an even better billing system. My entire staff is dedicated to these goals.

My best personal wishes.

Katherine Isolda

Katherine Isolda
President

kr

company, executives write *letters* to their employees in special situations. (Be
sure to note the special format of the letter in the next case example.)

Case Example 5
Complimenting an Employee

Situation   Susan Furman, an account executive with Frankel, Thomas & Paine,
gave an outstanding presentation to International Iron & Steel, a large conglom-
erate. In fact, her presentation did what was thought to be impossible for a small
ad agency: It won this huge account away from a major New York City firm that

had had the account for several years! In so doing, Susan not only put her firm "on the map" with this important new client but also brought in substantial new income for her agency. Sincerely appreciative of Susan's incredible accomplishment, Margaret Frankel, president of the agency, writes the following letter.

Simpson Building 500 Westerly Boulevard
Louisville, Kentucky 40202 • 606-555-2000

March 13, 19--

Dear Susan,

Congratulations on winning the International Iron & Steel account! All of us at FT&P are <u>very</u> proud of your accomplishment. I've never seen so many smiling faces around the office. Kudos to you!

Susan, I am well aware that luck had little to do with winning this prestigious account. You put many, many hours into developing your superb campaign. You pushed our Creative Department and Production Department hard--harder, I'm sure, than they've ever been pushed before. But they knew, as you did, that the goal was worth the effort. And they delivered for you because your confidence is contagious.

All the executives at International Iron & Steel who attended your presentation praised it as brilliant and bold. They're right.

Frank Thomas, Agnes Paine, and I appreciate your consistently excellent work, Susan, and we thank you for winning what is now our most prestigious account. To show our appreciation, we have a special reward for you. We look forward to telling you all about it when you return from your well-deserved vacation.

Sincerely,

Margaret Frankel

Margaret R. Frankel

Ms. Susan T. Furman
1200 Oak Court
Lexington, KY 40506

Analysis   Frankel's letter is excellent.

1. She expresses admiration and appreciation in the first paragraph.
2. She acknowledges the hard work Susan did to obtain this account.
3. She brings other executives into the picture.
4. She mentions a special reward to be given Susan later.

MAINTAINING GOODWILL WHEN WRITING "NO"

Whenever you must say "no" to a request or share unwelcomed news with someone, maintaining goodwill is slightly more difficult. But with a keen sensitivity to people's needs and feelings, you will still be able to develop letters that are friendly, helpful, courteous, and tactful.

Case Example 6
Saying "No" to a Request

Situation Baron's Sporting Equipment sells athletic goods to high schools across the country. Not surprisingly, then, the company receives hundreds of requests each year to buy advertising space in various high school yearbooks and newspapers. The volume of the requests is such that the company must turn them down. (Besides, such publications are more useful for local, not for national, advertising.) At the same time, of course, the company must maintain the goodwill of each school, as Martin Kyoto does in the letter on the next page.

Analysis The reply is effective and maintains goodwill, despite having to refuse the request.

1. Martin is friendly. His tone throughout the letter is personal and cheerful.
2. He is tactful. He doesn't simply say "no"; he explains why he must refuse the request.
3. He is helpful. Using his past experience, he describes techniques that he found most helpful in the same situation.
4. Martin is courteous. His attitude is clearly positive and comforting.

Explaining a delay is not exactly saying "no," but it *is* a negative situation, one requiring extra sensitivity on the writer's part, as shown in the next case example.

Case Example 7
Explaining Delays to Customers

Situation Palo Alto Electronics Inc. has not been able to supply customers with certain parts because of a strike in the plant of its major supplier. Many customers complained, of course, although most understood that it was clearly not PAE's fault. Now that the strike has ended, John Li writes to each customer as shown on page 24.

Analysis John's letter is on target.

1. He shows courtesy simply by taking the time to write this letter. He thanks Roy for his patience. Also, the tone of John's letter shows courtesy.
2. He tactfully explains what PAE intends to do to end the backlog of customer orders.
3. John is helpful—he tells Roy that he will try to give Nu-Way Aviation "top priority."
4. He is also very friendly to a long-time customer.

BARON'S SPORTING EQUIPMENT
435 Elm Street Pineville, LA 71360
504/555-9050

January 2, 19--

Mr. Sean McGeough
Business Manager
"The Islander"
Long Island High School
Southampton, New York 11968

Dear Sean:

I wish it were possible for Baron's to purchase advertising space in "The Islander." Unfortunately, however, we cannot do so.

First of all, Sean, Baron's market includes all of the 25,000 high schools across the country, and many of those schools request yearbook contributions. Obviously, the number of requests alone is prohibitive. Secondly, if we were to make any exceptions, we would then be unfair to all the other schools.

I certainly understand your problem, Sean, because I, too, sold yearbook ads a long, long time ago. Based on my experience, I suggest targeting local business firms and stores--they're the ones who will benefit most from advertising in your yearbook.

I hope that you understand our position, and I wish you success in your efforts to make "The Islander" a real winner. I'm sure you'll succeed!

Sincerely yours,

Martin Kyoto

Martin Kyoto
General Manager

klr

PALO ALTO
ELECTRONICS

500 El Camino Real • Palo Alto, CA 94306 • 415 555-1234

April 22, 19--

Mr. Roy Brankowski
Senior Vice President
Nu-Way Aviation Inc.
Fullerton, CA 92631

Dear Roy:

I want to thank you for your patience during the past few
months! Like you, we were flooded with customer
complaints--all justified and very understandable.

As you saw on last night's news, National Industries and the
union have settled their differences and signed a three-year
pact. Now that the strike is over, we can finally return to
"business as usual."

In an effort to end the backlog of orders from our
customers, we're putting our production, clerical, and
order-fulfillment staff on mandatory overtime. Naturally,
Roy, we'll try to give your orders top priority. Please
call me, of course, if there is any special order I should
know about.

Despite these temporary problems, I hope that Nu-Way Aviation is enjoying a solid first quarter. Please let me know
if you have any plans to visit Atlanta soon. I'd like to
introduce you to a few new tennis courts near our office!

Cordially yours,

John J. Li

John J. Li
Manager, Public Relations

TLR

1. Analyze each of the following messages and point out its goodwill-building characteristics.

   a.

F I N D L A Y ' S
Tryon, Minnesota 38967

May 12, 19—

Dear Mr. and Mrs. Mittiga:

Welcome to Tryon! It's always satisfying to extend warm greetings to newcomers. Findlay's has been doing it for the past 50 years.

I think you'll enjoy living in Tryon, a city rich in tradition and an unprecedented pride in its past, present, and future. We're known as the "city of lakes," but we're also known for our friendly people.

I hope you'll drop in to Findlay's very soon. It's got everything for you and your home. When you arrive just look for the young man at the Information Desk, show him this letter, and ask to speak to me. I'll be delighted to meet you and present you with a special gift for your home.

Let's get acquainted!

Sincerely yours,

Bette Findlay

Bette Findlay
President

   b.

Dear Fran:

I greatly appreciate the way you managed the Open House yesterday. It was elegantly done; and arranging the tour through both our electronically equipped offices and automated factory so that our 57 guests saw everything they came to see—with no bottlenecks or delays--took a lot of planning and synchronizing.

It was an enormously successful affair, Fran,
judging by what I saw and heard, and I am grateful to you for putting it over so well. Good
show!

Sincerely,

J. T. Sykes

J. T. Sykes

cc Carla D. Krantz

(*Note:* The recipient is an employee in the human resources department of
Ryder Steel; Carla D. Krantz is the human resources manager.)
c.

CAREER & MANAGEMENT COUNSELING ENTERPRISES

430 Massachusetts Avenue N.W.   Washington, D.C. 20001

August 14, 19—

Mr. Philip Marcil
Marcil Associates
1800 Market Street
Philadelphia, Pennsylvania 19103

Dear Mr. Marcil:

It was good to talk with you yesterday and to
learn that you can be with us at our October 15
seminar. The topic you suggested, "Motivation
Through Employee Participation," seems just
right; it ties in beautifully with this year's
theme of personnel development.

Our meeting, which is held in the Green Room of
the Broadmoor Hotel (3601 Connecticut Avenue,
N.W.) starts off with a social hour at 5:30.
Dinner begins at 6:30, followed by your talk at
7:30. We hope you will plan to speak for about
30 minutes and then to answer questions for another half hour.

If you would like to be picked up at the airport, please tell me when you expect to arrive and I'll be there. I have made a reservation for you at the Diplomat Hotel.

                                   Sincerely yours,

                                   Elizabeth Nelson

                                   Elizabeth Nelson
                                   Program Chairperson

EN:rs

2. Contemporary Sound Inc., a firm that manufactures audio equipment, sells its products only through authorized dealers (retail stores, for example). Recently an individual wrote to the company to place an order for two tape decks that he saw advertised in *Audio Systems Dealer,* a trade journal. In terms of goodwill building, what do you think of the response that follows?

Dear Sir:

We are unable to fill your order for the Contemporary Sound tape decks about which you inquired. This equipment is sold only through authorized dealers.

Obviously, the information provided is correct and helpful. (Some organizations would toss away the incoming letter without answering it.) But as long as there is to be a response, why not this one:

Dear Miss Traylor:

Thank you for asking about Contemporary Sound tape decks. While it is true that we are the distributors of these decks, we sell only to authorized dealers. The dealer nearest you is South Side Electronics in Fairfield. Why not pay them a visit? I'm confident they will be delighted to see you.

3. Often in corresponding with customers, a business writer must say "no." In doing so, he or she tries to be friendly and tactful. Mission: To get customers to accept the no and *remain* customers.

Compare the two "no" letters below. Which one is more likely to keep the customer's friendship? Why?

Dear Madam:

Sorry but we cannot permit you to return for credit the draperies you purchased, since we are not able to dispose of them. It is too bad that these drapes do not fit the windows you bought them for, but since they were sold to you well under the regular price and on an "all sales final" basis, there is little we can do about it.

Trusting you will appreciate our position in this matter, we are,

Very truly yours,

Dear Mrs. Kirkendall:

I appreciate your request to return for refund the draperies you recently purchased from Avery's.

You will remember, Mrs. Kirkendall, that these drapes were offered at a greatly reduced price (actually, 40 percent off) and that for this special sale all merchandise was advertised "Not returnable." As much as I would like to make an exception in your case, I'm afraid I cannot, since this sale was a closeout on the Beekman line, and we do not plan to restock it.

I know you will understand our position. Mrs. Kirkendall. Incidentally, our interior design consultant tells me that many people purchased these drapery materials for use as upholstery coverings and bedspreads.

Sincerely yours,

WRITING PERSON TO PERSON

When you walk into a store, you expect personal service from the people who work in that store—the clerks, the salespeople, the cashiers, the manager. You don't expect to receive service from the store itself. Only *people* can provide you with personal attention, advice, suggestions, and similar service. When you order merchandise by mail or by phone, you are not face to face with a clerk or cashier, but the same principle applies: Only a person, not the company itself, can provide you with service. Of course, "the company" benefits because the salespeople or clerks represent that company and reflect its policies and attitudes. But only a person, not a company or store, can provide personal service and attention.

When you write a business letter, you represent your company. Your reader may expect service from your company, but only *you* can deliver that personal attention! Once again, when you do deliver that personal attention, your company will benefit—and so will you, of course.

That's our goal in this chapter: to show you how to personalize your letters to ensure that they are warm, friendly, and tactful, not cold, stuffy, and brusque. Success lies in talking to your reader person to person!

ADDRESSING READERS BY NAME

In a normal conversation with someone (either face to face or on the telephone), you would ordinarily address that person *by name* from time to time. The formality or informality obviously depends on how well you know the person you are talking to:

MRS. WILSON: Is there a discount for buying in larger quantities?

YOU: Yes, Mrs. Wilson, we offer a 25 percent discount for bulk orders of 5,000 or more

PHIL: Does our leasing agreement cover this?

YOU: I'm sure it does, *Phil*, but let me double-check.

In writing, too, use the reader's name from time to time. Doing so helps make the message more personal—more like a normal conversation:

Dear Jim:

Thanks very much for rushing my last order to us overnight. We were out of stock on several of

the items, so I appreciate your giving special
attention to this order.

In fact, Jim, ...

Always be sure that the reader's name (and title, for that matter) is precise in every detail!

1. Spellings can be tricky.
   Caryn, Caren, Karyn, Karen
   Carol, Carole, Carrol, Carroll, Caryl
   Leslie, Lesley, Lesly
   d'Amato, D'Amato
   van Buren, Van Buren, VanBuren
   Johnson, Johnston
   Follow your reader's use of initials, hyphens, and similar details precisely.
   P. J. Dempsey
   A. Lloyd Chester III
   Frank J. Fasano Jr.
   Ellen Brooks-Grayson
2. Do not overlook the need for personal titles such as *Mr., Ms., Mrs.,* and *Miss* on envelopes and inside addresses. (Use *Ms.* when you do not know which personal title a woman prefers.) Use *Dr., Professor, Captain,* and so on, when appropriate.
   Mrs. Myrna Lopes
   Senior Marketing Representative
   Hanover Square Industries
   1301 Rockaway Parkway
   Brooklyn, New York 11236
3. Be sensitive to business titles in address blocks. The "*Senior* Marketing Representative" does not want to be addressed "Marketing Representative."

If you are not sure of the spelling of a person's name or precise title, *find out.* Check recent correspondence. Refer to a business directory. Ask a coworker. If necessary, call that person's company and ask a receptionist or a secretary there for help. Once you learn the correct name and title, copy it precisely in *your* personal name and address file for future use.

TALKING *WITH,* NOT *AT,* YOUR READER

Some studies have shown that many gentle people can change their personalities when they get behind the wheel of a car. Suddenly, when confronted by traffic, they become combative, unfeeling, even dangerous.

In a similar way, many people who are normally gracious and friendly in person become overly stiff and formal when writing a letter. When confronted by blank paper, a computer screen, a dictating machine, or a stenographer, they forget how to talk normally with their readers. Instead, they talk *at* their readers!

Dear Madam:

As per our discussion of last week, enclosed please find the signed agreements concerning the leasing of automobiles for all DenCo sales representatives. After both copies of the agreement have been signed and the original copy has been returned to our office, the agreement will then officially be in effect.

If there should be any questions concerning this matter, please call the number listed on the letterhead above.

Sincerely,

If you discussed the agreements with her last week, then you know her name. Use it in the salutation! Also, try to be less stodgy in the tone of the letter:

Dear Mrs. Ivanson:

I have enclosed the agreements we discussed last week concerning the auto leases for your sales representatives. You're probably as eager as I am to make the leasing arrangements final.

If everything meets with your approval, Mrs. Ivanson, please sign both copies of the agreements. Keep one copy for your files, and return the original to us in the envelope provided.

All of us here at Central Auto Leasing look forward to working with you. Please be sure to let me know if there is anything further that we can do for you.

Sincerely,

The second example uses a businesslike tone without being overly formal or pompous. The writer talks with the reader *person to person*, almost as if they were face to face.

True, you shouldn't write exactly as you talk face to face:

Good morning, Pam!

You're probably really eager to get those leasing agreements finalized—right? I thought so! Well, what are we waiting for?

Don't get *too* carried away with the "write as you talk" idea. Most readers will find the above message a little too cute, a little too corny.

USING PERSONAL PRONOUNS

The words *I, you, he, she, it, we, they, me, my, your*, and so on are personal pronouns. If you omit personal pronouns as you talk with someone, you will surely have a difficult time! Your conversation will not sound normal. Likewise, your *written* messages will sound "normal"—personal, helpful, and friendly—when you use personal pronouns.

In the previous letter to Mrs. Ivanson (page 31), note how often personal pronouns were used:

> *I* have enclosed . . . *we* discussed . . . *your* sales representatives. *You're* . . . *I* am . . . *your* approval . . . *your* files . . . to *us*. . . . All of *us* . . . with *you*. . . . let *me* know . . . *we* can do for *you*.

By contrast, the earlier "Dear Madam" letter included only two personal pronouns: "*our* discussion . . . *our* office. . . ."

At times, emphasizing "you" (rather than "I") is especially helpful. Compare these examples:

Dear Mr. Chung:

You will be pleased to learn that you have been accepted as a preferred charge customer at Frankel's. Your new credit card is enclosed.

Dear Mr. Chung:

I am happy to welcome you as a Frankel's preferred charge customer. I have enclosed your new. . . .

In the first example, the emphasis on "you" is appropriate: The purpose is to focus attention on the *reader.* The second example focuses attention on the writer.

ASSESSING THE RELATIONSHIP

How well do you know the person you are writing to? Is this your first letter to this person? How well developed is your relationship with this person? These are the kinds of considerations that determine how formal or informal you should be in each situation.

Again, there is no formula to determine what is correct. "Dear Bob:" is certainly appropriate if you and your reader are on a first-name basis. If not, then use "Dear Mr. Chung:" as your salutation. Both are considered appropriate for standard business letters. For very formal situations, use the salutation "Sir:" (or "Madam:").

Complimentary closings offer a greater range of formality and therefore more choices. Observe the following ways in which you can sign off your letters:

Informal	Cordially,
Best wishes,	Cordially yours,
See you soon!	Very cordially yours,
Warmest regards,	*Very Formal*
Formal	Yours truly,
Sincerely,	Very truly yours,
Sincerely yours,	Yours very truly,
Very sincerely yours,	Respectfully yours,

The "formal" closings are standard for business letters (that is, they are appropriate for use with salutations such as "Dear Bob:" *and* "Dear Mr. Chung:"). Of course, be sure to avoid mismatching salutations and closings. If you use "Dear Mary:" in your salutation, don't sign off with "Very truly yours," and if you use "Dear Sir:" don't sign off with "See you soon!"

Case Example 1
Acknowledging a First Order

Situation   Dan Shallcross worked long and hard to convince Roseanne Ausiello, chief purchasing agent for the House Beautiful chain of paint stores, to try his company's Luxor-Sheen brand of house paints. Months later, Ms. Ausiello places a large order for Luxor-Sheen. Here are two ways in which Dan's sales manager might have responded to this order.

Dear Madam:

This is to acknowledge receipt of Purchase order 43-6357 for 1,250 one-gallon cans of Luxor-Sheen paints. The total for this purchase, $4,656.79, will be charged to your account.

Please be assured that this order will receive our prompt attention.

                    Sincerely,

Dear Ms. Ausiello:

I was very pleased to receive your first order for Luxor-Sheen paints. As you requested, we will deliver the entire shipment of 1,250 one-gallon cans to your warehouse on December 3 and will charge the total ($4,656.79) to your account.

Thank you, Ms. Ausiello, for your confidence in our products! For several reasons, I'm sure that your stores will have success with the Luxor-Sheen line. First of all, in all categories (shine, color fastness, price, durability, ease of application, shelf life, etc.) Luxor-Sheen matches or beats every other brand of paint available today. Second, our new television and radio ads have been tremendously successful in drawing new customers to Luxor-Sheen.

Dan Shallcross and I are very flattered that your prestigious chain of stores will be carrying our brand. Within the next ten days or so, Dan will call on your store managers with the special free display racks we promised. In the meantime, please let me know if I can help in any way.

Sincerely yours,

Analysis

1. Letter A falls short on several counts. It lacks warmth and friendliness; it sounds as if it were written out of obligation.
2. Letter B, on the other hand, is warm, cordial, and friendly. It makes Ms. Ausiello important (and she is), and it wisely ends by bringing Dan Shallcross into the picture. This letter sounds as if it were written not out of obligation but out of desire on the part of the sales manager to communicate with a customer—quite a difference! Note the generous use of personal pronouns in this letter as compared with Letter A.

Case Example 2
Responding to a Price Inquiry

Situation Mrs. Dorothy Greco ordered a book by mail from Robertson Press and sent a check for the full amount listed on the invoice ($27.95). Along with her check she wrote a note questioning the price of the book. Reason: In the Robertson catalog the price was listed as $24.95, and she questioned this discrepancy. Review these two responses to Mrs. Greco's inquiry:

Dear Mrs. Greco:

This letter will acknowledge receipt of your in-quiry of August 2 concerning the price of <u>Modern Home Renovation</u>, by Levitt and Sommers. The price in our catalog is $24.95; the price on our invoice is $27.95.

With regard to this matter, please be informed that it is common practice in the publishing industry to raise book prices in subsequent printings after the initial publication as a result of increases in manufacturing costs. The price of $27.95 is, therefore, correct.

Trusting that this explanation will be satisfactory, I am,

Very truly yours,

B Dear Mrs. Greco:

It is easy to understand how two different prices for the same item could be confusing. As you point out, the catalog price for <u>Modern Home Renovation</u>, by Levitt and Sommers, is listed as $24.95 but the invoice showed a price of $27.95. Please allow me to explain why.

As publishers reprint books, manufacturing costs often increase--that is, the costs of paper, printing, and binding. Because there is no way to predict future costs, we (like other publishers) usually add this note in our catalogs: "Prices subject to change." We originally published <u>Modern Home Renovation</u> at $24.95 and listed this price in our catalog; since then, we have reprinted and have increased the price to reflect our current higher manufacturing costs. Unfortunately, our catalog does not always show the latest prices.

Thank you for giving me the opportunity to clear up this matter, Mrs. Greco. I hope that you find <u>Modern Home Renovation</u> a superlative guide to redecorating and redesigning, as <u>The New York Times</u> described it.

Sincerely yours,

Analysis Here's why Letter B is more effective:

1. The language in Letter A ("This letter will acknowledge…please be informed…") is neither friendly nor warm. Overall, the letter is rather unfriendly and stiff.
2. Letter B, on the other hand, is conversational and friendly. It talks *person to person* with Mrs. Greco. It has a genuine "from me to you" approach.

Case Example 3
Turning Down Requests

Situation A would-be subscriber has ordered a magazine with a circulation that (for advertising reasons) is limited to architects. In other words, anyone other than an architect who enters a subscription must be turned down.

Dear Ms. Gilchrist:

<u>Modern Architecture</u> has a "restricted circulation." This means that the publication is available only to registered architects.

Therefore, this magazine cannot be sent to outsiders.

               Sincerely,

Dear Ms. Gilchrist:

I appreciate your asking us for a subscription to <u>Modern Architecture</u>. Thank you, too, for your glowing comments on the June issue. We're flattered!

Ms. Gilchrist, <u>Modern Architecture</u> is what is known as a "restricted publication." Let me explain what this means. In the publishing industry, certain magazines guarantee advertisers that each issue will reach a specific number of specialized readers--in the case of <u>MA</u>, registered architects. Each year an independent company audits our figures to ensure advertisers that we do, indeed, meet our claims. As a result, we can accept subscriptions only from architects. I am sure that you will understand our situation.

Robertson Press, the well-known book publishing company in Cleveland, develops an annual compilation called <u>The Best From Modern Architecture--19--</u>. I suggest that you check in your local bookstore to see if this book suits your needs.

               Sincerely yours,

Analysis

1. Letter A sounds as if the reader has been rejected by a prestigious club to which she had no right to apply. It is rude, curt, and insulting.
2. Letter B explains what "restricted circulation" means, making it very easy for the reader to understand the business reasons why she cannot have a subscription. Because it is understandable, courteous, and personal, the "rejection" is really little more than a polite explanation. Ms. Gilchrist will surely understand without feeling turned down.

Case Example 4
Responding to an Unsolicited Job Application

Situation Cosmotron Computers, like other large companies, receives a great many job applications. Most applications must be turned down, of course. There may be no open positions; or if there is an opening, the applicant may not be qualified; and so on.

Mary Ellen Curtis applied for a job in Cosmotron's Advertising Department. Judging from her résumé, she has several years' excellent experience in advertising and may be well qualified for any number of different jobs. However, there are simply no openings presently.

Consider these responses to Miss Curtis.

```
Dear Miss Curtis:

Your application for a position with Cosmotron
has been received.

Unfortunately, there are no vacancies in our Ad-
vertising Department at this time.  Further, we
expect no vacancies in this department in the
near future.

Your interest in Cosmotron is appreciated.

                        Yours very cordially,
```

```
Dear Miss Curtis:

I appreciate your interest in a position with
Cosmotron Computers.  Thank you for sending us
your letter and resume.

Your qualifications are indeed impressive, Miss
Curtis, and I wish that we were able to make use
of your obvious talents.  At the present time,
however, our Advertising Department has no open
positions.
```

Naturally, I will be happy to keep your letter and resume just in case a job should open in Advertising. If so, you may be sure that I'll contact you. In the meantime, of course, I suggest that you continue your job search with other companies. Thank you--and good luck!

Yours sincerely,

Analysis

1. Letter A expresses no feeling, no appreciation (despite use of the word *appreciation*), no well-wishing. Miss Curtis is sure to realize that the writer probably sends this stock letter to both well-qualified candidates and *un*-qualified applicants. There is nothing personal in the letter—no "from me to you" feeling.
2. The writer of Letter B took the time to express his personal feelings about Miss Curtis's letter and résumé and to write her not a stock letter, but a letter suited to this particular situation. When she reads Letter B, Miss Curtis will realize that it was written *person to person*.

ACTIVE VOICE AND PASSIVE VOICE

One way to ensure that your messages will be more personal is to use *active voice*. Active voice means that the subject in the sentence is *doing* the action. Passive voice means that the subject is receiving the action.

The difference between active voice and passive voice sentences will be obvious when you compare the following examples.

Active Voice	*Passive Voice*
I delivered the shipment to Detroit.	The shipment to Detroit has been delivered.
She canceled the order.	The order has been canceled.
We discussed both problems.	Both problems were discussed.
I approved your raise.	Your raise has been approved.

Do you see why the passive-voice sentence is the poorer choice in each pair? The active-voice sentence is stronger because it is clearer and more direct. Each active-voice sentence immediately tells you *who* did *what*.

Here are some of the weak passive-voice sentences that were included in earlier examples of negative letters:

Please be assured that....
Please be informed that....
Your application for a position with Cosmotron has been received.
Your interest in Cosmotron is appreciated.

Instead, how about these active-voice sentences?

I am pleased to assure you that....

We are pleased to inform you that....

I received your job application this morning.

I appreciate your interest in our company.

On the other hand, when sensitive issues or negative matters are being addressed, the passive voice often provides a way of sparing the writer from "pointing a finger" at the reader—or back at the writer!

Active Voice	*Passive Voice*
You may not smoke in this store.	Smoking is prohibited in this store.
You should not have deducted the 10 percent discount.	The 10 percent discount should not have been deducted.
We don't think you deserve a refund.	In this instance, a refund does not appear to be justified.
You have the experience required for this position.	The position requires at least five years' experience.

PROJECTS

1. Rewrite the following statements, giving them a more personal flavor.

   a. Carlton's display rooms are open to the general public Wednesday afternoons from 3 to 5:30.

   b. Unfortunately, requests for copies of our contract forms must be denied.

   c. Customers are advised to place their orders early because these Hogan irons are in short supply and great demand.

   d. Your letter stating that you received 12 Big Tom Lawn Mowers instead of 12 Big Tom Lawn Sweepers has been referred to the writer. This error is regrettable.

   e. The beneficiary form X-388 is being returned because it has not been signed.

   f. Should further copies of the brochure be required, requests should be addressed to our Publications Office, specifying requirements.

   g. In acknowledgment of your letter of April 12, a catalog was mailed today.

   h. The suggestion of a "Car Pool Campaign" appears to be very timely, and the writer pledges full support.

   i. Subject report was received and read carefully.

   j. In order to minimize costs, it is necessary to maintain clerical productivity at the highest possible level commensurate with equitable employment practices.

   k. It is recommended that employees who are in disagreement with company policy concerning automobile leasing communicate with the assistant marketing director or the undersigned for clarification of the company's position.

   l. Recreational facilities at Wilderness Lodge are free to guests.

2. Personalize the following letter from a manufacturer to a dealer.

Dear Sir:

Enclosed please find ten copies of a new price schedule, which will take effect November 16.

Particular attention should be given to the new discount policy (page 4). Although there is an increase in the list price of several items, the more generous discounts offered actually mean a reduction in net prices on all merchandise.

Your next order is eagerly anticipated and will be given prompt attention.

Very truly yours.

3. Edit the following conversation so that it is suitable for a written communication.

Look, Mr. Nesbitt, you'd be crazy not to take advantage of the special price on these cars. I've got them marked down to the point where I'm not going to make a dime on them--in fact, I'm going to lose money--but I've got to get rid of them so that I'll have room for the new models. Five days--that's all the time I can give you to make up your mind.

4. The following letter was written by a special-sales representative to an individual with whom he is well acquainted (a long-time customer). Rewrite it so that it would be suitable for a potential customer who is not known to the writer.

Dear Paula:

Thanks for stopping by our exhibit at the Tulsa Business Show last month. I was very pleased to see your name among those who signed up for a demonstration of the Tutor-Trainer.

I will be in Topeka the week of April 11, and any day that week that is convenient for you would suit me fine. Just tell me where and when. I need to know right away, though, because I've got several other people to see while I'm in town. By the way, the demonstration should'nt take more than an hour. Bring your friends!

I look forward to seeing you again. What did you think of our exhibit--quite an extravaganza, eh?

Yours,

5. Rewrite the following sentences in the active voice.
   a. The speaker's presentation was enjoyed by the entire audience.
   b. The display signs will be shipped by August 19. *I will ship the display signs on Aug 19.*
   c. Every complaint received by the company should be looked on by employees as an opportunity to make a friend.
   d. A business reply envelope is enclosed for your convenience.
   e. Your support of our new line of video recorders is much appreciated.
   f. Interest is paid from the date of deposit.
   g. Submission of advertising copy is required two months prior to the publication date of the magazine.
   h. Caution is advised when entering or leaving the construction area.
   i. Early registration for the convention is recommended.
   j. A total of 412 responses were received from the *Fleet Owner* advertisement.
6. The following special announcement was issued to passengers on Skymaster Airlines recently. Rewrite it, correcting any errors you find and making the message more personal.

To Our Passengers:

Effective August 1, the price of alcoholic beverages will be increased to $2 a drink. Regretfully, Skymaster has found it necessary to make this adjustment due to substantial increases we have experienced in our costs. Light refreshments are still being served complimentary. It is appreciated that you chose Skymaster Airlines, and every effort will be made to make your flight enjoyable.

SKYMASTER AIRLINES

Stop

MAKING YOUR LETTERS EASY AND INTERESTING TO READ

Few business writers simply dash off a perfect letter—or even a near-perfect letter—on the first try every time. Generally speaking, the longer the letter and the more complicated the subject, the more time you should spend reviewing and revising the message.

As one writer, Robert Louis Stevenson, put it, "I must write with pains so that my reader may read with ease." Your readers, too, will "read with ease" if you edit your messages. Each word, each sentence, each paragraph must be reviewed carefully and, if necessary, revised. *Careful editing*—that's the key to effective letter writing.

REVIEW WORDS AND PHRASES

One often-quoted "rule" of letter writing is *to keep each letter as short as possible.* Following this advice, the sales manager of Advanced Systems wrote this letter to a potential customer who wanted to make an appointment to discuss how Advanced Systems might be able to tailor its programs to her company's needs.

```
Dear Ms. Dunphy:

Please let's meet in my office at 10 a.m. on
May 3.

                    Yours truly,
```

If brevity were a plus, this message must surely be a masterpiece! It is obviously short; it contains no "unnecessary words." It is also easy to read; after all, it is only about ten words long. But the letter is neither friendly nor interesting. This message does not attempt to establish goodwill or to impress Ms. Dunphy with cordiality. Also, the letter makes no attempt to presell Ms. Dunphy on Advanced Systems or its products.

The objective in writing such a letter is not to keep it short. The objective is to make friends and to persuade the reader to buy your company's products or services.

```
Dear Ms. Dunphy:

I'm delighted to hear that you'll be in Boston
the first week of October and that you're eager
```

to see Advanced Systems' newest business programs. We're just as eager to show them to you!

Ms. Dunphy, I've arranged a special product display for you on Wednesday, October 3. Could you
be here about 10 o'clock? At that time our chief
programmer, Dr. Frances Stallmaster, will be on
hand to describe the technical features of our
programs and explain how we can individualize
them to meet your company's specific needs.
Please let me know if this date and time are convenient for you.

I hope that you will be able to join Frances and
me for lunch afterward in our executive dining
room. We are looking forward to seeing you in
October. Have a pleasant trip!

Sincerely yours,

This letter will not win an award for brevity. Yet it is not long. Unlike the first
letter, which was cold and lifeless, this letter is warm and friendly. Although it
is obviously longer, this letter provides an excellent setting for the meeting
ahead.

Clutter Words and Phrases

Although short letters are not necessarily better, clutter words and phrases add
no value to any message, short or long. Read the following pairs of sentences
carefully. Note how the underscored clutter words and phrases in the first
sentence hide the simple, straightforward message in the second sentence.

In the event that you can attend the conference,
please let us know. (Better to simply say "if.")
If you can attend the conference, please let us
know.

We were not able to ship the order due to the
fact that the truckers were on strike. (Better
to avoid the clutter and, instead, say "Because.") We were not able to ship the order because the truckers were on strike.

For your information, I have sent Allied Distributors a copy of the standard leasing agreement.
(How helpful are the words For your information?

Not helpful at all.) I have sent Allied Distributors a copy of the standard leasing agreement.

<u>In view of the fact that</u> our vice president de-
mands three estimates, we have asked three suppliers to submit bids. (Better to say "Because.") Because our vice president demands
three estimates, we have asked three suppliers to
submit bids.

   Likewise, redundancies also add clutter. A redundancy is a repetition, as shown
in these examples:

Please be sure to <u>plan in advance</u> how you will
present the contract to the union delegates.
(Planning is always in advance. Therefore, <u>in
advance</u> is redundant.)
Please be sure to plan how you will present the
contract to the union delegates.

The Lubbock, Texas, franchise has won the sales
award for three consecutive years <u>in a row</u>.
(<u>Consecutive</u> means "in a row.")
The Lubbock, Texas, franchise has won the sales
award for three consecutive years.

We were pleased and delighted to receive your order. (Why overkill with <u>both</u> "pleased and delighted"? Either one will do.)
We were delighted to receive your order.

Of course, we will give this shipment our prompt
and immediate attention. (Why <u>both</u> "prompt and
immediate"? Choose one.)
Of course, we will give this shipment our immediate attention.

   In addition, there are many, many other useless, repetitive, or roundabout
words and phrases that can detract from the simplicity of your message and
make it unnecessarily lengthy. Here are more examples:

Instead of . . .	*Say . . .*
it is my opinion	I think
a large majority of agents expressed the opinion that	most agents think

Instead of . . .	*Say . . .*
we are at the present time	we are now
at that point in time	then
at this point in time	now
we held a meeting to discuss	we met to discuss
during the period from May 1 to May 5	from May 1 to May 5
during the time that	during (*or* while *or* when)
a check in the amount of $500	a check for $500 (*or* a $500 check)
in compliance with your request	as you requested
in accordance with your request	as you requested
on or before March 30	by March 30
I regret to inform you that	I regret that (*or* I'm sorry that)
I would like to call your attention to	please note that
subsequent to	after
attached hereto	attached
enclosed herewith	enclosed
large in size	large
blue in color	blue
basic essentials	essentials
meet together	meet
plan ahead	plan
consensus of opinion	consensus
absolutely essential	essential

Develop a sensitivity to such words and expressions as you edit your letters.

Pompous Words and Phrases

When writing letters, business workers must often discuss important issues, explain sensitive decisions, or describe critical plans. Perhaps because they realize the importance of their writing, they sometimes force their messages to sound important by using stuffy, showy words and phrases. Whatever the reason, the result—pompous writing—sounds arrogant and self-important and can make the writer appear out of step with the times.

Sometimes the culprit in a pompous-sounding sentence is one word. True, having a rich vocabulary is a great asset and is considered a strong measure of intelligence. Your vocabulary helps you to understand what you read and hear; at the same time, it contributes to your ability to speak and write well. Do all that you can to improve your vocabulary. But don't use your business letters as vehicles to display your intelligence. Avoid showy words; instead, select simpler words whenever possible.

For example, compare the italicized terms in the following sentences. In each case, note that the second sentence is easier to read.

1. I want to *cogitate further* on the matter before giving a *definitive* answer.
I want to *think about* the matter a little more before I give a *final answer.*

CHAPTER 4 · MAKING YOUR LETTERS EASY AND INTERESTING TO READ **45**

2. I'm sure that you are *cognizant* of the fact that our invoices are payable on receipt.

I'm sure that you are *aware* that our invoices are payable on receipt. (*or* I'm sure you *know* that....)

3. *Personnel* who work weekends will be *provided with overtime compensation.*

People who work weekends will be *paid overtime.*

4. I cannot *comprehend* Paragraph 14 in this agreement.

I cannot *understand* Paragraph 14 in this agreement.

5. I plan to *utilize* these displays at the next sales conference.

I plan to *use* these displays at the next sales conference.

6. We are *contemplating* an *initial* order of 500 units.

We're *considering* a *first* order of 500 units.

7. She *has a strong proclivity for* television commercials rather than print ads; her *rationale* is that TV is more cost-effective.

She *prefers* television commercials rather than print ads; her *reason* is that TV is more cost-effective.

Sometimes changing one word or two words is not enough: the entire sentence must be revised. Note these examples:

1. A buyer for a department store tries to stress the importance of speed in handling incoming shipments:

```
It is imperative, for purposes of product
availability at sales premises, that Receiving
Department personnel expedite deliveries of in-
coming shipments.
```

Surely the buyer should simplify this:

```
When we receive merchandise deliveries, we must
be sure to rush the goods to the appropriate
sales floors as soon as possible.  Instead,
merchandise has often been left lying on the
loading platform.
```

2. Here is how one comptroller explains the need to be careful with procedures for handling cash:

```
It is a fundamental truism of effective cash
control that responsibility for receiving and
disbursing funds be divided among personnel.
```

Perhaps the comptroller thinks this sounds important. How much clearer the following message is:

```
The main check in handling cash is to separate
```

duties by having one person receive the money
and another pay out.

3. A human resources supervisor explains the usefulness of job descriptions as follows:

Individuals who know their responsibilities are
in a position to concentrate their efforts on
the requirements of their job rather than con-
tinually struggle to ascertain what their duties are.

The sentence should be revised as follows:

When people know their specific job duties,
they won't waste time deciding what to do.

4. A manager discusses the efficient use of machines:

High-level volume and quality of work are not
attainable unless operators are properly
trained and the machines utilized are in suitable condition for work operation.

Instead, how about:

For high quality and high production, we must
have properly trained operators and well-main-
tained machines.

5. An administrative assistant writes:

We have ascertained that the group attending
the seminar will be composed of five department
heads and three personnel managers.

Here is a clearer, less pompous alternative:

Five department heads and three personnel managers plan to attend the seminar.

When you are tempted to write _conflagration_, should you really be saying
fire? When you are about to write _draconian_, should you consider instead _strict_
or _cruel_? When you read _pedestrian_ in your draft copy, should you change it
to _commonplace_? Choose the simplest word that conveys your thought precisely.

Bias-Free Words

Far worse than using pompous words is using biased words. Women, too, are employed in businesses, by fire departments and police departments, by the Postal Service, and so on. As a result, words such as *businessman, fireman, policeman,* and *mailman* are biased terms. They are unfair to an entire group of people.

To ensure that your writing is not biased, note the following suggestions.

Instead of . . .	*Say . . .*
businessman	business person *or* business worker
fireman	fire fighter
policeman	police officer
mailman	mail carrier
salesman	sales representative *or* salesperson *or* salesclerk
stewardess	flight attendant

You will note that each of the biased terms indicates gender. (Except for the last term, *stewardess*, all are masculine.) And there lies the problem. To be bias-free, a word must *not* indicate gender, because gender labels force incorrect assumptions.

This new financial magazine will be of interst to businessmen throughout the country. (But not to business<u>women</u>? Say <u>business people</u> or <u>business-men and businesswomen</u> instead.)

Many an insurance man has found this Sales Technique seminar very effective in his sales career. (Are insurance <u>women</u> cut off from this seminar? Say "Many <u>insurance agents have</u> found this Sales Technique seminar very effective in helping <u>their</u> sales careers.")

Similarly, note how this sentence makes an assumption:

A business executive must be sure to communicate well with <u>his</u> subordinates. (There is nothing wrong with the term <u>business executive</u>, of course. But note "<u>his</u> subordinates." Is <u>every</u> business executive a man?)

A business executive must be sure to communicate well with <u>his or her</u> subordinates. (<u>His or her</u> is somewhat awkward, but it makes no gender assumptions. Another alternative follows.)

Business executives must be sure to communicate
well with their subordinates. (Make both the
subject and the pronoun plural to avoid overusing
terms such as his or her.)

Jargon

Technical terms that are peculiar to an industry are described as "jargon." What
makes the use of jargon "right" or "wrong" is the target audience. If you are
talking with someone in magazine publishing, the term *kill fee* will be understood.
If you are writing to someone in the securities field, then discussing "the prime"
is appropriate. But in other cases, using the same terms may be "wrong"—that
is, when your readers don't understand your jargon.

Use jargon only when your listener or your reader is sure to understand.

Clichés

Clichés are phrases that have been worn out through overuse. As a result of
their overuse, clichés have little impact, perhaps none, on today's reader.

How often, for example, have you heard the following clichés?

neat as a pin	clean as a whistle
clear as day	green with envy
quick as a wink	good as gold
light as a feather	abreast of the times
sadder but wiser	a checkered career
at the crack of dawn	a herculean effort
it goes without saying	a bolt from the blue
once in a blue moon	in these troubled times
easier said than done	beat a hasty retreat

When they were new and fresh, these clichés evoked strong, sparkling images.
Today, however, the same clichés (you can probably name hundreds of others)
have lost all their original punch. As a result, using them will make your writing
lackluster and dull. Worse, using clichés will show you to be unimaginative.
Develop some original phrases instead.

Vogue Words

Like teenage fads, some words come and go. A famous person says "parameter"
in a speech televised nationwide and afterward thousands of people sprinkle the
word (often incorrectly) into every routine conversation and written message.

The bureaucrats we hear on news shows and read about in the morning papers
seem to have an especially strong effect on spreading vogue words. Thanks to
them, no one ever mentions a simple "alternative"; instead, it's always a *"viable*
alternative." We no longer hear of someone struggling to make a decision but,
instead, *"interfacing* with a problem." We no longer witness disagreement on a
particular matter but, instead, *"polarization* of an issue." We no longer hear of

someone offering an opinion but, instead, "taking a *stance*" or "adopting a *posture*."

In most cases, vogue words have a specific, legitimate (although limited) use. The problem is that people try to force them to become everyday words. In the process, naturally enough, vogue words are often misused. Learn to spot—and quickly reject—vogue words.

REVIEW SENTENCES

Sentence length is an important factor in making your letters easy to read.

Long Sentences

Probably no other single writing fault hinders readability so much as the long, rambling sentence.

```
Because of our limited warehousing facilities, we
are studying the possibility of contracting with
public warehouses, of which there are several in
this area, that offer storage and handling facil-
ities, charging their customers only for the
amount of space occupied and the length of time
it is used.
```

Despite the fact that this sentence uses no pompous words or difficult words, it is still difficult to read because it is long. With only slight adjustments, it can be simplified:

```
Because of our limited warehousing facilities, we
are studying the possibility of using public ware-
houses.  Several in this area offer storage and
handling facilities.  Most charge only for the
amount of space occupied and the length of time
it is used.
```

These three shorter sentences deliver the message more clearly and more directly than does the one-long-sentence version. Here is another example.

```
One of the greatest advantages of electronic pho-
tocopiers is their ability to make copies
quickly, both enlarged and reduced, but photo-
copiers also have disadvantages, the first being
that they are expensive for large runs and the
second that employees tend to use them for unau-
thorized copying.
```

To make this thought interesting to read, use shorter sentences:

One of the greatest advantages of electronic photocopiers is their ability to make copies
quickly, both enlarged and reduced. However, photocopiers also have disadvantages. First, they're
expensive for large runs and, second, employees
tend to use them for unauthorized copying.

No foolproof "rules" are possible, but recheck sentences with more than 20 words to determine whether they should be revised.

Short Sentences

Is the solution to readability using only very short sentences? No, of course not. Too many short sentences make your message choppy and disconnected.

Dear Mr. DeNora:

Thank you for your recent letter. You are correct! We made an error in our June statement.
We did not credit your account properly.

You should have received a credit for $125 for
merchandise returned on May 23. We have enclosed
a revised statement. It shows the proper credit.
We appreciate your help. Thank you.

As you see, using only very short sentences provides no remedy.

Dear Mr. DeNora:

You are correct! As you point out in your recent
letter, we made an error in our June statement.
We did not credit your account for $125 for mer-
chandise returned on May 23.

Mr. DeNora, we have enclosed a revised statement,
which shows the proper credit.

Thank you for your help!

The revised message is more readable because it uses sentences of varying lengths.

Note that certain sentences (called *elliptical expressions*) are grammatically incomplete but are perfectly acceptable for occasional use.

I know you need to have a revised schedule soon.
When?

The standard industry discount in such cases is
20 percent. Correct?

REVIEW PARAGRAPHS

Even the most ambitious readers don't look forward to tackling long, solid blocks
of copy. Paragraph breaks provide visual breathers for your reader. When faced
with one long paragraph in your rough draft, look for ways to break that long
paragraph into two or more shorter paragraphs.

At Allied Securities, all our registered representatives are trained to design an investment
strategy tailored to the needs of each individual
investor. The specific strategy depends on many
factors. First, is the investor seeking income?
If so, then part of the strategy may be to invest
in bonds that will pay interest on a regular basis. Is the investor seeking growth? If so,
then stocks may be more suitable. Also, how much
risk is the client willing to accept? Whether
the investor wants growth or income, a critical
factor in investing funds is safety of principal.
All investments have a certain degree of risk
(except U.S. Treasury obligations, which are considered "guaranteed" safe investments). Each
investor's risk tolerance must be carefully evaluated. In addition, what is the investor's tax
situation? If the investor is seeking income and
is in a high tax bracket, then perhaps a tax-free
municipal bond will be most appropriate. If
taxes are not an important consideration, then
perhaps a higher-yielding corporate bond may be
more appropriate.

Notice how much easier the copy is to read when it is properly paragraphed,
as follows:

At Allied Securities, all our registered representatives are trained to design an investment
strategy tailored to the needs of each individual
investor. The specific strategy depends on many
factors.

First, is the investor seeking income? If so,
then part of the strategy may be to invest in
bonds that will pay interest on a regular basis.
Is the investor seeking growth? If so, then
stocks may be more suitable.

How much risk is the client willing to accept?
Whether the investor wants growth or income, a
critical factor in investing funds is safety of
principal. All investments have a certain degree
of risk (except U.S. Treasury obligations, which
are considered "guaranteed" safe investments).
Each investor's risk tolerance must be carefully
evaluated.

What is the investor's tax situation? If the investor is seeking income and is in a high tax
bracket, then perhaps a tax-free municipal bond
will be most appropriate. If taxes are not an
important consideration, then perhaps a higher-
yielding corporate bond may be more appropriate.

An alternative way to break copy into paragraphs is to enumerate the three
topics, as follows:

At Allied Securities, all our registered representatives are trained to design an investment
strategy tailored to the needs of each individual
investor. The specific strategy depends on three
factors.

1. First, is the investor seeking income? If so,
   then part of the strategy may be to invest in
   bonds that will pay interest on a regular
   basis. Is the investor seeking growth? If
   so, then stocks may be more suitable.
2. How much risk is the client willing to accept?
   Whether the investor wants growth or income, a
   critical factor in investing funds is safety
   of principal. All investments have a certain
   degree of risk. Each investor's risk tolerance must be carefully evaluated.
3. What is the investor's tax situation? If the
   investor is seeking income and is in a high
   tax bracket, then perhaps a tax-free municipal
   bond will be most appropriate. If taxes are
   not an important consideration, then perhaps a

higher-yielding corporate bond may be more appropriate.

Yet another alternative is to provide headings for the subtopics:

At Allied Securities, all our registered representatives are trained to design an investment
strategy tailored to the needs of each individual
investor. The specific strategy depends on three
factors.

The Investor's Goals
First, is the investor seeking income? If so,
then part of the strategy may be to invest in
bonds that will pay interest on a regular basis.
Is the investor seeking growth? If so, then
stocks may be more suitable.

Safety of Principal
How much risk is the client willing to accept?
Whether the investor wants growth or income, a
critical factor in investing funds is safety of
principal. All investments have a certain degree
of risk. Each investor's risk tolerance must be
carefully evaluated.

Tax Liability
What is the investor's tax situation? If the investor is seeking income and is in a high tax
bracket, then perhaps a tax-free municipal bond
will be most appropriate. If taxes are not an
important consideration, then perhaps a higher-
yielding corporate bond may be more appropriate.

REVIEW THE TOTAL MESSAGE

To make sure that your messages are indeed easy to read and interesting, you must review the total message, not just its individual parts. Does it accomplish your objectives?

Dear Mrs. Dykstra:

Thank you for calling to tell me about the change
in shipping instructions. As I mentioned, the

order had not yet been packed when I called our
warehouse. We will now ship the entire order to
your Danville, Illinois, warehouse.

I've enclosed a price list for our Mercury product line. The next time I visit you, I'll probably have a new Mercury catalog for you, too.

My best regards.

Is this message effective? The letter contains no pompous words or clichés, and it is certainly easy to read. But unless you know the writer's objective—the reason for sending this letter—you really cannot tell whether it is effective.

In this particular case, the writer wanted to send an important customer a new price list. As he began writing, he opened the letter by referring to the recent conversation he had with Mrs. Dykstra. Then, in his rush to complete several other letters, he overlooked the real purpose of his message: to explain that his company suddenly announced an increase in all wholesale prices. Perhaps it is obvious to the writer that the price list is new, but it may not be obvious to the reader. Mrs. Dykstra may gloss over the most important point, just as the writer did.

Farfetched? Not really. When business writers do not carefully review their letters, their messages are often off target. To emphasize the key point, that the enclosed price list is new, the writer should revise the message:

Dear Mrs. Dykstra:

Thank you for calling to tell me about the change
in shipping instructions. As I mentioned, the
order had not yet been packed when I called our
warehouse. We will now ship the entire order to
your Danville, Illinois, warehouse.

I've enclosed a new price list for Mercury products. Please note that these new prices become
effective on September 30. If you know of any
Mercury products that you'd like to order, at the
present prices, I'll be happy to hold up shipment and payment for a month or so. Just let me
know. (By the way, the next time I visit you,
I'll probably have a new Mercury catalog for you,
too.)

My best regards.

In this case, slight revisions solve the problem. Remember: Review the total message to make sure that your letters are on target.

PROJECTS

1. Rewrite the following in simple, easy-to-understand language.

   a. In a subsequent letter, we will evaulate the relative desirability of various and sundry investments in effectuating the overall objectives of the company.

   b. It is apparent and obvious, therefore, that sound knowledge of letter composition and cultivation of the accurate thinking by which it must be accompanied should constitute an exceedingly worthwhile accomplishment.

   c. Verification that functional requirements of products are satisfied at minimal cost is established by design value reviews prior to final engineering release.

   d. A number of business decisions are capable of easier resolution as a consequence of advance cost estimates.

   e. Many top-management groups seek to inject more incentive into pay practices by gearing increases to differences in performance.

   f. Business failure itself is an everyday occurrence in our country.

   g. The two important considerations in determining the internal communications system or systems that will be most appropriate for a given organization are speed and cost.

   h. Mere availability of a potential statistical method has not led automatically to practical applications.

   i. What is the receptivity of the organization to change?

   j. Clear-cut job descriptions, preferably in writing, for all supervisory personnel are indispensable to manager development.

2. Reduce the number of words in each of the following, at the same time making each statement clearer and more to the point.

   a. We are making this analysis for the purpose of providing a basis for improving the sales picture.

   b. In the majority of instances, we ship goods to our customers under a c.o.d. arrangement.

   c. In view of the foregoing facts and figures, it seems appropriate to suggest an entirely new customer service policy.

   d. I have your letter of September 14 before me and am happy to tell you that we will be able to supply the uniforms you want in the colors and sizes you requested in your letter.

   e. Would it be possible, do you think, for you to engage the Crown Room for our use as the meeting place of our task force on May 19?

   f. It is the consensus of opinion of our Personnel Relations Committee that work stoppages would decrease impressively and substantially if the equipment were kept in constant and complete repair.

   g. Are you sending the invitations out in the mail in plenty of time so that those who are being invited will have sufficient advance notice in which to respond?

   h. The accountants in our department individually and collectively agree with the decision arrived at to cease and desist the practice of amortizing product-development costs over a five-year period.

i. The regional managers held a meeting for the purpose of discussing the distribution of sales territories in the various geographic areas.

j. Mr. Collard gave a talk on the growing increase in the popularity of bonus compensation systems for personnel in management positions.

3. Suggest one or two words that can be substituted for each of the following expressions. Indicate whether the expression can be omitted altogether.

a. in regard to or in reference to

b. along the lines of

c. due to the fact or for the reason that

d. in favor of

e. in order to

f. in the majority of instances

g. in the neighborhood of

h. in view of the above

i. on behalf of

j. Hoping to hear from you, I remain

k. with the exception of

l. attached (or enclosed) please find

m. enclosed herewith

n. continued patronage

o. I have your letter

p. subsequent to

q. taking the liberty of

r. would like to state (and all the would-like-to's and wish-to's)

4. Tell why each of the following expressions is redundant.

a. new innovations

b. absolutely necessary

c. ask the question

d. consensus of opinion

e. enclosed you will find

f. necessary requirements

g. other alternative

h. reasonable and fair

i. temporarily suspended

j. totally unnecessary

5. Study the following; then rewrite each, removing unnecessary words. In some cases, you may wish to substitute a different term.

a. exactly identical

b. basic fundamentals

c. connect up

d. free gratis

e. repeat back

f. past experience

g. four in number

h. at a distance of 40 miles

i. at a price of $175

j. the color of the Gizmo is dark green

k. round in shape

l. throughout the entire year

m. during the year of 19—

n. came at a time when

o. if it is possible, please

p. the reason is due to

q. in view of

r. according to our records

s. at all times

t. during the time that

u. held a meeting

v. in this day and age

w. made the announcement

x. at an early date

y. a substantial number of people are of the opinion

z. fully cognizant of

aa. encounter difficulty in

6. Can you think of a simpler word for each of the following? (For some, you may need more than one word.)

a. acquiesce

b. aggregate

c. apparent

d. approximately

e. ascertain

f. assist

g. commensurate with

h. communicate with

i. conclusion

j. construct

k. demonstrate

l. difficult

m. discrepancy

n. disseminate

o. equitable

p. equivalent	**x.** preclude	**ee.** submitted
q. expiration	**y.** predisposed	**ff.** subsequent to
r. feedback	**z.** previous to	**gg.** sufficient
s. initiate	**aa.** procure	**hh.** terminated
t. inquire	**bb.** provided	**ii.** transmitted
u. interrogate	**cc.** purchase	**jj.** utilization
v. modification	**dd.** render	**kk.** verification
w. permit		

<table>
<tr><td>

CHAPTER

5

</td><td>

MAKING YOUR LETTERS PERSUASIVE

</td></tr>
</table>

We mentioned earlier that practically every letter you write is a sales message. Obviously, when your principal objective is to persuade someone to buy, you employ all the elements of effective persuasion and selling. And the same is true when you respond to requests for information about your product or service. You consider each request as a chance to win a customer.

But as we've shown in various letters in the first four chapters, persuasiveness is also present in many other letter-writing situations: apologizing to customers and others for errors and delays, saying "no" to requests that you can't grant, collecting money from delinquent accounts, and so on. In such letters your objective is to sell an idea, a point of view, an attitude, or simply a favorable company image.

POSITIVENESS

Imagine a salesperson greeting a customer with this approach: "You don't want to buy a set of encyclopedias, do you?" Such a negative question makes it easy for the prospect to say "no," and the possibility of making a sale has been lost. A more positive approach would have been: "Wouldn't you and your family like to be the proud owners of these 18 handsome volumes?" Although the latter approach will not guarantee a sale, the prospect will have a little harder time saying "no" convincingly.

Becoming adept in the art of persuasion, so important in all human relationships, requires positiveness—stressing the favorable and playing down the unfavorable. Let's make it clear that being positive does not mean bending the truth. You wouldn't tell a prospect that your photocopier makes better copies than Brand X when you know it doesn't. On the other hand, you might direct your prospect's attention to the fact that your machine costs $200 less than Brand X.

Let's look at some examples of positiveness in business letters.

Case Example 1
Explaining a Delay in Delivery

Situation   The Time-Plus Watch Company has received an order from Kirby's Discount Store for 16 men's Criterion digital watches. However, this particular watch has been sold out, and a new shipment is not due for about ten days. An order service correspondent, distressed that she could not fill the order immediately, wrote this letter:

Dear Mr. Kirby:

I am very sorry that we are out of stock on men's Criterion digital watches, and I know you will be disappointed that we do not expect a new shipment from the factory for another ten days. Can you wait that long?

Sincerely yours,

Analysis The correspondent may have made the problem worse than it actually was. Here's why.

1. The situation should not have been represented as seriously as the correspondent wrote. What might she have said?

Dear Mr. Kirby:

Thank you for your order for 16 men's Criterion digital watches. This model has been so popular this Christmas season that the factory is a little hard-pressed to keep up with demand.

We do, however, expect a new shipment about November 14, and I'll make certain that the watches are sent to you the same day they are received here.

I think you'll be pleased, Mr. Kirby, at how quickly these new Criterions are recognized by shoppers as genuine bargains. Indeed, we're so convinced of their appeal that we've tripled our usual order. So we can take care of your future needs without delay.

Sincerely yours,

2. The writer of the second letter has chosen not to imply that ten days is a long time to wait, emphasizing the rapidity with which shipment will be made when new stock is available.
3. The last paragraph is, in effect, a compliment to Mr. Kirby for choosing such a popular product. Assuming that the statements are correct, this is a reassuring paragraph for a customer.

Case Example 2
Suggesting a Substitute for Merchandise Ordered

Situation Mark Hearell is junior sales correspondent of Metro Luggage Manufacturers. A luggage store owner, Marianne Travis (who has an open account at Metro) writes to place an order for the following vinyl garment bags: 15 black, 15 brown, 6 dark blue, 6 lemon yellow, and 4 white.

Metro has discontinued the lemon yellow garment bag but can fill the remainder of the order. Here is the letter Hearell wrote to the customer.

```
Dear Ms. Travis:

I am sorry that we no longer manufacture the
lemon yellow vinyl garment bag, but we are ship-
ping you today the remainder of your order.
Thank you for your business.
```

Analysis Hearell exhibits a negative, no-can-do attitude in his letter. The following is a more sensible response.

```
Dear Ms. Travis:

Thank you for your order for 46 vinyl garment
bags.  We are delighted to have it.  I am sending
you immediately the black, brown, dark blue, and
white garment bags.  We no longer manufacture
these bags in lemon yellow.

I'm enclosing a tearsheet from our current cata-
log in which all our garment bags are shown in
eight different colors.  Perhaps you will find
another color that you like since we don't have
lemon yellow.  Incidentally, two very popular
bags at the moment are gold and maroon.  I can
send you either or both of these colors immedi-
ately.  To save time, why not telephone me col-
lect at (456) 555-2075.

                              Sincerely yours,
```

Analysis The second letter is exactly as it should be—positive, friendly, and helpful. Whether Travis sends a replacement order for the lemon yellow bags, at least the writer has tried, in a very persuasive manner, to please the customer.

Sometimes, through oversight or lethargy, we fail to give people the precise information or help they ask for. This is a form of negativism, telling our readers that their requests deserve only casual consideration.

Case Example 1
Responding to an Order for Merchandise No Longer Produced

Situation   The Modern Press prints many books in ring binders, such as cookbooks, how-to books, and self-improvement manuals. After a book has been in print a few years, the publisher may decide to issue a new edition and let the old one go out of print. The new edition may be of a different size and format, bearing little resemblance to its predecessor.

Such a situation is the subject of the exchange of letters that follows. Mrs. Shirley Hamm, in Denver, purchased the first edition of a ring-binder cookbook. After she had used it for six or seven years, the cover began to fall apart, and so she wrote the publisher the following letter:

Ladies and Gentlemen:

I purchased the <u>Martha Johnson Picture Cookbook</u> at a local bookstore about seven years ago, and I have enjoyed using it very much. Now the cover is falling apart, and I would like to have a new one.

Could I purchase a new five-ring binder for this cookbook from you? Please let me know what the price would be.

Sincerely,

Here is the response Mrs. Hamm received:

Dear Mrs. Hamm:

Thank you for your letter of November 2 concerning your <u>Martha Johnson Picture Cookbook</u>.

It is company policy to replace all defective books. However, the first edition is out of print and is no longer available. It has been replaced with a newer edition in an eight-ring binder. Therefore, I cannot send you a cover for your book.

I am sorry I cannot help you. I know how difficult it must be to use a book in the condition you describe.

                              Sincerely yours,

Analysis The general tone of the letter to Mrs. Hamm is good, but there are some serious problems with it.

1. The first paragraph expresses appreciation for the letter, and the last paragraph offers an apology that seems to indicate that the writer is sympathetic with Mrs. Hamm's problem.
2. Unfortunately, the writer missed the point in the response given. For example, the term *company policy* is irritating, conjuring up visions of a big rule book that the organization hides behind when a "no" answer must be given.
3. Most serious, though, is that Mrs. Hamm's problem was really not dealt with. The fact that the first edition is out of print has little to do with the availability of a binder. Following is one way Mrs. Hamm might have been given satisfaction:

Dear Mrs. Hamm:

I wish we had a binder available to fit your first edition of the <u>Martha Johnson Picture Cookbook</u>, but unfortunately, we do not.

Actually, Mrs. Hamm, we do not manufacture any of the books we publish, and when new books arrive at our warehouse from the printers, we don't receive extra covers or binders. I checked to see whether there might be a copy or two of the first edition of the cookbook that I could send you, but no luck!

The company that manufactured the binder for your cookbook is Permadex Corporation, Norwood, Pennsylvania, 19704. I talked with Permadex's production manager, Mr. F. C. McCulloch, and I learned that he has no binders left from the original printing. However, he does have exactly the same binder (five rings, 8½ by 10 inches) with a blank cover.

If you think this would be a satisfactory solution to your problem, I suggest that you write

to Mr. McCulloch. He tells me that the price
is $4.60, including the cost of mailing.

Good luck!

Sincerely yours,

4. The second letter gives Mrs. Hamm the precise information she requested. Also, the writer's attitude is very likely to elicit from Mrs. Hamm the reaction that we spoke about earlier: "That's a fine company!"

GOING THE EXTRA MILE

The advertising slogan of a large bank in the East is "At Union Federal we do more than we have to. We have to." Certainly, going beyond what is really required in business letters can pay big dividends in terms of goodwill building. Let's look at an example.

Case Example 1
Responding to an Order for
Unknown Merchandise

Situation Baldwin's Book Nook, a retail store, received a request from a customer for an out-of-print book. The customer knows the approximate name of the author (Wernke or Werner), the title (*Practical Handbook of Mathematical Tables*), the approximate date of publication (between 1925 and 1930), and the publisher (Wolff).

Olivia Baldwin, the store owner, decided to write Wolff Publishers, from whom she still buys books. The reply she received was as follows:

Dear Mrs. Baldwin:

The book you inquired about is no longer in
print, and there is no record of it in our files.

Yours very truly,

Analysis The response is not adequate. Here's why.

1. If the writer had possessed the "can-do" attitude, he might have produced a more helpful response.

Dear Mrs. Baldwin:

I appreciate your request in behalf of a customer for information about a handbook of math-

ematical tables that you believe was published by Wolff in the 1920s.

I have searched our archives very carefully and talked to several old-timers here, but I can find almost no information. You may remember that we had a fire in one of our warehouses several years ago, and many of our records and old books were destroyed. One of our executives distinctly remembers the book, but he could supply no details.

You probably know, Mrs. Baldwin, that there are many organizations throughout the country that specialize in what is called "bookfinding," and I'm led to believe that they often turn up books that have been out of print for 60 or more years. I'm enclosing the Classified section of the current edition of <u>Atlantic's</u> magazine. Under "Books" you will find a list of about a dozen organizations that specialize in locating hard-to-find books. Perhaps your customer will want to write some of them, supplying all the information he has about the handbook.

I'm afraid this is the best I can do, but I wish your customer every success in his search.

Sincerely,

2. With the second letter, even if the customer cannot locate the book he wants, the publisher's correspondent will have shown a willingness to be as helpful as possible. This, of course, builds goodwill for Wolff Publishers in the eyes of Mrs. Baldwin as well as for Baldwin's Book Nook in the eyes of the customer.

EXAGGERATION

In your quest for persuasiveness, be careful not to get carried away with enthusiasm. Exaggerating can destroy your credibility.

In our hard-sell society we are accustomed to hearing such terms as *fabulous selection, sensational styling, dramatic advancement, dynamic breakthrough, unmatched performance, incredibly low-priced, terrific values, unique* (or the illiterate *most unique*) *features, tremendous savings, unbelievable bargains, once-in-a-lifetime opportunity,* and *fantastic offer.* And we have learned to quickly dismiss such claims as "sales puff" and let them slide by. That's exactly what your readers will do when they see such terms in your letters—let them slide by without placing any confidence in the writer's statement.

Beware of *more* and *most*, too, in your attempt to be persuasive:

1. I am *more than* happy to refund your money. (Ecstatic?)
2. We are *most* apologetic about the error. (Humbled?)
3. All of us at Musselman's are *more than* anxious to see that you are *most* pleased with your purchases. (Stubbornly determined?)
4. Rankin's is *more than* concerned about the delay. (Distraught?)

Flattery

Another form of exaggeration is flattery. While some flattery is all right, it can be overdone, leaving your reader suspicious of your sincerity. Following are examples.

Overdone

I am at a loss for words, Mr. Bandino, in attempting to express my profound gratitude for that tremendous order for Widgets and the beautiful check that accompanied it. A thousand thanks!

Reasonable

Thank you very much, Mr. Bandino, for your order for 240 Widgets and your check for $8,640. I really appreciate this expression of confidence in this new product.

Overdone

The success of the convention of the Society for Public Relations is a glowing tribute to your genius as an organizer and moderator. It was a magnificent performance, Linda, and I'm convinced that it will never be duplicated.

Reasonable

I want to compliment you, Linda, on the success of the convention of the Society for Public Relations. The programs were excellent, and I feel sure that everyone who attended came away as pleased as I was with the whole affair. Well done!

Overdone

Your selection as president of the Utah Wholesalers Association for the coming year is a signal honor, Mr. Krafft, and I couldn't possibly have been more delighted to see this recognition of your imagination, talent, dedication, and leadership qualities. Surely the Association is on the threshold of its greatest year ever!

Reasonable

I think the Utah Wholesalers Association chose well, Mr. Krafft, when it named you president for the coming year. I congratulate not only you but the election committee as well for its good judgment. I'm confident you will bring strong leadership to the UWA in 19—.

Overstatement

Beware of the overstatement! For example:

1. Believe me, Ms. Forbes, such an error will not happen again. (The promise of perfection is hazardous; all too often the same mistake *will* occur.)
2. Come in, and you'll see: Every car at Reston Motors is priced just a tiny fraction above cost. (A catchy slogan but probably not true. How much is "just a tiny fraction"?)
3. Everyone stands ready at all times to make your shopping at Kahn's a thoroughly delightful and long-remembered experience. (Perhaps, but highly unlikely.)
4. Nothing is as important to Cushman's as a satisfied customer. (Not even a healthy net profit?)
5. Everything that can be done will be done to guarantee your entire satisfaction. (Rubbish. How about pricing the merchandise below cost?)
6. The success of our organization rests entirely in the hands of customers like you. (This sounds good, but it's not so. Success hinges on several things, including intelligent buying, promotion, and management.)

DIGNIFY YOUR READER

Effective selling in business letters requires that the writer respect the reader's pride and dignity. "Killers" of persuasiveness include talking down, lecturing, and making insinuations and accusations.

Talking Down

By talking down we mean assuming an air of superiority—to be condescending. Here are examples.

1. When you've been in the business as long as we have, you will learn that....
2. It seems unlikely that the mistake could have occurred at this end. Our insistence on the highest standards of quality assures the efficient....

3. Although it is very large and successful, Conover-Crane makes no distinction between small customers like you and giant corporations.
4. It is natural that you might assume that because of our position in the industry, we are insensitive to suggestions from the public. However....
5. The reason we include order blanks in our catalog is to prevent the kinds of errors that were made in your recent letter.

Lecturing

Some writers can't resist the temptation to lecture to their readers. Beware of such preachments as these:

1. I am sure it is obvious to you that we cannot sell our products at cost.
2. Surely you know that our policy has always been that....
3. We're proud of our service, but we're not magicians.
4. It should be no surprise to you that without a profit you couldn't stay in business.
5. We think it is important to your business to attract and hold customers.
6. You've been in business long enough to know that when expenses exceed income, there is no profit.

Insinuations and Accusations

Readers bristle with indignation when a writer makes insinuations and accusations. The following examples show why readers react negatively.

1. *You claim* that the carrel panels arrived in a damaged condition. (*You claim* is an insinuation that the reader is not telling the truth.)
2. *It is hard to believe* that *all* the volumes in your new encyclopedia could, as you put it, be "coming apart." (*It is hard to believe* insinuates that the reader is stretching the facts. Too, emphasizing the word *all* and using the phrase as *you put it* are obvious attempts to ridicule the reader.)
3. *I am amazed that you think* our Gewgaws are too high-priced. (An accusation of stupidity.)
4. *The mystery is that you seem to be the only one* who did not receive the revised price list. (In other words, "You obviously received it but simply chose not to use it.")
5. *You neglected to* sign the second and third copies of the certificate. (Never say "you neglected to." This is better: "I'm returning the second and third copies of the certificate for your signature.")
6. It seems to me that the *fair thing* for you to do is to pay all crating and shipping costs. (An insinuation that the readers is being unfair. This is better: "Since an exception was made in accepting your returned shipment for full credit, I believe I am justified in asking you to pay all crating and shipping costs.")
7. The packaging protection for these instruments is certainly adequate for ordinary handling, as our many customers will attest. (An accusation that the customer was careless.)

MORE ABOUT GENDER BIAS

If you want to make your communications persuasive, you must also avoid gender bias. A few years ago it was standard practice in communications to refer to unnamed individuals as *he*, for the assumption was that the masculine gender also embraced the feminine. This is not uncommon today in many companies. For example, note the following office letter (memorandum) addressed to all employees in a large business firm. (*Note:* Interoffice letters—memorandums—are discussed in detail in Chapters 16 and 18.)

McPHERSON ASSOCIATES

INTEROFFICE MEMORANDUM

TO: All Employees   **FROM:** M. J. Southall
SUBJECT: Performance Ratings   **DATE:** July 14, 19--

Quite often an employee raises the question about how performance ratings affect <u>his</u> salary increases. A simple answer is that these ratings have an important bearing on whether an employee receives an increase and how much <u>he</u> receives.

Our performance rating form emphasizes the employee's fitness in the following eight categories.

1. <u>His</u> knowledge of the job.
2. <u>His</u> quality and quantity of work.
3. <u>His</u> attendance and punctuality. (If an employee is habitually late or absent, <u>he</u> will obviously be penalized.)
4. <u>His</u> judgment--that is, <u>he</u> must justify the utmost confidence of <u>his</u> supervisor.
5. <u>His</u> reliability. (This means that <u>he</u> can always be counted on.)
6. <u>His</u> attitude. (Every employee is expected to have a positive attitude toward <u>his</u> job, <u>his</u> coworkers, and <u>his</u> supervisor.)
7. <u>His</u> ability to learn quickly. (No employee can be highly rated if <u>he</u> is extremely slow in catching on to <u>his</u> responsibilities.)
8. <u>His</u> personal characteristics. (This means <u>his</u> appearance, manners, honesty, and <u>his</u> tact.)

The supervisor who rates employees is required by policy to discuss the preformance rating with each employee before <u>he</u> releases it to the Personnel Department. It is <u>his</u> responsibility to tell the employee frankly what <u>his</u> strong and weak points are and to make suggestions for improving <u>his</u> performance.

M.J.S.

Unless every employee in the organization is a "he," this memorandum will be offensive to those who are not. It is very easy to remove such biased language. For example:

McPHERSON ASSOCIATES

INTEROFFICE MEMORANDUM

TO: All Employees   **FROM:** M. J. Southall
SUBJECT: Performance Ratings   **DATE:** July 14, 19--

Many employees have raised the question about how performance ratings affect <u>their</u> salary increases. A simple answer is that these ratings have an important bearing on whether an employee receives an increase and how much.

Our performance rating form emphasizes the employee's fitness in the following eight categories.

1. Knowledge of the job. (To score high in this category, employees must have an exceptionally thorough knowledge of <u>their</u> jobs.)
2. Quality and quantity of work.
3. Attendance and punctuality. (<u>Those</u> who are habitually late or absent will be penalized.)
4. Judgment--that is, employees must justify the utmost confidence of <u>their</u> supervisors.)
5. Reliability. (By this is meant, of course, that employees can be counted on to do <u>their</u> work well and on time.)
6. Attitude. (Employees are expected to have a positive attitude toward <u>their</u> job, <u>their</u> co-workers, and <u>their</u> supervisors.)

7. Ability to learn quickly. (Employees who are extremely slow in catching on to <u>their</u> responsibilities cannot be highly rated.)
8. Personal characteristics. (This means appearance, manners, honesty, and tact.)

The supervisors who rate employees are required by policy to discuss the performance rating with each employee before <u>they</u> release the rating to the Personnel Department. It is the supervisor's responsibility to tell employees what <u>their</u> strong and weak points are and to make suggestions for improving <u>their</u> performance.

M.J.S.

The second memorandum shows how easily bias can be removed by just a slight rewording of the message. In achieving unbiased writing, however, avoid the use of *he or she* or *she or he* construction, which is considered awkward. Where feasible, switch your sentence to the plural form so that you can use *they, their*, and *them*. In many instances, it isn't even necessary to use a pronoun. In each item in the list we've omitted *His*—it is not needed. Also note the omission of *he* and *his* in the sentence following item 8; it is understood that this refers to every employee.

GRAMMAR AND PUNCTUATION

Correct grammar and punctuation can be very important in winning your reader's confidence. Whether we like it or not, educated people are offended when they see commas, periods, and other punctuation marks in the wrong place or missing entirely. They cringe when the subject and verb in a sentence are not in agreement, when participles dangle, when sentences are incomplete or run on, and so forth. The idea that it doesn't matter whether you follow standard grammar rules as long as people understand in a general way has not been accepted in business. The standards of language usage in business are high, and although many writers violate them, the standards are still there.

If you feel insecure about your grammar, invest in a good handbook of English usage and learn how to use it. Few people can remember all the nuances of correct grammar and style. But good writers know when they don't know and do not hestitate to reach for a reference book when in doubt. (One of the most popular manuals for secretaries and word processors is *The Gregg Reference Manual*, by William A. Sabin, published by McGraw-Hill Book Company.)

Writers who use electronic equipment soon learn that punctuation marks have a special significance for them. Most systems—especially word processing systems—have their own sets of computer commands, which may resemble traditional characters or punctuation marks. These commands may be used for underlining as well as for formatting, printing in boldface or italics, and other elements of letter preparation. Learning to distinguish these commands from traditional characters and punctuation will go a long way toward saving you time and frustration if you are using electronic equipment to write and send your letters.

APPEARANCE

The way your letters look can greatly influence your reader's attitude toward and acceptance of your message. Good balance on the page (top, bottom, and side margins) and the correct setup of the date line, inside address, salutation, body, complimentary close, signature block, and reference initials and notations will also help you to sell your message.

On the other hand, poor typing (bad erasures, strikeovers, skipped spacing, and so on) actually can "unsell" your message. When you produce a sloppy letter, you are in effect saying to the reader, "You're not important enough for me to take the time to do better."

A well-balanced, attractive letter is illustrated on page 73. The style is modified block, perhaps the most popular form in business. (A second popular style is the block style, which differs only in that the date and signature block align on the left.)

LOGIC IN COMMUNICATIONS

Some people have the habit of jumping to conclusions and making statements based on a personal bias or whim instead of provable facts. For example:

1. For the third time this quarter, we received a shipment from you that came a week later than promised. Obviously, our orders are very low on your priority list.
2. Murchison told me on the telephone that his check was mailed to us five days ago, and we still don't have it. What's wrong with our mail room?
3. October was a bad month for absences in our shipping room—World Series fever, no doubt.
4. In the first half of the year, there were 24 absences—16 women and 8 men—but of course it is well known that women are treated as second-class citizens in our company.
5. Since Miss Eberly did not list references on her employment application, it must be assumed that she had none to suggest.

Poor logic can destroy your rapport with your reader. Let's look at two examples of fuzzy thinking.

Case Example 1
Responding About Terms That Cannot Be Granted

Situation Lawrence Dennison, a retail furniture dealer, wrote to a supplier asking for an extension of 30 days in paying for merchandise purchased a couple

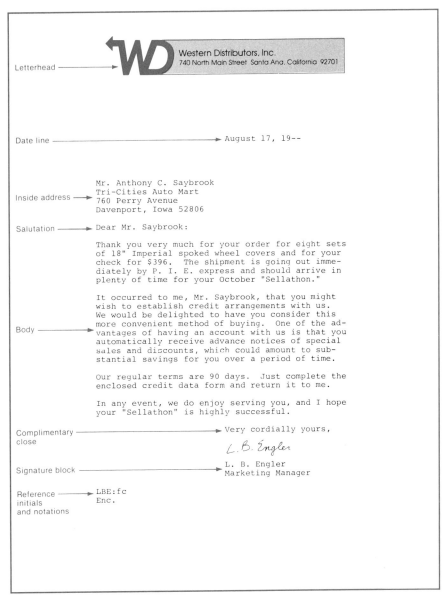

Letterhead → **Western Distributors, Inc.**
740 North Main Street Santa Ana, California 92701

Date line → August 17, 19--

Inside address →
Mr. Anthony C. Saybrook
Tri-Cities Auto Mart
760 Perry Avenue
Davenport, Iowa 52806

Salutation → Dear Mr. Saybrook:

Body →
Thank you very much for your order for eight sets
of 18" Imperial spoked wheel covers and for your
check for $396. The shipment is going out imme-
diately by P. I. E. express and should arrive in
plenty of time for your October "Sellathon."

It occurred to me, Mr. Saybrook, that you might
wish to establish credit arrangements with us.
We would be delighted to have you consider this
more convenient method of buying. One of the advantages of having an account with us is that you
automatically receive advance notices of special
sales and discounts, which could amount to substantial savings for you over a period of time.

Our regular terms are 90 days. Just complete the
enclosed credit data form and return it to me.

In any event, we do enjoy serving you, and I hope
your "Sellathon" is highly successful.

Complimentary close → Very cordially yours,

Signature block →
L. B. Engler
L. B. Engler
Marketing Manager

Reference initials and notations →
LBE:fc
Enc.

of weeks ago. He also requested the usual cash discount of 4 percent, even though he isn't entitled to it. The manufacturer is willing to grant the 30-day extension but not the cash discount. The account supervisor wrote Dennison as follows:

Although we will be pleased to grant you an extension of 30 days in paying your account, I must
tell you that the discount cannot be allowed.
Discounts are given only to our prompt-paying
customers. I'm sure you will understand.

Analysis   The account supervisor's response can be improved.

1. Lawrence Dennison was presumptuous in asking for a discount to which he obviously knew he wasn't entitled. But that is no reason to brand him as a slow-paying customer.
2. A more logical response follows.

```
Of course we're glad to allow you an extra 30
days to pay the July 17 invoice.

As to your request for a cash discount, I'm
sure you know that it can be offered only when
payment is received within ten days of the in-
voice date. If we made exceptions, many of our
customers who now observe the ten-day provision
would no longer feel obliged to do so.
```

Case Example 2
Announcing Business Hours

Situation   A mail-room supervisor, upset because employees bring mail to the department after the announced closing hour of 4:30 and expect it to be sent out the same day, issued this notice:

```
This is to notify all employees that mail cannot
be accepted after 4:30 for processing.  This pol-
icy has been in effect for over two years.  Of
course, overnight express mail is still an excep-
tion.
```

Analysis   The supervisor's notice needs to be clarified.

1. What do you think the supervisor meant? Probably this: Ordinary postal matter received after 4:30 will not be processed (placed in the mail) that day will be sent out the next morning. However, overnight express mail will go out that day even if received after 4:30.
2. A more logical communication follows.

```
Will you please help us?

A couple of years ago we set a policy that when
ordinary outgoing mail is received in the mail
room after 4:30, it will be held for processing
and mailing until the next morning.  The reason
is that mail-room employees leave at 5, and we
are not authorized to keep them beyond that
hour.
```

Of course, you may bring your outgoing mail to us up to 5; we'll put it in safekeeping and make sure it goes out early the next morning.

Overnight communications are exceptions to this policy. We'll continue to get them in the mail the same day we receive them, even if they arrive in the mail room after 4:30.

Thank you!

ANSWERING LETTERS PROMPTLY

When letters from customers and others go unanswered for long periods of time, it can be very difficult when a response is made to get off on the right foot with your readers. Their annoyance at the delay is apt to make them reluctant to accept what you have to say, no matter how persuasive the message.

Because delays in answering correspondence are often costly, some firms lay down this rule: Respond to all letters within 48 hours. This is a reasonable policy in most situations, and the well-organized correspondent sorts the incoming mail every day—often several times a day—to make sure that important letters get priority attention.

Even if you can't give a specific answer to an inquiry or request, because you don't have the information, it's wise to acknowledge the letter quickly and indicate when a specific reply will be forthcoming. For example:

Dear Mrs. Krantz:

I will attend to your request for information about Louis F. Foreman's employment here as soon as possible. At the moment we are transferring our personnel files to microfilm, so I don't have access to the necessary documents.

I expect to be finished with the microfilming by the end of next week, at which time I'll do my best to get you the information you need.

Yours very cordially,

There are situations, however, when an immediate response to a communication may not be wise. For example, a person who lacks the necessary qualifications applies for a job vacancy; an applicant for credit is sized up as a poor risk and must be turned down; an individual writes for a special favor that has to be denied; and so on. In these situations and in similar ones where the respondent immediately knows that the answer must be no, it is sometimes wise to let the communication "season" a bit before replying to it. An immediate response is likely to elicit this reaction: "They didn't even take the time to think about my request [or application, problem, suggestion, and so on]." When a response is made, the writer may write something like this:

```
Dear Mr. Harper:

I'm sorry to be late in responding to your letter
of May 12, but I wanted to get all the background
information necessary for evaluating your request
[or application, problem, suggestion, and so on]
intelligently.
```

PROJECTS

1. The following letter was received by the customer services manager of Executive Interiors Inc.

```
Dear Sir or Madam:

Can you please tell me how to remove stains
from marble?

About six months ago our company purchased a
marble-top DuBoise coffee table (Model 661)
from you.  Recently we discovered that the top
was stained in several places--mostly rings
left by glasses and cups.  We have tried sev-
eral cleaning fluids and detergents, but noth-
ing seems to work.

I would greatly appreciate your advice.

                        Sincerely yours.
```

Here is the response the customer received:

```
Dear Madam:

Re your inquiry regarding the removal of
stains from marble, we are extremely sorry
about this difficulty.  As you perhaps have
discovered, marble stains very easily, and
once the stains are allowed to penetrate, they
are very difficult to remove--often impossi-
ble.  People should be warned not to set wet
glasses or cups on marble surfaces.
```

I am making inquiries about methods that may
be used to remove the stains, and I will let
you know when I have obtained the information.
In the meantime, I am sending you a copy of
Caring for Your Marble, which has been recently published. I believe it will be exceedingly helpful.

Yours truly,

Criticize the response in terms of appropriateness and helpfulness. What
would you have written?

2. The Lorick Manufacturing Company makes and sells air-conditioning equipment for industrial use only. Lorick's assistant marketing manager received
the following letter.

Gentlemen:

I am building a beach house near Beaufort,
South Carolina, which I am planning to air-
condition throughout. Please send me full information on your air-conditioning systems.

Sincerely,

Here is the response that was sent.

Dear Mr. Shuster:

Unfortunately, we do not distribute our products to individual consumers. We sell only to
business and industrial users.

Thank you.

Very truly yours,

Rewrite the response, supplying whatever details you need to give Mr.
Shuster the help he wants.

3. The following letter was written to School and College Charms Inc. by the
president of a college students' organization.

Dear Mr. Allenbough:

About a month ago I wrote for a free catalog,
but I have not received it. I am particularly

interested in the college pennant charm for
William and Mary.

Is this charm available? If so, how much will
it cost, including postage?

I would still appreciate having your catalog.

                    Very truly yours,

Here is the response as it was actually written (at the bottom of the incoming
letter).

Under sperate cover we are sending you a cata-
logue. Please be advised that we can give you
a pennant with WM on it for William and Mary.
If you want it in gold it will cost you $8.00
and 3.50 in sterling. The pennant will be in
color and the WM will be in either gold or
sterling according to what you order it in.

Criticize the response, and then prepare the one that should have been
written.

4. Rewrite the following letter, eliminating the negative and accentuating the
positive.

Dear Mrs. Lopez:

I am sorry to be so late in answering your inquiry about the availability of Monarch Cork-
Prest bulletin boards, but because you addressed our Memphis office, your letter was
delayed in reaching me. In the future, please
address all such inquires to the Neosho office, which serves your area.

The information you require is contained in a
small catalog that I am sending you. Please
read it carefully, and if you find that it
does not contain the information you want,
don't hesitate to write.

                    Yours very truly,

5. Rewrite the following sentences, putting the messages in positive terms.
  a. If you don't remit by August 14, you will not receive the 5 percent
  discount.

b. If the foregoing explanation is not clear and you feel that you need additional clarification, kindly advise.

c. We must know the exact size and color you desire in order to get your order to you by October 22.

d. Although I have no actual experience in writing advertising copy, my very thorough college training in advertising, plus my willingness to learn, leads me to believe I could handle your copy in a short time.

e. We cannot send the tarpaulin by parcel post as you requested, since it is too bulky; instead, we are sending it by freight.

f. If, in the future, you will address your orders to this office instead of to the Racine office, you will not experience the delays that you complain about.

g. Because the building is over 40 years old, we could probably get no more than $75,000 for it.

h. Unfortunately, about 5 percent of our shipments in February were delayed because of a local transportation strike.

i. Are you handicapped in your business for lack of capital?

j. You may not have expected to hear from me, but I have been requested by Mr. Meell to answer the letter you wrote to him about our new discount policy.

6. Cynthia Noblett is to teach a course in investments at Olive Grove Community College. In preparing for the course, she ran across an article in *Financial Journal* entitled "The Future of Mutual Funds." She would like to distribute this article to her students, and so she wrote asking if reprints are available. If they are, she wants to order 30. If there are no reprints, she wants permission to photocopy the article. Following is the response Noblett received.

Dear Miss Noblett:

Reprints of the article "The Future of Mutual Funds" are not available. I'm sorry.

The policy concerning reproduction of materials from <u>Financial Journal</u> is described on the title page of each issue.

                              Yours truly,

Note: The policy is that up to 50 reproductions may be made by educational institutions, provided no fee is charged for the copies and full credit is given to the magazine.

7. The following letter was sent by a furniture store chain to people who have just moved into the community. What do you think the reaction will be of those who receive the letter?

Hello Neighbor:

As a newcomer to Cranbrook, we welcome you to this fine community, and we know your going to enjoy living here.

Maxwell Furniture has served this community for over 50 years, we have three outlets--downtown Cranbrook, Park Village, and Ridgecrest. Each store fully stocked with the finest furniture for the most discriminatory buyer.

If you will stop by one of our stores, you will find a free gift waiting for you. To get your's you need only present this letter.

8. Each of the following interoffice messages contains faulty logic. See if you can find the flaws; then rewrite each.
   a. The Manchester terminal is no longer adequate for our West Coast needs; therefore, we are considering enlarging the Haleyville plant.
   b. DAILY CAFETERIA HOURS
      Breakfast—7:30—8:30
      Lunch—12:00—2:30
        Closed Mondays
   c. To All Sales Representatives:

      All credit cards bearing the company name must be surrendered to the accounting office immediately. In the future, if you wish to have credit cards, you must apply for them individually, paying the membership dues yourself (the dues are not legitimate company expenses).

      You may retain the Air Travel and Hertz cards issued by the company.

9. The writer of the letter that follows overdid it when he acknowledged a big order that a good friend and customer placed at the end of the year. Rewrite it so that it is more believable.

Dear Wally:

That was a really sensational order you just gave us, Wally. $46,000--wow! We are more

```
than grateful for this fantastic business,
friend.  Thanks to you, we're going to have an
incredible year, and everybody's rushing out
to buy the biggest Thanksgiving turkey around.

Gracias, amigo!
                              Very sincerely,
```

10. Rewrite the following so that they are free of excessive modesty, sarcasm, preachments, and insinuations.

a. I realize that I am not a systems expert, but perhaps you will allow me to venture some suggestions about simplifying the receiver report form.

b. When will you understand that we are Harrelson's—not Harrison's? We received their statement again, and presumably they received ours.

c. It is quite unlikely that the cartons were damaged when they left our warehouse. Our rigid inspection standards were designed to prevent this kind of thing from happening.

d. I was amazed to learn that you received only 36 copies instead of the 48 we sent you.

e. You say that you reported this difficulty to our representative on several different occasions. This seems strange, since we can find no record of any kind.

CHAPTER 6

REQUEST LETTERS

YOUR JOB

You have just been promoted to office services manager of Winston Associates, a management consulting firm in St. Louis. This position was created for the purpose of providing services to executives, department heads, supervisors, and others in the company. You see that all incoming and outgoing mail is processed quickly and efficiently, that office space is properly utilized, that furniture and equipment are adequate, that needed supplies are available, that company records are properly maintained, and so on. In other words, you provide almost every office service that will help others do their jobs better. In the process, you try to maintain the best relations with all the people who supply you with goods and services.

You often write letters asking for materials, information, services, and special favors. Some of your letters are to companies that stand to benefit from helping you. That is, they have products or services to sell and are eager to attract as many friends and customers as they can. These communications are often referred to as sales-opportunity requests, since they are looked upon by the recipients as a chance to make a sale, either immediately or in the future. Your boss is Herbert Barry, administrative vice president.

CASE 1

Requesting Free Materials

THE SETTING

When you are asked to find answers to questions about products, materials, and services, you often depend on the latest catalogs and price lists and other materials that manufacturers and distributors make available free to potential customers. You notice that a lot of the materials in the files are out of date and that there are very few catalogs of the major suppliers whose ads you've seen and been impressed with in various magazines that you receive.

Your Objective To obtain the presently available materials you need for an up-to-date resource file and to receive new materials as they are released.

BACKGROUND

Since you write on your company letterhead and your requests represent sales opportunities to those who receive them, you can assume that you will generally receive favorable responses without delay. Thus in writing simple request letters such as the type described, you do not need to do a selling job—it's to the recipients' benefit to help you in any way they can. So you could write almost anything and still get what you want! Yet there are two important guidelines that you should observe.

Guidelines

1. Use common courtesy in your request—ask rather than demand.
2. Include all the information the recipients will need in order to give you maximum help, but avoid irrelevancies, for they will only waste the readers' time.

SAMPLE LETTERS

```
Sirs:

Send me all the free materials you have.

                      Very truly yours,
```

Analysis   What do you think of Letter A? Very poor, isn't it? Why?

1. The letter demands rather than asks (Guideline 1).
2. The writer has not supplied sufficient information (Guideline 2).
3. The salutation *Sirs* is not acceptable in modern letter writing.

Note: Although the recipients are likely to guess what the writer wants (the job title in the signature block will be revealing), it's always wise to be perfectly clear; otherwise, additional correspondence may be required.

```
Dear Office Manager:

In consulting our files of catalogs of office
equipment and supplies and checking them off
against various manufacturers and distributors, I
discovered that I do not have your latest cata-
logs and price lists and other information con-
cerning your products.  (I have some materials,
of course, but they appear to be badly out of
date.)

I have just been promoted to the position of of-
fice services manager of Winston Associates, and
```

I think one of the first things I must do is build a good reference source for me and my staff to use in selecting appropriate equipment, materials, and supplies. For this reason I would like to request that you send me your latest catalogs and price lists and other product information you may have in your possession at your earliest convenience. In addition, I would be most grateful if you would put my name on your mailing list so that I will receive all new materials.

Thanking you for your cooperation, I remain,

Very truly yours,

Analysis Letter B accomplishes certain guidelines well while others not at all.

1. Certainly, B satisfies the first guideline: it is courteous. If you were the recipient, you would quickly be able to sense the writer's sincerity and gratitude.
2. On the other hand, the writer has completely ignored the second guideline—brevity. There is no reason for writers to tell their life's story in a simple request letter. Although the recipients will not be offended, their time will be wasted.
3. Note the deadwood and hackneyed expressions: "For this reason I would like to request" (say "Please"); "I would be most grateful if you would put" (say "I would appreciate your putting"); "Thanking you for your cooperation, I remain" (say "Thank you").

C Dear Office Manager:

May I have your latest catalogs and price lists and other information about your office supplies and equipment. I would also like to be placed on your regular mailing list so that I will receive all new sales and promotional literature.

Thank you.

Sincerely yours,

Analysis Letter C meets the two guidelines for simple request letters.

1. It is courteous.
2. The writer has given all the necessary information without overwriting.

"YOUR JOB" PROJECTS

1. The March issue of *Digest of Human Resources* featured the article "Modern Training," by B. L. Wentz, which you enjoyed reading. In the article, Wentz mentioned a booklet available from American Visual Productions, *Making Professional Transparencies,* which is free to business firms. (American Visual Productions sells audiovisual supplies and equipment.) You're thinking of preparing a series of transparencies for training new personnel in company procedures. Write for the free booklet. (*Hint:* It's a good idea to mention the source of your information as well as the use you expect to make of the free materials.)

2. The director of human resources at Winston Associates has shown you a copy of *Building Good Public Relations by Telephone* and told you that the booklet is available free in quantity from Southern Bell Telephone Company (Mrs. Janette Simms, Customer Relations). You want 12 copies by April 11 for use in a special class you are conducting for secretaries, receptionists, and others in the company. Write for them (*Hint:* Be sure to mention the date you need the booklets. Use your own judgment as to whether you should specify the reason for your request.)

SUPPLEMENTARY PROJECTS

3. You are a purchasing manager, and one of your responsibilities is to make arrangements for moving employees who have been transferred by the company from one location to another. The December 14 issue of *Purchasing Weekly* contained an advertisement of Agena Transfer and Storage Company; the ad invited readers to order free copies of a new booklet, *Getting Ready to Move.* You want 50 copies, which you will distribute to employees who are being transferred to new locations. Write the letter (address Bernard C. Trotter), including whatever details you think are important.

4. The sponsor of a public-affairs television program, "Zero In," invited listeners to send for a free copy of *The Office of the Future,* which describes new developments in electronic office communications. You want three copies—one for yourself and one each for the president and financial vice president of your company. (You are a regular viewer of "Zero In," a program that you thoroughly enjoy each Sunday.)

STYLE CHECKUP

Choose the term in parentheses that correctly completes the sentence.

1. While transcribing the dictation, Mickey (accidently, accidentally) erased the first paragraph.
2. We're very (anxious, eager) to show you our new fall fashions.
3. Not only is orange juice delicious, it is also a (healthy, healthful) beverage.
4. I hope, Mrs. Gainer, that you have a (real, really) successful Open House.

CASE 2

Requesting Product Information

THE SETTING

The medical office supervisor has asked you to order two lie-down couches for the admitting office. You must ask for yellow vinyl foam pads to match the present office decor.

You find in a supplier's catalog a couch that fits the supervisor's needs exactly. However, even though the color illustration shows the couch in yellow, the only colors listed in the description below the illustration are black, ivory, green, and red.

The lounge is priced at $140 for one and $130 each for two, with shipping charges prepaid. Before you place a definite order, you want to make sure the couch is available in yellow.

Your Objective   To learn whether the couch is available in yellow and, if so, to place an order for two.

BACKGROUND

In this request letter situation, you are again in the driver's seat. You will place an order if the color you require can be supplied. Certainly, it is to the recipient's advantage to give you all possible help.

Although persuasiveness is not necessary, you should observe certain guidelines in writing requests for product information.

Guidelines

1. Use ordinary courtesy in your request.
2. Be very specific about what you want to know and what your plans are if the color you require is available.
3. Say no more than is necessary for the supplier to provide the help you need.

SAMPLE LETTERS

  Gentlemen:

Is the emergency couch in your catalog available in yellow vinyl as illustrated? Please advise.

                    Yours truly,

Analysis This writer ignores the basic guidelines referred to earlier.

1. Although the writer is not actually discourteous, neither is there any expression of courtesy.
2. It is quite possible that the supplier will know exactly what item is being referred to in the catalog. However, more details should have been given—stock number and catalog page number, for example.
3. Because it is not clear whether this is an order, Letter A will require two additional letters: a "yes" or "no" response from the supplier and an order letter (if yellow is available).
4. *Please advise* is a dead phrase and should be avoided; the complimentary close *Yours truly* is considered old-fashioned.

B

Gentlemen:

I notice that on page 50 of your current catalog, you illustrate the emergency couch No. M612 in the color of yellow. However, in the description below the illustration, only the colors of black, ivory, green and red are indicated. Does this mean that the yellow color illustrated is not available?

If it is not, then I shall not place an order, since we must have the yellow couch to match our present decor. If yellow is available, however, I will place an order for two.

Cordially,

Analysis Letter B is slightly better than A in that it is more specific. However, note the following.

1. Letter B contains deadwood and repetitions that could be eliminated (note that the word *yellow* appears four times).
2. Also, it is not clear whether this letter represents an order or is simply an inquiry ("If yellow is available, however, I will place an order"), so two more letters may be required. Always make one letter do when you can!

C

Gentlemen:

The yellow vinyl emergency couch (M612) illustrated on page 50 of your current catalog seems to be exactly what we want for our medical department admitting room. I notice, however, that yellow is not among the colors listed below the illustration.

If yellow vinyl is available, please consider this my order for two couches. I understand that the price is $130 each when the couch is ordered in lots of two and that you pay shipping charges.

Yours very sincerely,

Analysis   Letter C meets all the guidelines referred to earlier.

1. Although there are no courtesy terms per se (except *please* in the second paragraph), the tone of the letter is pleasant.
2. The writer is very specific about what is wanted and places an order for two couches if yellow vinyl is available. Thus additional letters will be avoided. Note that mention is made of the price and prepaid shipping costs—not essential, but nearly always a good idea.
3. There are no wasted words; the message is simple, straightforward, and complete.

"YOUR JOB" PROJECTS

1. Early this week you received a letter from a large publishing firm in which you were urged to join its new Executive Book Club. The circular enclosed illustrated a wide variety of management books but none in your field of interest (office administration). You are interested in general management subjects, but you want some assurance that your field is adequately represented before you join the club. Write the editor in chief, Glenna Rabon, for specific information. (Although there may not be books now available on office administration, some may be planned for the future.)
2. An advertisement in *Business Week* by Regency Paper Corporation describes a duplicating paper ("Super Versatile") that is suitable for all reproduction methods—spirit, stencil, phtocopier, and so on. You want to know what sizes are available, and you would also like to have samples of the various colors that may be obtained. Write to Patrick Dowling.
3. You are planning a new layout of your department and are thinking of using modular offices, which will save space and still provide privacy for the people who will occupy them. You saw a new line of office modules featured in an advertisement placed by Lowe-Franklin Interiors in the April issue of *The Office Administrator.* The firm is located in Seattle, and you decide to write for the name of a dealer in or near St. Louis.

SUPPLEMENTARY PROJECTS

4. As the assistant training director of Michaels Inc., you are considering establishing a visual aids library for staff training, including motion pictures, filmstrips, overhead transparencies, and various electronic transmission devices. You are interested not only in the equipment (hardware) but in the

materials used as well (software). A business friend suggests that you write Training Media Unlimited, in Minneapolis, for information. It is an outstanding company, you were told.

5. The executive vice president of Salten Products Company has asked you (her assistant) to find out about accommodations, including costs, at Best Western Golden Valley Inn, Chambers, Arizona, for a three-day conference of 40 executives and managers. The date is not firm, but August 18 to 20 is being seriously discussed. Write the manager, Joseph Ricci, for information, supplying whatever details you think are important. (*Hint:* You need only discuss the number of conference participants and the proposed date in this letter.)

STYLE CHECKUP

Choose the term in parentheses that correctly completes the sentence.

1. A cardinal rule of cash control is that only one individual should have the authority to (disperse, disburse) money.
2. Be sure to (disperse, disburse) copies of the president's announcement to all the warehouse and factory buildings.
3. Were you able to (elicit, illicit) Sanford's opinion?
4. The company attorney warned the credit staff against (elicit, illicit) methods of collecting money due from customers.

C A S E 3 Requesting an Appointment

THE SETTING

The American Society of Office Administration will hold its annual convention to the Hilton Hotel at O'Hare Airport (near Chicago) from October 9 to 12, and you will attend. For several months you have been thinking about installing a new mail-handling system in the company and have been especially interested in the literature you received from Putnam Lowes, in Northbrook, Illinois, which is fairly close to O'Hare. While you are at the convention, you would like to visit Putnam Lowes (Alfred C. Cohen, vice president) to see the company's new compact electronic mailing system and decide whether it will fill your needs.

Your Objective To obtain an invitation to visit Putnam Lowes and learn about the new mailing system.

BACKGROUND

Those who drop in on a company without an appointment are frequently disappointed. Often the person they hoped to see is not available, or the time chosen for the visit is not convenient. So it's a good idea always to arrange ahead for an appointment, either by telephone or through a letter. If you don't know anyone in the company, a letter is best.

Since Putnam Lowes should consider your request a sales opportunity, you should have no difficulty getting an appointment. Again, however, there are specific guidelines that it is wise to observe.

Guidelines

1. State the reason for your visit to the particular city or area (if it is not confidential). By doing so, you make it clear that the trip is not being made expressly to call on the recipient.
2. Ask for an appointment, and give the reason.
3. Suggest a specific time. If you are limited to a specific date, say so. However, if the hour is relatively unimportant, you may suggest a time, allowing the recipient to choose another one that is more convenient.
4. Tell where you may be reached in case there is a reason for the recipient to get in touch with you (for example, an emergency may arise that could result in the cancellation of the appointment).

SAMPLE LETTERS

Dear Mr. Cohen:

I plan to be in the Chicago area two weeks from Tuesday, and I am expecting to visit your office at that time. The best time for me is the afternoon of October 10, and unless I hear from you to the contrary, I will see you then.

Yours,

Analysis   The letter will probably result in a friendly invitation to visit Cohen (or his delegate), but it is extremely poor. Here are the reasons why:

1. The tone is brash and arrogant—there is not the slightest bit of warmth or courtesy.
2. No inkling is given of the purpose of the writer's visit to Illinois or to the offices of Putnam Lowes.
3. The writer demands rather than requests. It would have been much better to say "May I?" rather than "I am expecting to."
4. The time suggested could mean anytime from, say, 12:30 to 5 p.m. Most

executives have appointments, and if visitors merely drop in at their convenience, they may have to wait or be turned away.

B

Dear Mr. Cohen:

I will be attending the annual convention of the American Society of Office Administration at the Hyatt Hotel near O'Hare Airport from October 9 to 12.

While I am in the area, I would like to visit Putnam Lowes in Northbrook and see the new electronic mailing system that you introduced a short time ago. Our present system for mail handling is somewhat antiquated, and I am greatly intrigued by the literature you have sent out on your equipment. Would you or someone else be available to see me on Tuesday, October 10? This is the only day I am free, but the hours are flexible. I suggest 2:30 p.m. If this is not a convenient time, please feel free to suggest another hour.

I will be stopping at the Hyatt, arriving early in the afternoon of October 9 and departing around noon on the 12th. I look forward to hearing from you. Incidentally, I will be renting a car, and since I know Northbrook quite well, I'm certain I'll have no trouble finding your building.

Sincerely yours,

Analysis   This is an excellent letter for these reasons:

1. The tone is friendly and courteous.
2. The writer states the main purpose for being in the Chicago area and then asks to visit Putnam Lowes, indicating the purpose of the visit. The details given about the present antiquated mail-handling system are optional, but they will whet Cohen's desire to give the writer every courtesy.
3. A specific date and hour are suggested, but the latter is left to the discretion of the recipient.
4. The writer indicates where she or he can be reached.
5. The matter of getting from the Hyatt to Northbrook may be of some concern to Cohen, and the writer eliminates this problem by mentioning the rental car and familiarity with Northbrook.

"YOUR JOB" PROJECTS

1. You are planning to attend a seminar of the Computer Research Council in Tulsa from October 7 to 10. While you are in Tulsa, you want to visit the showrooms of Delacorte Interiors, a large manufacturer of office furnishings whose catalog you recently received. Winston Associates is planning to open a branch office in Little Rock, and you are shopping for furnishings. Write to the chief decorator, Mrs. Shari Limon, for an appointment; suggest a date and time for your visit. The afternoon of the tenth is the only time you have, and you must catch a plane back to St. Louis at 5:15. You are to stay at the Roadside Inn in Tulsa.

2. At the seminar of the Computer Research Council, you met Alan Kallaus, director of computer systems at Cygnet Foods, Inc., in Houston. Kallaus was elected program chairperson of the council for the coming year, and he asked you to assist him in planning the program and obtaining speakers. You agreed to do so.

   A month later you are planning a trip to Houston on company business. While you are there, you would like to visit Kallaus and share some of your ideas for the council's program for next year (the seminar will be in Tucson from October 9 to 12). You became quite friendly with Kallaus in Tulsa and are now on a first-name basis. Write for an appointment—suggest that he be your guest for lunch at your hotel (Albert Pick Inn, telephone number 555-3841) at 12:30 on the ninth (a Friday).

SUPPLEMENTARY PROJECTS

3. The information received from Golden Valley Inn (see Project 5 on page 89) is quite satisfactory, and you have decided to visit the inn to make final arrangements for your company's conference. Write the manager, Joseph Ricci, to tell him of your plans. Any day during the coming week would be satisfactory to you, and you suggest that Ricci indicate his preference. While you are at the inn, you would like a tour of the facilities (which you expect Ricci will arrange whether you request it or not).

4. The Omaha office of the company you work for (Mid-Regional Insurance Company, headquarters in Cleveland) has asked for someone from the home office to help it straighten out its inventory control system, and you have been selected to go. One of your equipment suppliers, DataRecord Corporation, is located just outside Omaha, and while you are there, you would like to see the new computerized payroll system the company has been advertising. You have communicated numerous times by telephone and by mail with Data-Record's customer service manager, Elaine Bando, and feel that you know her personally. Write to Bando, asking her to arrange an appointment for you with someone at DataRecord who will be able to demonstrate the equipment you want to see. You have the morning of September 4 free, and whatever time is convenient for your host will be OK with you.

STYLE CHECKUP

Choose the term in parentheses that correctly completes the sentence.

1. Kikta asked that a steel (partition, petition) be erected as a safeguard against pilferage.
2. If more accidents occur, Blaine says she will (partition, petition) the Labor-Management Council for action.
3. One (perquisite, prerequisite) enjoyed by U.S. Congress members is free mailing privileges.
4. A (perquisite, prerequisite) for the position of controller is an M.B.A. degree with specialization in accounting.

Requesting a Routine Favor

THE SETTING

Barry has been fully aware for several months that the company library is in urgent need of expansion and general renovation. It has, like Topsy, "just growed" and is quite inadequate for current needs. Andrea Follett, the head librarian, has discussed the problem with Barry, and he has asked the two of you to study the matter carefully and submit a proposal. Permission has been given by top management to provide additional space and purchase new equipment and furnishings.

You are not especially concerned at this point about obtaining equipment, since there are several suppliers from which Follett often receives catalogs and other promotional materials. However, you are greatly concerned about the space that will be required and the appropriate layout. Follett recommends that you write to the executive director of the Special Libraries Association, in Chicago, for help. She suggests that you ask about model layouts of various types of company libraries and recommendations for the latest in library equipment.

Your Objective   To obtain information that will permit you and Follett to proceed intelligently with your proposal to Barry.

BACKGROUND

In the first three cases in this chapter, you wrote only request letters that were considered sales opportunities by those who received them. Thus without using persuasion, you were in a favored position to obtain what you asked for. In the "request" cases that follow, however, you will deal with requests that may or may not represent sales opportunities for the recipients. Here you will ask for favors that will be of benefit to you but of little, if any, benefit to those to whom you write. These are somewhat more challenging.

In the letter to the executive director of the Special Libraries Association (J. T. Lipscomb), you will ask a routine favor—routine because your company is a member of the SLA and it is a function of that organization to serve its members. However, you will want to say the right thing, even though you don't have to sell anything.

Guidelines

1. Be very courteous, and show your gratitude for help.
2. Provide sufficient background to make it as easy as possible for Lipscomb to understand your problem and be of maximum help.
3. If appropriate, offer to reciprocate the favor.

SAMPLE LETTERS

Dear Mr. Lipscomb:

Do you have model layouts and recommended equipment for company libraries? We need help, and I am confident that SLA (of which our library is a member) is in an excellent position to supply it.

                    Yours very sincerely,

Analysis   There are two reasons why this letter is so ineffective.

1. Probably Lipscomb will have little difficulty granting this request, but he has been given very little information to guide him. Yet there is little excuse for such a telegraphic message and for the demanding tone.
2. Although membership in the SLA entitles the writer to certain services, help is nearly always more generously given when those requesting it exercise good human relations.

Dear Mr. Lipscomb:

Our company is planning an expansion and modernization of its library, and I have been asked to assist in putting together a proposal for the project.

The library was organized many years ago when we were a very small company, and during the early years it satisfied our needs quite well. The recent rapid increase in the number of our personnel--especially engineers, chemists, scientists, and executives--has added new demands that we simply cannot meet with our present space and equipment.

It occurred to me that perhaps the SLA has available various model layouts and recommendations for equipment and materials. If so, I would be grateful if you would share this information with me. I hesitate even to think about the amount of additional space we will need until I have a professional opinion from an organization such as yours.

If you do have resource material and there is a charge for it, we will be happy to pay for it. If you do not have the information I need but know where it can be located, I would appreciate your recommending a reliable source.

Thank you very much, Mr. Lipscomb. If we are successful in our plans, I will make it a point to share the results with you, complete with diagrams and photographs.

                              Yours very cordially,

Analysis   Letter B is much more effective than Letter A.

1. Letter B opens with a quick explanation of the nature of the request.
2. A brief history is provided so that the recipient will have a clear idea of the problem.
3. The request for help follows, along with further details. Note the compliment *until I have a professional opinion from an organization such as yours.*
4. Observe that an offer is made to pay for the materials if there is a charge. This is not likely to be the case here, but in other situations it is extremely important.
5. The writer asks to be referred to another source if the SLA cannot be of assistance.
6. The letter ends with a warm thank you and an offer to reciprocate.

"YOUR JOB" PROJECTS

1. Last week you attended the monthly dinner meeting of the Modern Management Society, of which you are a long-time member. The speaker, Dr. Dianne Lewisohn, spoke on the topic "Management Communications in the Computer Age," and you thoroughly enjoyed her talk. In her talk Lewisohn mentioned

that there are outstanding corporate communications programs. She indicated that many of these companies would be willing to share their ideas and materials with others. She did not, however, mention any names.

You think that Barry would be interested in seeing the materials referred to, and so you decide to write Lewisohn at Boston University to ask for the names of some companies whose corporate communications programs she considers outstanding.

2. Recently you received the annual report of McComber and Tichenor, an engineering firm in Baltimore that is unknown to you. It impressed you greatly—the design, layout, typography, color, and copy were superb. You know that the top executives in Holdridge-Plowman have not been happy with the company's annual report (it is produced by the firm's local advertising agency). Barry suggests that you write to McComber and Tichenor to learn the name of the organization that produced the report. You address the president, Carl M. Tichenor.

SUPPLEMENTARY PROJECTS

3. Your supervisor, Annabelle Froelich, is the financial vice president of Claybaugh Plastics Corporation. Last week she heard a speech at the Finance Research Council, in Indianapolis, by Ronald McMillan, president of Mayfair Food Distributors. The subject was equipment leasing, and Froelich found the presentation informative and the ideas intriguing. McMillan compared his company's experience in leasing trucks, automobiles, warehousing vehicles, and other equipment with that of outright purchasing. He said that his company's executives had prepared a complete report on their experience and that he would share it with anyone who requested it. Froelich asks you to write a letter to McMillan for her signature; in the letter you are to request a copy of the report.

4. The report requested from McMillan (Project 3 above) arrived, and Froelich thinks it is excellent. She wants to make a dozen photocopies of the report for distribution to the regional managers so that they can discuss it at next month's long-range planning meeting in San Francisco. Write a letter requesting permission to reproduce the materials (again for Froelich's signature). Since the report is not copyrighted, permission to reproduce it is not actually required; however, it is a courteous gesture to ask for this privilege.

STYLE CHECKUP

Choose the term in parentheses that correctly completes the sentence.

1. We plan to (envelop, envelope) the Twin Cities area in our advertising campaign.
2. Enclosed is an addressed, stamped (envelop, envelope) for your reply.
3. The ammunition is to be delivered to the (ordnance, ordinance) depot.
4. By city (ordnance, ordinance), unleashed dogs are not allowed in the park.

CASE 5

Requesting a Special Favor

THE SETTING

Herbert Barry, to whom you report, is concerned about the amount of money that is spent by the company on printing office forms. He suspects that there are too many forms and that there is little control over the people who determine the need for them, design them, and order the number of copies that are to be printed. You have been asked to make a study of forms usage in the company and find out how other companies handle this problem. You decide to write the systems manager in 25 large organizations for information.

Your Objective To obtain sufficient information that, when tabulated, will help you provide a guide for developing a forms policy.

BACKGROUND

When you request assistance such as that needed for your study, you are really asking a special favor. The information you want will require a good bit of thinking and perhaps research, and probably few, if any, of the companies you write to will have anything to gain from helping you. For this reason, you can't expect everyone to respond. You can, however, increase your chances of getting a response if you follow certain guidelines.

Guidelines

1. Provide complete details about what is wanted and why.
2. Make it possible for the recipient to provide information with a minimum of trouble.
3. Be tactful, reasonable, and grateful.

Note: When you know the title of the person you are writing to but not the name, your inside address may look like this:

```
Systems Manager
ABC Corporation
Address


Dear Sir or Madam:
```

SAMPLE LETTERS

 A Dear Sir or Madam:

Would you please tell me how you handle forms design, standardization, and control in your company? I would appreciate all the information you
can give me.

                    Very truly yours,

Analysis   The letter is courteous, but it is very poor for these reasons:

1. The information given is too skimpy. The recipient might or very likely might
   not understand what the writer wants to know.
2. A response to the letter will require much time and thought, and the writer
   has made no attempt to make it easy for the reader to provide the information.
   Indeed, the request is unreasonable, and for this reason it is likely to elicit
   few replies.

B Dear Sir or Madam:

Would you take just a few minutes to give me the
benefit of your experience?

Our company is making a study of forms usage with
a view toward establishing a forms control policy, and we are asking 25 top organizations to
tell us how they handle this problem. I would be
very grateful if you would answer the following
questions in the space provided.

1. Is the responsibility for forms design, standardization, and control centralized in your
   company? Yes _____ No _____
   a. If your answer is yes, what is the title of
      the person who has this responsibility?
      _____
   b. Does this person have authority to approve
      or disapprove all the forms used in the or-
      ganization? Yes _____ No _____
      Exceptions: _____
2. Are most of your forms:
   a. Reproduced in the office? _____
   b. Done by an outside printer? _____
3. Have you used committees (representatives of
   various departments) to control forms usage?
   Yes _____ No _____ If yes, was the plan

a. Satisfactory _____ b. Excellent? _____
c. Unworkable? _____

4. In round numbers, how many employees are there in your company? _____

5. Please estimate the number of official forms that are in use in your company. _____

6. Is it your personal opinion that more forms are used in your company than are needed? Yes _____ No _____ If yes, please estimate the percentage that you think might be eliminated without negative effects. _____%

If you care to make additional comments, I would be very pleased to have them. You may use the back of this letter if you wish.

Please use the enclosed stamped, addressed envelope to return your response.

Thank you!

                              Sincerely yours,

PS: Would you like a copy of the results of this study?
Yes _____ No _____

Analysis   This letter is effective for these reasons:

1. The purpose for which the information is needed is clearly stated.
2. The letter is complimentary in tone ("benefit of your experience," "25 top organizations").
3. The questions are set up so that they are easy to answer. The recipient will not have to compose a letter.
4. A stamped, addressed envelope is enclosed. Not only is this a courteous gesture, but it could elicit a larger response. (People hesitate to throw away a stamped envelope!)
5. You may want to offer to share the results of your study with the recipient. The PS shows how the invitation might be written.

"YOUR JOB" PROJECT

1. You are a member of the Employee Relations Committee at Winston Associates. One of your assignments on this committee is to study the feasibility of publishing a magazine for company employees. You need to find out what type of magazine would be most suitable, how large it should be, how often it should be published, and how much it will cost.

You decide to write to 100 different companies throughout the country for help. You want sample issues from them (two or three different ones, if possible). You would like to know how often the magazine is published, whether the company has a professional staff of editors whose sole job is to publish the magazine, the employees' reaction to the magazine, the number of copies printed, and whether the magazine is restricted to employees or is available to others. You would also like a statement from each company as to the main purpose of the magazine (some magazines feature management information, others emphasize employee activities, and so on). And you would like to know the annual cost of publishing the magazine.

Prepare a letter to send to the 100 companies you have selected, making it as easy as possible for each recipient to respond.

SUPPLEMENTARY PROJECTS

2. The company for which you are the purchasing director is planning to hold a series of management seminars in which all department heads will explain the objectives, organization, and methods of operation of their departments. Several months ago at a meeting of the St. Louis chapter of the American Association of Purchasing Agents, Professor C. Fred Bernstein, of the University of Kansas City, used a set of flip charts, including diagrams and cartoon drawings, to show the entire purchasing procedure in a typical business firm. You would like to use those charts in your presentation. Write Professor Bernstein (at the end of his talk you met with him and congratulated him on the excellence of his presentation), and ask if you may borrow the flip charts. You realize that this is a big favor to ask, so you need to be persuasive.
3. Professor Bernstein very kindly allowed you to use the flip charts requested in number 2 above. You had many compliments on your presentation at the seminar, and much of your success was due to the flip charts. Write Bernstein a letter that will be sent the same day that the flip charts are returned.

STYLE CHECKUP

Choose the term in parentheses that correctly completes the sentence.

1. If we (exceed, accede) to your demands, we will lose money.
2. Our objective is to (exceed, accede) last year's profit.
3. The advertisement in this week's Sunday supplement received numerous (adverse, averse) reactions from readers.
4. Although I am not (adverse, averse) to change, I think Kinder's proposal will prove to be far too costly.

CASE 6

Requesting the Services of a Speaker

THE SETTING

You have been elected vice president of the St. Louis chapter of the Modern Management Society. One of your responsibilities is to plan the monthly dinner meetings and obtain interesting speakers for these occasions.

For the March 25 meeting you have selected the topic of organization planning, a subject in which a number of members have expressed interest. It has been suggested that Professor William F. Kinsolving of Drury College (Springfield) be invited to speak to the group on this topic. Several of the members are familiar with his writings and have heard him speak. The chapter has a small budget for guest speakers—it can pay an honorarium (fee) of $100 plus all expenses.

Your Objective   To persuade Kinsolving to accept the invitation.

BACKGROUND

Letters asking someone to give a speech, write an article, or perform some other special service are of the persuasive type. Of course, those who earn most of their income from such endeavors don't need to be sold; if the fee is satisfactory, they are usually available. The people who must be persuaded are those whose services are in demand but who have limited time for travel and speaking. And when they are available and willing, they accept an invitation because they want to—not for money. Indeed, many speakers will not accept an honorarium or even reimbursement for travel expenses.

Guidelines   Guidelines for writing letters to speakers whom you can pay little or nothing for their services follow:

1. Describe the setting in which the speaker is to make the presentation—organization, membership, interests, topic, and so on.
2. Say why you are especially interested in having the speaker. Bestow appropriate compliments when you can do so honestly.
3. Indicate where the meeting is to take place, the date, and the time; also, give the recipient some idea of the length of the presentation expected.
4. Briefly mention what you can do in the way of an honorarium and expenses (if anything).
5. Keep the letter fairly brief. There is no point in giving all the details about the arrangements in the first letter. This information can be supplied when you have an acceptance.

SAMPLE LETTERS

 Dear Professor Kinsolving:

The St. Louis chapter of the Modern Management Association is planning to concentrate on the topic of organization planning at its March 25 dinner meeting.

Would you be willing to serve as our speaker for the evening? We are in a position to pay you an honorarium of $100 plus all expenses. I look forward to having your acceptance.

                    Very truly yours,

Analysis   This is not a satisfactory letter to Professor Kinsolving for these reasons:

1. Too little information is given concerning the group and the meeting.
2. The letter lacks enthusiasm and offers no real incentive for Kinsolving to accept the invitation.
3. The inference is given that Kinsolving will be swayed in his decision by the honorarium and expenses, yet a person of his importance is quite likely to be insulted.

 Dear Professor Kinsolving:

The St. Louis chapter of the Modern Management Society, which meets monthly, plans to devote its March 25 dinner meeting to organization planning. Our members will be highly honored if you can accept the invitation to be our speaker on that occasion.

Most of our members are supervisors, department managers, and young executives. Although our group is fairly small--the average attendance at our dinners is about 50--our lack of size is more than compensated by our enthusiasm! You would find a very receptive audience. Most of the members are well acquainted with your writings in the field of management, and many have heard you speak. Certainly, all of us hope that you might be prevailed upon to share some of your expertise with us.

The meeting will be at the Berkshire Inn in Manchester.

The social hour begins at 6 o'clock and is followed by dinner at 6:30 and the program at 8. We think a presentation of 45 minutes or so would be about right, although you may certainly have more time if you need it. We are prepared to pay you an honorarium of $100, plus all expenses. I realize that this is a modest compensation for a person of your stature, but I'm confident that your enthusiasm for the subject will provide the major incentive!

Just as soon as I hear from you, I will give you more details. If you prefer, you can call me collect at 555-4190.

Yours very sincerely,

Analysis   If you will compare Letter B with the guidelines on page 101, you will agree that if Professor Kinsolving is available, he will be tempted to accept this warm and friendly invitation. Note the effective way in which the compensation is handled.

If Professor Kinsolving accepts the invitation, he should receive a warm and enthusiastic response. The letter should also contain such details as:

1. The room in which the meeting will be held and a cordial invitation to participate in the social hour.
2. An offer to make a hotel reservation if he plans to stay overnight (likely).
3. Instructions on the best route from Springfield to Manchester if Kinsolving plans to drive.
4. A request for a brief résumé that the program moderator can use to make an appropriate introduction.
5. Instructions on how to handle expenses so that the speaker can be properly reimbursed.

"YOUR JOB" PROJECTS

1. The annual convention of the National Association of Corporation Financial Officers is to be held in Des Moines from October 9 to 12. Barry has been asked to obtain a speaker for the banquet, which is the windup of the convention.

   Since the conference leaders and speakers will have dealt with professional subjects and issues, the banquet will be looked on as a social affair—a "winddown" in a relaxed and informal atmosphere. Therefore, the banquet speaker is expected to deliver an amusing yet inspirational address.

Several members have heard Leonard Winkler, a syndicated newspaper columnist, speak at large conventions and recommend him highly. Not only were his remarks humorous and entertaining, but they were inspirational as well. Barry decides to try to engage Winker for the NACFO banquet. He has learned that this speaker's fee is $2,000, an amount that has been authorized by the NACFO board of directors. Winkler pays his own expenses.

You are to draft Barry's letter to Winkler, supplying appropriate information. Although in this instance it is to the speaker's advantage to accept the invitation (a large portion of his income is derived from public appearances), this should not prevent you from being friendly, complimentary, and persuasive. Winkler is to choose his own topic, but you are to suggest that he select something light.

Place: Hotel Fort Des Moines; date: October 12; time: dinner hour at 7, followed by the speech at about 8:30 (Hawkeye Room); time suggested: 40 minutes or so; probable size of audience: 600 (corporation executives and their spouses).

2. The Missouri Management Society is planning a statewide workshop for information processing managers at the American Motor Lodge in Kimberling, Missouri, from November 2 to 6. There will be panel discussions on such topics as reprographics, telecommunications, systems integration, records management, and computer security. The discussions will be led by executives from various companies. The workshop will end with a luncheon on Friday, November 6, and you have been asked to engage a speaker for the occasion. The theme of the workshop is "Information Processing Today and Tomorrow," and you would prefer that the speaker focus on this topic.

Dr. Donald Klingle, coauthor of *The Information Management Handbook* and a professor of office administration at Baruch College, is your choice. Although there is no budget for the speaker, you know that Dr. Klingle's publisher often pays his expenses for making such appearances because they promote sales of his book.

A cocktail hour beginning at noon will precede the luncheon, and the speech is allotted 45 minutes, starting at 2 p.m. The lodge's banquet room is equipped with a standard slide projector and an overhead projector, which the speaker may use. About 100 people are expected to attend the luncheon.

Write a letter asking Dr. Klingle to be the speaker.

SUPPLEMENTARY PROJECTS

3. You are in charge of the program of the Western States Management Society, which will hold its spring meeting at the St. Francis Hotel in San Francisco from July 14 to 16. The theme of the convention is "Management *Is* Communication," and you have been looking for a keynote speaker—one who can open the meeting dynamically and set the stage for the rest of the program.

Miss Berna Tillstrom, of Portland, Oregon, is a well-known authority in management communications. She has written widely on the subject and is a consultant to several large corporations. Your committee has suggested Tillstrom as the keynote speaker, and you are to write her a letter of invitation.

Your budget for a keynote speaker is $500, plus all expenses. You expect an audience of about 300 from 11 western states. The keynote address will be at 9:30 on Monday morning, the 14th, and an hour has been allowed for it.

4. Berna Tillstrom (see above) accepted your invitation and did an excellent job as keynote speaker. All who heard her were delighted and several speakers who appeared later on the program referred favorably to her remarks. Write a thank-you letter to accompany the check for the honorarium and expenses.

STYLE CHECKUP

Choose the term in parentheses that correctly completes the sentence.

1. It will be easy to (adapt, adopt) your policy statement to fit our needs.
2. At the meeting the committee decided to (adopt, adapt) the resolution of the Policies Committee. (That is, the resolution was accepted as written.)
3. We've had only (averse, adverse) reactions to the change in hours of work.
4. The sales representatives are (averse, adverse) to the idea of large territories.

CHAPTER 7

RESPONSE LETTERS

YOUR JOB

You are a sales correspondent for Wallingford's, whose logo includes "Products of Distinction." It is located in Fargo, North Dakota. This company sells a wide variety of products to companies that purchase them as gifts to important customers, as awards to employees, and as promotion devices. Included are such articles as pens, desk sets, medallions, matchbooks, wall plaques, desk nameplates, personalized luggage, and key tags. Most of the products are sold by mail.

You answer inquiries about products, prices, discounts—in fact, all communications from business people who have seen your firm's catalog and are considering purchasing something from your firm.

CASE 1

Responding Favorably to a Product Inquiry

THE SETTING

L. D. Moberly, sales director for Olympus Products Corporation, writes for information about the Accutrax electronic calculator, model G-7. The price of this model is $49.95 each, and there is a 10 percent discount for quantities of 50 or more.

The illustration of the G-7 Accutrax in your catalog shows the vinyl carrying case only in tan. Moberly wants to know if the case can be obtained in blue, with his company's logo imprinted on it in yellow. He has enclosed a black-on-white rendering of the Olympus logo.

The carrying case is available in blue (and other colors). Also it is possible to imprint the logo on the case in any color desired. The charge for the imprint is $1 each.

Moberly indicates that he would plan to order 80 model G-7 calculators.

Your Objective   To supply the information requested and persuade Moberly to place an order.

BACKGROUND

The request from Moberly illustrates the type that many businesses depend on to survive. Such inquiries are the result of the expenditure of a great deal of money for advertising, colorful catalogs, and superb service. Unfortunately, some of the people who handle such inquiries ignore the investment made to attract letters from prospective customers and make the mistake of treating them routinely.

To supply information to potential buyers, many large firms prepare special booklets and brochures, lavishly illustrated for sales appeal. Depending on the number of inquiries, these companies accompany their promotion pieces with a personal letter, a form letter, or a printed message on a card or special letterhead. A well-written personal letter is best, but because of the expense it is often not feasible to send one.

In some cases, as in this one, a personal letter is a must. Here the writer should give the message a definite sales flavor. A hard sell should certainly be avoided, but the message should be persuasive in tone. When you are in a position to provide what the inquirer wants, follow these guidelines.

Guidelines

1. Be friendly and positive.
2. Express your appreciation for the opportunity to be of service.
3. Subtly try to persuade the recipient to take favorable action.

SAMPLE LETTERS

A

Gentlemen:

The Accutrax electronix calculator (G-7) about which you inquired can be obtained in blue at no extra cost--that is, $49.95, less a 10 percent discount on quantities of 50 or more.

Your company logo can be imprinted on the case. However, there is a charge of $1 for this extra service.

                    Yours very truly,

Analysis   Although this letter provides the basic information requested, it is not an effective sales message.

1. Assuming that Moberly signed the letter he wrote, he should have been personally addressed.
2. The carrying case, not the calculator itself, is available in blue—a good example of carelessness in responding to product inquiries.
3. The letter lacks friendliness and positiveness.

4. In the third sentence, the psychology is poor. The word *However* introduces a negative idea that the reader might not even have considered.
5. There is absolutely no attempt to make a sale. The writer seems to have said, "Take it or leave it."

B

Dear Mr. Moberly:

I am very pleased to tell you that the carrying case for the model G-7 Accutrax electronic calculator is available in blue. The price is the same as for the tan case illustrated in our catalog.

Yes, we can imprint your company's logo in yellow on the carrying case exactly as in the sample you sent. Certainly, yellow would look very striking on the blue background. The charge for imprinting a company logo is $1 each; thus the net price for 80 model G-7 Accutrax calculators would be computed as follows:

```
80 G-7 calculators at $49.95    $3,996.00
Add logo imprint at $1              80.00
Total list price                $4,076.00
Less 10% discount                  407.60
Net price                       $3,668.40
```

I would be delighted to have your order, Mr. Moberly. Delivery is guaranteed within 15 days after the receipt of an order.

                    Yours very sincerely,

PS: I think you will be interested in the enclosed booklet of instructions that comes with each Accutrax. It contains everything one needs to know in order to become proficient in operating the calculator. We think that there isn't another compact electronic calculator on the market that has the versatility of the G-7 Accutrax. Please note the warranty on page 12; it covers one year on parts and labor.

Analysis   Letter B is an improvement over Letter A.

1. The favorable answer concerning the blue carrying case is supplied first. When you can give an emphatic "yes," you set a positive tone right away.
2. Then the information about the logo is introduced (note the reference to the complementary colors of blue and yellow). The charge of $1 is mentioned casually—no apology is made for it.

3. The calculations of the total net price are shown. These figures are not necessary, but they will be helpful, perhaps persuasive.

4. The letter closes with an invitation to place an order. If delivery can be expedited, this fact should be mentioned.

5. The PS is simply an extra attempt to close the sale.

" YOUR JOB" PROJECTS

1. Ripley Builders Supply (Marian Ripley, owner) writes to place an order for 20 Pro-Flex T-shirts—5 small, 8 medium, and 7 large. Each shirt is avocado green and will have "Ripley Builders" printed on the back in white. Mrs. Ripley sends a check for $262.80 (each shirt is $12.95, and the shipping charge is $3.80). She asks for delivery by October 7, which is a date that is satisfactory to you.

In her letter Mrs. Ripley asks about the availability of bowling ball bags, which are not shown in your catalog. You have just placed a large order for high-quality bags of expanded vinyl; they feature a modern luggage-style design, a handy inside pocket, strong Krylar welting, a fiberboard bottom, and a matching identification tag. These are expected in your warehouse on October 20 and will be priced at $16.99. The bags will contain no lettering, and your company is not equipped to handle this. You must decide whether you will mention the lettering. You enclose a brochure that describes and illustrates in color the bag you will have in stock.

2. Gerald Hembley, a vice president of Far Western Insurance Company, recently had lunch with a business friend, Phyllis Duggan. Duggan had in her possession a Blair electronic notebook cassette recorder that she had just purchased from you and with which she is highly pleased.

Hembley obtained your name and address and wrote asking for your latest catalog, mentioning specifically the recorder and his interest in various types of small electronic devices useful in the home and office and on trips.

The Blair electronic notebook cassette recorder has been a very popular item, and you have received numerous glowing reports on its quality and effectiveness. Write to Hembley, and enclose your general catalog along with a special brochure entitled *Electronically Speaking*.

SUPPLEMENTARY PROJECTS

3. As a sales correspondent for a large book publisher, you receive on June 2 an order for 40 copies of *Contemporary Zoology*, by Clayton and Bagley, from Professor C. T. Janicki, of Clemson University. He expects to use this book in his class that begins September 16. Janicki indicated that this is the first time he will have used this text. It sells for $16.75, less a 20 percent discount. A teacher's manual is available without cost to instructors.

Contemporary Zoology is being published in a new second edition, which will be off the press in early August. Although you have plenty of copies of the first edition, you think it wise to let Janicki know about the new book. It will be priced at $18.48, less a 20 percent discount. For the first time, a workbook is being published to accompany the text, and, of course, there will be a new teacher's manual.

Write Professor Janicki, and enclose a circular that fully describes the second edition, the workbook, and the teacher's manual. The reviewers who read the manuscript of the second edition were enthusiastic. One included in her remarks, "A superb revision of the best textbook in the field—one I thought couldn't possibly be improved."

4. Professor Janicki (see Project 3 above) places an order for 40 copies of the second edition of *Contemporary Zoology* as well as the workbook. In the same letter he mentions that he is to teach a new course in anthropology, which begins in late January, and asks for your recommendations for a text.

Your company publishes a highly popular book entitled *Introduction to Anthropology*, by Charles F. Winters. You write Professor Janicki that you are sending a copy of the book for a ten-day examination. If he decides to adopt the book for his course, he may keep the book you are sending as a desk copy (no charge). Otherwise, he is to return the text to you (there is no charge for the trial examination). Enclose with your letter a special circular that describes the primary features of *Introduction to Anthropology* and lists materials that can be purchased to accompany it—a laboratory manual, a teacher's guide, objective tests, and transparencies.

STYLE CHECKUP

Choose the term in parentheses that correctly completes the sentence.

1. Tim chose a red blazer and three pairs of slacks in (complimentary, complementary) colors.
2. The president's remarks about Cathy's report were highly (complimentary, complementary).
3. Black looked upon her administrative aide as a trusted (confident, confidant).
4. Are you really (confident, confidant) that you can do the job?

C A S E 2
Explaining a Pricing Policy to a Prospective Buyer

THE SETTING

Verna Littlefield, sales promotion manager of Cross-Continent Inns, has purchased a mailing list of 5,000 sales managers of large companies throughout the country. She plans to write them a letter encouraging them to choose a Cross-Continent

Inn for their meetings and conventions. To attract interest, she will attach to the letter a vinyl key tag (with ring) in the shape of a telephone on which Cross-Continent's toll-free number is imprinted. This will be followed by the message "Call us toll-free for the finest in conference accommodations" and the company logo.

Such a key tag is shown on page 42 of your gift catalog. The price of each tag ranges from 45 cents in quantities of 100 to 25 cents in quantities of 2,000. She wants to know what the price would be for 5,000.

The minimum price is 25 cents each, regardless of the quantity ordered.

Your Objective   To tactfully explain your pricing policy to the inquirer's satisfaction and encourage an order.

BACKGROUND

Frequently prospective buyers inquire about prices shown in a supplier's catalog either because they do not understand them or because they hope to obtain a more favorable price than quoted. Verna Littlefield, in the case problem, has reason to be puzzled; the price scale seems to indicate that the greater the quantity ordered, the lower the price. On the other hand, every supplier reaches a point where a minimum price must be established; otherwise there is no profit.

Responding to such inquiries is often a challenge to the writer. He or she must adhere to the company policy yet make every attempt to obtain an order. Guidelines for such letters follow.

Guidelines

1. Express appreciation for the inquiry.
2. Explain tactfully the minimum price at which the product can be sold and the precise reason.
3. Try to convince the inquirer that the minimum price quoted in the catalog is a favorable one.
4. Ask for an order.

SAMPLE LETTERS

Dear Ms. Littlefield:

I am sorry that we cannot offer a price of less than 25 cents on the phone key tags you wrote about, even though your requirements are 5,000.

I feel sure, however, that you will agree with me that at 25 cents each these phone key tags are realistically priced. The total cost to you for

5,000 would be only $1,250, and I hope that we may have your order soon.

Yours very cordially,

Analysis Letter A is weak in three respects:

1. The opening sentence is negative.
2. No explanation is offered as to why 25 cents is the minimum price, regardless of the quantity ordered.
3. The attempt to make a sale is feeble. In our opinion, it is poor sales psychology to mention the total price of $1,250.

 Dear Ms. Littlefield:

Thank you for writing about the phone key tag shown on page 42 of our gift catalog.

The minimum price at which we can sell each tag, Ms. Littlefield, is 25 cents. The reason is that the cost of manufacturing each tag in quantities of 2,000 is very nearly the same as for quantities of 5,000.

Just in case you haven't actually seen this clever phone key tag, I'm enclosing one for your inspection. I think you'll agree that it would be an excellent attention getter in your sales promotion letter.

The tag is available in red, white, orange, and black, and you are allowed up to six printed lines in gold, silver, black, red, blue, green, yellow, or white. We can reproduce your logo exactly as it is shown on your letterhead, including the color.

I would be pleased to have your order. We guarantee delivery within ten days of the receipt of an order.

Very cordially yours,

Analysis Here the writer has taken advantage of a sales opportunity. Note the following.

1. The thank-you opening is positive and specific as to the subject.
2. In the second paragraph the writer gives a logical reason why the minimum

price per tag is 25 cents. (If Littlefield has promotion literature printed, she knows how little it costs to increase the quantity from, say, 20,000 to 30,000.)

3. The writer showed imagination in sending a sample key tag. This could easily convince Littlefield that the item is well worth the price.

4. Although the catalog contains a complete description of the phone key tags, some of the information is repeated in the letter (fourth paragraph). This is fine so long as the writer doesn't overdo it.

5. The letter ends with a request for an order—a good rule to observe.

"YOUR JOB" PROJECTS

1. In early January, C. Joseph Vetter wrote to ask about the Autopulse computer phone dialer, Number 160-405 in your catalog. This unit is priced at $88.50 each; however, when three or more are ordered, the price is $82.50 each. Vetter says he will order only one unit now but plans to purchase two additional units in February. Therefore, he asks if he will be entitled to the lower price on the single-unit order because of his intention to purchase two more in February.

You must adhere to the price of $88.50. Reductions in price on multiunit orders are given for the purpose of encouraging larger purchases and to reduce the cost of handling and shipping. Write the letter.

2. A week after you wrote to Vetter (see 1 above), you received an order for six Autopulse computer phone dialers ($82.50 each). In the same letter Vetter also placed an order for four Trim-Line cordless telephones. The price of the phones is $280.75 each; however, for quantities of three or more, the price is $265 each. Vetter enclosed a check for $1,618. Write Vetter an appropriate letter to accompany your check for the overpayment of $63.

SUPPLEMENTARY PROJECTS

3. You are a sales correspondent for Comet Business Systems, a firm that sells stationery by mail to business firms and others who purchase in large quantities. Recently you received an inquiry about the cost of Linen-Craft stationery from Mrs. Katherine M. Lewis—she wants to know how much 500 letterhead sheets, 200 envelopes, and 100 business cards would cost.

You would be pleased to have Mrs. Lewis's business. However, the minimum quantity in which each item of stationery can be sold and the price of each item in that quantity are as follows: letterheads (1,000), $41.75; envelopes (1,000), $48.25; and business cards (1,000), $21.50.

Write the appropriate letter to Mrs. Lewis. Incidentally, you consider these prices excellent compared with those offered by most stationers.

4. Renfrow Wholesale Automotive Supply Company placed an order for 3,000 ledger cards from Comet Business Systems (see 3 above), indicating the size of 8½ by 11 inches. A quantity of 3,000 cards in this size sells for $135.75.

However, the office manager, Jacqueline Riessen, sent a check for $84.15, which is the price for 3,000 ledger cards in the 6⅜ by 9¼ size.

Renfrow is a long-time customer, and you have corresponded many times with Riessen and are on a first-name basis. You're almost certain that she has made an error. Your records show that Renfrow has always ordered the smaller size. When you telephoned Riessen's office to obtain clarification she was away on a business trip. You decide to take a chance and send the size she has been ordering. Write the letter.

STYLE CHECKUP

Choose the term in parentheses that correctly completes the sentence.

1. The reception is in honor of Dr. Chaim Koslov, the (imminent, eminent) scientist.
2. The need for a tight cash control system is (imminent, eminent).
3. The only drawback to my new apartment is that I have a lot (further, farther) to drive to work.
4. Milano asked the group to give the proposal (further, farther) study.

C A S E
3

Responding to "Problem" Letters

THE SETTING

In the past couple of days you received three letters to which you must respond.

Letter A: Sybil Darnell, manager of human resources for Meteor Manufacturing Company, has written about a five-piece luggage set in your catalog priced at $139.95. Darnell mentions that the luggage is to be her company's gift to an employee who is soon to retire. She asks whether it is possible to purchase only three of the five pieces. The answer is "no."

Letter B: S. T. Lucknow, vice president of Reynolds Corporation, writes asking about a canvas tote bag that he was given at a convention several years ago and that he still uses. He wants to purchase 2,000 for advertising purposes. This tote bag is no longer available—it proved to be too expensive as a giveaway ($3.99 each). You are now featuring a vinyl tote bag that, with the company's imprint, is priced at $1.25 each.

Letter C: Cheryl Mankeweicz, of Home Search, a national real estate franchise organization, ordered 15,000 ballpoint pens imprinted with the word *President*. The pens are available in various barrel colors, with blue or black ink, and with a medium or fine point. Mankeweicz chose a red barrel and supplied copy for the imprint but neglected to specify the color of ink desired and the type of point (medium or fine).

Your Objective   To encourage the recipient to take action that is favorable to the writer.

BACKGROUND

The three situations above are fairly common in business. Some prospective customers, as in Letter A, make requests that seem to be perfectly reasonable to them but that are not feasible to the supplier. Others ask for information about products that were discontinued long ago (B). And still others (C) place orders that are impossible to fill until additional information is supplied.

Of course, each of these situations should be considered by the letter writer as a sales opportunity. Guidelines for the first two inquiries follow.

Guidelines for A and B

1. Express appreciation for the inquiry.
2. Explain clearly why you cannot give what the customer asks for. Do this in such a way that you gain support for your position.
3. Do everything possible (commensurate with honesty and good taste) to make a sale.

Guidelines for C

1. Thank the customer for the order.
2. Tactfully ask for the additional information you need. Be very careful to avoid accusations such as *You neglected* or *You failed.*
3. Drop the issue as quickly as possible so as not to blow its seriousness out of all proportion. One way to get off the subject is to call the customer's attention to a new product, a new policy, and so on.

SAMPLE LETTERS

Dear Miss Darnell:

Thank you for your interest in the DeLuxe five-piece luggage set on page 28 of our catalog. It is a handsome set--with the look of expensive antiqued leather and the rugged durability of vinyl. It has been one of our most popular gift items.

The manufacturer makes the luggage set available to us only as a five-piece ensemble, and I'm afraid it isn't feasible for us to break it up.

I think you will agree, however, that it would be difficult, if not impossible, to purchase just three pieces of luggage with the beauty and quality of this five-piece set for the very low price of $139.95. Incidentally, all pieces nest inside each other for space-saving storage.

I hope I may have the pleasure of serving you, Miss Darnell. As shown in our catalog, each piece of the DeLuxe Luggage set will be stamped in gold with three initials at no extra cost. Just send me this information when you place your order.

                    Sincerely yours,

B Dear Mr. Lucknow:

Thank you for asking about the Carry-Eze canvas tote bag that we stocked briefly several years ago. Although it was a very handsome article, the manufacturing cost was so high that we were forced to price it at $3.99, and few companies could afford it as a giveaway in large quantities. The bag was discontinued in 1985.

I think you might be interested in our Super-Toter, a vinyl bag of the same size (15 by 18 inches) as the Carry-Eze. Enclosed is a flyer that illustrates and describes the Super-Toter. Note that it is available in a variety of colors, and your message or logo can be printed in any standard color in a 10- by 10-inch area. The price of each bag is only $1.25.

I think, though, that to really appreciate the features of the Super-Toter, you will have to see it. I am mailing a sample to you in a separate package.

Please be assured that we will be delighted to have an order from you.

                    Yours very cordially,

Dear Cheryl:

Thanks a lot for your order for 15,000-red-barrel "President" ballpoint pens.

So that I can get our production staff right to work on this order, I need to know two things: the color of ink (blue or black) and whether you want a medium or fine point. When you placed a similar order in May, you chose blue and a fine point, but I want to be absolutely sure before I duplicate it.

Have you seen our new key-chain knife? In case you haven't, I'm enclosing one. The price is only 87 cents in quantities of 500 or more. The name <u>Home Search</u> would look mighty handsome on the sheath!

                    Best Wishes,

Analyses   As you examine the sample letters on pages 115–117, compare the content with the guidelines provided.

"YOUR JOB" PROJECTS

1. Criticize each of the following responses to Letters A, B, and C in the case problem.

   a. Dear Miss Darnell:

   The DeLuxe luggage you inquired about in your letter is sold only in the five-piece set pictured in our catalog. Therefore, we are unable to break the set and supply the three pieces you want. By doing so, we would be left with two extra pieces that no one would want.

                       Yours very truly,

   b. Dear Mr. Lucknow:

   Sorry, but we no longer carry the canvas tote bag you asked about--in fact, it was discontinued years ago!

In its place we now feature a cheap vinyl bag
at the price of $1.25 each. Your order,
which includes your message, will be greatly
appreciated.

                         Thanks,

c. Dear Cheryl:

When you sent me your order for 15,000 red-
barrel "Presidential" pens, you failed to
indicate the color of ink you prefer (blue or
black) and whether you want a medium or fine
point.

     Please advise.

                         Sincerely,

2. Vulcan Metals Company will hold its annual sales convention on November 16 at a large Miami Beach hotel, and all top executives and sales managers, supervisors, and representatives will be present. This is a special year, however—the seventy-fifth anniversary of the company's founding.

   The executive vice president, R. B. Moeller, writes asking for a sample of the Porta-Desk—a combined carrying case and binder illustrated in your catalog—believing that this would be a handsome and useful item for everyone to have. He would expect to order 250 with a black vinyl cover and white lettering. The price of the Porta-Desk is $9.50 each in quantities of 200 or more and includes custom imprinting of the company name and/or logo on the cover.

   Moeller receives the sample and is delighted with it. He places an order for 250 and encloses a check for $2,375 (there is no shipping charge) and a glossy print of the Vulcan Metals Company logo. In his letter Moeller also asks that the following line be imprinted in fairly large letters at the bottom of the cover: DIAMOND ◇ JUBILEE. This extra line is not included in the $9.50 price—the extra cost will be $1.50 each. Write Moeller, giving him this information and assuring him that the Porta-Desk can be shipped so that it arrives at least three weeks before the convention begins.

SUPPLEMENTARY PROJECTS

3. Whitmore Wholesale Auto Parts received an order from Gilbert Sauerwein, manager of Gil's Auto Parts Store, for 36 wheel-cover locks. Sauerwein asked to be billed for $119.76 plus the shipping charge ($5.50). The store has established credit with Whitmore, so there is no problem in shipping the locks at once and sending a bill later.

However, Sauerwein made an error in his computation of the amount. The wheel-cover locks are sold in sets of 12 at $9.98 a set (three locks are installed on each wheel cover). Thus the total of the order should be only $29.94 plus the shipping charge (in this case, $3.65).

As an employee of Whitmore Wholesale Auto Parts, write Sauerwein an appropiate letter. Assume that shipment is being made immediately.

4. The sports director of Camp Wildwood, Sarah Willets, has written your company, Universal Sports and Leisure Inc., to place an order for 24 children's life vests. She says that she saw these swimming jackets at another camp and liked them so much that she decided to buy the same brand. She is not certain of the sizes and colors available, the shipping charges, or the price.

Following is an excerpt from your current catalog describing these vests. You photocopy the information and enclose it in your letter. (Your catalog is now being printed, and a copy will be sent to Willets when stock is received.)

```
YOU WON'T HAVE TO WORRY ABOUT CHILDREN IN THE
WATER WHEN THEY'RE WEARING "SAFE-TEE" LIFE
VESTS!  Three different sizes of foam-filled
vests are made to fit each child's age group.

No. ST 205.  Ages 2-5 years.  Chest sizes 20-24
inches.  Yellow.  No. ST 504.  Ages 5-7 years.
Chest sizes 24-27 inches.  Blue.  No. ST 707.
Ages 7-9 years.  Chest sizes 27-30 inches. Red.

Priced at $18.95 each.

Shipping cost anywhere in continental U.S., $5
per dozen.

Send personal check or money order or your
Visa, MasterCard, or American Express card num-
ber.
```

STYLE CHECKUP

Choose the term in parentheses that correctly completes the sentence.

1. I do not mean to (imply, infer) that Rossiter was willfully negligent.
2. I (imply, infer) from your remarks that Logan's application for credit was refused.
3. We are (loath, loathe) to take legal action to collect the money due us.
4. The people I talked with (loath, loathe) the company's attitude toward chemical-waste disposal.
5. The (party, person) I talked with on the telephone was very cooperative.

CASE 4

Responding With a Gentle "No"

THE SETTING

Many of the letters you receive are from individuals who have invented or developed products that they wish to sell to Wallingford's either outright or on a commission basis. Wallingford's would then distribute the products to its customers by mail order or through retail stores.

Mrs. Frieda Burleson, of Sayre, Oklahoma, writes that over the years she has gathered hundreds of home-canning recipes, many of which were handed down from generation to generation. She expects to put the recipes together in book form and have it published as *Never-Fail Canning: A Down-Home Guide to Food Preservation*. In her letter Burleson praises this unique collection and requests that Wallingford's publish and sell the book.

Wallingford's has a small book section in its general catalog; it features mostly how-to books on auto repair, appliance servicing, carpentry, and physical fitness. None of these books, however, is actually published by Wallingford's; all are purchased from well-known publishers at substantial discounts and marked up for retail sale. This section of the catalog, you suspect, inspired Burleson to write.

Your Objective   To explain why it is not feasible to say "yes" to the request and still retain the goodwill of the individual who wrote.

BACKGROUND

Those whose primary responsibility is to build or maintain good public relations must often respond to letters in which people offer ideas and suggestions that are not feasible for the company to adopt. These individuals may or may not be customers, but this should have almost no bearing on the kind of response they receive. As long as their ideas and suggestions are well intentioned and sincere, they deserve a friendly and sympathetic letter, even when the answer to their question is essentialy negative.

Follow these guidelines in responding to inquiries such as that posed by Mrs. Burleson in the case problem:

Guidelines

1. Express appreciation for the letter.
2. If possible, comment favorably on the idea or suggestion submitted; then explain tactfully why you must turn it down.

3. Where feasible, offer suggestions as to how the recipient may proceed with this idea elsewhere.
4. Extend warm wishes for success.

SAMPLE LETTERS

Dear Mrs. Burleson:

Wallingford's does not publish the books listed in its catalog. These books are purchased from publishers. Therefore, I am unable to express interest in examining your collection of canning recipes.

The only suggestion I can offer is that you submit your materials to various cookbook publishers; perhaps one of them will be interested in your collection.

Incidentally, I think you might have trouble getting any publisher interested in your home-canning book, Mrs. Burleson. I do know that the U.S. government issues many free booklets on the subject; too, manufacturers of containers, spices, and canning equipment offer free materials on methods of food preservation.

                        Very cordially yours,

Analysis   We object to Letter A for four reasons:

1. The tone of the letter is without warmth—a big-business approach seems condescending.
2. The phrase *I am unable to express interest in examining* is haughty; the writer is saying, in effect, "I don't want to see your collection of recipes." This may be perfectly true, but it need not have been stated.
3. The second paragraph is somewhat helpful, but the writer might have done a little more than he or she "had to."
4. The last paragraph is gratuitous. We think the writer has no business discouraging Burleson. Even though the statement may be accurate, it should be left to a publisher to point out these things. And there is always the chance that some publishers will be interested in Burleson's book.

Dear Mrs. Burleson:

Thank you for writing about the home-canning recipes that you are assembling for publication.

Although your idea for "never-fail canning" is very interesting, I'm afraid that Wallingford's is not in a position to publish your collection. You see, Mrs. Burleson, we do no book publishing; the books listed in our general catalog are purchased from various publishers.

I suggest that you proceed as follows:

1. Visit your local library and examine books on food preparation and preservation. Write down the names and addresses of the publishers whose books you like best.
2. Write each of these publishers a letter. Describe your proposed book in detail, and if possible, enclose a table of contents.

I am told that it is not a good idea to simply send your complete manuscript to a publisher at the outset--that it's better first to obtain some expression of interest and then submit the manuscript.

I do wish you every success in getting your materials published. If this happens, perhaps one day you might see your book listed in Wallingford's catalog! I hope so.

Sincerely yours,

Analysis   Letter B satisfies all the guidelines listed earlier.

1. Although the "no" message will not make Burleson happy, she should surely be aware that the writer did everything possible, short of saying "yes," to help and encourage her.
2. If this letter strikes you as too time-consuming for a busy correspondent, remember that it might simply be a form letter with appropriate insertions.

"YOUR JOB" PROJECTS

1. LeRoy Pruitt, assistant to the president of Mahan Technical College, which was recently established, writes asking Wallingford's to participate in the school's Awards of Merit program. He proposes that Wallingford's contribute $1,000 to the outstanding graduate each year in the field of retail merchandising. The contribution would be called the Wallingford's Award, and the recipient would be chosen by the faculty.

Each year Wallingford's receives hundreds of similar requests, and the board of directors feels that it is not financially feasible to grant any of them. Obviously, if an exception were made for one institution, it would be difficult to refuse hundreds of others. Write a letter to Pruitt, explaining Wallingford's position. At the same time, try to salvage as much goodwill as possible.

2. The Sunnyvale Senior Citizens Club president, Marion Sherron, writes requesting a cooperative arrangement whereby the club members take the responsibility for distributing the Christmas catalog to residents of the community at the rate of 35 cents a copy. This would help the club earn money for its various activities. Sherron says that the club has had this kind of arrangement with the telephone company for the past two years in distributing directories.

Actually, Wallingford's catalogs are sent by mail to a select group of people—mainly those who have placed orders with the company in the past and those who write requesting a catalog. The reason why the catalogs are not distributed on a house-to-house basis or mailed indiscriminately is that they are so expensive to publish—each one is nearly 500 pages in length and extravagantly illustrated in color. Telephone directories are in an entirely different catagory; subscribers are entitled to a copy, and much of the expense of directory preparation and printing is absorbed by revenue from Yellow Pages advertising.

Respond to Marion Sherron.

SUPPLEMENTARY PROJECTS

3. You are an assistant in the public relations department of Peerless Music Company, located in East Lansing, Michigan. Peerless manufactures and sells musical instruments to retail stores, schools and colleges, and professional musical organizations. Today you received a letter from Horace King, instructor in music at Pine Crest Academy, who has purchased several instruments from Peerless in the past. He requests that Peerless donate to Pine Crest Academy all their used instruments and "factory rejects" for use by students who cannot afford to purchase their own instruments.

Actually, Peerless does not have used instruments, and there are no such things as "factory rejects." Instruments turned out by the factory must meet exacting specifications, and the few that come off the assembly line with flaws are reprocessed until they are perfect in every way.

You are to write Mr. King, giving him this information. When you receive requests such as this one, you suggest that the correspondent try placing an ad or article in local newspapers asking people to give their no-longer-used instruments to the school for distribution to the students. It is surprising how many instruments are available, and those who have tried this idea have been pleasantly surprised at the results.

4. You are the assistant to Mrs. Selena Kemper, director of the Marshaltown Chamber of Commerce. One of your responsibilities is to handle much of her correspondence. Today Mrs. Kemper received a letter from Beatrice Lacy, head of the Marshaltown Beautification Committee, saying that the committee

plans to publish a booklet, *Keep Marshaltown Beautiful,* which will be mailed to community residents. Ms. Lacy wants the Chamber to give the Beautification Committee enough money ($800) to cover the expense of publishing and mailing.

Mrs. Kemper is not authorized to spend the Chamber's money except for salaries, office expenses, and advertising and promotions. You are to respond to Ms. Lacy, telling her that donations of the type Lacy suggests are not authorized by the Chamber of Commerce. You suggest that Lacy arrange to call on a dozen or so leading business firms in the community (most of whom belong to the Chamber), asking for contributions to Lacy's project. Write the letter for Mrs. Kemper's signature. Don't forget to compliment Ms. Lacy on her idea, and give as gentle a "no" as possible.

STYLE CHECKUP

Choose the term in parentheses that correctly completes the sentence.

1. The president's (principal, principle) concern is productivity.
2. Our compensation policy is based on the (principal, principle) of equal pay for equal work.
3. The sales compensation plan described will go into effect October 1, (providing, provided) the marketing director approves it.
4. (Provided, Providing) transportation is Alicia's responsibility.

CHAPTER 8

TRANSMITTAL AND CONFIRMATION LETTERS

YOUR JOB

You are the exhibit manager of the Capital City Convention Center, a large building complex in Austin, Texas, that was designed by the city expressly for large gatherings of people—for business, educational, political, professional, hobby, and social events. At many of these gatherings or conventions, manufacturers, distributors, and others purchase exhibit space to display their products and other items, and one of your main duties is to sell the exhibit space and collect the money for its use. You also purchase equipment, supplies, and fixtures, which are rented to exhibitors, as well as various services.

CASE 1

Transmittal Letters

THE SETTING

In your job you often transmit checks in payment of purchases, contracts with suppliers of services and with purchasers of exhibit space, and other materials. Today you have several things to transmit.

Your Objective   To identify what is being transmitted and, if necessary, provide an explanation concerning it.

BACKGROUND

When you send a check, a contract, or some other valuable or hard-to-replace document, it is usually a good idea to send a transmittal letter with it. The main reason is to provide a record of *when* you sent *what* to *whom* and, if appropriate, *why*.

Guidelines for transmitting important papers follow.

Guidelines

1. Identify what is being sent. If it is a check, state the amount and, if you prefer, the check number.

2. Tell why the check or other document is being sent if you think that the recipient will be puzzled.
3. When ordering merchandise or services, be certain that your address is clearly indicated.
4. Explain anything about the transmittal that you think is important for the recipient to know.
5. Unless you need to provide full details about what you are sending, make the message brief.

SAMPLE LETTERS

Two checks, a contract, and a package must be put in the mail today. Judge these messages on the basis of thoroughness and brevity.

Transmitting a Check

Dear Office Manager:

Enclosed is my check for $55 for a two-year sub-scription to <u>Fortune</u>.

                    Very truly yours,

Analysis   Letter A is well done. Here's why.

1. Transmitting a check for a magazine subscription usually requires only a one-sentence message. Letter A does this succinctly.
2. It is assumed that the letter above will contain the address to which you want the magazine sent. If there is any doubt, put your name and address inside the letter.
3. The salutation may be omitted in a transmittal letter when there is no specific person to address, as below.

Enclosed is my check for $55 for a two-year sub-scription to <u>Fortune</u>. Please address the maga-zine as follows:

        Tracy G. Spurrier
        2220 South River Road
        Manchester, NH 03102

            or

        Trace G. Spurrier, Advertising Department
        Corelli Engineering Associates
        4730 Harvey Road
        Manchester, NH 03102

                    Very truly yours,

B

Dear Mrs. Benjamin:

The enclosed check for $477.75 is in payment of your invoice (Number 17X203).

Yours very truly,

Analysis This transmittal letter accomplishes what it sets out to do.

1. Unless some explanation is required about the payment being transmitted, the letter should be very brief.
2. On the other hand, if there is a difference between the amount of the invoice received and the check transmitted, the letter must explain it. Let's say that you received a circular from Vu-Way Corporation announcing a special 15 percent discount during December on an overhead projector that is ordinarily listed at $172. You placed an order on December 16, but the invoice you received from Vu-Way showed $172 as the amount due.

Dear Mr. Ballachey:

Enclosed is our check for $146.20 in payment of your invoice (Number 3671).

You will see that I took advantage of the special 15 percent discount that you announced on December purchases of the Vu-Way overhead projector:

List price	$172.00
Less 15% discount	25.80
Net amount due	$146.20

I'm certain that the $172 figure was an inadvertent error, but if there is any question, please let me know.

Very truly yours,

Transmitting a Contract

C

Dear Ms. Pfaff:

Enclosed is the original and one photocopy of the contract for exhibit spaces 75 to 77 at the Greater Austin Kennel Show, scheduled for May 6 to 9. Would you please sign both copies and return the original to me? Thank you.

Sincerely yours,

Analysis   Letter C transmits the contract effectively.

1. Letter C, like all letters that transmit contracts for signature, is brief and straightforward.
2. This letter of transmittal also requests a signature. Thus it employs the courteous tone used in general request letters.

D Dear Miss Elan:

Enclosed is a signed copy of the maintenance contract on the Capital City Convention Center.

Please note the insertion on line 3 of Section C.
The sentence beginning with "Texas Maintenance
Company agrees to clean all furniture in the
reception foyer" was changed to read, "Texas
Maintenance Company agrees to clean and wax all
furniture in the reception foyer. . . ." I'm
sure that in the retyping of the contract, the
words <u>and wax</u> were inadvertently omitted.

                                        Yours very cordially,

Analysis   Letter D employs a tactful and factual technique for pointing out changes.

1. Sometimes it is necessary to point out alterations or omissions in a contract that is being transmitted. Letter D does this.
2. The alteration is noted objectively, thus not making a bad impression on Elan.

Transmitting Materials Separately

E Dear Mr. von Fischer:

Fifty copies of <u>Get Acquainted with Austin</u> were
sent to you today by United Parcel Service, and
you should have them very soon.

We're delighted that your association chose Austin as its convention headquarters and sincerely
hope your visit with us will be very productive
and enjoyable.

                                        Sincerely,

Analysis   Letter E is an example of an effective transmittal letter.

1. Letter E alerts von Fischer to the shipment of his books, as is often done

when weight or bulk dictates that what is being transmitted must be sent separately.

2. Since the books are being transmitted separately, the transmittal letter includes shipping information for the recipient.

3. Also, the letter provides a record of the transaction for the sender.

"YOUR JOB" PROJECTS

1. Recently you ordered 6,000 copies of the booklet *Austin—Convention Center of the Southwest* from Commonwealth Printers, in Fort Worth. This is the first printing of this new booklet, and you are delighted with it. The statement received shows $9,600, the correct figure. Transmit the check in payment, saying whatever you think is appropriate.

2. You are planning to set up a business conference at the Adolphus Hotel in Dallas on May 19 and have telephoned the hotel to reserve a private room for your meeting for the day. The reservation is assured, provided you pay for the room ($125) in advance. Transmit your check, addressing Bernard Kloppman, the reservations manager.

3. On May 24 you sent a contract to Mrs. Patricia Knowles for exhibit spaces 112 to 116 for the Southwest Antique Show, which will be held from September 15 to 18. You asked her to sign the document and return it to you. When the contract was received, it was accompanied by a letter from Knowles saying how much she is looking forward to the show in Austin. However, the contract was not signed—an oversight, you're certain. Write the appropriate letter.

SUPPLEMENTARY PROJECTS

4. Recently the firm you work for entered into an agreement with a local computer company. The company will provide services for your computer equipment and offer consulting services on programming and systems analysis. When you received the contract (the original and a photocopy—you are to return the latter after signing it), you discovered two errors:

Line 16: The term *input* should be *output*.

Line 33: The term *systems analysis* should be *systems analyst*.

You make the corrections on both the original and the photocopy and initial the changes in the margins. Then you return the copy. In your opinion, the errors are not serious enough to require the initials of the computer company on your copy. Transmit the contract.

5. As manager of accounts receivable, you receive a check from Mrs. K. D. Fielding for $277.63 in payment of her account. According to your records, which you have checked very carefully, Mrs. Fielding owes only $214.47, which gives her a credit balance of $63.16. You decide to send Fielding a check for the overpayment rather than show a credit balance in her account. Write an appropriate letter.

Choose the term in parentheses that correctly completes the sentence.

1. Do you believe the new fringe benefits will (affect, effect) employee turnover?
2. Yes, I think the new fringe benefits will have a favorable (affect, effect) on employee turnover.
3. Porter Brothers apparently received poor (advise, advice) from its advertising agency.
4. The broker said, "I would (advise, advice) you to sell."

Confirmation Letters

THE SETTING

The Association of Rare-Book Dealers has chosen Austin for its convention, to be held from December 27 to 31. Grantland-Corning Inc. plans to exhibit its products at the convention, and the executive vice president, Philip G. Paxton, has telephoned you about the availability of space and the cost. He has asked for a prime location and has agreed to the price of $2,400, half of which is due immediately and the remainder when he arrives for the convention. You are to follow up the conversation with a letter.

Your Objective   To confirm in writing the agreement reached by telephone.

BACKGROUND

It is nearly always wise to confirm in writing any important oral agreement, whether made on the telephone or in person. Too often people forget conversations or learn later that they misinterpreted what was said.

Many people make it a practice to confirm the receipt of something—an important document, money or substitutes for money, a valuable article, and so on. Others insist on confirming by letter messages sent by telegraph or cable.

Guidelines
1. When confirming an oral agreement, be very specific about the details agreed on. If documents are available to support the details, send them.
2. When you are the person who stands to gain most from the oral agreement, use the opportunity to build goodwill.

3. When confirming receipts, say specifically what has been received and, if you think it is important, when it was received.
4. Provide any details about the document or article that might be valuable for the record.
5. Express appreciation when confirming receipts, if appropriate.
6. If sending a letter to confirm an important telegram or cablegram that was garbled in transmission, repeat the message exactly as it was originally written. Apply this guideline only if the letter of confirmation has no other purpose.

SAMPLE LETTERS

As you read the following communications, pay special attention to tone, specificity of information conveyed, and thoroughness, according to the guidelines above.

Confirming an Oral Agreement

Dear Mr. Paxton:

The space we talked about in our telephone conversation yesterday has been reserved for you. I'm sure you will be very pleased with its location. I will appreciate your check in payment of half the cost of the space within the next few days.

        Yours very sincerely,

Analysis   Letter A could easily confuse Paxton. Here's why.

1. Letter A leaves a good deal of room for argument about the location of the exhibit space and the cost. On arriving in Austin and observing the space reserved, Paxton could say "I thought you said my space would be at the main entrance to the exhibit hall" and "I understood you clearly to say that the cost would be $1,400—not $2,400."
2. The writer doesn't even mention the date, which is extremely important. In other words, then, the letter might as well not have been written.

Dear Mr. Paxton:

As agreed in our telephone conversation yesterday, I have reserved Exhibit Space K for you at the convention of the Association of Rare-Book Dealers, to be held from December 27 to 31. The enclosed diagram shows the exhibit area layout, and I have checked Space K in red so that you will know precisely where you will be situated in relation to the other exhibits. This is an excellent location--in the mainstream of convention traffic--and I'm sure you will be happy with it.

Details concerning electrical outlets and other facilities are described on the back of the exhibit area layout. The cost for the four days is $2,400, and I will be pleased to have your check for half that amount ($1,200). The remainder is to be paid when you arrive at the convention.

I extend a warm welcome to Austin and hope the convention will be a very successful occasion for you and your company.

Very sincerely yours,

Analysis   Letter B is a vast improvement over Letter A.

1. Here the writer's interpretation of what was said in the telephone conversation is clearly stated. If Paxton has any rebuttal to make, he can put it in writing so that matters can be cleared up before he arrives in Austin. Note that a diagram of the exhibit hall is enclosed and that the agreed-on space is checked in red.
2. Although a confirmation letter need not always contain a sales message, this one does, since the writer is in the business of selling the convention center's facilities and, in the process, building goodwill for the city of Austin.

Confirming Receipts

Dear Mr. Paxton:

Thank you for your check for $1,200 as the first payment on Exhibit Space K for the convention of the Association of Rare-Book Dealers, to be held from December 27 to 31.

As you requested, I will be on the lookout for a carton addressed to me from your company, and I will let you know when it arrives. I appreciate your concern for the safety of the rare illuminated manuscripts you plan to put on special display.

Sincerely,

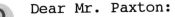

Dear Mr. Paxton:

An insured package from Grantland–Corning Inc. arrived in today's mail. Although I signed for the package, I did not open it. Yet I suspect it contains the rare illuminated manuscripts that you were so anxious about, since you did not refer to any other shipment.

I have placed the carton in our vault for safe-keeping, and you may pick it up any time you like.

                    Sincerely,

Analyses   Letters C and D are well done. Here's why.

1. Letters C and D both accomplish the purpose of a letter confirming a receipt: to ease the sender's mind that the document or article has arrived.
2. At the same time, the letters give the writers an opportunity to make records for later reference.

Confirming a Telegram

Dear Sheila:

A few minutes ago I sent you the following tele-gram: PLEASE INSTRUCT ALLEGHENY MANUFACTURERS TO SUBSTITUTE 16 MOLDED PLY "PIERRE RANCO" CHAIRS (CATALOG NUMBER 496) FOR THE 16 "ALLENTON" SIDE CHAIRS THAT I ORDERED MARCH 22. URGENT THAT SHIPMENT ARRIVE HERE NOT LATER THAN JUNE 10.

                    Sincerely,

Analysis   This confirmation letter serves its purpose well.

1. Letter E's only purpose is to confirm what the telegram said. Thus it repeats the message exactly as it was originally sent.
2. Note that the writer thoughtfully includes when the telegram was sent, thus giving the receiver the time of its transmission, should it be somehow significant.

Confirming Time and Sequence

```
 TO:      BARNARD CASEY, CHICAGO                        FROM:  GUILLERMO RAMIREZ
          MARY ROSE DALLAH, NEW YORK
          WILLIAM ROGERS, MIAMI
          MIKE RUSSELL, NEW YORK
          HERBERT WILLIAMSON, NEW YORK
          TAMARA WILSON, LOS ANGELES

 SUBJECT:  MARCH 12 TELECONFERENCE                       DATE:  MARCH 10, 19--

          FOLLOWING IS THE CONFIRMED TIME AND SEQUENCE FOR THE
          TELECONFERENCE WEDNESDAY, MARCH 12, ABOUT POSSIBLE CHANGES IN
          MODERN MODE'S DESIGN, SPACE RATES, AND ADVERTISING POLICIES.

          1:30-1:45 P.M. (EST)    ARRIVE AT TELECONFERENCE FACILITIES AND SET UP DISPLAYS.
                                  TELECONFERENCING FACILITIES FOR EACH REGIONAL OFFICE
                                  ARE:  NEW YORK--HARBRACE HOTEL, 395 WEST 66TH STREET;
                                  MIAMI--MILLIKIN CORP., 4333 S. DUNE STREET; CHICAGO--
                                  GREAT LAKES INN, 316 N. WACKER DRIVE; LOS ANGELES--
                                  ERCOM CORP., 797 LA JOLLA, STUDIO CITY.
          1:45-2:00 P.M. (EST)    HERBERT WILLIAMSON IN NEW YORK WILL TALK ABOUT CHANGES
                                  IN THE MAGAZINE'S READERSHIP AND FINANCIAL PICTURE.
          2:00-2:15 P.M. (EST)    DERECK MEYERS IN NEW YORK WILL DISCUSS PROPOSED
                                  CHANGES IN DESIGN.
          2:15-2:30 P.M. (EST)    MIKE RUSSELL IN NEW YORK WILL DISCUSS CONTROLLING THE
                                  CIRCULATION BASE.
          2:30-2:45 P.M. (EST)    MARY ROSE DALLAH IN NEW YORK WILL DISCUSS POSSIBLE
                                  ADVERTISING RATE CHANGES.
          2:45-4:30 P.M. (EST)    OPEN DISCUSSION OF HOW THE ABOVE CHANGES ARE LIKELY
                                  TO AFFECT SALES OF ADVERTISING.

          THE TELECONFERENCE MUST END PROMPTLY AT 4:30 P.M. (EST). BECAUSE OF THE
          AGENDA AND TIGHT TIME RESTRICTIONS, IT IS IMPORTANT THAT WE START ON TIME
          AND ADHERE STRICTLY TO THE SCHEDULE.
```

Analysis   Memo F serves well as a confirmation message.

1. Scheduling an event so that it's convenient for everyone can be complicated. Often you'll make arrangements by telephone so that you can resolve time conflicts and other problems without delay. While you are discussing these matters by telephone, however, there's always the chance of confusion as to who, when, and where. So it's usually a good idea to follow up oral conversations in writing. As with confirmations of other oral agreements, the main guideline here is to be very specific in supplying details.

2. Guillermo Ramirez, assistant to the publisher of *Modern Mode* magazine, wrote the memo on a word processor in the magazine's New York headquarters. Copies were sent to the electronic files of the addressees in New York, and a hard copy of the memo was sent by telecopier to the regional sales managers in Chicago, Miami, and Los Angeles. By means of electronic technology, Ramirez was able to confirm time and sequence for all the meeting attendees.

"YOUR JOB" PROJECTS

1. The administrative vice president of the University of Austin, Dr. Lynn Hossboch, has telephoned you about engaging the main auditorium and other facilities of the Capital City Convention Center for the exclusive use of the School of Law—specifically, for the school's commencement exercises on Saturday, May 14. There are no bookings on that date, and you agree to make the reservation. The fee is $3,000, and includes seating for 1,500, a first-rate sound system, maintenance services, parking facilities and attendants, and

other services. A 20 percent advance is required as insurance against cancellation or a change in plans.

The details concerning the stage setting, the music, the seating of graduates, and other matters will be discussed later when Dr. Hossboch, along with several assistants, visits you at the center. The important thing now is to confirm the reservation, giving only basic details. Write the letter.

2. For the School of Law commencement exercises (see 1 above), you engaged six ushers from Professional Services Inc. at $50 each. The young women and men supplied by the firm were very friendly and gracious; they were appropriately attired for the event and did an outstanding job. Transmit your check to Professional Services Inc. (Grant Braden, with whom you became acquainted), and put anything you think appropriate in your letter.

SUPPLEMENTARY PROJECTS

3. The Program Committee of the Montana Internal Auditors Association, of which you are a member, is planning an afternoon meeting and dinner on June 12 at the Executive Motor Inn in Missoula. The committee chairperson has asked you to make reservations. You talked to the assistant manager of the inn by telephone and made tentative reservations for (a) a private meeting room for ten people, (b) single sleeping rooms for six (yourself, Judy Patterson, Leo Frailey, Peter Musette, Jane Logan, and Morris Haritan) for one night, and (c) dinner (to be selected from the menu) for ten in a private dining room. The hotel is to supply the meeting room without charge and is to bill MIAA for the dinner. Each person staying overnight is to pay for his or her own room (the rate is $50). Confirm your reservation request by letter.

4. This morning Mark Stoll, the representative of Seaway Stationers, called on you (a public relations supervisor) to discuss your needs for stationery and supplies. You placed an order for 10,000 letterheads, 8½ by 11 inches, with 7,500 matching envelopes; 5,000 letterheads, 7¼ by 10½ inches (Monarch), with 3,000 matching envelopes; and 2,000 business cards for Marcia Jorgenson, director of public relations. Although you gave Stoll this information, plus samples that he is to match exactly, you decide to confirm the order in writing. Prices are in accordance with Seaway's May 1 schedule.

STYLE CHECKUP

Choose the term in parentheses that correctly completes the sentence.

1. Voelker said she would (appraise, apprise) the president of the committee's recommendations.
2. The office equipment dealer will arrive tomorrow to (appraise, apprise) the value of the typewriters we offered to sell.
3. The (canvas, canvass) tote bag is much more expensive than the vinyl.
4. Did you (canvas, canvass) the dealers for their opinions?

CHAPTER 9

SALES AND SALES-PROMOTION LETTERS

YOUR JOB

You are the assistant manager of Golden State Coastal Inn, a large hotel in Oceanside, California. Although the hotel provides accommodations for individual visitors, much of its business comes from large organizations that use its facilities for meetings and conferences. The hotel provides sleeping rooms for conference participants, meals, meeting rooms, and banquet facilities. A wide variety of recreational activities are available, including tennis, golf, water sports, sightseeing tours, and various indoor games. Your job involves not only managing the hotel's daily business affairs but also handling advertising and promotion, customer services and relations, and general public relations.

CASE 1

Writing a Sales Letter

THE SETTING

You have obtained a directory of the Under-40 Presidents' Club, a list of the names and addresses of over a thousand men and women who became company presidents before reaching the age of 40. You think that the various companies these presidents represent would be excellent prospects for the services offered by Golden State Coastal Inn, and you decide to write each club member a letter.

Your Objective   To sell the advantages offered by the inn and to trigger requests for additional information.

BACKGROUND

We have mentioned several times that nearly every letter that one writes sells something, even if it's only a point of view, an idea, or goodwill. But the true sales letter attempts to persuade people to spend money for a product or service immediately or to put them in the mood to do so later.

Four basic elements are usually present in an effective sales letter. You can look upon them as your guidelines.

Guidelines

1. Attracting the reader's *attention*
2. Building the reader's *interest* in the product or service
3. Creating a *desire* for the product or service
4. Inducing the reader to take *action*.

These make up what is often called the AIDA concept—attention, interest, desire, and action. To illustrate, let's look at the letter below. *Tennis Monthly*

TENNIS MONTHLY
435 South Ironwood Drive • South Bend, Indiana 46675

Dear Subscriber:

    Don Budge . . . Jack Kramer . . . Pancho Gonzales . . . Rod Laver . . . Fred Perry . . . Margaret Court . . . Bill Talbert . . . Billie Jean King . . . John Newcombe . . . Arthur Ashe . . . Lew Hoad . . . .

    Pardon me for name dropping, but I have exciting news about these and other all-time tennis greats that I want to share with Tennis Monthly readers. You know, of course, that each of these players blazed the pro circuit in one era or another, leaving an indelible imprint on tennis history. But did you know that they were also prolific writers on the subject?

    Tennis Monthly has arranged to issue in book form the major writings of twenty of the greatest names in tennis. The first is Don Budge on Tennis, followed by similar books by those named above plus many of today's headliners whose names are instantly recognized by every tennis enthusiast.

    I think you'll find every volume in this series immensely exciting. Each will be profusely illustrated by America's leading tennis artist, Eklund Nillsen, and will be handsomely bound in a rich-looking leatherlike cover. The price of each book will be only $9.95, including postage.

    Use the enclosed card to order your copy of Don Budge on Tennis. I'll accept your personal check now, or I can bill you later. As each volume is released, I'll send you advance notice. I won't think you'll want to miss a single one!

    SPECIAL BONUS! If your order reaches me before May 15, I'll include--absolutely free--a beautifully illustrated 24-page booklet, Back to Fundamentals. It could make a big difference in your game!

              Sincerely,

              Chris Hemby

              Chris Hemby

Attracting attention
Those who receive *Tennis Monthly* will be familiar with these names, so their attention is captured at once.

Building interest
Once attention has been gained, the writer then explains the reason for "name dropping," gradually building sufficient interest on the reader's part to want to learn more.

Creating desire
By the end of the third paragraph, it is expected that the reader has become interested enough to want to own them.

Inducing action
The assumption now is that a sufficient desire has been created to lead the reader to wonder, How do I get this series? This question is answered in paragraph five, and as an incentive to take action a bonus is offered in the last paragraph.

magazine is publishing a series of books, each written by a well-known tennis champion. It is hoped that subscribers to the publication will want to buy one or more of the books in the series.

The Salutation in Sales Letters

Ideally, the reader's name, title, and address, as well as a personal salutation, should be included in a sales letter. But if you're sending a letter to many thousands of people, including all these items is not usually practicable—it is too expensive, since the information must be individually typewritten. Large mailings are usually processed by some means—that is, printed. Although the computer has reduced greatly the cost of inserting a personal salutation, advertising copywriters are not convinced that the merits of this pseudopersonal touch justify the extra expense.

Sometimes you can provide an appropriate impersonal salutation, such as in the letter on page 137 and with such titles as *Dear Homeowner, Dear Antique Collector,* and *Dear Professor,* but more often than not, you won't find one that is suitable. Some solve this problem by using *Dear Friend,* but it's really not appropriate in most business cases and offends some people.

Thus in large mailings, many writers simply omit a salutation and in its place use a headline of some sort. Here are two examples.

- DO YOU REMEMBER . . .
  when Apex was selling for $120 a share back in 1980?

- LOOK BEFORE YOU LEAVE!
  Let our colorful booklet, <u>Island Hopping in the Caribbean</u>, guide you to the greatest adventure of your life.

Openings for Sales Letters

There are many different types of openings that you can use to attract attention in opening your letter. Three of the most popular are a special offer, a quotation or anecdote, and a provocative statement or question.

A Special Offer

- TWO FULL WEEKS TO ENJOY
  THE BEST DAILY NEWSPAPER IN IOWA
  WITH OUR COMPLIMENTS!

- You'll save $26.50 if you order
  <u>Art Treasures of the Ancient World</u>
  before December 1.

- WITHOUT A CENT OF COST TO YOU
  we'll mail you a handsome pocket diary.

A Quotation or an Anecdote

- It was Tuesday, May 12, when John and Sara Beadling first came to see me. I remember because it was a fateful day for me--and, as it turned out, for them.

- I was about four when my father took me to my first circus (in the small town where I grew up, any outfit that had a merry-go-round, a few clowns, an elephant, and a tiger was called a circus). But what I remember most vividly was the medicine man who sold bottles of pink fluid, which he promised would cure any sickness or ailment--from fallen arches to baldness to arthritis. He did a lot of business at one dollar a bottle, and it was then I first learned the meaning of the word <u>gullible</u>.

- Charles Caleb Colton is credited with having first said, "Imitation is the sincerest flattery." If that's so, then we've got every reason at Mowbray's to. . . .

A Provocative Statement or Question

- Children should be seen and not hurt.

- There's an underground in this country of about 40,000 men who use neither a safety razor nor an electric shaver. Yet they're the cleanest-shaven men in America.

- One day soon you'll be able to do all your shopping from your own living room!

- How would you like to have a profitable business of your own for less than $3,000?

The Sales Message

Before you begin to develop your sales message, you will need to do some hard thinking about what to emphasize. If you try to tell your reader everything there is to know about your service or product, you'll wind up with more material than anyone has the patience to wade through. So you have to ask this question:

What is the outstanding feature of my product or service that is most likely to appeal to the readers being addressed? For example, in the sales letter to the Under-40 Presidents' Club, will the members be attracted most by the luxurious accommodations of Golden State Coastal Inn? Or the beautiful surroundings and recreational facilities? Or your expertise in hosting meetings and conventions? Or the special rates? Of course, all these matters are important, and if appropriate, they might be mentioned in your letter. But you should choose one dominant theme and build your message around it. This is often referred to as the *central selling point* or *central theme*.

Preparation of the Under-40 Presidents' Club Letter

We come now to the preparation of the letter to the members of the Under-40 Presidents' Club. You know your objective, of course: to persuade readers to choose Golden State Coastal Inn for their company's next important meeting. But what will be the central theme? How will you attract immediate attention? What ways will you choose to develop interest, build desire, and induce action?

Before answering these questions, let's try to visualize the typical members. We know that they are relatively young, reasonably affluent, probably physically active, dynamic, and aggressive. Probably, too, they are good managers—cost-conscious and eager to get their dollar's worth when they spend money.

It is likely that such people would be interested more than anything else in making the most productive use of their time when they have a meeting. Meetings away from home can be very expensive, and although most program planners allow time for relaxation and fun, their main purpose is to make sure that at the end of the conference everyone who attended will feel that it was a highly rewarding educational experience. The theme we might choose for this letter, then, is the expertise that Golden State Coastal Inn has in putting on the best conference possible in terms of facilities and services.

Now that we have chosen the "expertise" theme, how do we attract the attention of the readers? Here are two possibilities.

- ```
  "Thank you--
  for helping us put on the best conference we
  have ever had.  Your superb facilities, ser-
  vice, and know-how and helpful attitude all add
  up to one word:  professionalism."
  ```

- ```
  Pardon us for crowing just a bit, but the above
  message was received a few days ago from the
  vice president of one of. . . .
  ```

- ```
  KNOW-HOW
  That simple word is the difference between an
  outstanding company meeting and a merely pass-
  ```
  ```

able one. That difference is Golden State Coastal Inn. We <u>know how</u>.

Eighteen spacious, carpeted meeting rooms, each seating 25+ people; two large auditoriums, one seating 150 and the other 350; three special banquet rooms accommodating from 160 to 300. . . .

These are only a few of the extraordinary facilities Golden State Coastal Inn can offer you for your company meetings. But there's more.

SAMPLE LETTER

Let's take the opening used in the first example and develop the theme.

Golden State Coastal Inn

"Thank you--
for helping us put on the best conference we have ever had. Your superb facilities, service, and know-how and helpful attitude all add up to one word: <u>professionalism</u>."

Pardon us for crowing just a bit, but the above message was received a few days ago from the vice president of one of the country's largest manufacturing companies. And it's typical of many we get from top executives who choose Golden State Coastal Inn as their host for meetings, conference, seminars, and conventions.

At Golden State we know how to help you make your meetings really successful. It's what we were designed to do, what we're mainly in business for, the reason we like to think we're the ideal convention headquarters. Golden State Coastal Inn is not just another magnificent resort center that offers everything any meeting goer could ask for--all sports, including a championship golf course and tennis courts; outstanding cuisine; big-name entertainers; an almost ideal climate; elegant nearby shopping malls; and a stunning view of the Pacific Ocean. We're all those things, of course, but we are more.

By "more" we mean that we really are professionals when it comes to arranging space for your specific needs and providing every service you require to make outstanding meetings and conferences. At Golden State you'll find a staff that is dedicated to personal and friendly hospitality.

Skeptical? Let me prove what I have said. Please look over the enclosed colorful folder, which shows our spectacular setting and elegant facilities. Then, to learn more about our professional side, mail the enclosed card for your free copy of <u>So You're Having a Meeting</u>!

Sincerely yours,

Analysis The central theme—getting the most from your meeting dollar—is a thread that runs throughout the letter.

1. Attention is obtained by the testimonial at the beginning.
2. Interest is achieved by expanding on the testimonial and the idea that although Golden State Coastal Inn is a magnificent resort hotel, with all the attractions and services anyone would want, its fame has been earned largely from its expertise in hosting meetings and conventions.
3. Action is induced by inviting the reader to let Golden State prove its claims—by encouraging the reader to send for a free booklet.

"YOUR JOB" PROJECTS

1. The Pacific Coast Association of Reading Teachers will be holding its annual meeting at the Oceanside Civic Center from August 11 to 14. You have obtained a membership roster of this group and plan to write a sales letter to the members encouraging them to stay at the Golden State Coastal Inn during the convention. Plan and write the letter. Assume the following:
   a. The regular daily rate at the inn is $50 (double occupancy). However, you are offering the members of PCART the special rate of $100 for three days.
   b. Golden State Coastal Inn is only three blocks from the civic center—a pleasant and easy walk. Complimentary limousine service is also available every 15 minutes in the early morning and late afternoon.
   c. You will enclose a colorful brochure that illustrates some of the many outstanding features of the inn.
2. A new organization, the American Association of Administrative Assistants, has just been formed. It is made up principally of women who have risen in rank from secretaries and clerical supervisors up to managers and executives. Write a letter to the new president, Miss Jennifer Webster, inviting the group to consider Golden State Coastal Inn for its annual meetings. Assume that

you will send your special brochure and a postcard that the members can use to request a copy of *Golden State Plans a Meeting. Note*: In some respects, this letter will resemble the one illustrated on page 141.

SUPPLEMENTARY PROJECT

3. You are the membership director of The Art Collector's Guild, a group formed for the purpose of selling lithographs and etchings by outstanding modern artists. You have obtained the mailing list of the Under-40 Presidents' Club, and you want to write to the members of the club, encouraging them to become members of the guild. Your budget does not permit you to send an individually typewritten message, so your letter will have to be "processed" (printed in some fashion). Here are some details (they are not necessarily given in the order in which they might be featured in your letter) supplied by the advertising manager:
    a. The guild is offering original art for the people who appreciate its aesthetic value as well as its economic value.
    b. Enclosed with the letter will be a folder (announcement) that shows samples of the art that will be available to members.
    c. Each work is signed by the artist, numbered, authenticated, and framed.
    d. The cost of each work will be less than half its appraised value—from $60 to $100.
    e. The artists who are represented are only those whose works have been displayed in galleries and museums and recognized by critics for their beauty and financial potential.
    f. Those who join risk nothing—they are not required to purchase a single work of art.
    g. The membership fee is $20, and subscribers will be billed for this amount only after they have received a free, framed original etching or lithograph, which they must request.
    h. A postage-paid card is to be enclosed, and all the reader has to do to enroll as a member and receive a free original etching or lithograph is to complete the card and mail it.

STYLE CHECKUP

Choose the term in parentheses that correctly completes the sentence.

1. Between (you and I , you and me), I am planning to promote Rachel to a supervisory position.
2. The food served in the company cafeteria and that served in the executive dining room are (equally as good, equally good).
3. Although she was a little embarrassed at her anniversary luncheon, Eileen seemed (kind of, rather) happy to receive the glowing tributes.
4. I think Ramsing was (somewhat, sort of) upset by the error on the income statement.

C A S E 2

Following Up an Inquiry

THE SETTING

You received 51 requests for the brochure *So You're Having a Meeting!* as the result of the sales letter (Case 1). This is about a 5 percent return, which is considered very good. One of those who received the brochure, Carl E. Bingham, president of Consolidated Business Equipment, Inc., of Butte, Montana, later wrote asking about accommodations for a company meeting of 120 sales and executive personnel. The meeting is scheduled for December 3 to 7.

In your letter to Bingham, you told him that his group can be accommodated on the date requested, and you suggested that he make reservations by September 10, since December is a popular month at Golden State Coastal Inn for meetings. It is now September 15, and you have not heard from Bingham. Space is still available, but it is filling up rapidly.

Your Objective   To persuade Bingham to make a reservation for his meeting.

BACKGROUND

Business firms are usually not satisfied when their first response to an inquiry produces no results, and many set up a follow-up system. Four or more letters and telegrams may be sent. The theory is that the large amount of money which has been spent to get people interested enough to make an inquiry is wasted when prospects are permitted to slip away.

Observe these guidelines in your first follow-up letter.

Guidelines

1. Gently remind the prospect that you genuinely want a favorable decision about the product or service you are selling.
2. If you can honestly give a logical reason for taking immediate action, do so, but don't cry wolf simply as a ruse.
3. Briefly reinforce the advantages of choosing your product or service.
4. Do not be pushy—keep your message low-key and friendly; an overaggressive attitude will do more harm than good.

SAMPLE COMMUNICATIONS

Dear Mr. Bingham:

I cannot hold the tentative reservation I made

for your group beyond September 25. Please write
or telephone immediately about your intentions.

                    Very truly yours,

Analysis Letter A is almost certain to annoy Bingham. Here's why.

1. Bingham did not request that accommodations be reserved—he merely inquired about their availability from December 3 to 7.
2. The writer puts Bingham on the defensive, and this may cause him to say, "Those people are too pushy for me; I'll just ignore that presumptuous message."

(Telegram)

I HOPE YOU PLAN TO BE WITH US FOR YOUR DECEMBER
MEETING. ACCOMMODATIONS ARE FILLING UP, AND I
URGE YOU TO MAKE RESERVATIONS NO LATER THAN SEP-
TEMBER 25.

Analysis Telegrams usally attract special attention, and the one shown is well written. But there are some special precautions that you must take with telegrams.

1. Some people associate telegrams with crisis situations and may be annoyed when there is no crisis.
2. Although telegrams are very effective for follow-ups in certain situations, we think that this situation does merit such an "alarm" at this point.
3. If the writer feels that a panic button situation really exists, she or he will probably find that a telephone call is more effective.

Dear Mr. Bingham:

When you wrote me in July about accommodations
for your December 3-7 meeting, I tentatively reserved a block of meeting and residence rooms for
your group. Although you did not ask me to do
so, I wanted to make certain I had an appropriate
record in case you decided to choose Golden State
Coastal Inn.

If you are still thinking about being with us
(and I certainly hope you are), Mr. Bingham, I
suggest that you let me hear from you not later
than September 25. This is the latest date on
which I can <u>guarantee</u> accommodations.

Since I last wrote you, we have been building a
solarium with an indoor pool plus a very spacious

sauna. I hope yours is one of the first groups
to these new facilities!

                              . Sincerely yours,

Analysis   Letter C effectively meets the four guidelines listed on page 144.

1. It is friendly, tactful, and low-key, yet it has an appropriate air of urgency.
2. If Bingham is still a prospect, this letter is quite likely to trigger favorable action.

"YOUR JOB" PROJECTS

1. Arthur O. Lasser, executive secretary of the United Air-Conditioning Institute (Gallup, New Mexico), wrote asking about accommodations at the Golden State Coastal Inn for a meeting scheduled for March 16 to 18. You responded enthusiastically, answering specific questions about exclusive golf privileges, the availability of various types of audiovisual equipment, and so on, and urging Lasser to make reservations by December 15, if possible.

   It is now January 6, and you have heard nothing further from Lasser. You decide to write a follow-up letter. You think that the letter should have a definite sales flavor—that it should emphasize three of the things about Golden State Coastal Inn you are proudest of: the people, the facilities, and the climate. Also, you will include a gentle reminder that space is filling up rapidly and that Lasser should make reservations now while accommodations are still available.

2. Mr. Bingham (see the letter on page 145) telephoned you on September 25 to say that Consolidated Business Equipment is still favorably considering Golden State Coastal Inn for its December 3–7 meeting. At that time you reminded him of the necessity for making reservations quickly—certainly not later than September 25. He had not responded by October 2, when you received a letter from the marketing director of a large company in South Dakota specifically requesting accommodations for a December 3–7 meeting for about 100 people. You decided that you should first send a telegram to Bingham explaining your problem and asking for an immediate response, either by wire or by telephone. Prepare the telegram.

SUPPLEMENTARY PROJECTS

3. It has been three weeks since you wrote to L. D. Moberly of Olympus Products Corporation about the G-7 Accutrax electronic calculator (see letter B on page 108). Just this week it was announced that an additional discount of 10 percent will be offered during the next 30 days on this calculator—the offer ends June 30. Write a follow-up letter.

4. You telephoned Gerald Hembley (Project 2, page 109) on December 12, and Hembley said he expected to place an order for a dozen cassette recorders within a few weeks. It is now January 4, and you have not heard from Hembley. Today, you received notice that the price of the recorder will be increased from $39.95 to $49.99 each on February 1. Write the appropriate follow-up letter to Hembley.

STYLE CHECKUP

Choose the term in parentheses that correctly completes the sentence.

1. The kerosene heater saves fuel costs, (like, as) the dealer said it would.
2. (Fewer, Less) people are buying new cars this month.
3. Our profits were (fewer, less) than expected in the first quarter.
4. The accounting manager feels that we must raise prices (regardless, irregardless) of the effect it may have on sales.

C A S E
3

Welcoming a New Customer

THE SETTING

Shortly after receiving your telegram, Carl E. Bingham (Case 2, Project 2) telephoned you that Consolidated Business Equipment Inc. definitely wants reservations for the company's meeting scheduled for December 3 to 7. He apologized for the delay and asked you to send him the necessary papers for his signature. (It was stipulated in the material Bingham received from you that those who reserve conference accommodations for sizable groups must sign a written agreement covering various details—rates, services, method of payment, and so on.)

Your Objective   To welcome Bingham and his group to Golden State Coastal Inn, transmit the necessary papers for signature, and reaffirm your determination to make this new relationship a happy one.

BACKGROUND

After expending a good deal of money and effort to win new customers, alert business people adhere to this motto: "Now that I've won these customers, I'll do everything possible to keep them." It makes absolutely no sense to turn handsprings to attract customers and then virtually ignore them. Remember the old saying, "A bird in the hand is worth two in the bush."

Obviously, very large companies can't afford to write a long, personal letter to everyone who places a first order. Yet many do acknowledge the occasion with a printed card or note. If a first order comes from an especially important buyer, a personal letter of welcome *is* often written. Even if it's a form message, it is the first step toward building good customer relations.

Golden State Coastal Inn, a relatively small enterprise, makes it a practice to welcome every new convention group with a personal letter to the person who made the arrangements.

Follow these guidelines in welcoming a new customer.

Guidelines

1. Express your pleasure in receiving the order or the new customer's intention to purchase your services.
2. Supply whatever information the customer may have requested or you think might find useful.
3. Tactfully request any information or action that you require.
4. Make it clear that it will be a personal pleasure for you to be of maximum service.

SAMPLE LETTERS

Dear Mr. Bingham:

Enclosed is a contract for your signature, along with several menus from which you may select one for each of your three dinner meetings.

Would you please sign both copies of the contract and return one to me, along with your menu selections. Thank you.

Cordially yours,

Analysis While parts of it are effective, Letter A lacks some qualities of a good letter.

1. Letter A is brief and courteous. One could say that everything has been said that must be said.
2. Yet Letter A lacks a very important ingredient: warmth. Bingham will have a hard time reading into this message any sign of "glad to have you—welcome!"

Dear Mr. Bingham:

It was very pleasant talking with you yesterday and learning that Consolidated Business Equipment Inc. will be with us for its December 3-7 meeting. Welcome!

The enclosed contract includes a detailed summary of the accommodations, services, and equipment you require as well as the various prices we agreed on during our conversation. If you approve this agreement, please sign both copies and return one to me. If anything is amiss, however, please telephone or write me.

You will see that I have enclosed several menus for your three dinner meetings. Would you please indicate your choice for each dinner by simply circling the appropriate number and placing the date alongside it.

I would consider it a favor if you would ask for me just as soon as you arrive here. My office is just to the right of the reception area. I'd like to give you a personal tour of the inn and show you the accommodations that have been reserved for you.

Yours very sincerely,

Analysis No doubt you quickly spotted the things that make the letter effective:

1. It opens with a reference to the telephone conversation and a hearty welcome.
2. In the next two paragraphs, the writer tactfully handles the business details, leaving room for dissent if Bingham objects to anything in the contract.
3. The last paragraph says, in effect, "I'm eager to meet you and make sure that everything I've arranged will have your complete approval."

"YOUR JOB" PROJECTS

1. Clarice Hailey, president of Très Chic Sportswear, recently visited you at Golden State Coastal Inn for the purpose of seeing whether the inn would be suitable for a district sales meeting that is planned for July 17 to 20. Yesterday you received a letter from her in which she asked for reservations for 60 people; 50 will share rooms, and 10 will have private rooms. She requested the following information.
   a. The actual off-season rates, which are described in the literature you sent her only as "special rates from March 15 to December 15." (Your regular rates are $50 per person for double occupancy and $65 per person for single occupancy. Off-season rates for the same accommodations are $35 and $50, respectively.)
   b. May she reserve six tennis courts for the exclusive use of her group on the afternoon of July 19? (The answer is "yes," and there is no charge for

this service. Tennis racquets and shoes can be rented at the pro shop. Tennis balls and other supplies can be purchased at the same place.)

c. At what hours is limousine service available to and from the airport? (Courtesy limousine service is provided every 30 minutes from 7 a.m. to 11 p.m.)

d. May she substitute menu No. 4 for 7, which was originally requested for the dinner meeting on July 19? (This can easily be arranged.)

Write the appropriate letter, assuming that you will send a standard contract for Hailey's signature. She may return either the signed original or a copy.

2. While you were out of the office on August 22, R. Donald Terhune telephoned for reservations for a two-day seminar of the Western Cost Accountants Association scheduled for September 8 to 10. Although this group has previously held meetings at the Golden State Coastal Inn, Terhune, the new president, was not present. However, the message you received indicates that he has complete information and is ready to contract for accommodations if they are available. He is very eager to have an immediate response, since time is very short.

You have just had a cancellation for the dates Terhune requested, and you can accommodate his group. When you tried to return Terhune's call later, you were told that he was on an out-of-town trip and could be reached at the Parkside Hotel, in Fresno. However, you were unable to get in touch with him, and so you decided to send him a telegram at the Parkside Hotel and, at the same time, send a letter to his business address confirming the telegram. Write both messages.

SUPPLEMENTARY PROJECT

3. The Broadmoor Manufacturing Company (Oklahoma City), which manufactures a complete line of house paints, distributes its products through retail paint stores, building supply firms, discount marts, and mail-order houses. Broadmoor's line is a top-quality line, yet it sells for about 20 percent less than nationally advertised brands. A fairly new company, Broadmoor has not achieved national attention as yet.

For over three years, Broadmoor's sales representative, Milton McDow, with considerable help from the home office, has been trying to persuade Laughlin's, a thriving specialty paint store in Stillwater, Oklahoma, to purchase Broadmoor's De Luxe paints for its customers. The dealer, Vernon Mullis, carries many lines of paints and is well satisfied with sales and customer acceptance.

Broadmoor had no outlet in Stillwater or in all of Payne County, where Stillwater is located. McDow and his sales manager, you, have paid many visits to Stillwater to talk with Mullis, and although you have become good personal friends, Mullis continues to say, "I've got all the brands I can sell. I think your paint is great—and I like the price—but I'd have to give up one of my popular brands to stock yours. I just don't have the space."

This week, without prior warning, you happened to see a large order for Broadmoor's De Luxe paints from Laughlin's—signed by Vernon Mullis. Although you and McDow had lately begun to feel that you were making some headway with Mullis, this order caught you almost totally by surprise.

You and all the others at Broadmoor are, of course, delighted at this turn of events. You tried to telephone Mullis to express your appreciation, but he had left on vacation. So you decide to write him a letter.

Prepare the letter, using whatever theme you think is appropriate. (We recommend that you bring McDow, the representative who worked so hard to obtain this customer, prominently into the picture.) Use your own imagination in forecasting the future of Broadmoor paints at Laughlin's, and present other ideas that you think will convince Mullis that he made a very wise decision. You may decide to have one of Broadmoor's trucks loaded immediately with Laughlin's order so that it can be delivered to Stillwater without delay.

STYLE CHECKUP

Choose the term in parentheses that correctly completes the sentence.

1. There is really no excuse for (this kind, these kinds) of errors.
2. Unfortunately, this is the (last, latest) set of travel posters we have, and there is no plan to reprint them.
3. The author sent an autographed copy of her new book to both Carey and (myself, me).
4. The responsibility for refreshments will be shared by Mark and (myself, me).

CASE 4

Winning Back Former Customers

THE SETTING

Until two years ago, Creighton Lighting Company had held its annual dealers meeting at Golden State Coastal Inn every March for three years in a row. Although you sent your usual promotional literature during these two years, the company has not returned. You decide to write a special follow-up letter to the executive vice president, Agatha Lupino.

Your Objective To win back Creighton Lighting Company as a customer or learn the reason why the company did not return.

BACKGROUND

"Once a customer, always a customer" is an axiom every business would like to make a reality. But in our competitive world, customers do stray. Sometimes they are lured away because a competitor offers better prices or services or because they received special favors or attention. Alas, too many customers are lost because they are taken for granted or feel they have been mistreated. In some cases the reason customers leave is simply a mystery.

Guidelines   Because there are so many different methods used to win back old customers—offering more generous credit terms or special discounts, sending new-product announcements or keep-in-touch letters or "What did we do wrong?" questionnaires, and so on—there are no specific guidelines that apply. Obviously, you want to trigger an order or receive some indication that the former customer will give your company favorable consideration. Therefore, the tone of your letter should be friendly and persuasive—never accusatory or demanding.

SAMPLE LETTERS

Dear Mrs. Lupino:

We've missed you!

For three years in a row Golden State Coastal Inn had the pleasure of being your host for your annual dealers meeting in March. For this reason we had begun to think of Creighton Lighting Company as a favorite "perennial." We enjoyed having you here, and think you were pleased with our accommodations and service.

But for two years now you haven't chosen us for your March meeting, and it is only natural that we ask ourselves, "What did we do to those nice folks at Creighton Lighting Company that would cause them to stay away?" We can't come up with a reason that satisfies us.

If there was something at Golden State Coastal Inn that did not measure up to your expectations, we'd like to know about it. Honestly. I'm enclosing a little questionnaire that I hope you will complete and return to me in the envelope

provided. Please be perfectly frank in your answers.

Thank you.

Yours very sincerely,

Analysis Letter A makes effective use of the "What did we do wrong?" theme. There are pros and cons about using this theme.

1. Some promotion people object to this approach because it invites adverse criticism.
2. Others say that it is an excellent device—that some positive remedy for a problem can be prescribed only if the real truth is learned.

Dear Mrs. Lupino:

I wish you were here this morning as I write this. I'd like to seat you in one of our Lektric Carriages and take you on a grand tour of Golden State Coastal Inn. So many new features have been added that I could spend two or three hours just pointing out the wonderful changes that have taken place since you were here in [year].

Perhaps you can get an idea by quickly reading our new colorfully illustrated booklet. <u>Present-ing . . . the New Golden State Coastal Inn</u>. I hope it will persuade you to plan to hold your next dealers conference here!

Yes, we've got a new look, but there is one thing that hasn't changed: our friendly hospitality. Why not give us a chance to demonstrate it? Re-member, winter rates are in effect through March 15, and now would be a good time for you to make your reservation.

Yours very sincerely,

Analysis Letter B uses the "See how much better we are now" theme.

1. We do not necessarily think it is better than Letter A: only the reactions from the recipient can indicate whether it is.
2. If there are a large number of follow-ups to "lost" customers, the writer might use Letter A for half of them and B for the remainder to see which one "pulls" better.

"YOUR JOB" PROJECT

1. Write two letters, each with a different theme, attempting to win back customers (organizations) who, after having been good patrons for several years, have not returned to Golden State Coastal Inn for the past two years. Use your imagination in making the invitation attractive. Here are some themes you may choose from:

   a. What went wrong?

   b. Expansion of recreational facilities.

   c. New facilities for meetings.

   d. Headline performers in the supper club nearby.

   e. New restaurants or menus.

   f. New services such as sightseeing trips, recreation programs, and other activities designed especially for spouses and children of those attending meetings.

   g. Big-name sports events nearby, such as golf and tennis tournaments, boat races, baseball and basketball games, stock car races, and rodeos.

SUPPLEMENTARY PROJECT

2. You are the sales manager for Macklin Wholesale Hardware Company. Mrs. Hazel Maples, the owner of Maples Hardware, a retail store in Catesburg, was a loyal customer of yours for many years. Although she was sometimes slow in paying her account, she always came through and was considered an excellent credit risk and a valuable customer. Three years ago a new credit supervisor became impatient with Mrs. Maples because of an overdue balance and wrote her a threatening letter. She paid immediately but was highly indignant. All efforts to pacify her were unsuccessful, and she has placed no orders since.

   Last month a new sales representative, Donna Ewell, was hired to represent Macklin in Jefferson County, where Catesburg is located. You decided to visit Maples Hardware and introduce Ewell to Mrs. Maples. Although Maples received you hospitably, she was a bit standoffish, obviously still rankled by her unpleasant experience three years ago.

   You were greatly impressed by the expansion and remodeling of Maples Hardware. It is a thriving establishment, and you want very much to have the store's business again. However, no sales pitch was made, and past events were not recalled; you left Mrs. Maples with a copy of your latest catalog (greatly enlarged) and a friendly handshake.

   After you return to the office, you decide to write Mrs. Maples. You hope your letter will set the stage for winning her back as a customer. Prepare the letter, using whatever theme you think is appropriate.

STYLE CHECKUP

Choose the term in parentheses that correctly completes the sentence.

1. There is an excellent view (outside of, outside) my window.
2. The Quik-Snak Deli manager said she would have our lunch delivered (inside of, within) 30 minutes.
3. Lisa (can, can't) hardly wait to start her vacation.
4. The buying habits of apartment dwellers are quite (different from, different than) those of homeowners.

CHAPTER 10

CUSTOMER-TO-SUPPLIER LETTERS

CASE 1

Placing Orders With Suppliers

YOUR JOB

You are the purchasing manager of Tri-State Sports Mart, with headquarters in Biloxi, Mississippi. You place orders for sporting goods from several suppliers with nearly all of whom you have established credit.

THE SETTING

You are preparing an order to go to Mid-Continent Sports Equipment in Omaha.

YOUR OBJECTIVE

To write up your order in such a way that there is no doubt about what you want and what the cost will be.

BACKGROUND

Orders can be placed in four different ways: (1) by telephone, (2) on a purchase order form (which Mid-Continent uses where they have credit), (3) on an order blank furnished by the supplier, and (4) by letter.

Usually, an order is placed by letter only when the company does not use purchase order forms or when there are no order blanks on hand from the supplier. When you use a purchase order form or the supplier's order blank, there is no need to write a letter. Some people, however, for record-keeping purposes, attach a note to the order something like this:

```
Here is our purchase order No. 45872 [or your or-
der blank] for various goods.  I would appreciate
your prompt shipment.
```

If you have established credit with a supplier, it is understood that you will be billed after the merchandise has been received. Otherwise, you are required to send your check in payment or ask that the amount be charged to your credit card, which you identify by name and number. For this order let's assume that you will order by letter, enclosing your check for the amount.

Guidelines

1. Show catalog number, if any; quantity; name of item; size or color, if appropriate; price per item; shipping charge, if any; and total amount.
2. Indicate method of payment.

SAMPLE LETTERS

Ladies and Gentlemen:

Please send me the following: 3 golf bags No. GB470, gray, at $77.00, total price $231; 3 golf bags No. WGB 165, navy, at $46.50, total price 143.40; 6 putters No. P161, at $47.80, total price $143.40; 44 dozen Acme balls No. GB68, at $9.50, total price $418.00; and 6 ball shaggers No. SH413, red, at $27.25, total price $163.50. Shipping charges, $8.50. Total of order, $1,103.90.

Enclosed is my check No. 460 in the amount of $1,103.90.

Very truly yours,

Analysis   Letter A contains all the information required. However, it is poorly set up and will be difficult for the supplier to read.

Ladies and Gentlemen:

Please send me the following:

Qty	Cat. no.	Item	Size or color	Price each	Total price
3	GB470	Golf bags	Gray	$77.00	$ 231.00
3	WGB 165	" "	Navy	46.50	139.50
6	P161	Putters	--	47.80	143.40
44 doz.	GB68	Acme balls	Assorted	9.50	418.00
6	SH413	Ball shagger	Red	27.25	163.50
		Add shipping charges			8.50
		Total			$1,103.90

Enclosed is my check No. 460 in the amount of
$1,103.90.

                                  Very truly yours,

Analysis   Letter B is far superior to letter A because it is set up in columns so that it is easy to read.

"YOUR JOB" PROJECTS

1. Demands by customers make it necessary that you keep a small stock of books on sports. You are to place an order with Specialty Books as follows: three each of Nicklaus: *How to Win at Golf* at $16.95; Crenshaw: *How to Putt Like a Pro* at $11.50; Evert: *My Life on Court* at $15.75; Payton: *Confessions of a Running Back* at $18.25; Jordan: *Making the Right Moves in Basketball* at $14.50; and Arnold: *Surfing For the Beginner* at $11.95.

   Set up column heads and enter the information required. Assume that this is the first order you have placed with Specialty Books and that your order is to be accompanied by check. Shipping charges amount to $6.40.

2. You are to place an order for 16 bowling shirts from Torrington Mills with whom you have not established credit. Of the 16 shirts, 4 are to be small, 6 medium, and 6 large. Each shirt is priced at $18. You have chosen white as the base color of the shirts, and the lettering "NAPA PARTS" is to appear in bright yellow across the back. For the lettering design, you refer to the circular arrangement shown on page 16 of the supplier's catalog.

   This is to be a COD order, which requires you to pay half the total amount when you send in your order and the remaining half when the merchandise is received. Shipping charges are to be paid by the supplier.

SUPPLEMENTARY PROJECTS

3. The store owner of Gadgets 'n Things wants to place an order with House of Novelties. You will need the following headings for the order: Quantity, Article, Catalog number, Price each, and Total amount.

   The order consists of 4 giant thermometers, No. H5450, at $12.99; 6 rotating spice racks, No. K-2161, at $19.99; 12 food umbrellas, No. F2280, at $3.49; 6 umbrella hats, No. F4207, at $2.99; 6 clip-on magnifying lenses, No. S3099, at $8.99; 3 E-Z pull exercisers, No. F5213, at $9.99; and 4 shoe racks, No. H5205, at $14.99. Gadgets 'n Things is in the same state as House of Novelties and must pay a 4 percent sales tax. The shipping charges are $7.55.

4. As sales training director of Milford's, C. L. Blount wants to order 25 copies of *Winning the Sale* by Sara Banker and published by Becker's, Inc. Each copy of the book is priced at $14.80, and the supplier pays mailing charges. Blount will use MasterCard No. 6353 0542 5601 4953. Place the order.

Choose the term in parentheses that correctly completes the sentence.

1. Please (try to, try and) reach Mrs. Jurgenson this afternoon.
2. The fringe benefit package you propose is (very unique, unique) in the broadcasting industry.
3. Among those (who, that) commented favorably were the president and the human resources manager.
4. Worley is the kind of coach (who, that) can inspire the players.
5. We intend to make things right (irregardless, regardless) of who was to blame for the damages.

CASE
2

Thanking a Supplier for a Special Favor

THE SETTING

Tri-States Sports Mart, of which you are the purchasing manager, has had several calls lately for "junior"-size golf clubs and other equipment designed for ages six to nine. Tri-State's regular suppliers have been of little help, saying that the demand for such equipment is not great enough to warrant stocking it. You telephone one of your suppliers, Cliff Weaver of Universal Sports Company, and he says he would look into the matter and get back to you. After several telephone calls, Weaver finds a manufacturer who has a complete line of "junior" sports equipment—Winhurst, Inc. Weaver telephones the manufacturer and talks with the marketing coordinator, Cathy Bloomfield. Bloomfield telephones you in Biloxi and tells you she is sending a complete catalog of youth equipment. You immediately place an order with Winhurst for five sets of junior clubs, including woods and irons as well as bags, carts, and gloves.

When you receive the equipment from Bloomfield, you are delighted with their quality and the colorful assortment of bags. You drop a note to Bloomfield, telling her how pleased you are with the equipment. You also write to Cliff Weaver who went to considerable trouble to help you.

YOUR OBJECTIVE

To write a letter of appreciation to Cliff Weaver.

BACKGROUND

Business managers often cooperate with one another when problems arise such as the one you were faced with. It costs little or nothing to go this extra mile, and it could possibly result in favors (even orders) from unexpected sources.

SAMPLE LETTER

Dear Cliff:

Through your kindness, I feel that I really hit the jackpot! The "junior" golf equipment received from Winhurst is really great. I couldn't be more pleased. These clubs, bags, and gloves are every bit as handsome and professional as traditional quality golf equipment.

Thanks very much, Cliff. If I can reciprocate in any way, just let me know. You'll see that I'm sending a copy of this letter to Cathy Bloomfield so you'll both know how I feel.

Sincerely,

copy to Cathy Bloomfield

Analysis   This is a very appropriate letter to a friend who did a favor for someone else. It's folksy in tone, but there's nothing wrong with that in this situation. The idea of sending Cathy Bloomfield a copy is good—now both she and Cliff will have something in common.

"YOUR JOB" PROJECTS

1. On March 11, the "Bears," a team in the Hattiesburg (Mississippi) PeeWee League, ordered 16 baseball uniforms from Tri-States Sports Mart, sizes small to large in the six-to-nine-year-old category. After the uniforms were made up, they were sent to Hattiesburg by United Parcel Service. The manager of the "Bears," Dean Drissell, received the uniforms on April 16, three days before the first game of the local baseball season. For some reason, however, the baseball caps that were ordered did not arrive. Drissell telephoned you to ask about this oversight. You found no defensible reason except poor order filling.

    However, Jennifer Dietz, a Tri-States sales representative, is visiting the home office and is ready to drive from Biloxi to her home base in Jackson on April 18 and will pass through Hattiesburg en route. The delivery takes place, and everyone is happy. Drissell telephones you that the caps were delivered "in the nick of time" and expresses grateful thanks for the "special delivery."

You are to write Drissell, apologizing for the error in not sending the caps along with the uniforms and expressing relief that everything turned out all right. Add whatever details that occur to you.

2. Tri-States Sports Mart has a number of films on sports that they lend to their customers without charge. The Tennis Anyone? store in Baton Rouge asks to borrow the film, "The Great Years at Wimbledon." The film was sent immediately. The owner of Tennis Anyone? writes to you, expressing appreciation for the film. The audience thought that the film was very exciting and praised the coverage of the most important finals in the history of that tournament. She (Glenna Wisnewski, owner of Tennis Anyone?), returned the "Wimbledon" film and asked if there were other films on tennis that she could borrow. You have two others: "Legendary Finals of the U.S. Open" and "A Brief History of the Davis Cup." The "U.S. Open" film is on loan at the moment, and you expect it back in about a week. The "Davis Cup" film can be sent immediately. Write the appropriate letter to Glenna Wisnewski.

SUPPLEMENTARY PROJECTS

3. The Texas Association of Cost Accountants recently held a convention at the Best Western Caballero Motor Hotel (Mrs. Marie Valdez, manager) in El Paso. At the conclusion of the convention, Tina Coulter, the executive secretary of the Association, writes to Mrs. Valdez, praising the hotel on its superb facilities—the magnificent auditorium and meeting rooms, and for the excellent food and service. Coulter thinks that this was the best convention the Association has had in many years and credits the Best Western Caballero Motor Hotel with helping to make it a memorable experience. Respond to Miss Coulter's letter, adding whatever details you think appropriate.

4. A few weeks after the meeting of the Texas Association of Cost Accountants, Mrs. Valdez (see Project 3) received a letter from the executive secretary of the Texas Bar Association, requesting accommodations for the week of July 13. In his letter, the executive secretary (Lewis Padgett) mentioned that he had been referred to the Best Western Caballero Motor Hotel by Tina Coulter, of the Texas Association of Cost Accountants, mentioning the fine service and accommodations offered by the hotel. Mrs. Valdez responds to Lewis Padgett favorably and is now ready to write Ms. Coulter for the recommendation. Write the letter for Mrs. Valdez's signature.

STYLE CHECKUP

Choose the term in parentheses that correctly completes the sentence.

1. Our survey shows that in 70 percent of the homes, the television set remains (stationary, stationery).

2. For personal correspondence, many executives use Monarch-size (stationary, stationery).

3. We have sufficient facts to (disapprove, disprove) Roe's allegations.

4. I (disprove, disapprove) of the idea of a standard dress code for everyone.

CASE 3

Customer Not Given
an Expected Discount

THE SETTING

Wilson Springer is a sales representative of Honeycutt's, a manufacturer of luggage and certain sports items. He calls on you frequently at Tri-State Sports Mart.

On his last visit, Springer said that the popular Excello sports bag will be on sale during April at 20 percent off the regular price of $34.50 to dealers, or a net price of $27.60. The company already offers dealers a discount of 5 percent on cash orders and you assume this same discount will be added to the special 20 percent discount on the Excello sports bag.

Therefore, when you placed an order for six Excello sports bags, you sent a check for $157.32. After your order arrived at Honeycutt's, an accountant wrote that you owe $8.28 because the regular 5 percent discount is not in addition to the special discount of 20 percent. You write to the accountant, Rita Diaz, that since the regular 5 percent discount was not mentioned in the advertisement you assumed that it could be taken.

You are to write to Diaz and explain your situation.

OBJECTIVE

To persuade Diaz to allow you the regular 5 percent cash discount in addition to the special 20 percent discount.

BACKGROUND

The issue of discounts is often raised between suppliers and customers. The amount of the discount may be rather small (as in this case). The issue is whether it is wise to argue over a discount when the amount is quite small. Frequently the supplier will give in to the customer if there's a risk of losing the customer's business. However, if one customer receives a discount and another doesn't, in normal situations it is unfair to others who do not receive the discount.

SAMPLE LETTERS

A

Dear Ms. Diaz:

I disagree with you that I owe you $8.28. Your advertising leaflet announcing the 20 percent discount on Excello sports bags made no mention of the 5 percent that we cash customers are allowed on all cash orders. As far as I am concerned, my account with Honeycutt's is paid in full.

Yours very truly,

Analysis This letter seems harsh and severe, and it needn't. We think that since Honeycutt's did not refer to the regular 5 percent discount on cash orders, customers have the right to subtract the $8.28 from the discounted selling price of 20 percent. Thus, it's possible to state the case much more tactfully and still win the argument.

B

Dear Ms. Diaz:

When I placed my order for six Excello sports bags on the basis of your announced 20 percent discount, I assumed that your regular 5 percent discount on cash orders would also apply. I can find nothing in your advertising flier on this matter.

I will do whatever seems fair to you. I don't want to be made an exception, but I do think my logic is sound, don't you? Incidentally, I think the Excello sports bag is great--a terrific bargain, too.

Sincerely yours,

Analysis Letter B is better than A. Here the writer applies logic to the communication, and the tone is conciliatory. In other words, A was a demand; B is a gentle request. We think that Honeycutt's will have just as good a chance—perhaps better—in earning the extra discount.

"YOUR JOB" PROJECTS

1. Assume that you are to respond to letter B to Ms. Diaz. She is right; there should have been a 5 percent discount allowed because it is a cash order. The fact that this information was not included in the flier is an oversight; someone slipped and omitted it.

2. Midtown Sports Center, in Birmingham, places an order on May 15 for 60 Excello sports bags, expecting to receive the 20 percent discount. Because Midtown did not place its order during the month of April, the 20 percent discount for later orders will have to be denied and the regular price of $34.50 will be charged. However, because Midtown sent a check with the order, the customer will be entitled to the regular 5 percent cash discount. *Note*: You will have to do a little math to find out how much Midtown owes and ask for the amount due. Address your letter to Ronald Goucher.

SUPPLEMENTARY PROJECT

3. You are the sales manager of Mirador Promotions. Recently the executive director of the Ocean Shores Chamber of Commerce, Marvin Zuckerman, ordered 3,000 bumper stickers advertising the community's main attraction, Yaupon Beach. The stickers featured a lighthouse motif. In the copy that you received for the art, however, the name *Yaupon* was spelled as *Youpon*, and this is the way it was printed on the stickers. You had no way of knowing that a spelling error had been made.

When Zuckerman received the stickers and a bill for $300, he was aghast. In his letter Zuckerman admitted the typographical error on his order and blamed a new typist. He also pointed out that the chamber is a new organization and its funds are very limited. Obviously, he cannot use the stickers with the beach's name misspelled, and he added that "in the interest of future business with your company, I think you may want to do the job over at no cost to us." He did not send payment with his letter.

You must deny the request. However, because the artwork and layout have been done, you can deduct $40 from the next printing. Respond to Zuckerman, using whatever theme you think is appropriate.

STYLE CHECKUP

Rewrite the following sentences to eliminate excess words

1. I am enclosing for your information a copy of our standard lease.
2. As to your question about exchanging the Handyman tool kits for the Professional kits, I would say that this is acceptable to us.
3. I take great pleasure in announcing to all our dealers a clearance sale on all Star outboard motors.
4. Please return the postcard as soon as conveniently possible for you to do so.
5. I wish to ask your opinion about the series of ads that appeared in *Home Digest*.

Customer Dissatisfied With Merchandise

THE SETTING

Faustin's, a large mail-order sporting equipment organization, sends out catalogs not only to wholesalers and retailers but also to individuals. Tri-State Sports Mart always leafs through Faustin's promotional literature but has had few occasions to place an order. Recently, Faustin's made a big hullabaloo about a brand-new concept in golfing equipment: stainless-steel heads for drivers and various other clubs whose heads are ordinarily made of wood. Faustin's claims that these all-metal "sticks" (called "Steel King") not only will get more distance on the fairway but also are much more accurate—"no slices, no hooks." The ad also said, "Satisfaction guaranteed or your money back. Endorsed by leading professionals."

You are intrigued by these all-metal clubs and decide to order three sets (five clubs in a set) at a price of $240 to dealers. You decide to have some of the staff who play a lot of golf try these metal clubs—the same set, so that the new ones remaining won't look used.

After several trials, all players voiced dissatisfaction. Not only are the clubs awkward (they lack balance); they do not get the distance or accuracy of the regular woods.

You decide to write Faustin's (Oscar Faustin, president) about your dissatisfaction with the clubs, giving the reasons for your disappointment. You plan to return all three sets of clubs (even though one has been used).

YOUR OBJECTIVE

To persuade Oscar Faustin to accept the returned clubs and remit the total cost of them to you.

Guidelines

1. Start the letter stating your intentions to return the three sets of golf clubs.
2. Supply reasons why the merchandise is being returned.
3. Ask for a refund.

Note: There is no point in showing your anger or making accusations.

SAMPLE LETTERS

 Dear Mr. Faustin:

Now when I see your guarantee "endorsed by leading professionals," I'll be very wary. This is
my assessment of the truth of your advertising.
A half dozen of our staff members tried the Steel
King all-metal clubs (all players have handicaps
of 12 or better), and they were enormously disappointed. Not only are the Steel King poorly bal-
anced; they positively do not cure a slice or a
hook.

I'm taking you at your word, "Satisfaction guaranteed or your money back." The clubs are being
returned to you today by Bulldog Trucking. I assume I will have your check for $720 plus $8.88
for freight.

Never again will I believe a Faustin's ad.

                    Yours very truly,

Analysis Letter A states the truth, but the author's criticism is overdone.
There appears to be little justification for the last sentence in the letter.

 Dear Mr. Faustin:

I'm returning by Bulldog Freight the three sets
of Steel King golf clubs which I ordered from you
on July 11. I gave these clubs what I think was
a fair trial on the golf course.

Six of our staff members who are experienced
golfers (all with handicaps of 12 or less) gave a
highly unfavorable report. The distances you
claim and the elimination of hooks and slices
just did not justify your statement, "endorsed by
leading professionals."

I assume you will send me your check for $720 for
the cost of the clubs plus freight charges of
$8.88.

                    Sincerely yours,

Analysis   Letter B gets across the most important points concerning the golf clubs and does so without calling Faustin a liar or a cheat.

"YOUR JOB" PROJECTS

1. You often order sports articles and other items from Fabray Industries in Chicago. A popular item recently at Tri-States Sports Mart is a set of 18 colorful paintings, 30 by 48 inches, each illustrating a famous hole on golf courses throughout the United States. The set is called "The 18 Greatest Golf Holes in the United States."

   A new customer, the Shreveport Athletic Club (Michael Burns, director) ordered a set of these illustrations and sent a check for $90. Burns stated in his order letter that he plans to have the paintings framed and placed in the Trophy Room of the club.

   You decide to place the order with Fabray Industries and have them ship the set directly to the customer. Shortly after the shipment was received by Michael Burns, he wrote you that the set of prints had been badly damaged in shipment. The tube in which they were sent was flattened and the illustrations creased so badly that they are unusable. Burns returned the lithographs to you, adding "Please make sure that the package is strong enough to avoid damage to the contents."

   You telephone Theresa Chung at Fabray Industries and tell her what happened, asking that a new set of "The 18 Greatest Golf Holes in the United States" be sent to Burns at the Shreveport Athletic Club. You extract a promise that a heavier tube will be used which is more sturdily constructed and damageproof.

   a. Write a letter to Chung at Fabray Industries reviewing the situation and expressing your disappointment.

   b. Write the letter you believe Chung should send to Tri-State Sports Mart.

2. As purchasing manager, you have placed a first order with Beaufort Sports Gear for 40 pairs of Breton socks. During the past two weeks pro shops that bought these socks have told you that they are poorly made and that holes form in the toes and heels after only two or three wearings. You refund the customers' money and substitute Regent socks that have long been popular for their appearance and durability. Obviously, Breton socks are shoddy merchandise even though their price was not low ($2.50 a pair at wholesale). You write to Glenna Sloan, sales correspondent for Beaufort Sports Gear, asking for a refund of $100 and permission to return the 30 pairs of Breton socks that you have not sold. You do not plan to reorder the Breton socks.

   Write the letter to Miss Sloan.

SUPPLEMENTARY PROJECT

3. You are the assistant manager of Best Western Caballero Motor Hotel, a large hotel that counts among its customers individuals as well as groups of people

attending conventions. A few days ago you received the following letter from C. J. McFarland, president of Midwest Manufactured Homes, Inc., whose executives recently concluded a three-day meeting at the hotel.

Ladies and Gentlemen:

Thanks to the inefficiency of your staff, the fall meeting of Midwest Manufactured Homes Inc. was a big disappointment.

As you very well know, the materials that were shipped to your hotel two weeks in advance for use in our group sessions were misplaced by someone there and were never found (they arrived here today from your hotel). The entire program had been built around these materials, and as a result of their being misplaced, we had to improvise. This was both awkward and unproductive.

Your statement for $1,998.65 arrived today, and I am tempted not to pay it. In any event, it would seem that we are entitled to some kind of discount for the inconvenience we suffered at your hands.

I expect an explanation from you before I authorize payment.

Very truly yours,

Most businesses investigate carefully each complaint before responding. In McFarland's case, the investigation showed that the materials in question arrived at the hotel several days before the meeting. The part-time custodian who signed for the materials (they arrived late in the evening) did not know what to do with them, so he locked them up in the Lost and Found Room. He left the hotel to go on vacation the following day, and his whereabouts were unknown. Later, someone piled several pieces of luggage on top of the carton so that it was hidden from sight. Although the Lost and Found Room was searched at the time, no one thought to lift the luggage to see if there was anything underneath.

Certainly, Best Western owes McFarland an apology; however, you have no authorization to give him a discount on his statement.

Write an appropriate letter to Mr. McFarland. (*Note:* You ignore the request for a discount.)

Each of the following contains errors in the use of possessives. Make the necessary corrections.

1. Who's employment application was received first?
2. Theirs a bonus for those who exceed they're production quota.
3. The mistake was ours—not your's.
4. I can't understand Sarah not meeting her deadline.
5. Phil will preside, and you can depend on him doing a good job.

Customer Complains About a Delay in Shipment

THE SETTING

In addition to sports equipment, Tri-State Sports Mart also sells trophies—brass plaques, silver cups and trays, and various "statues" of sports figures—baseball hitter, tennis player, bowler, skier, boxer, etc.—silver-plated and mounted on a pedestal. Your major supplier for such articles is Paterno Trophies, Inc., which has always given you dependable service. On July 26 you placed an order with Paterno Trophies for tennis trophies as follows:

1. One male tennis player on a brass pedestal, engraved "Men's Junior Champion, Kenwood Tennis Tourney, July 19—"
2. One female tennis player on a brass pedestal, engraved "Women's Junior Champion, Kenwood Tennis Tourney, July 19—"
3. One female tennis player as described above, engraved "Women's Senior Champion, Kenwood Tennis Tourney, July 19—"
4. One male tennis player, as described above, engraved "Men's Senior Champion, Kenwood Tennis Tourney, July 19—"
5. Two female tennis players on a brass pedestal, engraved "Women's Doubles Champions, Kenwood Tennis Tourney, July 19—"
6. Two male tennis players as above, engraved "Men's Doubles Champions, Kenwood Tennis Tourney, July 19—"

On your order you emphasized the rush in getting these trophies. The banquet at which these trophies are to be awarded is August 30.

By August 12 you have not received the trophies, and you telephoned Gail Moyers at Paterno Trophies to see how the order was being handled. Moyers assured you that the trophies would be sent no later than August 15. When the trophies had not been received by August 18, you became very irritated but were given assurances over the telephone by Moyers that the trophies were being sent that day.

When the awards banquet was held on August 30, you had not received the trophies you were promised. They did arrive on September 2, however, and everyone was delighted with them. Your customer was furious.

BACKGROUND

No matter how good one's intentions are, there will be occasions when everything goes wrong. The situation described could hardly be more frustrating to both the customer and the supplier. The customer can only emphasize the disappointment at the poor service and ask for an explanation, and the supplier can only try to explain what happened.

YOUR OBJECTIVE

To write a letter to Paterno Trophies expressing your disappointment and ask for an explanation.

Guidelines

1. Express truthfully your feelings about this unfortunate development.
2. Request tactfully for an explanation.
3. Give the supplier warning about future handling of orders.

SAMPLE LETTERS

Dear Gail:

This is to notify you that we will place no further orders with your company. The manner in which you handled my order placed July 26 for six trophies has caused me no end of embarrassment, and I'm expecting the Kenwood people to deliver me the same message I'm sending to you.

                    Yours truly,

Analysis   Letter A is probably what most people would be tempted to write—and with good reason. The awards banquet was a disaster; no other term seems to describe the affair as accurately. Yet Paterno Trophies, Inc. has heretofore been a reliable supplier, and we think it might be to Tri-State's disadvantage to completely sever relations with them over this error. In any event, before this drastic step is taken, it might be wise to invite Paterno Trophies to state their side of the story.

Dear Gail:

I don't need to tell you how I feel about the way you people at Paterno Trophies handled my order of July 26 for six tennis awards for a valuable customer. The banquet at which the awards were to be presented was, of course, a dismal affair, and I as the guilty party was never quite so humiliated.

My temptation is to say that we will place no future orders with Paterno Trophies. Yet, in all my past dealings with you I have found you to be very dependable in terms of service and outstanding in the quality of the trophies you design and produce.

Before I take any further action, I do think I'm entitled to some sort of explanation that would give me reason to continue to order from you.

Cordially yours,

Analysis   Letter B is a better letter than A, in our opinion, simply because we believe that a usually reliable supplier deserves a second chance. Paterno Trophies no doubt feels great anguish over their slip-up and have probably been expecting a letter such as A. Incidentally, if you think this situation is unbelievable, you would be wrong—such errors occur frequently in business!

"YOUR JOB" PROJECTS

1. Assume that you work for Paterno Trophies and have been given the responsibility to respond to Letter B from Tri-State. Actually, you discovered that the trophies *were* sent August 18 but to another customer in a different state. Say whatever you think is appropriate in persuading Tri-State to continue to receive orders from you.

2. A week ago Finch's Department Store, in Little Rock, ordered 24 "Champ" table tennis paddles and one gross (12 dozen) of balls from Tri-State Sports Mart. Today Elwood Finch telephoned that he now wants to include in the order four table tennis nets. As you wrote down the new order, you were told that the paddles and balls have already been received by Tri-State and are on their way to Finch. After three days Finch writes saying that he has received the paddles and balls and wants to know what happened to the nets.

The company from whom the table tennis equipment is purchased is Glencoe Manufacturing Company in Houston, and the nets have just been ordered. It will take three to five days for the order to be filled and shipped. You follow up with Glencoe and are told that the order went out the same day it was received and should now be arriving in Biloxi within two or three days. Write Elwood Finch an appropriate letter.

3. Suzanne Weger of Fairchild's Sports-O-Rama wrote to you saying that the 16 fielder's gloves, 8 catcher's mitts, and 12 batting helmets she ordered a month ago have not arrived. You wrote to her immediately saying that the gloves and mitts have been received, but the helmets are being held up. The manufacturer is having difficulty getting the sizes specified. You have telephoned the manufacturer twice about delivery. Each time you were told that the helmets would be shipped "in a week." Soon after you placed a telephone call to the manufacturer—two days after receiving Weger's letter—the helmets arrived. You immediately wrote to Weger that the helmets were being shipped today from Biloxi. You wonder whether anyone at Tri-State bothered to tell Weger why the order was held up and find there is no record that the customer was given a single status report during the time of the hold up.

Write Mrs. Weger, telling her the order is being shipped at once, explaining the delay and apologizing for not having written sooner.

SUPPLEMENTARY PROJECT

• •

4. Wickham Automotive Parts, Inc., a wholesaler in Duluth, Minnesota, received an order for various auto parts from Eileen Di Garmo at Raytown, Missouri, in the amount of $2,755.30. The terms of the order are 5 percent discount if paid within ten days of the receipt of the parts. The shipment was due to arrive in Raytown on September 11 but for various reasons was delayed two weeks. When the merchandise was finally received by Di Garmo, she wrote that she was greatly annoyed about the delay, saying she felt justified in taking the 5 percent discount even though her check was written a month after receipt of the goods. The amount was $2,617.53, or $137.77 less than it should have been. Write Di Garmo a letter on behalf of Wickham Automotive Parts, making it very tactful, but stressing that she still owes your company $137.77, the amount of discount she took in defiance of the rules.

STYLE CHECKUP

• •

Choose the word in parentheses that correctly completes each sentence.

1. He seems unable to (adopt, adept, adapt) to new situations.
2. Mr. Symonds was (adverse, averse) to the committee's suggestions.
3. The plan is so good that I believe we should (adopt, adept, adapt) it.
4. Under these (adverse, averse) conditions, we cannot raise prices.
5. JoAnn proved to be quite (adopt, adept, adapt) in copywriting.

CHAPTER 11

SUPPLIER-TO-CUSTOMER LETTERS

YOUR JOB

You are assistant to the sales manager, Barbara Weeks, at Brunswick Paint and Hardware Company, in San Antonio, a wholesaler whose main customers are retail stores and building supply centers in various parts of the country. Your job requires you to be a "troubleshooter" in dealing with customers, which includes working directly with sales representatives to give customers what they need and refereeing any dissensions between customers and your company.

CASE 1

Thanking a Customer for an Order

THE SETTING

You receive an order from The Paint Pot in Denton, Texas, which has not ordered from you before. The order is for 50 gallons of Satin Touch white enamel, and the amount is $422.88. A check for this amount accompanied the order, which includes shipping charges. However, the customer did not deduct the 5 percent discount for paying cash. The amount is $20.80. The Paint Pot's general manager is Margaret McDougle.

BACKGROUND

When new customers place a sizable order from Brunswick Paint and Hardware Company, it is your responsibility to see that they are welcomed. This first letter is warm, friendly, and personalized. When you joined this company, you quickly learned the importance of good customer relations, for without satisfied customers, the company could not stay in business.

YOUR OBJECTIVE

To write a letter to Margaret McDougle welcoming The Paint Pot as a new customer and thanking her for payment.

Guidelines

1. Thank the customer for the order and for payment.
2. Mention the earned discount that was not taken, enclosing your check.
3. Indicate when shipment will be made.
4. Emphasize the good feeling you have to have that first order.
5. Sign off on a cheerful note.

SAMPLE LETTERS

Dear Mrs. McDougle:

This will acknowledge receipt of your order for 50 gallons of Satin Touch white enamel in the amount of $422.88, including shipping charges. Our check for $20.80 is enclosed--your discount for paying cash.

Yours sincerely,

Analysis   Letter A contains the correct information, but it lacks the personal touch that we believe a warm, personal communication should have, particularly on a first order. Obviously, no one at The Paint Pot will not be offended by the letter. (Indeed, they might not have expected to receive any communication.) However, a much more personalized letter will go a long way in establishing good relations at the outset. Note that in Letter A no mention was made about when shipment will be made.

Dear Mrs. McDougle:

Thank you very much indeed for your order for 50 gallons of Satin Touch white enamel and for your check for $422.88, including shipping charges. The order is being shipped today by Cannonball Express.

We consider it a major "event," Mrs. McDougle, when a new customer joins our family of quality paint and hardware stores. According to our representative, Samuel Horowitz, The Paint Pot is a very reputable store in the Greater Denton area. I'm sure you've met Sam. I telephoned him when your order arrived, and he is a mighty excited young man.

You'll find Sam Horowitz very knowledgeable about Brunswick products, and I hope you'll call on him for any help he can give you.

Incidentally, I'm enclosing our check for $20.80, your discount for cash payment. Again, welcome!

Sincerely yours,

Analysis   Letter B is the personalized, friendly welcome we spoke about earlier. Bringing the sales representative who calls on The Paint Pot into the picture makes sense; sales representatives are often left out, and with this letter, relations between Horowitz and McDougle will be off to a good start.

"YOUR JOB" PROJECTS

1. You receive the following order from Lowery's House and Garden Center in Durant, Oklahoma: 4 one-gallon cans of House Beautiful redwood stain; 20 quarts of Deluxe clear shellac; 20 quarts of Rust-No-More enamel; 50 9-inch paint rollers, and 60 2½-inch Clean Flo paint brushes.

   This is your first order from Lowery's. The owner, Philip Lowery, sends a check for the amount of the order, $950.

   Write a welcome letter to Lowery's, sending your check for $47.50, the discount for a cash payment. The sales representative for southeastern Oklahoma is Barbara Sauer, and she will be calling on Lowery soon to find out whether she can be of any special service.

2. You received a purchase order from Mrs. Harold Becker, owner of Becker Building Center, in Loris, South Carolina, for 25 five-gallon cans of Silver Bright roof coating. Becker Building Center was a good customer of Brunswick Paint and Hardware for several years, but has not placed an order for over two years. Becker had a fine credit history, and Mrs. Becker sends no check, presumably assuming that her credit is still good. (It is.)

   You are short of Silver Bright roof coating and can send Becker only 15 cans at this time. The remainder will be shipped within a week. Write the appropriate letter, assuming that Mrs. Becker is to be welcomed back as a valued customer.

SUPPLEMENTARY PROJECTS

3. You work in the Order Fulfillment Department of the Executive Office Supply Company. This week you received a large order for stationery and supplies from Renfro Stationers in Hays, Kansas. Renfro was a good customer of the Executive Office Supply Company for many years, and you tried by mail to lure Carl Renfro back into the fold, but there was no response to your letters. The sales representative from Executive Office Supply called on Renfro but could get no response from him except "I've found a better supplier."

The Executive Office Supply Company is delighted, of course. Renfro's credit history while purchasing from Executive is excellent. Unfortunately, the catalog from which Renfro placed his order is three years old and many of the brand names of the articles carried, as well as the prices, have changed. In addition, there is a much larger selection of products now than there was three years ago.

Write a letter to Carl Renfro, welcoming him back as a valued customer and telling him that a new catalog is being sent immediately so that he will have the latest information on Executive products.

4. Nicholls Paper Company has been in business for 25 years. The early years were very difficult—getting a foothold in a highly competitive market is always difficult. By the end of the fifth year, however, the company was thriving and looking forward to significant growth in the future, and that growth came about dramatically. Nicholls Paper believes, of course, that its products and services are unsurpassed and management has been innovative, which account in large measure for the company's success. On the other hand, the "star" of this particular drama is the customer. As the 25th year closes, the president of Nicholls Paper Company wants a letter of appreciation to go out to all customers in good standing, and you have been asked to construct a draft of the letter.

Read the two letters that follow. Which do you prefer? Why?

a. Dear (customer's name):

On December 15 Nicholls Paper Company will celebrate its Silver Anniversary--our 25th year in business!

There are several reasons why we think we have reached this milestone. We have honestly tried to offer the best possible products at the best possible price, employ personnel who are innovative and dedicated, and create an atmosphere of "Service to our customers comes first."

Yet no matter how much we pat ourselves on the back, we can't give ourselves all the credit for our exciting growth. Our customers have done their share by sticking with us loyally and recommending us to their friends. So you have played an important role in the growth of our enterprise.

Thus we salute you on our Silver Anniversary and promise you in the years ahead the same high-quality products and services that you are accustomed to.

Cordially yours,

b. Dear (customer's name):

On December 15 Nicholls Paper Company will celebrate its Silver Anniversary--25 years of continuous service to our customers.

I think it is especially fitting, as we reflect on our years in the paper business, that we give credit for our success to good customers such as you. No matter how smart we think our management was, the high efficiency displayed by our employees and the high-quality products and services we've offered all pale in importance when compared with the excellent customers we've been blessed with. So as we pause to congratulate ourselves on our success, we place much of whatever glory we've earned right at the feet of our customers.

So we salute you, (customer's name), on our Silver Anniversary. We're very much aware that none of the good things that have happened to us could have happened without you. Thanks to you, we hope to be in a position to continue for another 25 years. Together we can do it!

Very cordially yours,

STYLE CHECKUP

Awkward construction sometimes produces amusing (and unintentional) results. Rewrite each of the following, expressing what you think the writer had in mind.

1. After a thorough inspection and approval of our attorneys, you will receive a new contract.
2. This will acknowledge your letter of May 10 regarding the Musical Giant organ, which we finally located in our files.
3. As one who has a fine credit reputation, I am reluctant to suggest legal action to collect the amout due us.

4. Being reduced to half the original price, you can't expect these motors to remain in stock very long.
5. You will find us unsurpassed in merchandise, service, and prices.

CASE 2

Customer Takes an Unearned Discount

THE SETTING

Lone Star Builders Supply ordered paint from Brunswick Paint and Hardware Company on June 10 in the amount of $2,150. The terms of the sale were 5/10 receipt of goods (ROG). This means that the customer (in this case, Leon Spangler, treasurer) will be allowed a discount of 5 percent if the order is paid for within 10 days after receipt of the merchandise. The merchandise arrived at Lone Star Builders on June 13. Lone Star's check for $2,042.50 was received by Brunswick on June 30.

BACKGROUND

The main purpose of offering discounts to customers is to encourage them to pay for their purchase promptly. Brunswick Paint and Hardware Company offers other terms such as 5/10 n/30, which means that customers who pay for their purchases within 10 days of the invoice date may take a 5 percent discount; in any event, payment is expected for the net amount within 30 days. Usually, suppliers are quite strict in applying these discount terms. All customers are to be treated alike—both large and small. If some customers are allowed to "bend" the policy, then all will be entitled to do the same, which means that there is no discount policy at all.

YOUR OBJECTIVE

To write an appropriate letter to Lone Star Builders Supply asking for an additional $107.50, the amount of the discount taken but not earned.

Guidelines

1. Thank the customer for the check that was received.
2. Call attention to the invoice terms and indicate that Spangler did not meet the requirements to earn a discount.
3. Ask for a check for the amount owed or offer to add the amount to Lone Star's next order.

SAMPLE LETTERS

Dear Mr. Spangler:

You still owe us $107.50 on your purchase of June 10 (Purchase Order No. 641Y) because you did not fulfill your part of the bargain by sending us your check several days past the due date of June 23. May I expect your check at once?

Very truly yours,

Analysis   Obviously, this is a brusque letter which will do nothing but offend Spangler. Even though the message is correct, the method of approaching the customer is atrocious, probably losing a valuable customer.

Dear Mr. Spangler:

Thank you very much for your check for $2,042.50, which we very much appreciate.

I do not like to offend you, but there is a slight error in the amount of the check. The discount terms required payment by June 23 in order to receive a 5 percent discount, and your check did not arrive until the 30th. I know it isn't easy to keep track of such matters--we make our share of mistakes, too.

I hope you will see your way clear to send us the amount of $107.50. I dislike having to ask you for this because I know how highly we value you as a customer. However, I must adhere to company policy and request a check for $107.50.

Cordially,

Analysis   Letter B is hardly an improvement over Letter A. Here the writer, rather than say outright what is wanted, tries not to say what must be said and thus is in the position of begging.

Dear Mr. Spangler:

Thank you for your check for $2,042.50 dated June 30 in payment of Purchase Order 641Y.

If you will look at our invoice, you will see

that the 5 percent discount is allowable only if payment is received within ten days of delivery of the merchandise. Our records indicate that you received the paint shipment on June 13; thus, to earn the discount of $107.50, you would have had to have your check in our hands by June 23. (Incidentally, this discount policy applies to all our customers--so we're not picking on you!).

I know you will want to send your check for $107.50. If you prefer, we can add this amount to your next order.

                              Yours sincerely,

Analysis Letter C is an effective way to tell Spangler that Lone Star owes Brunswick Paint and Hardware Company $107.50. It is direct yet friendly—it could hardly be more tactful. The idea that Spangler may wish the $107.50 added to his next order may soften the blow somewhat.

"YOUR JOB" PROJECTS

1. Vernon Blanchard, a retail store manager, sent a purchase order to Brunswick Paint and Hardware Company on July 1 in the amount of $165.20, terms 5/10 ROG. The date the shipment was received by Blanchard was July 6. Blanchard sent his check in the amount of $156.94 on July 20. Was Blanchard entitled to the 5 percent discount? If not, write him an appropriate letter. He may be asked to send $8.26 or whether Brunswick should add that amount to his next order.

2. On August 16, Abagail Carter ordered paint and hardware in the amount of $240, terms 5/10 ROG. The order was received by Carter on August 19. Carter forwarded her check in the amount of $228 on August 21. However, the check was returned by the bank on August 28 because of insufficient funds. When the check was run through again on September, it cleared (September 12). You have had trouble in the past collecting money from Carter and you decide to follow the strict discount policy to the letter. Write Carter asking for payment of $12, the amount of discount taken.

3. L. B. Bledsoe is a longtime credit customer of Brunswick Paint and Hardware Company. Bledsoe has always paid his account on time and usually takes advantage of the discount offered. Bledsoe purchased paint on August 20 in the amount of $600, and the order was immediately shipped, arriving on August 24. On that date Bledsoe sent a check for $570, taking advantage of the 5 percent discount. However, the check was unsigned. By the time you returned the unsigned check to Bledsoe for signature, it was August 27—too late for the discount. What do you think should be done in this situation? Write the appropriate letter, keeping in mind Bledsoe's overall credit record.

4. You are credit manager of Ingraham's Wholesale Carpeting, a firm that sells only to dealers—not to individuals. Mrs. Julia Thompson, owner of Carpet-O-Rama, ordered outdoor carpeting on October 16 totaling $2,600. It was her first order. The terms are 5/10 ROG, and the carpet was delivered October 20. Thompson mailed her check for $2,600 on October 21. Obviously, Thompson did not know about the 5 percent discount. Also, during October all outdoor carpeting is sold at 20 percent off the regular price.

Write an appropriate letter to Thompson, including in your letter whatever type of welcome you prefer, telling her to watch for special sales that are announced every few months. You are sending her a new catalog in a separate mailing and will add her name to your list of customers to notify when there are special reductions in carpeting prices. *Note:*

Cash payment	$2,600.00
Less 20% price discount	520.00
Total	$2,080.00
Less 5% cash discount	104.00
Amount owed	$1,976.00
	$2,600.00
	− 1,976.00
Amount owed Carpet-O-Rama	$ 624.00

STYLE CHECKUP

Each of the following contains errors in the use of possessives. Make the necessary corrections.

1. EAT AT FRAN'S AND FRED'S DINER.
2. Its not too late to make you're reservations.
3. The committee held it's meeting at the Alhambra Inn.
4. Your not being charged for this special service.
5. Mark and Glenn's electronic calculators cost less than $50 each.

C A S E
3

Customer Returns
Unsalable Merchandise

THE SETTING

A few days ago Brunswick Paint and Hardware Company received 12 one-gallon cans of avocado green EZY-Apply house paint from Alvarez Building Center, a customer for about two years. A note was affixed to the cardboard container, "Returned for credit." There was no previous communication with the senior partner, Luis Alvarez, about returning the paint, so you were somewhat surprised at this action. Not only were the lids rusted, which would render the paint unsalable as new merchandise; the labels were grimy and faded as if they had been stored in a damp place.

Brunswick Paint and Hardware discontinued the EZY-Apply line of paint over a year ago and encouraged their customers to change to the new featured brand Velvet-Sheen, a very high quality paint that is famous nationwide and that Brunswick has sold exceptionally well since the new brand was adopted.

You are not in a position to accept the returned EZY-Apply paint from Luis Alvarez for full credit. Indeed, you know that if the paint can be sold at all, its price will have to be greatly reduced.

BACKGROUND

Customers sometimes return to the supplier products that have not been selling well or have proved defective in some way. If the product is defective at the time it is received—or even a few weeks later—the customer is often given full credit. However, after the lapse of many months and evidence that the product was improperly cared for, the supplier has no alternative except to get the customer the best price that can be obtained. The key issue in accepting or rejecting returned merchandise is whether it is salable.

OBJECTIVE

To refuse to offer full credit to Alvarez for the returned paint and persuade him that the only alternative is to mark it down from the original price to such an extent that its low price may persuade customers to buy it.

Guidelines

1. Agree to do everything possible to "move" the paint.
2. Explain the steps that are to be taken if there is any hope of selling the paint.
3. Call attention to the new line of paints you are now featuring.
4. Extend good wishes.

SAMPLE LETTERS

Dear Mr. Alvarez:

To put it mildly, you gave us an unpleasant shock when you returned 12 gallons of EZY-Apply house paint for full credit! Obviously, we cannot re-fund the original amount you paid for the paint.

The containers are in terrible condition, and there isn't a chance that a customer would buy it.

Didn't you get the word that we were discontinuing the EZY-Apply line, replacing it with Velvet-Sheen? That was over a year ago. At the time the notice was sent, we told customers they should sell their remaining stock of EZY-Apply and purchase the Velvet-Sheen line. Obviously you didn't see this or chose to ignore it.

We are in no position to "move" those 12 cans of paint and will be forced to get rid of them either by lowering the price to not more than one-third of the original cost to you or donating them to charity. This means that the most we could send you would be a little over $2 each and even that seems ambitious.

Please, please never return a product without our permission to do so!

Very truly yours,

Analysis   The writer of Letter A is obviously angry at the return of the paint. Who wouldn't be? It smacks of cunning and underhandedness. However, it seems reckless to show anger; after all, Alvarez is a customer—perhaps not a big one but certainly important. Why risk losing Alvarez over a trifling sum of, say, $24 or less? We think Alvarez deserves better than the writer gave him.

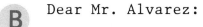 Dear Mr. Alvarez:

We will do everything possible to move the 12 gallons of avocado green EZY-Apply house paint that you returned to us. It seems to me that there is very little we can do--the lids are rusted and the labels are grimy and faded.

We will do this, however. We will put your paint in our Bargain Bin, marking down the price to $2.12, about a third of the price you paid for it. Even so, I can't promise you that the paint will be bought by our customers. It may turn out that we'll have to give it to some worthy organization or simply discard it. Time will tell!

If you have been receiving our catalogs, you will see that we are now featuring Velvet-Sheen paints. Since we adopted this brand over a year ago, we have had wonderful reactions from our customers, and the volume of business grows month by month. Just in case you have not seen our literature, I'm enclosing six color folders with complete price information to dealers. I think you'll agree that there is a superb selection of ready-to-use paints and dozens more can be mixed to suit anyone's taste.

Best wishes for a very busy and prosperous spring for Alvarez Building Center!

Sincerely yours,

Analysis   This is a much better letter than A. Although it contains essentially the same information, the writer uses tact and good sense in an effort to reject a request for full credit and hold on to Alvarez Building Center.

"YOUR JOB" PROJECTS

1. Frank Verdugo, owner of Verdugo's Hardware in Anniston, Alabama, is a customer of Brunswick Paint and Hardware Company. Recently he sent without notice 14 Little Gem hardwood miter boxes and asked for full credit. (He paid $46 for the boxes.) Verdugo wrote that almost invariably after he made a sale of the Little Gem the customer returned it, saying that it was poorly constructed and produced inaccurate miters.

   Brunswick Paint and Hardware Company does not handle the Little Gem miter boxes. The brand they sell is the Peerless Miter King, a box very superior in construction and performance to the Little Gem. You must return the miter boxes that Frank Verdugo sent you, explaining the situation. In your letter responding to Verdugo you suggest that he stock the Peerless Miter King, which wholesales at $4.25 and usually retails at $8.40. In fact, you decide to send Verdugo a Peerless Miter King without cost so that Verdugo may compare the two. Suggest that Verdugo return the 14 Little Gem miter boxes to the company that sold them to him.

2. Dale Bobbins, owner of Boone Hardware Center in Boone, North Carolina, recently ordered from Brunswick Paint and Hardware 16 4 × 8 waferboard sheets. A number of people had inquired about lumber for building Ping-Pong tables, tennis practice backboards, bookshelves, and so on. Bobbins telephoned you today to say that only three of the waferboards have sold to date and in all three cases those who bought the lumber expressed their disappointment. They felt that the waferboard sheets lacked the resiliency and strength of ¾-inch plywood. He wants to return the 13 sheets in exchange

for the ¾-inch plywood. He believes that the three that were sold represent inferior quality and he should not be charged for them. You told him you would consider the matter and write to him this week.

You decide to give permission to return the 13 sheets of waferboard for which he will receive full credit. Robbins is to pay freight charges ($9.75). You cannot, however, give him credit for those sheets of waferboard that were sold to customers. Write the letter for Brunswick Paint and Hardware.

SUPPLEMENTARY PROJECT

3. You are administrative assistant at Cornwallis, Inc., a manufacturer of office equipment. You have just received shipment of three secretarial desks from Edmondson's, a management consulting firm. Your records show that these desks and six executive desks were sold to Edmondson's (Janice Pierce, purchasing director). Mrs. Pierce wrote that the company was reducing its staff and equipment because of a falloff in business in recent months. These three secretarial desks that were returned cost a total of $795. According to Pierce, they are hardly used and look brand new.

Obviously, you can't accept used merchandise no matter what its condition and you must write Pierce to that effect. The desks will remain in your warehouse at Cornwallis awaiting word from Pierce as to how they should be disposed of. You are angry that anyone could be so naive not to realize that a manufacturer of high-quality furniture cannot accept used furniture for resale regardless of its condition. The following is a letter you may be tempted to write:

```
Dear Mrs. Pierce:

You should have known better than to ship those
three secretarial desks to us!  We don't deal
in used merchandise no matter what its condi-
tion.  We will take no action on these desks
until you let us know how you wish to dispose
of them.  If we return them, you will obviously
have to pay freight charges.  It is out of the
question that you are entitled to a $795 re-
fund!

                              Very truly yours,
```

Write a more tactful letter to Mrs. Pierce, keeping in mind that Edmondson's may again be a customer if business takes a turn for the better. Suggest to Pierce that she may wish to try to sell these pieces to local business houses.

Make the necessary corrections.

1. Every department manager and unit supervisor are encouraged to participate.
2. Not one of the June shipments have arrived.
3. Six months are too long to wait for payment.
4. A number of our employees participates in community activities.
5. The chairperson invited Karen and I to make a few remarks.

C A S E
4

Granting and Refusing Credit to Customers

THE SETTING (LETTER A)

Rebecca Harrelson is owner of the Clinton Hardware Store in Clinton, Texas. Harrelson writes a letter to Brunswick Paint and Hardware Company, placing an order for paint and hardware for $785.50. She asks that the amount be charged to her account. The fact is that Clinton Hardware has no account at Brunswick. It is the first order you have received from that store, and before you can ship the items ordered, you must investigate Harrelson's ability to pay. You write to her asking for a balance sheet and income statement for the current year to date. You also request a list of firms with which she has enjoyed credit privileges. Harrelson responds quickly, providing the information requested. She checked out OK; the profit picture of her store is very satisfactory and she has few outstanding debts. Her credit references gave good reports on her.

YOUR OBJECTIVE

To give a warm welcome to Harrelson as a charge customer.

BACKGROUND

The type of credit allowed Clinton Hardware Store is called *commercial* or *wholesale* credit. (The type of credit offered by retail stores to individual customers is called *retail* or *consumer* credit.)

Dear Ms. Harrelson:

Your order in the amount of $785.50 was shipped today on our usual credit terms of 30 days. We are delighted to welcome you as a charge customer at Brunswick and promise to do our utmost to see that your orders receive our careful attention.

Thank you for allowing us to number you among our valued charge customers.

Sincerely yours,

Analysis   The letter to Ms. Harrelson is friendly and tactful. She should be pleased to have recognition of your faith in her.

THE SETTING (LETTER B)

Lindley's House and Garden Shop (Cary Lindley, owner) in Brentwood, Georgia has ordered $660.40 worth of hardware items, asking that the merchandise be charged to his account. Lindley has not ordered before from Brunswick Paint and Hardware Company except on a cash basis. You write asking him for current financial statements as well as a list of firms with whom he has done business on credit in the past year. When you receive this material, it is not at all favorable. His current liabilities exceed current assets three times, and the references he supplied indicated that Lindley is not considered a good credit risk; one said that Lindley had owed him money for over four months with no attempt to pay.

BACKGROUND

Refusing credit is one of the most ticklish, if not *the* most ticklish, of all challenges to the letter writer. When you have to say "no" to a credit applicant, you are in fact saying that that person is not to be trusted, and that you have reason to believe that the applicant can't or won't pay. Such a serious indictment of an organization or firm must be handled with great tact.

   Some credit experts believe that poor-risk applicants need not be told that they are being turned down, saying "We lack sufficient information necessary to grant your request for credit." Others think it best to come right out and say "no," giving reasons for the response. Most agree, however, that if at all possible the customer should be "saved" and encouraged to pay cash for the time being. Obviously this is quite a challenge, and the person who can bring it off is somewhat rare.

SAMPLE LETTERS

A

Dear Mr. Lindley:

I am sorry that we do not have sufficient information on which to base an acceptance of your application for credit. When we receive suitable
information, we will let you know.

Very truly yours,

Analysis   This is one of those "no comment" letters that we object to. It does
nothing except to leave the applicant hanging. Certainly, the letter will not make
friends, and it's unlikely that Lindley will want to place future orders, even for
cash.

B

Dear Mr. Lindley:

Thank you for supplying me with the credit information I requested. I wish I could say, "Yes,
we'll be pleased to have you as a credit customer." However, on the basis of information I
have received about the condition of your business and the comments of your creditors, I must
give you a reluctant no at the moment. We truly
believe that it would not be wise for you to take
on other obligations at this time.

I say "at this time" because I am hopeful that
things will change for the better for you. If
so, please write me again when your financial
picture has changed.

In the meantime, I hope you will find it possible
to order from us on a cash basis. We are proud
of both our products and our services and will do
everything possible to see that you get what you
want when you want it.

Cordially,

Analysis   Although Letter B will not make Lindley ecstatic—indeed, it may
provoke him to say, "I will place no further orders from you," the writer does
leave the door slightly ajar, saying that Lindley will be welcomed as a charge
customer when he gets his financial house in order. Notice that the writer

avoided saying "I don't trust you." (This should be self-evident to Lindley.) Remember that businesses that are in poor financial condition now may become completely trustworthy in the future.

"YOUR JOB" PROJECTS

1. Stewart Walsh, manager of the Paint Shed in Rolla, Missouri, placed an order for paint totaling $360.28, asking that the amount be charged to his account. Actually, Walsh has purchased nothing from Brunswick for two years. The Paint Shed and Brunswick had a falling-out two years ago when the Paint Shed had to be threatened to place its account in the hands of an attorney. Walsh eventually paid and now wants to resume credit privileges, making no mention of past difficulties.

   You write a friendly letter to Walsh accepting his order on a conditional basis. Although you are very tactful, you clearly state your intentions to constantly audit his credit record and will terminate the arrangement the moment his account becomes overdue.

2. Assume that it has been two years since you granted Stewart Walsh credit privileges. True to his word, he has paid within 30 days for the materials he ordered on various occasions. You now consider Walsh a valuable credit customer. However, you recently received a letter from him asking that his credit limit be raised from the present $1,000 to $2,500. Respond to the letter.

SUPPLEMENTARY PROJECT

3. You are credit manager at Willock's, a large retail clothing store in Los Angeles. Write a form letter, enclosing a Willock's credit card, that can be sent to everyone who qualifies for credit at the store. *Hint:* You can do some subtle selling in such a letter.

STYLE CHECKUP

Which word in each of the following sentences is superfluous?

1. It seems unwise to revert back to the old system.
2. Isn't this the same identical problem we had last month?
3. In some departments, such as, for example, Manufacturing and Personnel, employee contributions exceeded the quota.
4. Up until today we had no idea that Barton was planning early retirement.
5. Can we divide up the responsibility between Rachel and Max?

CASE 5

Collecting Money Due From a Customer

THE SETTING

On September 7, Muriel Ivaroni, owner of Jayhawker Paint and Garden Shoppe, purchased paint on credit from Brunswick Paint and Hardware Company in the amount of $960. (Miss Ivaroni is a new credit customer, although she has frequently bought paint on a cash basis in the past.) The $960 order was approved by the sales manager, Gary Weeks, thinking Ivaroni would be in a position to pay her bills when due.

The paint was delivered to Jayhawker Paint and Garden Shoppe on September 20, but by October 31 nothing has been heard from Miss Ivaroni. Weeks asks you to follow up with Ivaroni to see if you can collect the amount due. So on November 10 you send a statement for $960. Nothing happened, and on November 25 you send a second statement, along with a printed reminder stating "Past due, please remit." It is now December 3, and there has been no response from Muriel Ivaroni. You must now consider other means of collecting the money.

YOUR OBJECTIVE

To collect the $960 due with the least possible hassle.

BACKGROUND

Most people who buy on credit pay their bills promptly. If this were not true, businesses wouldn't be able to be as generous as they are about allowing customers to "buy now and pay later." Yet there are customers in every business who must be prodded to settle their accounts. More often than not, a second statement to the customer is all that is necessary to get action. Yet there are those who ignore the reminders and the several letters that follow; they finally have to be threatened with legal action.

Because slow payers and nonpayers represent a very small percentage of the number of people and businesses who charge their purchases, the collection letter writer makes the assumption that every customer is good for the amount owed. It is only when repeated requests produce no results that a get-tough policy is introduced.

Collection Letter Series

Every organization has its own approach to the task of collecting overdue payments. Some businesses develop a *collection letter series*, which is a sequence of increasingly demanding reminders. Some even have several different series, each tailored for a particular type of customer. For example, the series for customers who usually pay by check might be slightly different from the series for customers who usually transfer their payments to the store's bank account electronically.

A collection letter series is often stored in the supplier's information processing system, which may be integrated with that of accounts receivable. In that case employees who handle collections may have electronic access to account information as well as to the form letters so that they can tailor the letters appropriately.

The following is a typical collection sequence:

1. A statement that merely indicates the amount owed is sent during the regular billing period.
2. A second statement is sent ten days or two weeks later, and a colorful sticker might be affixed that says "Did you forget?" or "Now Past Due" or "Please!"
3. A short reminder letter or two are sent. Even if the organization has sophisticated word processing equipment, it may purposely use obvious form letters for these reminders. This is so that the letters will appear to be routine and impersonal—the customers may find them less embarrassing.
4. Two or more letters are sent, each successively more urgent in tone. Although these letters may be part of a series of form letters, an automated office would probably personalize them as much as possible.
5. A personalized ultimatum is mailed. It says that the organization will resort to other collection methods if the customer doesn't pay by a specified date.

   As mentioned, the sequence above is merely typical. Some organizations resort to the telephone after, say, the second statement, and the third communication may be a telegram.

Appeals in Collection Letters

Several appeals may be employed in writing collection letters. Among the most-used are justice and fair play, pride, and fear. Following is a typical series of collection letters that a customer might receive after having ignored two or more statements.

First Letter—Gentle Reminder   The following is a form letter, obviously duplicated, with blank spaces for fill-ins.

```
Your account in the amount of $127.40 is now
overdue.  Perhaps your check is already in the
mail; if so, please disregard this reminder.
```

Second Letter—Stronger Reminder   The second letter may also be a form letter, and it may be similar to the first one.

Perhaps you did not receive the previous reminders about the outstanding balance of your account. Otherwise, I believe you would have sent us your check for $127.40 by this time. Your account is now 30 days overdue.

Third Letter—Appeal to Justice As you will notice, the following letter is a personalized, individually typed—rather than duplicated—letter.

If a friend of yours borrowed money from you and promised to pay it back in 30 days, you'd expect her to keep her side of the bargain, wouldn't you? Or if she couldn't, you would expect her at least to tell you why, wouldn't you?

That's the situation we are in. You bought a food processor from us on credit, which is the same as borrowing money, and agreed to pay us $127.40 for it in 30 days. Those 30 days have come and gone, and we still haven't received payment. And you haven't told us why.

Please use the stamped envelope to mail us your check for $127.40 right away.

Fourth Letter—Appeal to Pride If the customer still hasn't paid the account, another personalized letter similar to the one below would be sent.

This morning I asked to see your account, and I have it before me right now. You have done business with us for over three years, and you have maintained a fine credit record. Until now.

I say "until now" because your good credit reputation is in danger of being damaged. And all for the small amount of $127.40, which you've owed us for six weeks.

Probably you meant to settle your account long before this, but you simply haven't gotten around to it. Or maybe there is another reason. Whatever it is, please take care of this obligation immediately. I don't want to see you labeled "Bad Credit Risk"--and this could happen if you delay longer. Please send me your check at once. Before it is too late.

Fifth Letter—Appeal to Fear A letter similar to the one that follows gives the customer one last chance to avoid the unpleasantness and expense of having the account put in the hands of a lawyer or a collection agency.

The last thing I want to do is to put your account in the hands of a collection agency. It's unpleasant business--unpleasant for us and unpleasant for you. But I will be forced to take this action unless I have the $127.40 in payment of your account by July 10.

Help me to avoid this step by at least getting in touch with me and discussing your intentions. This is the last opportunity I can give you--the next move is yours.

Actually, many companies today (including Brunswick Paint and Hardware Company) have done away with the collection letter series. They believe that a customer who has not responded to two or three printed reminders is unlikely to respond to several letters, even though each letter is more demanding than the previous letter. Typically, the supplier will follow a scheme such as this:

1. Send one or two gentle reminders.
2. If no response is forthcoming, send a telegram something like this:

IMPERATIVE THAT YOU SEND US IMMEDIATELY YOUR CHECK FOR $960 TO PROTECT YOUR CREDIT STANDING.

3. If there is no response to the telegram, the supplier telephones the customer and in that discussion strongly hints that the account will be turned over to a collection agency if the check is not sent at once.
4. After a lapse of three or four days, the customer will receive a letter such as the following:

Dear Miss Ivaroni:

This is to notify you that your account has been placed in the hands of a collection agency, and all further communications about your indebtedness will be between the agency and yourself.

Very truly yours,

ACTIVITIES CONCERNING THE CASE PROBLEM

Since Ivaroni ignored the first two reminders, you sent a telegram. On receipt of the telegram, Ivaroni telephoned you explaining that she had been out of town on urgent business matters and promised to send the $960 that same day. She did so, the check arrived two days later, and Ivaroni's account now has a zero balance. Thus it is not necessary to take the last step indicated—writing a "Pay or else" letter.

"YOUR JOB" PROJECTS

1. Benders House and Garden Shoppe (owner, Arnold Bender) has been a good customer of Brunswick Paint and Hardware Company for the past two years and has always paid its bills promptly. Bender purchased paint and hardware items on November 3 for $152 on credit. The amount is to be paid by December 3 if Bender expects to receive a 5 percent discount. (In the past he has paid so promptly that he nearly always qualified for the discount.)

   You sent a gentle reminder December 6 and received no response. The following week you sent another reminder. Still no response. On December 16 you received a check from Bender for the amount due ($152), but the check was not signed. What is your assessment of this situation? Do you think the unsigned check was a deliberate attempt to stall payment? (Bender may be a little short of cash right now.) Or do you think it was merely an oversight? Send back Bender's check accompanied by an appropriate letter.

2. Chandler and Sons Hardware are credit customers of Brunswick Paint and Hardware and the store has been quite dependable about paying its bills, although they were several days late on numerous occasions. Chandler and Sons are already ten days behind schedule in paying for a $435.60 bill. You sent two tactful reminders two weeks apart and received no response. You're almost certain that something has come up that has prevented Chandler and Sons from paying that they owe. After receiving a telegram from you, followed by a telephone call several days later, Chandler and Sons sent their check in the mail for the full amount. When the check arrived, you deposited it in the bank, but a few days later the check was returned by the bank marked "insufficient funds (ISF)." What will you do? This is a pretty good customer, and you don't want to lose the business. Think about it and then write Chandler and Sons the action you are taking. *Hint*: You're likely to give Chandler and Sons a little more time.

SUPPLEMENTARY PROJECTS

3. Mildred Hunsinger is the treasurer of Babcock Farm Implements, Inc. Today she received a harsh letter from the Saar Corporation, one of Babcock's major suppliers. The writer, Leon Sykes, asks Babcock to either pay immediately

the $1,260 the firm owes the Saar Corporation or risk damaging its credit rating.

Actually, Babcock owes Saar Corporation nothing. All orders have been paid for promptly—not once has Babcock missed out on the discount for prompt payment. There is no hint as to what the $1,260 covers. The surprising thing is that Saar Corporation is considered a dependable supplier and Babcock has always had pleasant relations with them. Indeed, Hunsinger is personally acquainted with Leon Sykes and considers herself a friend of his.

Read the following letters, and state which one you prefer and why.

a. Dear Leon:

I think I have never before received such an outrageous letter until your diatribe arrived telling us in no uncertain terms that we are negligent in paying our bills. This is absurd!

When you examine your records carefully, you will see that Babcock Farm Implements owes Saar Corporation absolutely nothing. I expect you to send me an apology for this gross mistake. If I don't receive it, I cannot predict what our decision will be in considering placing future orders with you.

                              Very truly yours,

b. Dear Leon:

Because of your flagrantly worded declaration of our $1,260 indebtedness to you--totally inaccurate and insulting--you can expect no further orders from us. Even though we have made this decision, I still expect a letter of apology from you. Obviously, you are not getting a check from us--no way!

                              Yours very truly,

4. Write a letter for Leon Sykes to Mildred Hunsinger apologizing for the mix-up. You don't know how the error occurred, but there appears to be strong evidence that the computer was given faulty instructions and this letter should never have been sent. You don't want to lose Babcock as a customer.

STYLE CHECKUP

Each of the following sentences contains a comma error. Make the necessary insertions.

1. It is far better as you know to have too much merchandise than too little.
2. Macklin didn't use good judgment in his selections to say the least.
3. Better yet why not ask the Personnel Department to place the ad.
4. Kati and Carol will attend the third and fourth sessions respectively.
5. In other words you reduce the risk of injury by 50 percent.

CHAPTER 12 ADMINISTRATIVE COMMUNICATIONS

YOUR JOB

You are the executive assistant to the president of Computronics Inc., Glenn D. Newley. The company manufactures and sells various types of automated equipment for modern offices, including electronic typewriters, information processors, copiers, computer-based communication systems, personal computers, and phototypesetters. In addition to performing his regular duties as the chief executive officer of Computronics, Newley is active in a number of organizations in the electronics industry. You handle much of the correspondence addressed to the president, preparing some letters for his signature and others for your own.

CASE 1 Responding in the Executive's Absence

THE SETTING

Mr. Newley left yesterday for Des Moines and will not return to the office until January 16. The purpose of the trip is to investigate the possibility of purchasing a small firm that makes equipment for preparing microfilm and microfiche; the firm is rumored to be for sale. Among this morning's mail is the following letter from Mrs. Denise Wolff, vice president of Marathon Systems Corporation (a competitor).

Dear Glenn:

As you may have heard, I'm planning the program of the next convention of the National Micrographics Association. It will be in Dayton from June 16 to 17.

One session is to be a panel, "Dry-Processing Computer-Output-Microfilm Images." It is scheduled for June 17 from 2:30 to 4. Hal Weiss (Microsystems) was selected as the moderator, and he has lined up five panel members. Each one is to make a brief presentation and then answer questions from the audience. Yesterday I received a call from Hal. He said that he has been called to an important meeting in Tokyo and will be gone the last two weeks in June. Naturally, this puts me in a real bind.

Would you be willing, Glenn, to act as moderator in Hal's place? I know you would do a great job--certainly, no one knows more about COM than Glenn Newley! I'm in a bit of a rush for an answer because I have to get the program in the printer's hands by February 4.

I do hope you will say "yes." Of course, I'll supply complete details about the panel just as soon as I have your acceptance.

Sincerely,

Your Objective   To acknowledge Wolff's letter in Newley's absence.

BACKGROUND

The principal function of an "assistant to" is to relieve a top executive of as many routine responsibilities as possible. Often those who have this job walk a tightrope. Although they can make certain decisions for the executive, it isn't always clear *which* decisions are safe to make. Thus they have the challenge of doing all they can to ease the executive's burden without appearing to run the show. Making decisions in the executive's absence can be especially tricky.

When answering mail in the executive's absence, follow these guidelines.

Guidelines

1. Do not commit the executive to a course of action that that person may not wish or be able to follow.
2. Offer assurance that the matter inquired about will be brought to the executive's attention as quickly as possible.
3. Unless you are a personal friend of the writer of the letter you are acknowledging, don't indulge in personal chatter or asides—be businesslike.
4. Unless the matter inquired about is very urgent and requires the executive's immediate attention, do not suggest where the executive can be reached by telephone.

Dear Mrs. Wolff:

Mr. Newley left the office yesterday and will not return until January 16.

Although I cannot assure you that Mr. Newley will be able to accept your invitation to be the panel moderator at the NMA conference, his calendar is clear on June 17. And knowing his high opinion of that organization, I think it is quite likely that he will arrange to participate.

If you need to talk with Mr. Newley, you can reach him at (515) 555-7224.

                    Yours very sincerely,

Analysis Although the letter is well written and the tone appropriate, it is not satisfactory for two reasons.

1. The letter very nearly commits Newley to accepting the invitation, but for any number of reasons, he may not be able to do this. The statement about the clear calendar could make it very hard for Newley to say "no" without embarrassment.

2. It is generally not wise, except in genuine emergencies, to give out a telephone number where a traveling executive can be reached. This is not an emergency.

Dear Mrs. Wolff:

Mr. Newley is away from the office and is expected to return on January 16. Just as soon as he gets back, I will bring to his attention your invitation to moderate the panel at the NMA conference on June 17.

Often when he is on out-of-town trips, Mr. Newley calls in. If I am in touch with him before he actually returns, I will mention your letter. I know you are in a hurry for an answer.

                    Yours very sincerely,

Analysis This letter is very satisfactory.

1. The tone is appropriate.

2. The writer tells Wolff all she needs to know and assures her that the matter will be handled promptly.

3. The second paragraph is a courteous gesture, yet no actual promises are given.

"YOUR JOB" PROJECTS

1. The following is among the letters received while Newley is away on business in Des Moines.

Dear Mr. Newley:

The Elkhart Uptown Association cordially invites you to be the luncheon speaker at our March 27 meeting at the Elkhart Hoosier Lodge.

The EUA is a group whose aim is to promote the commercial and civic advantages of this community. Although our principal objective is to boost the city of Elkhart, we also engage in a number of philanthropic activities in the community.

As the president of a large manufacturing company located in Indiana, you would be an ideal speaker on the topic "Indiana--Today and Tomorrow." We will feature this theme at this year's meeting because presidents of nationally known Indiana firms are likely to be excellent prognosticators of future developments in the state and how cities like Elkhart can capitalize on the opportunities.

We would be pleased to pay all your expenses in addition to an honorarium of $250. May I hear from you?

Cordially yours,

Sidney F. Crenshaw

According to Newley's calendar, he has an all-day meeting on March 27 with the company's finance committee, of which he is the chairperson. When he telephoned you about another matter, you mentioned the letter from the Elkhart Uptown Association and the meeting already scheduled for March 27. He asked you to respond to Crenshaw, saying that he would be delighted to appear on the association's program at a later date. You know that Newley never accepts an honorarium and always pays his own expenses. Write the letter.

2. Here is another letter that arrived while Newley was out of the office.

Dear Sir:

We would like you to appear on a panel at our Spring Career Conference on June 17 at Brazil High School. This countywide conference is held each year to acquaint high school students with career opportunities in various fields. Computer science is an area in which many students have expressed interest.

Will you accept?   I do hope so!

                        Very truly yours,

                        Anna Schneider
                        Conference Leader

Since you know that Newley has accepted the invitation from Mrs. Denise Wolff to moderate a panel at the NMA convention in Dayton on June 17, he obviously can't accept this one. Actually, it is almost impossible for Newley to accept invitations such as that from Anna Schneider. However, he likes to have Computronics participate whenever it is feasible and generally suggests one of the regional sales supervisors as a substitute. The sales supervisor in the Brazil area is Melissa Lorenz. You find that Lorenz is available on June 17 and will be happy to appear at the Brazil conference. (She is always well received at these meetings.) She can be reached at 2200 Dixie Bee Road, Terre Haute, Indiana 47800. Write the letter.

3. Comment on the following response to an invitation to Newley; then write one that you feel is more appropriate.

Dear Miss Bettendorf:

Your letter to Mr. Newley arrived while he is away on business in Des Moines.

As Mr. Newley's assistant, I must decline on his behalf your invitation to be a judge in the annual Mt. Tabor Young Scientists Exhibit. Mr. Newley does not have time to participate in events of this nature. As president of Compu-tronics, he is a very busy man; every week he receives dozens of letters inviting him to do this or that, and he must turn down most of them.

I am sure you will understand the position Mr. Newley must take in this situation. Thank you, however, for your inquiry.

Very sincerely yours,

SUPPLEMENTARY PROJECT

4. You are the assistant to the vice president and treasurer of Caldwell Investment Corporation, Mrs. Helene Eisley. The firm is located in Houston. While Eisley is in New York on business during the week of January 6, a letter arrives from Henry L. Hemby, president of a large chain of discount stores. He will arrive in Houston on the morning of January 12, the day Eisley is expected to return, and he suggests a luncheon meeting at the Hyatt Regency Hotel, where he is stopping for a few days. Eisley's plane is scheduled to arrive at 4 p.m.—too late for a luncheon meeting. However, when you talk with Eisley by telephone, she suggests a dinner meeting at 7. (She feels it is very important to see Hemby.) Write an appropriate letter to Hemby; supply your own details.

STYLE CHECKUP

Rewrite the following sentences, each of which contains an example of bigwordism.

1. I expect the committee to ratify the agreement this week.
2. All shipping department employees who work on Saturdays should receive remuneration that is double their regular rate.
3. Jehle promised to scrutinize the letter carefully.
4. When did the accident transpire?
5. The ultimate result is likely to be a saving of 50 percent.

C A S E 2

Using Discretion in Writing for an Executive

THE SETTING

Computronics is considering setting up a center for manufacturing electronic parts in the south Atlantic area. Executives are studying the merits of several sites, including Savannah, Charlotte, Jacksonville, and Charleston. Until they reach a decision, the subject is not to be discussed with anyone outside the company.

While Newley is in Des Moines, the following telegram arrives:

HAVE IDEAL SITE FOR SOUTH ATLANTIC PARTS-MANUFAC-
TURING CENTER IN BRUNSWICK, GEORGIA. LOW, LOW
PRICE. IMMEDIATE REPLY REQUESTED.

S. K. VANDERGRIFT

You have no idea how Vandergrift learned about the plans for a south Atlantic manufacturing center—possibly from a sales representative in that region.

Your Objective   To decide how the telegram is to be handled and respond accordingly.

BACKGROUND

It is generally understood that all routine mail will be taken care of during an executive's absence for any length of time. If there are important decisions that only the executive can make, the mail is simply acknowledged with some indication of when an answer can be expected. Some correspondence will be urgent enough to justify a telephone call to the executive, some will be handled directly by the executive's assistant, and some will be referred to others in the company.

In any event, the important word in handling correspondence that arrives in the executive's absence is *discretion*. By that we mean that unless you are absolutely positive that anyone who requests information is entitled to have it, you do not reveal it. This includes information about where the executive is; the reason for absence from the office; the executive's private opinion concerning a person, another company, a proposal or suggestion, and so on; financial matters; and company plans or deliberations that have not been announced publicly. These rules apply not only to outsiders but also to people in the company.

When an executive is away and correspondence arrives from people soliciting information or opinions that you feel they are not entitled to, follow these guidelines.

Guidelines

1. Acknowledge receipt of the communication, saying that the executive is away from the office.
2. Say that you will call the executive's attention to the communication when that person returns. You may or may not supply the actual date, depending on the circumstances.
3. Make your message brief, civil but not especially friendly, and very businesslike.

SAMPLE LETTERS

 Dear Mr. Vandergrift:

Thank you for your telegram to Mr. Newley. He is at the present time away on business in Des Moines and will not return until January 16.

Although Computronics is planning a parts-manu-facturing center in the south Atlantic area, there has been no mention, to my knowledge, of Brunswick, Georgia. Currently under considera-tion are Savannah, Charlotte, Jacksonville, and Charleston. However, I will let Mr. Newley know about your proposal at the first opportunity, and I am sure he will wire or telephone you.

Yours very truly,

Analysis   Obviously, Letter A violates most of the guidelines suggested earlier.

1. Vandergrift should not be told (a) where Newley is, (b) whether a south Atlantic manufacturing center is under consideration, (c) the locations under consideration, and (d) that Newley will wire or telephone him.
2. As to d, this matter is not urgent, and so a telegram is not necessary, and Newley is not likely to want to speak personally to Vandergrift.

 Dear Mr. Vandergrift:

Your telegram arrived while Mr. Newley is out of the office. He is expected to return about Janu-ary 16, and your proposal will be brought to his attention at that time.

Cordially yours,

Analysis Letter B is an improvement over Letter A.

1. Although Letter B may seem abrupt, it contains all the information that Vandergrift is entitled to have.
2. In this situation the writer could hardly have been friendly. (*Thank you*, or *Mr. Newley will be pleased to see*, or *I am certain that Mr. Newley will appreciate*); otherwise, the message might easily be interpreted as an encouraging response.
3. There is no choice here but to be noncommittal.

"YOUR JOB" PROJECTS

1. The consulting firm of Ferris and Borichaud, employed to design a new corporate symbol (logo) for Computronics, has sent a rough sketch to Newley for his opinion. Since Newley will be out of the office for another two weeks, you decide to make a photocopy of the sketch for your records and send the original on to him, since the matter is of some urgency.

   You strongly dislike the symbol submitted, and you are convinced that Newley will have a similar opinion. Acknowledge the receipt of the sketch, adding whatever you think is appropriate.

2. While Newley is away, Miss Sigrid Untermeyer, the owner of a computer store in Fort Worth that sells Computronics products, writes to complain that a competing store is selling the Mitsikobi word processor for $800 less than the price of the same model manufactured by Computronics. Untermeyer says the Mitsikobi processor has even more features that appeal to business owners and that unless the price of the Computronics processor meets that of the competition, she will switch to Mitsikobi. She asks that Newley write her immediately.

   Newley is on a fishing trip in Florida and cannot be reached for at least a week. You will acknowledge Untermeyer's letter, telling her about the absence of Newley. In the meantime, you talked with the marketing director of Computronics, Clayton Valder, and learned that he is planning a trip to the Dallas–Fort Worth area in the next few days and will drop in to talk to Miss Untermeyer. He will telephone her from the Dallas airport to set up an appointment.

SUPPLEMENTARY PROJECT

3. You are the executive assistant to General Calvin T. Detmer, the commander of a large army base. While General Detmer is attending a meeting at the Pentagon, near Washington, D.C., a letter arrives from Colonel Beth Strawn, U.S. Army Signal Corps. About six months ago the army base where you are employed purchased a fleet of 12 Rexford buses for transporting army personnel. Colonel Strawn is planning to purchase six new buses for the Signal Corps base under her command and wants General Detmer's opinion of the Rexford vehicles. You know that the new buses have been a "disaster."

Many are in the repair shop constantly, and other methods of transportation have had to be provided. Indeed, the reason General Detmer is at the Pentagon is to discuss this problem and see what can be done to bring suit against Rexford Transportation Company for the failure of its equipment. He is expected to return a week from tomorrow. Acknowledge the letter from Colonel Strawn.

STYLE CHECKUP

Each of the following sentences contains more than one idea. Form two sentences out of each statement.

1. Thank you for sending a corrected invoice, and our check in payment is enclosed.
2. We appreciate your comments on the new displays, and we hope you will let us know what results you get from them.
3. After bringing down the new balances on the stock cards, I made spot checks against actual merchandise in the warehouse, and I found all of them in agreement.
4. One of the advantages of the salary plan as compared with the straight commission plan is that sales representatives can be held directly responsible for results, and the representatives can also more easily identify with the company.

C A S E
3

Referring Communications to Others

THE SETTING

The following letter was received from Julio Gomez, a manufacturer of shipping containers, while Newley is away on a two-week vacation.

Dear Mr. Newley:

Have you reached a decision about the new shipping carton for printwheels that I left with you
on January 11? Our supply of the cartons you are
now using is getting low, but before I replenish
it, I want to know whether you plan to use the
old cartons.

Please let me know by February 14, if possible.
I need at least two weeks' lead time for which-
ever carton you select.

                              Yours very cordially,

You know that when the proposed new shipping carton was left with Newley,
he said he thought it was excellent—better than the present one—but that the
final decision would have to come from Irene Currie, the manager of the shipping
department. As far as you know, Currie has not reached a decision.

Your Objective   To acknowledge Gomez's letter and tell him what you know
about the matter and to refer the problem to Irene Currie for action.

BACKGROUND

Often mail that is sent to an executive must be referred to another person in
the company for handling. If there may be a lapse of a few days before definite
action by that other person can be taken, you acknowledge the correspondence,
saying what is being done about it. Follow these guidelines on such occasions.

Guidelines

1. Respond promptly and courteously.
2. Be specific about what you are doing to obtain the information requested.
3. Do not commit the person who is to handle the matter to a specific course
   of action or time limit.
4. Do not criticize the employee—either directly or indirectly—for not having
   attended to the matter previously.

SAMPLE LETTERS

Dear Mr. Gomez:

Mr. Newley is out of the office, and I am handling his routine correspondence in his absence.

I am sorry you have not had an answer before this
time to your question about the new shipping carton for printwheels. Mr. Newley approved it at
least two weeks ago and asked our Shipping Department manager, Irene Currie, to follow up with
you. I am surprised that this matter was not
settled.

You may be sure, Mr. Gomez, that you will have a

decision from us this week. Ms. Currie is attending to the matter at my instructions.

                              Very truly yours,

This note should be included with a copy of the letter.

Irene, will you attend to the enclosed letter right away. Apparently, there was a bad slipup here. Note that the matter is somewhat urgent.

Analysis   The letter to Gomez is faulty in several respects.

1. Although the statement "Mr. Newley is out of the office" is fine, referring to Gomez's letter as "routine correspondence" is tactless. Beware of attaching labels, even though in your own mind they may be accurate.
2. The second paragraph implies that there is some infighting in Computronics; the writer shows annoyance with a fellow employee for not doing what was expected. Although the writer may be put out with Currie, this fact should not be revealed to an outsider. Currie will feel degraded, the writer will have made an enemy, and Gomez's problem will still be unsolved.
3. The statement "Ms. Currie is attending to the matter at my instructions" is officious. Flaunting authority, even when you have it, is in very poor taste.
4. The memo to Currie will further annoy her and widen the human relations gap.

 Dear Mr. Gomez:

Mr. Newley is out of the office for several days, and I want to give you some assurance about the new shipping carton for printwheels that you wrote about.

I talked this morning with Irene Currie, our Shipping Department manager, who has been asked to make the final decision on the carton. She told me that she will write to you no later than Friday of this week. I know that the opinions she asked for from the various departments were late in reaching her. This accounts for the delay in getting an answer to you.

                              Yours very sincerely,

This note should be included with a copy of the letter.

Irene:

Here is a copy of the letter from Mr. Gomez that I spoke to you about this morning, along with a copy of my reply. Please let me know if I can do anything further on this.

Analysis   Letter B is an effective response to Gomez.

1. Obviously, the writer telephoned Currie for up-to-date information before attempting to answer Gomez.
2. Rather than condemning Irene Currie, the writer explained the delay in a way that takes Currie off the hook.
3. The memo to Currie is fine. No accusations are made—indeed, there is an offer of cooperation.

"YOUR JOB" PROJECTS

1. The following letter arrived in Newley's absence.

Dear Sir or Madam:

I have invented a process for destroying confidential business documents without the use of the old-fashioned paper shredder. My device actually <u>dissolves</u> the documents electronically so that there is no longer the danger that company secrets can be stolen.

Before I describe the invention in detail (I have applied for a patent), I need to know what your company would pay for such a device. For an advance of $50,000 and a guarantee that you will manufacture and distribute the product, I will send you drawings and photographs.

I warn you that you will have to act fast--before someone beats you to it.

                    Yours truly,

                    Roscoe Grinch

Presidents and other executives of large companies receive many such proposals every year, and the electronics industry is no exception. Most of the ideas submitted are worthless; a few have possibilities. In many cases those who write are very vague about their idea or invention, fearful that it will be stolen. Obviously, a $50,000 cash advance and a guarantee to manufacture are unreasonable demands in view of the flimsy evidence given.

Acknowledge the letter in Newley's absence, mentioning that you are sending it to the director of new-product development (whose name is Tracy Sontagg). Then prepare the transmittal memo to Sontagg.

2. Dale R. Badham, a graduate student at the University of Wisconsin, has written to Newley to request an interview. He is preparing a thesis on the office of tomorrow and wants to get Newley's view of the subject.

Newley is often asked to participate in studies of this nature, and when he can find the time, he accepts. When he is especially busy—tied up in meetings for several days, for example—he asks you to refer such requests to Walter Scheaffer, vice president for research and development. This is the situation here. Write the appropriate communications.

SUPPLEMENTARY PROJECT

3. You are the assistant to Kenneth Overstreet, president of Sav-U-Mor Corporation, a franchisor of over 500 cleaning shops throughout the country. While Overstreet is on a two-week vacation, a letter arrives for him from Chester DeGarmo, one of two Sav-U-Mor franchisees in Greenville, South Carolina. He complaints bitterly about the other franchise shop, which opened two months ago, saying that "that fellow is hurting my business because of his terrible service and shoddy treatment of customers and is giving Sav-U-Mor a bad name throughout Greenville."

DeGarmo has been a highly successful franchisee, and you know that Overstreet considers it very important to keep him happy. He does excellent work and has established a fine reputation in Greenville. The new franchisee, however, has not been operating long enough for Overstreet to assess his potential.

You decide to refer DeGarmo's letter to Edwin Whitney, district manager of Sav-U-Mor Corporation, who is located in Columbia. You will ask him to make a confidential investigation of the situation.

Prepare the communications required in this situation.

STYLE CHECKUP

Rewrite the following sentences, each of which contains an example of bigwordism.

1. The president said she would deliberate on the proposal.
2. My initial reaction is very favorable.
3. The important thing is to obviate the necessity of renting more space.
4. We have had only nominal success with the new form.
5. What is Finney's rationale for changing the procedure?

CASE 4

Writing on Behalf of and for the Executive

THE SETTING

In late May Mr. Newley delivered the commencement address at Bryant College in Providence. Shortly thereafter, he received an enthusiastic thank you letter from the vice president for academic affairs, Dr. Elaine Wilkins, along with a check for $500. As he rushed off to a stockholders meeting in New York, he said to you, "Please thank Elaine for her very nice letter, tell her how much I enjoyed being with her and the Bryant College people, and return the check. Ask her to use it for some worthy cause—perhaps the general scholarship fund. You can write the letter and sign my name or write for your own signature, whichever you prefer."

Your Objective   To write an appropriate letter either for your signature or for Newley's.

BACKGROUND

Executive assistants often write letters for the executive, "forging" the executive's signature. When they are given this responsibility, they learn to make their letters sound as though the executive wrote them. Therefore, they must know how the executive reacts to situations, the executive's style of expression, and the writer-reader relationship.

On the other hand, some executive assistants write only on *behalf of*—not *for* the executive. Here one must still convey the executive's thoughts but is free to use one's own writing style.

Guidelines

1. Acknowledge receipt of the communication and check, saying that the executive is away from the office.
2. Repeat his words—that he enjoyed giving the commencement address and visiting with Dr. Wilkins.
3. Again using his words, explain the reason for the returned check, stressing how much he enjoyed the visit and suggesting that the money be used for a worthy cause.
4. Make your message friendly and affirmative, being sure not to alienate Dr. Wilkins over the returned check.

Dear Elaine:

You were very generous in your comments about my address at the Bryant College commencement. To tell you the truth, I enjoyed expounding on my "learning is forever" theme much more than anyone in my audience could have enjoyed hearing me. A great group of graduates (how proud you must be of them!), a distinguished faculty, and overwhelming hospitality--what more could a commencement speaker ask for?

I am returning your check for $500, not because I don't appreciate the generous gesture, but because I think the money can be put to much better use--in one of your scholarship funds, perhaps. But I'll leave the decision to you.

Thank you for your many courtesies while I was in Providence. It was an experience that I will long remember.

Sincerely yours,

Analysis   There is no objective way to analyze this letter written for the executive.

1. It can't be intelligently evaluated without knowing Newley's general style and his relationship to Dr. Wilkins.
2. If this letter matches in tone and style others that Newley has written on similar occasions, it can be said to do the job very well.

Dear Dr. Wilkins:

Shortly after your letter arrived, Mr. Newley had to fly to New York for an important meeting, and he asked me to express his sincere thanks for your generous remarks about his presentation at the Bryant College commencement and for the check you enclosed.

Mr. Newley spoke enthusiastically of the people at Bryant College--both the graduating class and the faculty. He appreciated especially the many courtesies you extended to him and asked me to be sure to tell you so.

Mr. Newley also asked me to return the $500
check, which is enclosed. He feels that the
money can be put to good use at your institution
and referred specifically to a scholarship fund.
I'm confident, however, that any decision you
make will be fine with him.

Very cordially yours,

Analysis   This is an excellent letter written on behalf of the executive.

1. The message is pleasant and sincere.
2. Note, however, that it is not highly personal, since the writer is speaking for someone else.

"YOUR JOB" PROJECT

1. Anna Schneider, a conference leader at the Brazil High School Spring Career Conference (see Project 2, page 201), wrote to Newley to thank him for sending Melissa Lorenz as a speaker on June 17. Schneider was extremely complimentary toward Lorenz—both as an individual and as a speaker. She drew the largest crowd at the conference, and the reactions of the students were uniformly enthusiastic.
   a. Respond to Schneider for Newley's signature.
   b. Respond to Schneider on behalf of Newley, using your own name.

SUPPLEMENTARY PROJECTS

2. Ernest Warren, an important stockholder in Orion Publishing Company, has written the president, Mrs. Maggi Presley, about a manuscript his son has written entitled "American Education at the Crossroads." (The son, Dr. Peter G. Warren, is a graduate school dean at a private university and is nationally recognized as an educator and scholar.) Ernest Warren states that he knows that such a book would have a limited market and expresses his willingness to subsidize the cost—he will pay all editorial and manufacturing expenses. He simply wants the Orion imprint on his son's book. (Ernest Warren and Maggi Presley are good friends, having met many times at the annual meeting of Orion stockholders.)

   Actually, there was no reason for Ernest Warren to make the offer to subsidize his son's book. Orion recently set up a scholarly books department; it publishes distinguished works on various subjects, including higher education. It is true that the company expects only a modest, if any, profit on these books, but the board of directors feels that a major house like Orion should engage in this type of publishing—not only as a public service but also for the prestige value these works offer.

   As her administrative assistant, you talked with Presley by telephone about

Ernest Warren's letter (she is on an out-of-town trip), and she asked you to tell Ernest Warren that Orion would be delighted to consider Dean Warren's book for publication on its own merits—not as a subsidized work. If Dean Warren will submit his manuscript to Presley, she will see that it receives priority attention from the editors in the scholarly books department.

a. Write a letter to Ernest Warren for Presley's signature.
b. Write a letter to Ernest Warren for your own signature.

3. You are the assistant to the director of product research for the Merit Tire and Rubber Company, Alfred Caine. A few days ago Caine visited several large dealers, including Charles Frantz, in El Paso. Later he wrote Frantz the following:

Dear Charlie:

When I was in El Paso, I forgot to ask you about the results of that tire mileage test you are making. How did our Super-Ms stand up against the competition? Are you planning more tests, or do you feel that you have all the evidence you need?

It was great being with you last week. Your new warehouse looks like a winner, and I hope we can automate the Duluth and Richmond warehouses to the same extent. With nothing to do but punch buttons, you're obviously planning to get in a lot of golf from now on.

Cordially,

Assume that instead of writing to Frantz personally, Caine gave you the details and asked you to send a letter over your own signature. Write the letter.

STYLE CHECKUP

Rewrite each of the following sentences to eliminate the redundancy or unnecessary word.

1. Leona's presentation follows after the kick-off speech.
2. Saunders repeated again the importance of making the sales budget.
3. Laytham suggested that we revert back to the old procedure.
4. Dorr is only a new beginner and needs much instruction.
5. Morgan described the new benefits, such as stock options, free medical insurance, tuition refunds, and so on.

CHAPTER 13

PUBLIC RELATIONS LETTERS

YOUR JOB

You are employed in the public relations department in the home office (Cleveland) of Hanover's, a large retailing firm that sells merchandise not only through its catalog but also through hundreds of retail stores all over the country. Your supervisor is Martha Lendon, assistant director of public relations. You handle a good bit of the mail addressed to the public relations department that relates to the public image of Hanover's.

CASE 1

Thanking a Correspondent for Favorable Comments

THE SETTING

Hanover's, which has been running a series of institutional ads in several national magazines on environmental matters, received a complimentary letter from Curtis Halverson, a member of the staff of the United States Chamber of Commerce. In his letter, Halverson also suggests several topics for future ads. You are to write Halverson for Martha Lendon's signature.

BACKGROUND

Public relations (PR) means educating people in favor of your company. *Public* includes nearly everyone, but especially the print and broadcast media; centers of influence in one's community; and, in some cases, nationwide, government officials, political leaders, customers, stockholders, and employees—any individual or group that can affect others' opinions of the company. Public relations letters are often friendly, and in some cases even "salesy," putting one's best foot forward to enhance the company's image in the eyes of others. But PR letters are not always friendly or even tactful. Often the company has to say "no" to unreasonable demands, to critics who have vested interests opposite the firm's, and to solicitors of endorsements, advertising, funds, and so on.

Your Objective   To thank Curtis Halverson for his excellent comments and express appreciation for his suggestions.

SAMPLE LETTERS

A

> Dear Friend:
>
> Thank you for your comments about our series of ads in national magazines on the environment. It was very thoughtful of you to write, and we hope you will continue to enjoy this series.
>
> HANOVER'S

Analysis This response is obviously a printed postcard designed for mass mailing. While the message is friendly enough, we can't imagine Curtis Halverson's deriving much pleasure from it. It is quite impersonal, for one thing, and there is no mention of Halverson's suggestions. There is some defense for such printed messages; perhaps the company will receive hundreds of communications about their public-spirited ads and find it impossible to answer each letter personally. However, as mentioned earlier, several form letters can be written, each tailored to a specific situation, and these can be set up to resemble individually typewritten letters at very little additional cost.

B

Dear Mr. Halverson:

You were very thoughtful to write praising our series of ads in several national magazines. I am delighted, of course, that you enjoy these pieces and find them stimulating and provocative. This is exactly what we and our advertising agency had in mind when the series was planned.

Your suggestion that we give more emphasis to creatures of the wild is very appropriate. We are now planning six ads which will emphasize the importance of protecting our wild life, especially endangered species. Watch for them, and if you have time, give us your impression of these ads.

Thanks for writing. Your letter boosted our spirits!

                                Cordially,

Analysis Martha Lendon accomplishes three things in this goodwill-building letter:

1. She expresses deep appreciation of Halverson's letter of praise and for his confirmation of the real purpose the company and its advertising agency had in mind.
2. She then compliments him on his suggestion, describing future plans that coincide with his own ideas.
3. She closes the letter with a hearty thank you.

"YOUR JOB" PROJECTS

1. Dr. Wilma Dehnert, vice president of human resources at Hanover's, recently wrote an article for *Atlantic* magazine entitled "The Unheralded Human Resources in the Corporate Domain." In the article, Dehnert emphasized the readiness of women to succeed in the higher echelons of corporate management, disavowing old-fashioned clichés that women shun responsibility, are too soft-hearted to make difficult decisions, lack the imagination and drive of typical top men executives, and lack the physical stamina and emotional stability to compete effectively with their male counterparts.

   Dr. Dehnert received 200 letters from readers of *Atlantic*, 90 percent of them favorable. She turned all responses over to the public relations department, asking that each "favorable" letter be responded to with gratitude. The letter will be processed in such a way that it will appear to be very personal. You are to draft a letter for Dr. Dehnert's signature.

2. About 10 percent of the responses to Dr. Dehnert were negative. However, Dehnert is determined to answer everyone who wrote, even if the writer's response was critical. Write a response that Dehnert can use in letters to the "negatives." Assume that Dehnert will enclose a report, *Women in Management: 20 Case Studies*. This report was presented before the American Association of Human Resources Directors at a recent meeting at which Dr. Dehnert was a featured speaker.

SUPPLEMENTARY PROJECT

3. At a state meeting of the Idaho Education Association in Boise, the general theme was "A Backward and Forward Look at Education." The keynote speaker on the occasion was Raymond D. Frankel, president of one of America's largest corporations who has been a very outspoken critic of vocational-technical education in high schools and colleges. Frankel believes that there is no place for "job training programs" in America's regular

educational institutions and that high schools and colleges have become essentially trade schools, and he abhors the tendency toward eliminating the liberal arts courses such as the classics, higher mathematics, history, foreign languages, science, fine arts, philosophy, and humanities.

The talk was highly publicized because of Frankel's position of influence in the corporate world. Frankel received 615 letters, 409 of which were highly complimentary, while 206 took violent exception to Frankel's stand. In the interest of good public relations for the company that Frankel heads, he plans to answer all letters. Frankel is not opposed to vocational education; however, he believes that schools and colleges should be divided into two strict categories—liberal arts and vocational-technical education and that the two areas become separate institutions.

Assume that you have been asked by Frankel to write to the 206 people who disagree with him. Prepare an appropriate response, although not changing Frankel's position. Remember, Frankel doesn't want to make enemies no matter how severe the critics were.

STYLE CHECKUP

Select the sentence from each pair that needs one or more hyphens.

1. **a.** Braxton's catalog is 96 pages long.
   b. Braxton's 96 page catalog is now available.
2. **a.** The air conditioning unit needs to be replaced.
   b. The air conditioning in the storeroom is not very effective.
3. **a.** We need another filing cabinet—one with four drawers.
   b. We need another four drawer filing cabinet.
4. **a.** The purchasing manager asked for inventory figures that are up to date.
   b. The purchasing manager asked for up to date inventory figures.
5. **a.** Mr. Solin said, "Let's roll out the red carpet for our visitors next Tuesday."
   b. Mr. Solin said, "Let's make sure our visitors get the red carpet treatment next Tuesday."

CASE 2 Apologizing for Inconveniences

THE SETTING

When Hanover's builds a new branch store or shopping mall, all those in the immediate vicinity suffer many inconveniences—heavy equipment blocking the roads, mud and dirt everywhere, rerouting of traffic, and so on. The company has developed a form letter to the residents near the new shopping area (in this case, the suburban community of Lakeside), apologizing for the inconvenience to homeowners and others in the vicinity.

Objective   To prepare a form letter to be sent to Lakeside residents that can easily be adapted to any geographic area.

SAMPLE LETTER

```
Dear Fellow Lakesiders:

Building a new store can be a messy business--as
you have undoubtedly noticed from the dust clouds
we stir up, the rerouting of traffic on East Main
Street, and the noise and general confusion we
create.

Although things are still unsettled, we are doing
everything we possibly can to eliminate inconven-
ience and discomfort for our friends.  The good
news is that we expect to finish the "dirty"
part of the job by June 1 and then get back to
normal.

Thank you for your patience.  Although we regret
being a nuisance, we think you will be proud of
this new Hanover's--a full acre of shopping
pleasure--which is scheduled to open on December 1
of this year.

                    Sincerely yours,



                    Martha Lendon
```

Analysis   Although this personalized letter from a high-ranking officer at Hanover's will do very little to alleviate the discomfort that Lakeside residents are enduring, many people will feel just a little better knowing that someone at Hanover's cares. The subtle sales message at the close of the letter is a fine ending for this note of apology.

"YOUR JOB" PROJECTS

1. While the new Hanover's was under construction, you receive a letter from Mr. and Mrs. Harrison Spaulding asking why it is necessary to destroy so many beautiful trees. They claim that many of the pine trees are 50 years old or older and were a haven for birds and squirrels.

    Answer the letter to the Spauldings. Here are some of the details:

    a. Every tree that could be spared was left standing.

    b. Before construction is completed, Hanover's plans to plant a great many trees, including pine, bay, sycamore, and maple.

    c. In addition, dozens of colorful shrubs are to be planted—pampas, crepe myrtle, azaleas, gardenias, roses, and red tips.

    d. The entire store area will be surrounded by a lush, green lawn.

    Add whatever details about the planned appearance of the building you think may be appropriate and write the letter to the Spauldings.

2. Assume that it is November 24 and the new Hanover's Shopping Mart is getting ready to open its doors for business as scheduled on December 1. Write an appropriate announcement (either a letter or a printed card) of the Grand Opening. Supply whatever details you choose to make the invitation to Lakeside shoppers appealing.

SUPPLEMENTARY PROJECT

3. Rothman's, a popular jewelry store in downtown Norman, has been in business for 35 years in the same location. In recent years, business has fallen off because more and more young people prefer to shop in the suburbs rather than downtown where the traffic is heavy and space for parking cars limited. The management decides to build a new and larger store in the Golden Maple Mall, now under construction. The plan is to keep the downtown store—there is a large contingent of customers who would be reluctant to shop anywhere else.

    Write a letter to your present customers, announcing the new store to be located at Cedar Road and Classen Boulevard. The store will open Wednesday, April 18. Include in your message anything that you think will entice customers to shop in the Golden Maple Mall.

STYLE CHECKUP

Each of the following sentences contains an error in usage. Make the necessary corrections.

1. This company doesn't hardly ever get its payroll out on schedule.
2. No tire dealer in Larchmont offers the discounts that we do.
3. Of the six possible locations for a retail store, Ridgewood is the better one.

4. Eileen and George only began work last Monday.
5. The Anniston distribution center has more space than any distribution center in the company.

C A S E 3

Saying "No" to a Request That Cannot Be Granted

THE SETTING

The public relations department at Hanover's has the responsibility for publishing *Grist*, a weekly paper for company employees. When *Grist* was first published, it was made available to anyone who requested it. The idea was that the paper would build good public relations with all readers. However, requests for the paper have become very heavy and the cost of preparing the paper (editing, printing, paper, etc.) has nearly tripled. The decision has been made by management to restrict the circulation of *Grist* to company employees. Outside requests must be denied.

Following are two possible rejection letters.

Dear Mrs. DiSalle:

Because of increased printing and distribution costs, the policy has been established to restrict the circulation of <u>Grist</u> to our own employees. Therefore, it is not possible to send the magazine to outsiders.

                    Very truly yours,

Dear Mrs. DiSalle:

I appreciate your asking to be put on the mailing list to receive our employee magazine, <u>Grist</u>. Your comments about its high quality are especially satisfying.

When <u>Grist</u> was first published, we were pleased to send it to all our friends. In recent months, however, the demand has become so great and the cost of printing and mailing so high that we have been forced to adopt the policy of limiting distribution to our own employees. It was a painful decision, but I am confident that you will understand why it was made.

I have entered your name and address in our computer bank, and if at some time in the future the decision is made to resume our regular distribution, you will hear from me.

Yours very cordially,

Analysis   It should be clear why Letter B is the better letter here.

1. Letter A is curt to the point of rudeness, and the label "outsiders" is unforgivable. It clearly excludes DiSalle and puts her on the defensive. What could be more impersonal?
2. Letter B is a gracious, personalized turndown. The writer has demonstrated that it is possible to say "no" without making an enemy.

"YOUR JOB" PROJECTS

1. Throughout the years Hanover's has bought numerous small companies and stores. In corporate lingo these are referred to as "acquisitions." In Hanover's annual report to stockholders, the figures concerning acquisitions or subsidiaries are not broken down. The financial statements show only total income, expenses, and profits for the entire corporation. Of course, financial records are kept for each of the major divisions; however, these figures are not available to the general public. C. R. McIvey (not a stockholder) writes asking for information concerning Yamaguchi Appliances, a firm that McIvey held stock in before it was acquired by Hanover's. McIvey wants to compare the present figures for Yamaguchi with those before Yamaguchi was purchased. This information is not available to the general public, although major stockholders are provided with this information on an individual basis and with the approval of the board of directors. McIvey's request cannot be granted. You are to write to McIvey. Be as tactful as you can in your "no" response. Remember that stockholders are VIP's in the corporate world, and McIvey may at some time purchase Hanover's stock.
2. Hanover's publishes a general catalog containing thousands of pages and is very hefty. The general catalog is available to individuals at $4.40. However, individual sections of the general catalog, such as automobile accessories, kitchen appliances, carpeting, and sports equipment, are often available and are free. Of course, authorized merchant stores located in hundreds of smaller towns have complete catalogs, some merchandise on display, and people to help the shoppers find what they want and place the order and arrange for delivery. Answer a request for a general catalog from Ms. Renee Fleming, referring to the authorized merchant in Stonington, which is only 12 miles away from Fleming's home town.

3. Like other large, nationwide retail store establishments, Hanover's has hundreds of authorized merchants that carry no merchandise but have facilities for placing orders and arranging to have them delivered. A Luther Jackson writes asking to purchase a franchise to operate as an authorized merchant for Hanover's in the town of Gurneyville (population 5,200). The nearest retail store operated by Hanover's is in Claremont, which is only 12 miles from Gurneyville. Hanover's does not consider Gurneyville a desirable location for such an operation. The town of Gurneyville is too small and too close to Claremont. Several executives are considering three new authorized merchant outlets in downstate areas. If Jackson is interested, he is to write them to be considered when a choice is made.

4. You received a letter this week from a Hanover's retail store manager in which was enclosed a complaint from a stockholder (Tyler Jacobsen) that Hanover's retail store in Macon, Georgia, will not accept MasterCard, Bank Americard, or Visa cards. Only Hanover's credit card is accepted. Jacobsen feels that Hanover's loses a great many sales by this practice. The facts are these. A large percentage of customers, on learning that Hanover's accepts only its own credit card, apply for a Hanover's credit card. If Hanover's accepted other credit cards, the store would have to pay a percentage of the sale to the issuer of the card—as much as 5 percent. Losses from Hanover's credit card holders are less than one-half of 1%. Finally, holders of Hanover's credit card (as is true of other cards) must pay interest on unpaid balances resulting in a substantial income for the store.

   You write to the stockholder (Tyler Jacobsen) explaining the situation, telling him the store will continue to assess the situation and be quick to change the policy if it appears profitable to do so.

SUPPLEMENTARY PROJECT

5. Rhodes, Inc. is a large manufacturer and distributor of household appliances. The company also operates over 50 retail stores in which Rhodes products are sold and serviced. Each retail store has a service department, and the service people fan out to outlying areas—often as far as 50 miles away.

   Henry Stabler operates a small appliance-service business in Mill Creek where Rhodes does not have a retail store. Stabler writes the president of Rhodes asking to be certified to work on Rhodes appliances, saying that he has 15 years' experience in servicing household appliances of all brands. He would like to enter into a contract with Rhodes to service Rhodes products in Mill Creek. At the moment the community of Mill Creek is serviced by Rhodes appliance repair people from the Whiteville some 60 miles away. Until such time as Rhodes finds it necessary to build more retail stores, the president prefers to keep the arrangements as they are now. Assure Stabler that should anything develop, Rhodes may wish to contract with outside service people, and he will be notified if an agreement appears to be feasible.

STYLE CHECKUP

Some writers have a hard time deciding between the verbs *effect,* which means "to bring about," and *affect,* which means "to act upon." *Effect* is also commonly used as a noun meaning "result" or "consequence." In the following sentences, choose the correct word in parentheses.

1. Our many warnings to the dealer had no (affect, effect) on his methods.
2. How will this new procedure (effect, affect) service to customers?
3. This policy went into (effect, affect) over a year ago.
4. I think the (effect, affect) on morale will be significant.
5. What (affect, effect) will rising costs have on prices?

C A S E
4

Handling Requests to Make a Donation or Purchase Advertising

THE SETTING

Almost every week the president of Hanover's in Cleveland or a branch store manager receives requests to make a contribution to this or that worthy cause or to purchase advertising. Most of these requests must be refused—no company, not matter how large, can afford to support every campaign for funds. A typical letter is from Ms. Dorothy Forbes, director of the Center for Helping the Homeless, which opened recently. Forbes asks Hanover's for a contribution to the Center. You are asked to respond for your supervisor, Martha Lendon.

BACKGROUND

Every business organization receives many requests for contributions. Although most organizations do contribute to various local compaigns, setting aside a percentage of profits for that specific purpose, they can never honor all the requests they receive. Some firms support only one united fund organization (called by that name, or Community Chest, or a similar name). Others give most of their contribution fund budget to a united fund group and, in addition, set aside money for other charitable organizations that do not share in the united fund.

In any event, requests for contributions must be screened very carefully. It is very hard to justify a "no" to one organization when you have just said "yes" to a similar one. More important, the charge of discrimination is always a possibility, especially among religious and ethnic groups. The subject of donations, then, is a very sensitive one in the public relations area.

Most large companies set up a special committee to study contribution requests, and the committee ponders over and discusses each request before reaching a decision. One purpose of such a committee is to share the responsibility for turning down a request. The negative decision of a group carries more weight than that of an individual; and certainly it is less painful to the person who has to convey the decision when he or she can say, "The Committee decided," rather than "I decided."

SAMPLE LETTERS

A

Dear Ms. Forbes:

Thank you for your letter in which you ask Hanover's to support your Center for Helping the Homeless. Our Donations Committee, which has the responsibility for allocating our budget for contributions, handles all requests for funds. I am therefore referring your letter to them. No doubt you will hear from the chairperson soon after the committee reaches a decision.

                    Yours very cordially,

Analysis In companies like Hanover's where all requests for donations are turned over to a special donations committee, a letter such as A is appropriate. Note that the writer is noncommital but tactful.

B

Dear Ms. Forbes:

Thank you for writing us to request a contribution to the Center for Helping the Homeless.

Each year we set aside a generous budget for contributions to local activities. In fact, last year we gave to various organizations the largest amount in our history. Even then, we were able to give to only a fraction of the groups that sought our help. I am sure you will understand that we cannot give financial support to all.

Reluctantly, then, we must refrain from participating this year. In your case the decision is particulary painful for us because we are well aware of the fine public service you are performing.

Best wishes in your drive, and I hope that at some later date we may be able to share in this effort.

Sincerely yours,

Analysis   Letter B, written by the chairperson of Hanover's donations committee, emphasizes the "We can't give to everyone" theme. It is sympathetic in tone, tactful, reasonable, and friendly.

BACKGROUND (CONTINUED)

Business firms receive many requests to purchase advertising space in school yearbooks, directories, programs for sports and cultural events, and so on. Although there is some advertising value in such publications, it is mostly "institutional" (public relations). Most businesses look on such advertising as a contribution, and the printed advertisement often consists of just the simple message "Compliments of the ABC Company."

Although many business firms support local community activities by purchasing advertising space, such requests are often so numerous that many must be turned down. Refusing such requests is a delicate matter—every organization needs money to support its activities, and local businesspeople are obvious sources. The solicitor's appeal is to the business people's conscience, their responsibility to the community they live in. Often, though, the solicitor emphasizes the theme "We keep you in business and you owe us something."

The president of Hanover's received the following letter from John C. Bowes of the Greater Cleveland Art League. The president writes "one-half page max!" and forwards the letter to Martha Lendon to handle. You are to draft a letter for Lendon's signature.

Dear Sir:

The Greater Cleveland Art League is having its annual ball on October 11 at the Kenwood Club in Shaker Heights. The proceeds from the ball will go toward establishing a scholarship fund for gifted young artists.

In connection with the ball, we are printing a special souvenir program. This program is designed by local young artists and printed in four colors.

Advertising space is available in these programs ($1,000 for a full page, $600 for a half page and $300 for a quarter page) and we hope you will want to be represented in the advertising pages. Hundreds of people will see your ad and know that your company supports this very worthy activity.

Another reason that I believe you will want to help us is that several of your employees are members of the League and will be proud that Hanover's name appears in the program.

May I put you down for a full-page ad on the program?

Sincerely yours,

John C. Bowes

SAMPLE LETTERS

A Dear Mr. Bowes:

I am sorry that we feel we should limit our contribution to $600 for a half page in the souvenir program of the Greater Cleveland Art League Ball rather than purchase a full page. Our check is enclosed.

Sincerely yours,

Analysis Of course, you know that no apology is necessary for not taking a full-page ad in the souvenir program. To express regrets by saying "only" $600 the writer is taking away all the positive effects of the donation.

B Dear Mr. Bowes:

Here is our check for $600 for a half-page ad in the souvenir program for the Greater Cleveland Art League Ball. Please include this simple message: "Compliments of Hanover's."

Congratulations on the fine job the League is doing in the Cleveland area. Hanover's salutes you and the other fine people who are working with this program.

Sincerely yours,

Analysis Letter B does what Hanover's wanted done: cements friendly relations with the league. Everything about the letter is positive.

"YOUR JOB" PROJECTS

1. The general manager of the Norwalk store received a letter from Jeanette Hruska, secretary of the Arts and Crafts Club at Norwalk High School. Hruska requested show window space for the week of April 11 to 17 to display the work of that organization—woodworking, decorative metals, graphic design, leather goods, and a variety of other things. She expects that about 50 objects will be shown. The store manager is agreeable to lending this display space at the time requested. Edmondson believes that doing so will build pride in the community and excellent public relations for Hanover's. You are to write the letter to Hruska for Clarence Edmondson's signature. In your letter, offer the services of Hanover's window display specialists and whatever help is required (including materials) in setting up the exhibit and dismantling it when the exhibit ends.

2. The manager of the Santa Fe Store of Hanover's is Charles Lester, and he received the following letter from the chairperson of the Youth Athletic Activities Association, Adele Chisholm.

Dear Mr. Lester:

The Youth Athletic Activities Association is conducting a campaign for money to help us in our work. The purpose of our organization is to encourage young people to participate in various sports programs. We are especially interested in sports activities for the disadvantaged who have little opportunity to learn to swim and to learn to play tennis, volleyball, basketball, and other sports.

Would you please help us in our drive? A very substantial contribution from your store would, of course, be greatly appreciated, but we would welcome any amount that you feel you can give us.

Gratefully yours,

Lester believes that a separate contribution for the Youth Athletic Association would be a mistake. Hanover's contributes heavily to the Community Chest and believes that individual contributions would open the door to others who choose to bypass the Community Chest. Write the letter of rejection to Adele Chisholm, stating in a frank but tactful way why the request is being denied.

3. The Patterson Guild is a small private school near Lexington, Kentucky. Beause of the high expense of operation, the administration has announced that the school must close its doors at the end of the current academic year.

Although the students understand the problem and appreciate the administration's attempts to deal with it, they are not willing to accept the school's fate and have decided to solicit funds from various large corporations to keep the guild in operation. The "Committee to Save Patterson Guild" (chairperson, Rachel DeVille) prepares a letter pleading for help from the national office in Cleveland.

The Contributions Committee at Hanover's home office has voted to send a check for $2,000. Write to Rachel DeVille, enclosing Hanover's check. Add whatever details you think appropriate in building good public relations.

4. An organization known as Patriotic Americans for Puritan Principles is soliciting funds to support its work. In his letter asking for money from Hanover's headquarters office, the president of the organization soliciting funds, Roscoe Bartley, points out that the objective of this organization is "to protect the American way our forefathers fought and died for." After a thorough investigation, Hanover's Contributions Committee found nothing favorable about the organization that Bartley represents. The committee's research revealed that it is a radical group. Write the letter of rejection by the Contributions Committee. *Hint*: Don't delve into the subject of unfavorable comments about the organization.

SUPPLEMENTARY PROJECTS

5. Canfield's, a manufacturer of sports equipment, has headquarters in Omaha, Nebraska. The firm sells all types of sports articles to various groups, including schools and colleges, amateur organizations, professional teams, and so on. The firm also has Canfield's retail stores throughout the nation where individuals, as well as teams, may shop.

Every year Canfield's in Omaha receives hundreds of requests from schools and colleges asking the company to purchase advertising in the yearbook. Obviously the company cannot afford to place ads in thousands of yearbooks that are published each year. Instead, they respond by referring the yearbook's business manager to the nearest Canfield's retail store. This is not simply "passing the buck"; generally speaking, a national advertiser would receive practically no benefit from this type of expenditure. Local stores, however, often buy advertising space because they *do* stand a chance of having the advertising pay off.

Write a form letter explaining this policy to yearbook business managers. Be very tactful. Incidentally, local managers of Canfield's understand and are in accord with the home office.

6. The president of Peerless Tire Company, in Akron, Ohio, received the following letter recently. It was from The Society for the Removal of All Billboards in America (chairperson, Peter B. Gould).

Dear Sir:

I am writing you on a matter of critical importance. Our organization seeks to abolish all

outdoor advertising. Not only are these ads
unsightly but they often make driving dangerous.

In support of our cause, we are planning a one-
page advertisement in several national magazines. If you agree with our position, and all
Americans who love their country should, you
will favor our cause by a contribution of a
minimum of $5,000.

May I expect an immediate response?

                              Very truly yours,

The president of Peerless Tire Company is outraged by this letter. He believes
that outdoor advertising, carefully controlled and monitored, is legitimate. Indeed,
Peerless's has billboards outside the city limits of the towns where Peerless
products are sold. After several attempts at a tactful rejection of the request,
the president of Peerless Tire Company decides not to respond at all since any
conflicting opinions between the two organizations will only offend Gould. Do
you think the president is justified in his decision to remain silent? Why or why
not? Assume that you think the president is wrong. What would you have
written?

STYLE CHECKUP

Correct any errors in comma usage in the following sentences.

1. The handbook, *Welcome to Tyson's* should be revised frequently.
2. Certain overhead costs such as rent and insurance cannot be reduced.
3. Melissa Culhane our representative in Boston won this month's award.
4. Did the contracts from Rhodes, Inc. arrive this morning?
5. The report had a special binding which made it more impresseve.

CASE 5

Responding to a Request That
Violates Company Policy

THE SETTING

Like other large organizations with both mail-order and retail store operations,
Hanover's offers credit privileges to shoppers who qualify. And like most other

businesses, Hanover's finds that it is sometimes difficult to collect money owed by customers.

Over the years, Hanover's has developed several sets (series) of collection letters. Each set is designed for a particular group of delinquent customers. The letters are essentially form letters, and they are revised from time to time to bring them up to date.

This week you received a letter from Professor G. K. Marsala in which she requested the form letters in Hanover's various collection-letter series. She is writing a book on retail credit and plans to use some of Hanover's letters as examples of effective collection letters.

At one time Hanover's released its series to authors and others; however, because the materials were not always intelligently handled, the company received adverse publicity. When federal laws were enacted to control methods of making collections, the matter became especially sensitive. Hanover's management then established the policy denying anyone outside the company access to these materials.

Your Objective   To deny the request, explain precisely why you must do so, and retain Professor Marsala's goodwill.

BACKGROUND

As you know, you will sometimes have to write a "no" response to individuals who ask for donations or special favors that would be too costly to grant or make requests that you consider downright unreasonable. You have seen examples of such requests in cases presented earlier. In this instance, however, the person making the request is not asking for money or for a favor that is completely unreasonable. Yet she must be turned down for reasons of "company policy," which means that granting the request would simply not be in the best interest of the company. The policy may have been established to protect company secrets, to avoid legal problems or unfavorable public relations, and for other reasons.

No matter how you feel personally about policies that are established by the company you work for—you may think that some are a bit foolish—you have no choice but to uphold them. Guidelines for writing letters that uphold company policies follow.

Guidelines

1. Express appreciation for the letter.
2. Describe the background that led up to the adoption of the company policy; then tactfully refuse the request on that basis. (Never give "company policy" as your only reason for a negative response.)
3. Do not give any indication that you disagree with the policy.
4. Express the hope that the requester will understand your position, and close on a positive note.

SAMPLE LETTERS

Dear Professor Marsala:

Concerning your request for copies of our collection-letter series. Unfortunately, I am very sorry to report that I cannot release these materials to individuals outside the company. I assure you that this is not my personal decision; it is company policy.

Thank you for writing, however.

Yours very truly,

Analysis   Letter A is very poor for several reasons.

1. The "ing" opening is awkward, and the first sentence is a fragment (incomplete).
2. *Unfortunately, I am very sorry* is an awkward phrase.
3. In the third sentence, the writer seems to be unable to defend the policy—a cardinal sin in letter writing.
4. The last paragraph (sentence) is fine, except the addition of the word *however* is unfortunate and unnecessary.

Dear Professor Marsala:

I appreciate your request for copies of Hanover's various sets of collection letters.

For several years Hanover's released those letters to a number of retailing specialists, Professor Marsala, including textbook authors. Indeed, you may have seen some of these letters in textbooks on business communications. About two years ago, however, the policy was established by management to deny public access to these materials.

There were two primary reasons. First, the letters were not always intelligently used; in some instances they brought us unfavorable publicity. Second, and more important, the Fair Debt Collection Practices Law established stringent regulations for making collections, and the new conditions affecting the content of letters make some letters especially vulnerable to misinterpretation by those who are not familiar with the law.

I hope you will understand our position, Professor Marsala, and I extend best wishes on completing your new book and getting it published. Your approach to the subject of retail credit sounds very interesting.

Sincerely yours,

Analysis   Letter B satisfies the guidelines established for writing a "company policy" letter:

1. The opening is courteous and friendly.
2. The writer traces briefly the history of the Hanover's collection-letter series in terms of their use by retailing specialists. This leads nicely into the next paragraph.
3. The situation is carefully explained. Although the explanation may be a bit complicated for an average reader, Professor Marsala should have no difficulty understanding it.
4. In the final paragraph the writer makes the assumption that Marsala will understand Hanover's position and then ends the letter with a pleasant, goodwill-building message.

"YOUR JOB" PROJECTS

1. Dorothea Costello, executive director of the Gulf Shores (Alabama) Chamber of Commerce, writes requesting a special price on the Bass Power motorboat described in Hanover's sports catalog. The chamber is making plans for its annual bass fishing tournament and wants to award the boat to the tournament winner. The catalog price of the Bass Power, including a 50-horsepower outboard motor and a trailer, is $6,375. Mrs. Costello asks for the special price of $4,000, since "we are a new Chamber and our funds are very limited." She offers assurance, however, that Hanover's will be given extensive publicity for the financial assistance.

   It is the policy of Hanover's national office not to participate in local promotions of this type. The decision is left up to the manager of the appropriate retail store, for the manager is in the best position to evaluate the return insofar as public relations are concerned. The Hanover's outlet nearest Gulf Shores is in Pensacola. Acknowledge Costello's request, and refer her to the Pensacola store manager, J. D. Rutledge. (*Hint*: Do not express an opinion as to how Rutledge is likely to handle this matter.)

2. Lloyd Demaret, a partner in an investment counseling firm, wrote asking to be put on the mailing list for six copies of the publication *Inside Hanover's*. This monthly bulletin contains confidential financial information, and its distribution is restricted to the officers of the company. You don't know how Demaret got his hands on a copy. Write an appropriate response to the request.

SUPPLEMENTARY PROJECTS

3. As a correspondent for Continental Book Publishers Inc., you have been asked to respond to the following letter, which was addressed to the president:

> Dear Sir:
>
> Our organization, Friends of the Botanical Gardens, is trying to raise money in order to build a new cactus garden. One of our members suggested that we sell vegetable gardening books, provided we can purchase them at a price low enough to enable us to make a profit. We are especially interested in <u>Joan King's Home-Grown Vegetables Guide</u>, which you publish (it is listed in your catalog at $12.95). What will be the cost to us if we purchase, say, 400 copies?
>
> An immediate response will be appreciated.
>
> > Very truly yours,
> >
> > (Mrs.) Greta Wylie

Company policy prevents you from allowing the discount requested. Continental sells *Joan King's Home-Grown Vegetables* primarily through retail bookstores, and if Friends of the Botanical Gardens were permitted to purchase the book at a discount and sell it to individuals, the company would be undercutting its local book dealers. Explain the policy to Wylie in a letter.

4. You are the assistant general manager of Woodbridge Building Centers, a small chain of building supply stores in Vermont. You receive a letter from the Laketown Tax Revolt Committee (George Kaneer, president) requesting the use of the company's name in a campaign to lower local taxes (one of Woodbridge's stores is located in Laketown, and the manager referred Kaneer to the home office). Woodbridge's policy is to endorse no local community action campaigns that have political overtones, and each retail store must adhere to this policy. Respond to Kaneer with a message that you feel is appropriate.

STYLE CHECKUP

Choose the term in parentheses that correctly completes the sentence.

1. The two recommendations are (alike, both alike) in many respects.
2. (All, All of) the inquiries received were acknowledged.

3. Susan (accidently, accidentally) opened a letter that was addressed to her manager and marked "Personal."
4. Cindy is an (all-around, all-round) athlete.
5. We do not doubt (that, but that) Sharpe calculated the totals correctly.

Responding to a Critic

THE SETTING

In support of its retail stores throughout the country, Hanover's advertises in several national magazines such as *Reader's Digest, Better Homes and Gardens*, and *McCall's*. Occasionally the firm also advertises certain products in small magazines whose readers are relatively young and active in politics, environmental issues, and various socioeconomic affairs. Recently Hanover's advertised its new PanaVistic Sound System in *Forefront*, a somewhat controversial periodical that speaks boldly on modern issues, often attacking public figures and social institutions.

Today you received the following letter from H. J. Douglass, the owner of an electrical contracting business in the Midwest.

```
Sirs:

Why would a reputable organization such as Han-
over's support, through advertising, a muckraking
periodical like Forefront?  I cannot understand
why you would assist in the desecration of our
treasured institutions and the character assassi-
nation of our respected leaders.  Your sales and
profits depend on protecting and sustaining our
American way of life--not on destroying it.

I expect to hear from you with an explanation im-
mediately.  It is not inconceivable that your
stores could be boycotted for such advertising
practices.  I for one have quit doing business
with your store in this city and have encouraged
others to do the same.

                        Yours truly,
```

Your Objective   To try to persuade Douglass to understand your point of view in a straightforward, no-apology manner.

BACKGROUND

All major companies receive letters from people who are highly critical of policies, or methods of doing business, or political leanings, or advertising practices, and so forth. Some critics mean well and state their positions calmly and with little venom. Others show their rage and make threats.

Of course, the company should not panic in such situations. At the same time, it is not wise simply to ignore irate critics. A low-key, tactful response is in order even when the critic has made almost libelous accusations. Observe these guidelines in responding to highly critical letters.

Guidelines

1. Express thanks for the letter.
2. Explain your position fully, presenting your points logically and persuasively.
3. Try to persuade the reader to understand your side of the problem.
4. Express appreciation to the writer for stating personal points of view and giving you the opportunity to state yours.

SAMPLE LETTERS

 A

Dear Mr. Douglass:

If we listened to every Tom, Dick, and Harry who disagrees with our various policies, we would get very little done. In the case of advertising, it appears that a good many misinformed people keep a list of publications whose editorial policies are at odds with their own beliefs. Obviously, we can't let these self-proclaimed censors dictate where we spend our advertising dollars.

Your threat of boycotts is noted. This is not the first time we have been threatened, but so far threats have been simply sound and fury, signifying nothing.

Yours truly,

Analysis Letter A is not a good business letter.

1. Obviously, the writer of Letter A is angry and makes no attempt to hide this feeling. Although there is a temptation to strike out at those who would dictate company policies and practices, one must keep in mind the purpose of the response: to win over the critic to the writer's point of view. Certainly, Letter A has not achieved that purpose.
2. Letter A will surely evoke a stinging retort.
3. Perhaps a much softer response will not succeed either, but it is always worth at least one attempt.

B Dear Mr. Douglass:

Thank you for writing us about our advertising in Forefront.

I am sure you will understand, Mr. Douglass, that by placing advertising in Forefront or any other periodical, we are not necessarily endorsing the editorial policy of that publication. By and large, we and other businesses select printed advertising media on the basis of results. We are constantly experimenting with various media, and whether we continue such advertising depends on the results obtained. In the opinion of our advertising staff, the readers of Forefront are prime candidates for the sound system that was advertised.

Obviously, we do have standards. For example, we will not advertise in periodicals devoted to scandal, immorality, or similar subjects that are offensive to a large number of people. However, in our opinion, Forefront does not fall within any of these categories.

Don't you agree, Mr. Douglass, that it would be presumptuous of us to adopt the policy of advertising only in those publications whose editorial policy we agree with? And who is "we"? One advertising manager will have a personal editorial preference for publications that another finds offensive. Yet neither can afford to base his or her business judgment on personal preference. As a business owner, you understand, I am confident, the role that economics plays in such decisions.

I appreciate your taking the time to express your viewpoint so frankly and giving me an opportunity to express ours.

Sincerely yours,

Analysis Letter B is a better response to what is admittedly a difficult situation.

1. Letter B is tactful and courteous, but it is also straightforward.

2. The writer has done just about everything that could be done to convince Douglass that the position taken is reasonable.
3. Note the attempt to get Douglass, as a business owner, to agree that personal bias should not affect good business judgment.

Note: Suppose that Douglass is not at all satisfied with the response in B and fires back a second rebuke. What then? Unless you feel that you must bow to Douglass's demand to stop advertising in *Forefront*, a second response will serve no purpose. We suggest, therefore, that you simply file and forget additional letters from this person.

"YOUR JOB" PROJECT
. . . .

1. Respond to the following letter, which was addressed to the president of Hanover's.

Dear Sir:

I am writing on behalf of the Pearl City Environment Association in protest of your support of a manufacturer that pollutes our river and air. This firm, which we know supplies the paper for your catalogs, is the R. S. Ogle Company. Every day of the week we see dirty, black smoke pouring out of the company's plant, and the Crystal River, on which the building is located, is fouled and filthy because of the chemicals Ogle dumps into it.

We have protested to the mayor of Pearl City many times and have met with the Ogle bigwigs on numerous occasions to discuss this matter. The only answer we get is, "We're working on it." Yet nothing happens--just more pollution to destroy the beauty of our city and the health of its citizens.

The only recourse left to us is to protest to those who support this company. You have the responsibility, in our opinion, to quit buying paper from the R. S. Ogle Company. I expect to hear from you.

Yours truly,

Gardner V. Pritchard

Note: Of course, Hanover's has no control over the practices of its suppliers. Although you may deplore the situation (if the accusation is true), you must select suppliers primarily on the basis of the quality of their work and service and their prices. Actually, however, Hanover's is proud of its activities in environmental affairs. For example, the company recently wrote a booklet on pollution control—*The Manufacturer's Responsibility for the Environment*—and distributed it to all its suppliers.

In responding to Pritchard, use whatever methods you think are appropriate to convince him that Hanover's is much concerned about environmental affairs and is willing to help in any way possible (short of automatically dropping Ogle as a supplier) to solve the problem.

SUPPLEMENTARY PROJECT

2. You are the assistant to the editorial director, Daphne Casserta, in the Centenary Book Company. This week Casserta received the following letter:

Dear Sir or Madam:

As president of the Fairmont Association for Decent Literature, I must express my shock and disgust at <u>Revolt of a Radical Realist</u>, by Chauncey Arcane, that you recently published. How can a company with your reputation champion the cause of this blatant revolutionist?

Our association considers such publishing offensive and irresponsible, and we protest on behalf of all parents. The language is filthy, and the ideas expressed by this author (!) are dangerous to our youth.

We have petitioned the Fairmont Library to remove <u>Revolt of a Radical Realist</u> from its shelves. Some members have even suggested that we should demand that all future books published by your company be banned from our classrooms and libraries. Think it over!

Yours truly,

Mrs. Mona Standish

You are to prepare a draft of Ms. Casserta's response.

STYLE CHECKUP

Choose the term in parentheses that correctly completes the sentence.

1. The internal auditor divides his time (between, among) the Burlington and Chandler branch offices.
2. Ben, Sarah, and Harry shared the collation of the huge report (between, among) them.
3. Of the 24 Penmaster desk sets you ordered, 16 are being shipped today; the (balance, remainder) will follow early next week.
4. Your account now shows a (balance, remainder) of $188.65.

CHAPTER 14

HUMAN RESOURCES COMMUNICATIONS

YOUR JOB

You are the manager of human resources at Strickland's, a large department store. You have a variety of duties, including finding people for job vacancies in the store, interviewing applicants, establishing fair wage and salary policies, setting up employee training programs, supervising employee services (cafeteria, storewide communications, medical care, recreation, and so on), and administering various other employee benefits.

CASE 1

Responding to Job Applications

THE SETTING

One of your responsibilities is to respond to those who apply by letter for a job at Strickland's. Today you received four application letters as follows:

1. Theresa Frattiano has applied for the position of housewares buyer, which you advertised in the *Milwaukee Journal*. Fratiano seems to have excellent qualifications for the job.
2. Jason Arledge has applied for the same job (housewares buyer). He has had considerable retail selling experience but mentions nothing in his application papers about buying.
3. Thomas Croft has applied for the job of advertising manager at Strickland's but will accept any important supervisory position in advertising. There is no vacancy in the advertising department, and none is anticipated. However, Croft's qualifications appear to be outstanding.
4. Jennifer Warhol has applied for a position in store display. She states that she is a recent high school graduate with no experience but that she has been told by several people that she has a special flair for art and design.

Your Objective   To respond to each applicant with an appropriate letter.

BACKGROUND

Most companies of any size receive numerous applications for jobs. Some of the letters are in response to ads placed in local newspapers; others come from people who have learned from friends or employees in the company about a job vacancy; and still others are written by individuals who simply take a chance that there is an opening for which they might qualify.

All applications should, of course, be acknowledged. In some larger companies, applications for jobs for which there are no vacancies or from obviously unqualified applicants for jobs that are available are acknowledged by means of a printed form letter or postcard. Usually, such messages make no distinction between the qualified and unqualified.

Strickland's policy is to treat every applicant as an individual, and although form messages are often used, they are personally typewritten and signed. A problem arises, of course, when an applicant must be turned down for a position because of lack of the required qualifications.

Responding to job applications can conceivably involve many different situations. Among the most typical are the following:

- Responding to a well-qualified applicant when a position is open.
- Responding to an unqualified applicant when a position is open.
- Responding to a well-qualified applicant when no position is open.
- Responding to an unqualified applicant when no position is open.

Because these situations call for different responses, the guidelines, sample letters, and analyses for each are discussed separately.

Well-Qualified Applicant—Job Opening   When you are responding to an individual who has applied for a position that is open and who seems to be qualified, follow these guidelines.

Guidelines

1. Express appreciation for the application.
2. Invite the applicant to come for an interview; give the date, time, and place.

SAMPLE LETTER

Dear Ms. Frattiano:

Thank you for applying for the position of house-wares buyer at Strickland's in response to our ad in the Milwaukee Journal.

I would be very pleased to discuss this position with you in person. Can you come for an interview on Tuesday, March 7, at 9:30 a.m.? Unless I hear from you to the contrary, I will expect you at that time. The second-floor receptionist will direct you to my office.

Sincerely yours,

Analysis   This is an easy letter to write, since there are only two matters to cover: a thank you for the application and a suggested date and time for a personal interview.

1. The writer was wise not to have dwelt on Frattiano's excellent qualifications. Many people who look very impressive on paper make a poor showing at the interview, and it's usually not wise to be too encouraging in the initial communication.
2. The letter assumes that Frattiano will know that she would not have been invited for an interview if she lacked the training and experience required for the job.

Unqualified Applicant—Job Opening   In writing to applicants who do not appear to have the qualifications to fill a job vacancy, follow these guidelines.

Guidelines

1. Express appreciation for the application.
2. Point out, if appropriate, those things that are favorable to the applicant, and then tactfully explain why the applicant does not appear to have the other necessary credentials.

SAMPLE LETTERS

Dear Mr. Arledge:

I have received your application for the position of housewares buyer, which was advertised in the <u>Milwaukee Journal</u>.

As mentioned in the ad, this position requires at least three years' experience in retail buying, and since you have had only selling experience, your application cannot be considered.

Cordially yours,

Analysis   This might be called a "tell it like it is" response to an unqualified applicant.

1. Although it is not wrong to tell Arledge that he lacks the required experience, we think it could have been done much more tactfully.

2. Did you spot the poor opening, *I have received your application?* Obviously, the application was received; otherwise, the letter would not have been written.

Dear Mr. Arledge:

I appreciate your application for the position of housewares buyer, which was advertised in the <u>Milwaukee Journal</u>.

Certainly, your experience in retail selling is impressive, Mr. Arledge. However, you may not have noted in the ad that this position requires retail buying experience (three years), which I do not find in your qualifications summary and must assume you do not have. If I am in error, I will be pleased to hear from you.

Thank you for your interest in Strickland's.

Yours very sincerely,

Analysis Letter B is a tactful way of handling this situation.

1. The writer points out what is apparently Arledge's major job asset (selling) and then refers to the need for buying experience.
2. The door is left slightly ajar in case Arledge has been a buyer and simply forgot to mention it—quite unlikely, but the writer has avoided a direct turndown.

Well-Qualified Applicant—No Job Opening Follow these guidelines in writing to applicants who appear to have the necessary qualifications for a position for which there is no opening.

Guidelines

1. Express appreciation for the application.
2. Indicate that the applicant's qualifications are adequate for the position in question and then explain the no-vacancy situation.
3. Offer to hold the applicant's papers in case an opening does occur, but do not be too encouraging when the likelihood of a vacancy in the near future appears to be remote.

SAMPLE LETTERS

Dear Mr. Croft:

I am sorry to inform you that there are no vacancies in our Advertising Department, and none is anticipated in the near future. Thank you, anyhow, for your interest.

Yours sincerely,

Analysis This letter has obvious flaws.

1. It is one of those form letters—every unsuccessful job applicant is sent the same message, regardless of qualifications.
2. Croft is highly qualified and deserves something better.

B

Dear Mr. Croft:

I very much appreciate having your application letter and the accompanying resume for a position in our Advertising Department.

Your resume seems to indicate that you could handle a supervisory position in advertising with skill and imagination, Mr. Croft, and I wish there were an opportunity to make use of your training and experience. Unfortunately, there are no openings at this time, and none is anticipated.

I will keep your papers handy and let you know if something turns up that I think you would be interested in. However, since I cannot make a prediction about when or if this might happen, I suggest that you continue your job search in other merchandising organizations.

Thank you--and good luck!

Yours very sincerely,

Analysis This letter has the individual touch that we spoke about earlier.

1. The writer lets Croft know that if there were a vacancy, he would certainly be considered for it.
2. Note, however, that no encouragement is offered. Some applicants, on receiving the least bit of encouragement, simply stop job hunting, thinking that they may be called at any time to fill the position applied for.

Unqualified Applicant—No Job Opening Human resources managers receive many inquiries from individuals who have few, if any, qualifications for the jobs that they want and for which there are no openings. In responding to these applicants, follow these guidelines.

Guidelines

1. Express appreciation for the application.
2. State that there is no opening for the job applied for.
3. Gratefully acknowledge the applicant's interest in the job and your company.

SAMPLE LETTERS

A

Dear Miss Warhol:

Although you would undoubtedly be a splendid addition to our store's display staff, there are,
unfortunately, no vacancies at this time.

I appreciate your letter and wish you success in
finding exactly the position you want in retailing.

> Sincerely,

Analysis   This is not the best letter to send to Warhol.

1. Although the tone of the letter is excellent, the writer has stretched the truth in order to be pleasant.
2. Warhol is a person with limited qualifications, and we think it is a disservice to her to lead her to think that she is an attractive candidate for the position of store display specialist.

B

Dear Miss Warhol:

I appreciate your application for a position in
store display at Strickland's.

There is no vacancy in this department, Miss Warhol, and I have no reason to believe that there
will be in the foreseeable future.

Thank you for your interest in Strickland's.

> Sincerely,

Analysis   Although there is nothing remarkable about Letter B, we think it is entirely suitable for the situation.

1. The writer chose not to embarrass Warhol and point out that she isn't really qualified for a job in store display, even if there were a vacancy.
2. Some people would tactfully suggest that she get some training in store display before taking further steps to find a job. This is a matter of personal preference. We think Warhol will discover this need on her own; on the other hand, it is possible that she will locate a trainee's job in a small retail store.

"YOUR JOB" PROJECTS

1. Today you received the following letter from Nancy Rafferty. It was addressed to the personnel manager.

Dear Sir or Madam:

I am writing to inquire about a summer job at Strickland's.

At present I am a student at Fillmore College, where I am majoring in retail merchandising. On graduation I hope to work in a large retail store such as Strickland's (my long-range career goal is to become a retail buyer), and I want to gain as much experience as possible while I am still studying.

Since the buyer's responsibility embraces several facets of retail merchandising, it is not particularly important where I am placed for a temporary summer job. I think almost any work in a reputable store would be very beneficial.

A brief resume is enclosed. May I hear from you?

Sincerely yours,

Strickland's does hire a number of young people for temporary summer jobs. However, it is too early to estimate how many will be needed this year and what the jobs will be. You expect to have this information two months from today. Although you are impressed with Rafferty's letter and résumé, you make no promises—only that she will hear from you later. Write the letter.

2. The following letter also reached you today. It is signed by L. Harvey Moore and addressed to "The President."

My dear Mr. President:

I am offering you the opportunity to put on your staff the most knoledgable financial person to be found anywhere. I am throughly experienced in acct'g, finance, systems, and edp.

```
I can begin work anytime, and I will expect to
hear from you very quickly that you won't me to
work for you.   I have had many offers, so you
must act fast.
```

```
                    Yours,
```

According to the company treasurer, there are no openings in the accounting and finance department. Write an appropriate response to Moore.

3. The credit manager of Strickland's, Hanna Gitlin, will retire next month, and you have been looking for a replacement—someone who has at least five years' experience as a credit manager in a large retail store. You placed an advertisement in the *Milwaukee Journal* and other big-city newspapers. Shortly after the job was advertised, the assistant credit manager resigned because he was not considered for Gitlin's job, and now his position must also be filled.

Alex Worsham, who recently received an M.B.A. degree with a specialization in credit management, applied for Gitlin's position. His educational credentials are very impressive, but he lacks experience as a retail credit manager. However, the assistant's job has no such experience requirement. Write Worsham, inviting him to come for an interview for the job of assistant credit manager. Choose your own date and time.

SUPPLEMENTARY PROJECT
. . . .

4. You are the supervisor of word processing at Careers Unlimited, a large home-study school. You will need six temporary typists during the months of June, July, and August, and you have advertised the positions in the local newspapers with the notation "Performance test required." Each applicant will be given a typing test, and the six who have the highest speed and accuracy scores will be hired. There were 78 applicants who showed up for the test. Write a letter that can be sent to the 72 individuals who did not place in the top six.

STYLE CHECKUP
. . . .

Correct the following run-on sentences.

1. We will add two new parking lots this year, the third will be added next year.
2. I will ship the cabinets this week, in the meantime, I am back-ordering the tables.
3. Debora and Elaine will arrive on Thursday, Donna on Friday.
4. Time and a half is paid for Saturday work, double time for Sunday.

CASE 2 Confirming a Job Offer

THE SETTING

Three weeks ago your supervisor of employee training left Strickland's to accept a similar position in her home town of Madison. You advertised the job in several papers and discussed it with a number of placement agencies.

Although you had 22 applications, you invited 15 people in for an interview. Here you discussed the requirements of the job, the salary, promotion opportunities, and other matters, all the while assessing each applicant's personal as well as professional qualifications. As each interview ended, you indicated that you would write to the applicant when a final decision had been reached.

The individual who impressed you most was Madelyn Anthony. She appeared to have the education, experience, poise, personality, and enthusiasm the position requires. You finally decided to offer her the position and telephoned her that she had been selected. She accepted the assignment enthusiastically. You will now write Anthony a letter confirming the job offer.

Your Objective   To make a definite written offer, outline the major points that should be confirmed, and extend a warm welcome to Strickland's.

BACKGROUND

Generally, very few people are hired for important positions at the time they are interviewed. It is customary to see as many applicants as possible before making a final decision; thus the interviewer's mind is usually not made up until everyone who applied has been interviewed and all application forms and other job papers have been reviewed. When the decision is made, it is common practice to telephone the successful applicant and then follow up with a written letter of confirmation.

The following guidelines are suggested for a letter confirming a job offer.

Guidelines

1. Express your pleasure at the applicant's acceptance of the job offer.
2. Confirm basic data about the position that should be on the record so that there will be no misunderstandings.
3. Enclose descriptive literature that the new employee will be interested in reading before reporting for work.
4. Extend a warm welcome.

Dear Madelyn:

Congratulations on being selected for the position that we discussed! You should feel very proud that although there were many excellent applicants, Stickland's selected you. Please confirm your acceptance of this offer by signing in the space below and returning this letter (or a copy) to me. I will see you on March 11 at about 11:30 a.m.

                          Sincerely yours,

                          Your Name
                          Human Resources Manager

Accepted: _____
Date: _____

Analysis   Of course, you have noticed that the writer ignored the guidelines on page 249.

1. Letter A is one of those "To Whom It May Concern" messages; it has no warmth and virtually no information.
2. A serious flaw in the letter is that the writer implies that Anthony should feel very fortunate in being chosen. This is poor psychology.
3. The theme of the letter should be that Strickland's feels fortunate in obtaining the services of Madelyn Anthony.

Dear Madelyn:

I am delighted that you have accepted the position of supervisor of employee training at Strickland's. You're exactly the kind of person I had in mind when I began to advertise the job!

Although we discussed this position when we talked in my office, I think you might like to look over the official description of the duties of the supervisor of employee training. I don't believe you'll find any surprises, but if you do, we'll discuss them when I next see you.

The annual starting salary is $24,000. Since employees are paid every other week, your biweekly

check will amount to $923.08, less required with-
holdings for social security and income tax and
other deductions of your own choosing (insurance,
savings bonds, and so on). The enclosed handbook, <u>All About Strickland's--A Guide to Employ-
ees</u>, covers the subjects of voluntary deductions,
salary reviews, maximum and minimum increases,
and promotion policies. Of course, your salary
takes effect your first day on the job.

I suggest a starting date of March 11. If for
any reason this is not a convenient date, please
let me know. You are to report at 9 a.m. to our
Medical Department (second floor) for a physical
examination. Afterward, I will see you in my office and get you settled in. Since there may be
delays in Medical (depending on the number of
emergencies that must be attended to), I'll leave
my calendar open and expect you only when I see
you.

I do not know whether you plan to live at home in
Waukesha and commute to Strickland's or find a
place in Milwaukee. If the latter, I suggest
that you get in touch with Martha Guile in the
Human Resources Department; she is our "resident
expert" on housing and will be happy to help in
any way she can. By the way, Strickland's is
quite generous in granting employees time off to
find suitable living accommodations.

I am really looking forward to seeing you again,
Madelyn. In the meantime, if you need to talk to
me, just telephone me collect at 555-4170.
Welcome!

                         Sincerely,

Analysis Letters confirming job offers vary a great deal, depending on the circumstances, but this one is typical.

1. Essential information has been covered—salary, starting date, and job duties.
2. Most of the miscellaneous facts that pertain to employees will be found in the handbook enclosed.
3. Often, when the date set for reporting to work is not convenient to an applicant, the employer makes appropriate allowances, as was done here.

4. The gesture concerning housing is a thoughtful one and will give Anthony a warm feeling whether she takes advantage of the suggestion or not.

5. Note the emphasis on how pleased Strickland's is to have Madelyn Anthony—not on how lucky Anthony is at having been selected.

6. The writer might have included a line for Anthony's signature so that she can indicate her acceptance of the job. This is overly formal, in our opinion. If Anthony has changed her mind since the telephone conversation, she will let Strickland's know.

"YOUR JOB" PROJECTS

1. Write a letter that may be sent to each of the unsuccessful applicants for the position of supervisor of employee training.

2. Theresa Frattiano (see Case 1, page 241) was interviewed by C. W. Malmquist, merchandising manager at Strickland's, for the position of housewares buyer. He liked her very much and later offered her the position. She readily accepted. Malmquist will now write Frattiano the appropriate confirming letter.

   Even though Frattiano will report to another executive, you consider it your obligation, as human resources manager, to write her a letter of welcome. Criticize the following letter; then write one that you think would be more appropriate.


```
Dear Theresa:

I am delighted that you have been selected for
the position of housewares buyer at Strick-
land's.

Probably no function in retailing is more im-
portant than buying.  The buyer's job requires
not only a thorough knowledge of merchandise
and sources of supply but also a special "sixth
sense" about what customers want.  Above all,
however, is the ability to provide constant mo-
tivation for the individuals who do the sell-
ing.

I think you are uniquely qualified in all these
respects, Theresa, and I'm certain you will be
a most valuable addition to our buying staff.

I'm enclosing a special handbook, All About
Strickland's--A Guide to Employees, which con-
```

tains information about office hours, store
policy, compensation policy, and employee services and benefits. I hope you will take time
to read it before you report to work on March
16. This will save Mr. Malmquist's time.

Please feel free to call on me or any other
member of the Human Resources Department if you
have any questions whatsoever about your duties.

Sincerely yours,

SUPPLEMENTARY PROJECT

3. As the district manager for Welles Fiberboard Products, you recently interviewed J. C. Senninger for the position of sales representative. He appeared
to be an excellent candidate, and you offered him the job, which carries with
it the responsibility for calling on customers in the states of Kansas and
Colorado. He accepted the position, and you wrote him an enthusiastic letter
confirming the agreement. You suggested October 17 as the date to begin
work.

On October 16 you received a short note from Senninger saying that he
was declining the offer. His wife Jennie had just learned that they were to
have a baby, and she did not want her husband to be away from home for
long periods of time.

You think highly of young Senninger (Joe) and fully understand his position.
Write him an appropriate letter.

STYLE CHECKUP

Rewrite each of the following sentences to eliminate the redundancy or unnecessary word.

1. I promise prompt and speedy delivery of your next order.
2. Only when the true facts are known can we make an intelligent decision.
3. It is vitally essential that all software sales representatives attend the
conference.
4. Our group will meet on Wednesday at 9:30 a.m. in the morning.
5. When you have assembled together all the customer complaints, please send
them to me.

CASE 3

Letters of Congratulations and Appreciation to Employees

THE SETTINGS

1. Beverly Hartness, a member of your staff in the human resources department, recently ran a week-long seminar on effective human relations for all store managers and supervisors. You were able to sit in on most of the two-hour sessions, and you found them excellent. Several of those who attended told you how helpful the seminar had been to them. Although you congratulated Hartness in person, you make it a practice to acknowledge outstanding performance with a personal letter.

2. Recently you were asked to speak at the Tri-State Human Resources Directors Association conference on the topic "The Use and Misuse of Merit Ratings." Although you know a great deal about merit ratings from your experience at Strickland's, you do not feel that you are an authority on the subject. Kermit Parkington, who manages the small company library, helped you collect materials on the subject from various libraries and other sources. He came up with several new reports, books, articles, and newspaper clippings that were extremely helpful to you in preparing your talk.

   Your remarks were enthusiastically received by those who attended the conference, and you will write Parkington to thank him for his help.

Your Objective To extend congratulations to Hartness and express appreciation to Parkington by letter.

BACKGROUND

One of the most effective ways to build and maintain good human relations and morale in an organization is to praise employees who do outstanding work and express appreciation for special assistance. Of course, you congratulate and/or thank these people in person. However, when performance or assistance is especialy noteworthy, you put your message in writing. Often a copy of such messages is placed in the employee's personnel file, but in any event, it is something she or he can keep and show to others. The message may be written on a regular company letterhead, on an executive letterhead (usually 5½ by 8½ or 7¼ by 10½ inches), or on a memo form. Whether you use a letterhead or a memo, the message should be personalized, including a salutation, complimentary closing, and signature.

In congratulating an individual for outstanding performance or for special help, follow these guidelines.

Guidelines

1. Compliment the employee warmly, or express sincere appreciation.
2. Point out any special things that deserve specific mention.
3. If appropriate, indicate the value of the service or performance to others as well as yourself.
4. Don't get carried away by superlatives; overly flowery language can strain credibility.

SAMPLE MESSAGES

Dear Beverly:

The seminar on human relations, which was recently concluded, was very competently handled, and congratulations are in order for a good job.

                    Sincerely,

Analysis   Letter A could have been more effective.

1. Letter A is grudgingly complimentary; it is hardly the warm, personal message that Hartness would have liked.
2. We get the impression that the writer would rather not have had to bother with this "chore."
3. Note the absence of personal pronouns, which are "musts" in letters of this type.

Dear Beverly:

Your seminar on effective human relations was splendid in every way, and although I complimented you in person, I want also to express my congratulations in writing.

I especially liked your case-problem method, which created a lively give-and-take atmosphere and got everybody into the act. It was wonderful how you so tactfully turned off the "marathon talkers" to give others a chance to participate. I certainly enjoyed the sessions I sat in on, and I have had excellent reports from many of those who attended them all.

Congratulations, Beverly, on an outstanding performance. You made me very proud.

                    Sincerely,

Analysis Letter B is much superior to Letter A, for three reasons.

1. Letter B's tone is warm and friendly.
2. The letter reveals the writer's pride in Hartness's performance.
3. Note the emphasis on some of the outstanding features of the seminar and its value to other employees. The letter has *soul*.

SAMPLE LETTERS

Dear Kermit:

Without your invaluable help, I'm afraid I would have fallen flat on my face when I spoke on merit ratings at the Tri-State Human Resources Direc- tors conference. But to my surprise, nobody ac- tually walked out!

Goodness knows, I'm not an experienced speaker, but you helped to make me look like a real pro. How can I possibly thank you enough?

                    Yours,

Analysis Letter A is an example of what we meant by *straining credibility*.

1. It is a bit flowery and, at the same time, self-effacing.
2. Although Parkington may be flattered and pleased, we think he is likely to be embarrassed instead.

Dear Kermit:

You'll be pleased to know, I think, that "our" speech at the Tri-State Human Resources Directors conference last week was very well received. In fact, I had nine requests for copies of it.

I'm so glad that I could present something really new on the old subject of merit ratings, and I certainly wouldn't have had access to many of the sources I quoted from without your help. Thank you!

                    Sincerely,

Analysis Letter B is effective and well-balanced.

1. The writer has been completely positive and expresses appreciation to Parkington in a very effective way.

2. There is no false modesty, no flowery superlatives.

3. Most important, the letter is *believable*.

"YOUR JOB" PROJECTS

1. Every other week the human resources department presents a two-day orientation program for new employees. All department managers at Strickland's appear on the program to discuss the activities of their departments and explain how they relate to other departments in the company. During last week's program, C. W. Malmquist, the merchandising manager, was out of town; he has asked Theresa Frattiano (see Project 2, pages 252 to 253) to speak in his place. Frattiano described her first six weeks at Strickland's, putting herself in the new employees' shoes and discussing the dos and don'ts of "learning the ropes" at Strickland's. The presentation was not only amusing but also informative, and it was evident that the employees thoroughly enjoyed it. (In your opinion, the talk was particularly effective because Frattiano is a relatively new employee herself.) Write an appropriate letter of appreciation and congratulations to Frattiano.

2. A reporter from the publication *Modern Human Resources Management* heard you speak at the Tri-State Human Resources Directors conference and later wrote to invite you to write an article for the magazine ("The Use and Misuse of Merit Ratings"). You agreed to do so. After you prepared the final draft of the article, you asked Ernest Akers, advertising manager of the company, who writes frequently for publication, to read the draft for clarity and correctness. He did so and offered many suggestions about organization, headings, style, and grammar. The editor of *Modern Human Resources Management* accepted the article, saying that it was superbly written and required virtually no editing. Write Akers an appropriate letter of appreciation.

SUPPLEMENTARY PROJECT

3. As a regional sales supervisor for Roble Business Forms, you received a letter from Earl McDowell, vice president of Chambers-Fox Corporation—a large and long-time customer—praising your new sales representative, Sally Boaz, who made her first call on McDowell a week ago. He mentioned her "wonderful personality and knowledge of Roble products." At the same time, he placed a large order for continuous invoice forms. Write an appropriate letter to Sally Boaz. (Letters from customers praising sales representatives are extremely rare.)

STYLE CHECKUP

Rewrite the following to eliminate excess words.

1. This is to acknowledge receipt of your kind order and express my appreciation for same.

2. Your order for 16 copies of Handel's *Messiah* arrived early this week, and they are being placed in today's mail.
3. Notwithstanding the fact that you promised to send your check by December 15, I am sorry to advise you that it has not arrived in this office as of this date, December 21.
4. In the event that you continue to ignore the terms of your contractual agreement with us, termination is an alternative that must be considered.
5. This is to acknowledge your letter, which arrived during the time that Mr. Kinkaid is on an extended business trip, which will take him from his desk for about seven days.

CASE 4
Congratulating a Coworker on a Promotion

THE SETTING

It has just been announced that Gerald Dembofski, chief accountant at Strickland's, has been named vice president and treasurer of the company. You have known Dembofski for about three years. Not only has he been very helpful to you in guiding you in the preparation of financial statements required of the human resources department; he has become a personal friend as well. You have frequently sought his advice on compensation and other financial matters and always received his full cooperation.

Your Objective   To write a sincere letter of congratulations to Dembofski.

BACKGROUND

In the typical business firm, hardly a day goes by that somebody doesn't receive a promotion or an honor or do something worthy of favorable comment. To write or not to write depends very much on your relationship to the person who was honored. There is no real reason to write to people you do not know personally or whom you do know and have no particular regard for. In the situation described, it seems very much in order for you to write to your friend Gerald Dembofski. On the other hand, if, say, the adjustments manager—a person who has always been cold and unfriendly to you—received a similar promotion, chances are that you would not write.

Let's assume that you do decide to write to the adjustments manager. What could you say that would have any real meaning? What do you think of this?

Dear Mrs. Vereen:

I was personally delighted to learn of your promotion to the position of vice president and director of customer relations at Strickland's.

Although I have not had the privilege of working closely with you, I know what a wonderful job you have done as adjustments manager and the excellent reputation you have throughout the company. Certainly, it seems obvious that you are the logical choice for the position to which you have been promoted.

I extend heartiest congratulations and wish you every success.

Very sincerely yours,

People have been known to write such a letter to a person for whom they have no particular liking or respect, calling it simply "good politics." We think it is completely phony. True, the recipient probably won't be offended, but she is likely to be very surprised and perhaps a bit startled at the writer's audacity.

In writing a letter of congratulations on an important promotion to a co-worker whom you greatly admire and respect, follow these guidelines.

Guidelines

1. If you have the opportunity to congratulate the individual in person or on the telephone, by all means do so. Then follow up with a letter that refers to the conversation.
2. Express appreciation for any favors or acts of friendship that have been extended to you, being specific about that person's value to you (if any) in doing your job.
3. Extend warm congratulations and best wishes.
4. Avoid effusiveness and superlatives unless the person to whom you are writing is a special friend and has profoundly influenced your career.

SAMPLE LETTERS

 Dear Jerry:

I can't think of anything that has happened during my tenure at Strickland's that pleased me as much as your promotion to vice president and treasurer.

I'm sure it's no secret to you that I simply
could not have functioned in my job without your
guiding hand, and it is impossible for me to find
the words to express my heartfelt appreciation.
Nobody but nobody can ever take your place in my
esteem!

I know you will do an absolutely smashing job in
your new position. Certainly, I can't think of a
soul who deserves this honor as much as you do,
and I'm thrilled and delighted that others recog-
nize your superlative talents.

Yours,

Analysis   Without knowing more about the relationship between the writer
and Gerald Dembofski, it is difficult to categorically denounce Letter A as a
gushy letter. However, if Dembofski is merely a friendly colleague who was of
considerable assistance, then the message truly strains credibility.

1. The statement in the first paragraph is very unlikely to be true; surely, certain
   personal triumphs must have been equally rewarding (or a great deal more
   so).
2. The second paragraph lays it on too heavily. It's not likely that one somewhat
   removed from the writer's domain of human resources management could
   deserve so much credit for one's job performance. Nor does the writer know
   whether another person might be equally (or more) esteemed later.
3. The last paragraph is plainly effusive. No matter how patient and helpful
   Dembofski was, it does not seem that he could be honestly accorded so many
   superlatives.

B

Dear Jerry:

Although I said it to you on the telephone, I
feel that I must put in writing my immense pleasure at your promotion to vice president and
treasurer.

You've been a great help to me for the past three
years, and my elation about your ascent to "the
throne" is tempered just a bit by the realization
that I'll be assigned a new mentor very soon.
Let's just hope that that person is as patient
and kind as you have been.

Hearty congratulations, Jerry, and warmest wishes

for success in your new role. I'm confident that
the right person was chosen for it!

                         Sincerely,

Analysis   This is an appropriate congratulatory letter to a person whom you
admire and respect and consider a personal friend.

1. Everything in the letter rings true.
2. Dembofski should be able to read the message with much pleasure and
   satisfaction.

"YOUR JOB" PROJECTS

1. Your administrative assistant, Grace Laviska, preceded you by five years at
   Strickland's; she worked for your predecessor before you arrived on the
   scene. She has been a conscientious, loyal, and efficient employee. Not once
   during the years she has worked for you have there been disagreements
   between you. Laviska really helped to break you in on the job when you
   became the manager of human resources. She offered suggestions born of
   long experience, yet not once did she try to tell you how to do your job or
   volunteer advice.

   Recently the president of Strickland's, Kenneth Grimes, lost his executive
   assistant because of retirement. Because you know this job would represent
   an important step upward for Laviska, you recommended her to Grimes.

   When you heard the good news, you were enormously pleased, yet at the
   same time, you think of Laviska as your "indispensable right arm" and are
   very sorry to have her leave you. Write Laviska a personal letter of congratulations. (You have already discussed the new assignment with her in person.)

2. Two weeks ago the president of Strickland's announced a new position in
   the company—director of community relations. The person chosen for the
   job was Ernest Akers, advertising manager (see Project 2, page 257). Although
   you are not a close personal friend of Akers', you have occasional contacts
   with him (he helped you with your article for *Modern Personnel Management*) and have a high regard for his work. You consider Strickland's
   advertising exceptionally creative, and on many occasions you have heard
   your friends outside the company refer to "those classy Strickland's ads."
   Write Akers an appropriate letter of congratulations. (You have not previously
   talked with him about this important promotion.) Assume that when Akers
   starts in his new position, you and he will have a closer relationship than
   previously.

SUPPLEMENTARY PROJECT

3. Assume that you were graduated from Bradley University, in Peoria. You read
   in the current issue of *Bradley Update*, a monthly magazine for students

and alumni, that Dr. Louise Misa has been appointed head of the Department of Behavioral Sciences at the university. You studied psychology with Professor Misa and had a special regard for her. She was known as a tough professor, but she was an excellent teacher, and under her rather stiff professional exterior was a very warm and friendly person with a delightful sense of humor. Today you are employed as a labor-management specialist for a large manufacturer of agricultural machinery in Cleveland, and you still remember and use much of what you learned in Misa's classes. Write her an appropriate letter acknowledging her promotion.

STYLE CHECKUP

In each of the following sentences, one or more words have been omitted. Supply the missing word(s).

1. This $15 calculator is as good, if not better than, the $50 one.
2. Representative Atkins made more calls last month than any salesperson.
3. The programmers had little knowledge and sympathy for the proposed changes in the software.
4. The walkways have been repaired and the sign replaced.

C A S E
5

Writing Letters of Sympathy

THE SETTING

During the past week, death touched the lives of two people who mean something to you. The mother of Loraine Carlson passed away. You had met Mrs. Carlson at a luncheon you hosted in honor of Loraine's first anniversary. A very warm and vivacious lady, Mrs. Carlson was obviously very proud of her daughter and told you how much it meant to Loraine to be employed at Strickland's.

The wife of a favorite professor at the college you attended also died during the week. The professor, Dr. J. H. Harrison, became a close friend when you were his student, and you attended many evening seminars in the Harrison home. Mrs. Harrison was a gracious hostess, and you became very fond of her.

Your Objective To write both Loraine Carlson and Professor Harrison a personal note of sympathy.

BACKGROUND

Perhaps the most difficult of all letters are those expressing sympathy to people who have suffered personal losses. The first question is, of course, should you write? Many people do not. Some express their sympathy in person and/or send a printed sympathy card with a very short note. Others prefer to send a gift such as flowers, a book, or a record or tape. In some instances, though, you will feel that it is appropriate to express your condolences by letter.

In writing letters of sympathy, follow these guidelines.

Guidelines

1. Always write in your own hand and on social stationery. Never use a company letterhead.
2. Make the message brief.
3. Express your sympathy sincerely, but don't be maudlin.
4. Try to recall something that is remembered as a pleasant experience involving the deceased.

SAMPLE LETTERS

 A

Dear Loraine:

Please accept my sincerest sympathy in your great loss. Although I met your mother only once (at your anniversary luncheon), it was a wonderful experience being with the two of you--you were obviously so proud of her and she of you. I liked her immediately and wish I could have known her better.

When a close relative of mine passed away a few months ago, a friend sent me the enclosed poem by Rachel Leighton. It gave me much comfort, and I hope it will do the same for you.

Sincerely,

Analysis   The writer faced a difficult task but responded effectively.

1. The letter is brief, warm, and sympathetic.
2. Note that the writer emphasizes a pleasant experience with the deceased rather than dwelling on the tragedy.
3. An appropriate poem or quotation can also be quite effective.

B Dear Professor Harrison:

The news of Mrs. Harrison's death has just reached me, and I want to extend to you my deepest sympathy.

I count those evenings in the Harrison home among the highlights of my college career. Flo (which she insisted we call her) was certainly a friend to the Humanities Seminar crowd; I will never forget her warmth, cheerfulness, and thoughtfulness. (And I have yet to taste a fondue that equaled hers!)

I hope that I will see you one of these days. Is there a chance that you will be coming to Milwaukee for any reason? I'm the personnel manager at Strickland's, and I would enjoy showing you how I'm putting to good use some of the things you taught me.

Best personal regards,

Analysis   Letter B is excellent as well.

1. The writer's tone is sympathetic, yet the emphasis is on pleasant events involving the deceased.
2. The final paragraph may help to take Harrison's mind off the tragedy.

"YOUR JOB" PROJECTS

Letters of sympathy are the most personal of all messages, and whether to write them is always a matter of individual choice. The two examples illustrated in the preceding pages are imaginary, of course. Those who choose to write messages of condolence will have highly emotional reasons for doing so. Because a really effective letter cannot be composed if the writer has not actually felt a deep personal tragedy, no projects are assigned for this case.

STYLE CHECKUP

Rewrite each of the following sentences to eliminate negative statements.
1. You failed to sign the contract that you recently returned to us.
2. Your order cannot be filled until we receive your bank credit card number.
3. Obviously, you overlooked the fact that we require 50 percent of the total amount on a COD order, as indicated on page 16 of our catalog.
4. Do not hesitate to tell me when you are unhappy with our services.
5. The cheapest electronic typewriter we sell is priced at $2,500.

CASE 6 · Writing a Reference Letter

THE SETTING

For about six months Edith McGrath was an editorial assistant on the monthly employee newsletter, *Strickland's Speaking*, which is published under your supervision. Although she was a competent editorial assistant and writer, McGrath proved to be unsatisfactory. She was constantly late for work, often called in "sick," showed little interest in the job, and frequently missed important deadlines, which proved to be costly. You talked with the employee on numerous occasions, but she did not respond to your warnings, and you finally had to let her go.

When McGrath applied to another firm for a similar position, you received a letter from the human resources director inquiring about her employment record at Strickland's.

Your Objective   To respond to the request for information about the former employee.

BACKGROUND

At some time during your business career, you are likely to be asked to supply information about a person who was under your supervision. Most companies check out all job applicants who are being considered for employment by writing not only to the references supplied by the applicants but to former employers as well. The following form letter is typical; it is addressed to the director of personnel, whose name is not known to the writer.

Dear Sir or Madam:

George Alexander has applied to us for the position of computer programmer. He lists your company as a former employer.

Would you please give us your assessment of this applicant--work habits, ability, character, potential, personality, and any other traits that would help us to evaluate him as a potential employee.

Your statement will, of course, be kept in strict confidence. An addressed, stamped envelope is enclosed for your reply. Thank you.

                    Very truly yours,

Responding to such a request can be very simple if you have a high opinion of the applicant and sincerely believe that that person would be an asset to the company applied to. Follow these guidelines.

Guidelines

1. Express your pleasure in writing in behalf of the applicant.
2. Describe the qualities that make the applicant an excellent candidate.
3. If appropriate, explain the reasons for the former employee's leaving the firm.
4. Add any personal testimonial concerning the candidate that you believe would strengthen that person's chances of obtaining the position.

Following is an example of a favorable response to the request for information about George Alexander. It satisfies the guidelines above.

```
Dear Miss Seaton:

It is a pleasure for me to write in behalf of
George Alexander, who has applied for the posi-
tion of computer programmer in your company.

I have known George Alexander for over three
years, first as a fellow programmer and later as
his supervisor.  I consider him an extremely com-
petent person, highly dependable, and very intel-
ligent.  He works well with people, and I con-
sider his record here outstanding.

When George told me that he was leaving us (he
had to return to the family farm in Iowa because
of his father's illness), I was very sorry to see
him go.  In my opinion, the organization that em-
ploys George Alexander will make no mistake.


                    Sincerely yours,
```

Writing a letter concerning a former employee with a poor employment record, however, can present problems. Recent federal laws give people the right to examine their personal files, and derogatory statements contained in those files could result in a legal suit. For this reason it is the policy in many companies to divulge only the dates of employment and the job title and duties.

The kind of letter you write about an incompetent employe will, then, depend on company policy. In our discussion we assume that you are free to say what is on your mind and that you choose to give other employers a completely candid appraisal of the former employee. This is what you would hope to get when you request information from former employers of applicants for jobs in your company.

SAMPLE LETTERS

Dear Mr. Phineas:

I do not feel competent to evaluate the qualifications of Edith McGrath for a position as an editorial assistant in your company. She was under
my supervision too short a time for me to make a
truly meaningful assessment of her.

Yours very truly,

Analysis   Some people, instead of saying anything negative about an applicant whom they really can't speak highly of, resort to a noncommittal letter. Letter A is of this type; in our opinion, it is poor.

1. It could be argued that even though the writer has said nothing bad about Edith McGrath, the letter is really a condemnation. In other words, what is left unsaid often speaks as loudly as an outright denunciation.
2. This is a dishonest letter, and we think it is unfair to the person who requested the information.

Dear Mr. Phineas:

Edith McGrath, about whom you inquired, was an
editorial assistant under my supervision for
about six months (March 15 to August 13 of last
year). I found her to be a helpful assistant and
a talented writer; the copy she produced was always sharp and interesting.

Personally, I see no reason why Miss McGrath cannot do a good job for you.

Cordially yours,

Analysis   Some letters discuss only the favorable qualities of a discharged employee, ignoring the request for information about character, dependability, performance, and so on. Although it is honest in some respects, Letter B is an example of a half-truth.

1. It is true that Edith McGrath was competent and wrote good copy for the employee news bulletin, but she was also undependable.
2. Still, those who use this approach may believe that it is unfair to condemn an employee who is basically competent but simply lacked interest in the job. We disagree with this theory; basic competence and outstanding job performance are often worlds apart.

C

Dear Mr. Phineas:

I appreciate your letter in which you inquire about the employment record of Edith McGrath.

Edith was an editorial assistant on our employee news bulletin for about six months (February 15 to August 13 of last year) and was directly under my supervision. Although she was an excellent writer and assistant, her overall job performance was not satisfactory. Her attendance was sporadic; she was absent from work a great deal, frequently missed deadlines, and showed little interest in her work. Although I discussed these matters with her a number of times, the problems were never resolved, and finally I had to let her go.

Perhaps, Mr. Phineas, the position Edith held here didn't challenge her enough--or possibly she had personal problems that she could not resolve. Basically, she is an intelligent and likable person, and I really felt bad that I could not motivate her to perform up to her capabilities.

Sincerely yours,

Analysis   It could be argued that the writer of Letter C has shot down Edith McGrath's chances at another job and, for that reason, is heartless. People will differ in their opinions as to how best to handle this matter. We think it is a suitable letter.

1. The writer has spoken the truth yet has given McGrath credit for the positive attributes she does possess.
2. We think the writer used good judgment in not being more apologetic for not having done a better job of motivating McGrath.
3. Although there is a chance that the writer is as much at fault as the employee, it is the employee's responsibility to adapt to the supervisor's personality— not vice versa.

"YOUR JOB" PROJECTS

1. Basil Jenkins joined Strickland's on February 16 of the current year as a general clerk in the department of human resources. He left the company on

August 22 of his own accord, giving this as his reason: "I don't like this job or this company." In fact, you were about to release Jenkins anyhow. His attitude was sullen, he was habitually late for work and often sneaked out before closing time, and his job performance was well below par.

Actually, it is your opinion that Jenkins was underemployed—that is, he appeared to be very intelligent, but because he felt that the job was far beneath his capabilities, he simply coasted. You explained that the best way to get a more challenging and important position in the company was to handle his present job in a highly capable manner. He refused to accept this advice.

Recently you received a form letter from Wassau Chemical Company (Abagail Franklin) asking for your assessment of Jenkins, who has applied for the position of assistant customer services manager.

a. Assume that it is the policy in your company to give only basic facts about an unsatisfactory employee, saying nothing derogatory. Write the letter.

b. Assume that you are free to supply complete details to Abagail Franklin about Basil Jenkins's employment record at Strickland's. Write the letter.

2. Three months ago Homer Cox announced that he was forced to resign from his position as supervisor of the recruiting section. His widowed father has been stricken with a terminal illness, and Cox must return to the family home in Racine to take care of his father.

Last week you received a letter from Paul Goshen, president of the Racine Manufacturing Company, asking about Cox's employment record at Strickland's and your assessment of his fitness for the position of assistant human resources manager. You think Cox would be excellent for the job. Write the letter.

SUPPLEMENTARY PROJECT

3. As a district sales manager of Mohawk Book Company, you hired Felicia Cherner for the position of sales representative. You explained that she will call on bookstores, libraries, and large business firms in Massachusetts. Vermont, and New Hampshire. She quickly proved to be an excellent choice for the job. Sales in her territory nearly doubled in the first six months, and judging from the information you received from customers as well as other sales representatives, she was extremely popular and effective.

Nearly seven months after Cherner joined your organization, she submitted her resignation. In her letter she said she really enjoyed selling and the people with whom she associated; however, she found that being on the road for weeks at a time was very tiring, and she missed seeing her family and hometown friends. Because you had no other position to offer Cherner, you reluctantly accepted her resignation.

A few days ago you received an inquiry about Cherner from Beacon Printers, where she has applied for the job of sales representative for the Greater Boston area. (Her hometown is nearby Wellesley.) Write a letter of reference in behalf of Felicia Cherner; address it to Marshall Rafferty.

STYLE CHECKUP

In each of the following sentences, change the passive voice to the active voice.

1. Your check for $267.16 was received today with much appreciation.
2. Shipment will be made this week of most of the electronic office equipment you ordered.
3. The Palmer House in Chicago was chosen for our conference.
4. The research for the media report was done by Arlene Johns.
5. Photo-Metrics was selected by the production manager to prepare the microfilm.

CHAPTER 15
EMPLOYMENT COMMUNICATIONS

YOUR JOB HUNT

You are approaching graduation, and the time has come for you to make definite plans for getting a job.

If your education and training have equipped you for a position for which there is a big demand, then all you may have to do is present yourself to the human resources department where an opening exists and ask for an application blank. If the job proves to be exactly what you had hoped for and you expect to hold on to it "forever," then you won't need to know a lot about employment communications.

However, for most people this isn't a realistic situation. When they are ready to seek a job, they often find that there are few openings in their chosen field and a large number of applicants going after those few jobs. And even those who have no trouble landing their first job may not keep it very long. Millions of people change jobs several times during their working lives. They may quickly find out that they don't like the type of business the organization is engaged in, or they're unhappy about working conditions and the lack of opportunities for advancement, or they don't get along with their supervisor, or they want to live in another area, or they simply get tired of what they're doing and want to try something entirely different. And one more thing: People who are happy in a position and are doing a good job may be laid off because of bad economic conditions.

The chances are great, then, that at some time in your career, you'll have a need to make use of the job-getting techniques discussed in this chapter.

CASE 1
Assessing and Conveying Your Qualifications

THE SETTING

Since we don't know your job interests and qualifications, we'll illustrate job-getting techniques and employment communications by using two fictitious people who are about to graduate and are getting ready to apply for a position.

Stephen R. Ludlum will receive his B.B.A. degree in June from the University of Baltimore, where he majored in marketing. He has seen a want ad in the

Baltimore Sun for a management trainee position in marketing research and has decided to apply for it.

Roberta R. Eubank will receive her A.A. degree in June from the College of San Mateo (California), where she majored in secretarial administration with a minor in accounting. The placement director of the college, Ralph Meadows, received a telephone call from Western Container Corporation, in Oakland; the firm is looking for an individual to fill the position of executive assistant to the controller. Meadows suggested to Eubank that she apply for the job.

Your Objective   To present the qualifications of Stephen Ludlum and Roberta Eubank for the positions they want.

BACKGROUND

The first step in getting ready to apply for a position that is known to be open is to learn precisely what the requirements are for it and then match your qualifications with those requirements.

The want ad that Stephen Ludlum is interested in is as follows:

LARGE COMPANY
seeks management trainees in marketing research. College degree required, pref. in marketing or bus. adm. Writing skill essential, plus ability to meet and work with clients. Some sales exper. helpful but not essential. Good starting salary, oppor. for advancement, excel. benefits. Send application and resume to Wilson Goddard, Box 417, this newspaper.

The notes made by Ralph Meadows when he talked to Western Container Corporation's human resources recruiter follow:

```
Exec. asst. to vp and controller (Carolyn May-
heu), Western Container Corp., Oakland.  Some
secretarial exp. req.  Must have good shorthand
and typ. skills and fundamental knowl. of ac-
counting.  Will assist in preparing numerous re-
ports.  Send data sheet and appl. to Miss Mayheu.
(Very good job.)
```

When Ludlum and Eubank are fairly confident that they are qualified to fill the vacancies described, they will be ready to set down on paper the things about themselves that will impress an employer.

Guidelines

1. The presentation of an applicant's qualifications may be called a résumé, a data sheet, a personal profile, or a qualifications summary. No matter what it is called, this brief history should enable prospective employers to determine quickly whether the applicant is worth their time to invite in for an interview. No one is hired for an important job without an interview, and the main purpose of the résumé is to secure that interview. Actually, then, it is a sales document. If it fails to impress an employer, then the applicant will probably receive an "I'm sorry" letter without getting the chance to appear in person to tell her or his story.

2. Since the résumé is your personal sales representative, make sure that it puts you in the best possible light. If possible, it should be typewritten (well-inked ribbon, clean type) on a good grade of white bond paper. If, however, you expect to use the résumé for several job applications, you may have to duplicate it. The best method is photocopying; be sure to insist on the sharpest reproduction possible.

3. Keep your résumé to two pages if you can. In some cases one page may be all you need, but don't squeeze and condense merely for the sake of brevity.

4. The résumé should make the most of all your assets. Obviously, you will not indulge in self-glorification; but at the same time, don't be modest about the things you have achieved that may attract an employer's interest. If, for example, you made the dean's list in college, or attended school on a scholarship, or were graduated with honors, by all means point this out.

SAMPLE RÉSUMÉS

The résumés for Stephen Ludlum and Roberta Eubank follow. As you examine them, refer to the discussion on the preceding pages.

Ludlum's Résumé

```
                    STEPHEN R. LUDLUM
                     518 Burnett Road
                Randallstown, Maryland 21123
                  Telephone: (301) 555-1234


    Position: Management Trainee in Marketing Research

EDUCATION

Degree: B.B.A. (June 1989), University of Baltimore
        Major:  Marketing  Minor:  General Business
```

CONTINUED

Marketing Courses:
| Marketing Principles | Advertising Media | Motivation Research |
| Marketing Research | Marketing Management | Principles of Distribution |

Other Business Courses:
| Business Statistics | Accounting 1 and 2 | Business Finance |
| Business Communication | Business Law | Electronic Data Processing |

Comments: B+ average in all marketing courses (on Dean's List past two years). Make A's on all research reports; two were exhibited as models of excellence.

EXPERIENCE

June–September, 1988   Warehouse clerk, Tracy's Discount Store, Randallstown, MD. Filled customer orders, maintained inventory, supervised two part-time helpers.

July–August, 1987   Salesperson, Higganbotham's Pharmacy, Randallstown. Made special deliveries, assisted customers, did stockkeeping.

June–September, 1986   Sales representative, Cavell Home Products. Sold housewares door to door.

1982–85 (various dates)   Laborer (street repair), filling station helper, carwash attendant

ORGANIZATIONS AND HOBBIES

Organizations: Webster Debating Club; American Marketing Association (student member): Tau Kappa Epsilon (Grammateus, 1987–88); Managing Editor of Scroll (student poetry magazine), 1986–87; tennis team, 1987–89.

Hobbies: Building and flying model planes, tennis, writing short stories

PERSONAL DATA: On request.

REFERENCES

Dr. Christine Hale, Professor of Marketing, University of Baltimore
Mr. A. T. Tracy, Tracy's Discount Store, Randallstown, MD 21123
Judge R. N. Toffenetti, 272 Burnett Road, Randallstown, MD 21123

Eubank's Résumé

```
                    Qualifications of
                    ROBERTA R. EUBANK
                      17 Cayuga Lane
              Redwood City, California  94064
                      (415) 555-2788

Position applied Executive Assistant to Miss Carolyn Mayheu
   for            Vice-President and Controller
                  Western Container Corporation

EXPERIENCE

At present        Administrative assistant to the Dean of
                  Faculties, College of San Mateo. In this
                  position, which I have held all this aca-
                  demic year while a student, I have the
                  following responsibilities:

                  1. Take all the Dean's dictation (often
                     heavy); type memorandums and reports,
                     many of which are statistical;  receive
                     visitors;  keep the Dean's appointment
                     calendar;  prepare minutes of all meet-
                     ings chaired by the Dean.

                  2. Write letters and reports for the
                     Dean's signature and others for my own.
                     Assist in research for reports and ar-
                     ticles.

                  3. Supervise two student clerks.

                  4. Prepare financial reports.

1988 (summer)     Clerk-stenographer at California Bank
                  (Redwood City branch).
                  Took some dictation and typed letters,
                  contracts, bank documents, and financial
                  statements.

1986-87           Salesclerk (after school and on Saturdays)
                  at The Factory Outlet Store, Redwood City.
                  Did floor selling and assisted in the of-
                  fice (customer accounts).
```

CONTINUED

EDUCATION

   <u>College</u>

      Attend College of San Mateo, majoring in Secretarial
      Administration. Will be graduated in June, 1989, with
      A.A. degree.

      Business Courses Completed:

         Shorthand (120 words a minute)
         Typewriting (78 words a minute)
         Business Communications (grammar, vocabulary, letter
         writing, report writing)--two semesters
         Secretarial Procedures
         Accounting (principles, cost, intermediate, data
         processing)
         Mathematics of Accounting and Finance--two semesters
         Computer Programming

   <u>High School</u>

      Graduated from Redwood City High School, 1987. Took the
      business curriculum, which included shorthand, typewrit-
      ing, secretarial practice, personal development, busi-
      ness English, office machines, and bookkeeping.

   <u>Scholastic Honors and Activities</u>

      National Honor Society (high school)
      Glee Club (soloist), Redwood City High School
      College of San Mateo Choral Ensemble
      Paid soloist at St. Andrews Episcopal Church, San Mateo
      Voted outstanding student in Secretarial Administration,
      1989

OTHER INTERESTS

      Skiing, scuba diving, working with handicapped children
      (music)

PERSONAL DATA

      Birth Date: January 12, 1970
      Physical: Weight, 120; height, 5'5"
      Health: Excellent

CONTINUED

```
REFERENCES (by permission)

    Dr. J. Willa Patrick, Chairman, Department of Secretar-
       ial Administration, College of San Mateo. Tel.: 555-
       1527

    Dr. Philip Caulfield, Dean of Faculties, College of San
       Mateo.  Tel.: 555-1744

    Rev. J. C. Butterfield, St. Andrews Episcopal Church,
       San Mateo.  Tel.: 555-4756.
```

Analysis   Note the following about Résumés A and B.

1. *Sections and headings.* The sections used in the résumé and the manner in which the information is displayed vary from person to person and according to the requirements of the position applied for. Usually, there are at least six sections: personal identification, position wanted, education, experience, personal information, and references.

2. *Personal identification.* You will want to identify yourself at the top of the résumé, including your name, address, and telephone number. You may or may not choose to give the document a name or heading. Note that Ludlum has not done so, while Eubank has (*Qualifications of*). If you decide to label your résumé, here are two possibilities:

```
                      Resume of
                  CARLOS C. NOGALES
                  1977 DuBlanc Avenue
               Monroe, Louisiana 71201
                   (318) 555-6107


                  ELLEN C. GRANVILLE
               Job Qualifications Summary
                  1642 West Rocks Road
               Norwalk, Connecticut 06850
               Telephone:  (203) 555-9150
```

3. *Position applied for.* Human resources managers strongly urge applicants to specify the job they are applying for. If you do not know the title of the job—or indeed whether there *is* a job opening—identify as closely as you can the work you are most interested in.

   Both Ludlum and Eubank know the title of the position they are applying for and have stated it. Note that Eubank includes the name and title of the person to whom she is applying as well as the company name. This is quite effective in personalizing the résumé and attracting favorable attention.

   If you don't know the exact title of the job you want, try to give the employer a hint. For example, rather than indicate *Advertising* as your job preference, you might say *Advertising* (*art, layout, design*). Instead of using *Sales*, you might use *Outside Sales Representative*. And *Computer Operator* is preferable to *Electronic Data Processing*.

4. *Education*. If you have had no experience in the position applied for, the main thing you have to sell is your education. Thus this will be your first side heading (see Stephen Ludlum's résumé). Ludlum and Eubank's setups for listing the courses that are of special importance differ slightly—there is no one best way to list courses. Note the emphasis Ludlum has given to marketing courses, followed by his achievements in these courses and the research reports written. This is a good example of adapting the résumé to fit the specific job applied for.

Eubank has included her high school education, while Ludlum has not. This is a good idea in her case, since it gives her an opportunity to list additional business training and, later, indicate that she was an honor student and active in music. Obviously, Ludlum felt that his high school education and achievements were not worthy of mention. Or perhaps this information was omitted in order to limit the résumé to one page. In any event, it is standard practice for those who have mainly education to sell to name the high school graduated from and list any courses or activities that an employer might be interested in.

5. *Experience*. The job that Roberta Eubank is applying for requires experience as a secretary, and since she meets this requirement nicely, she lists experience before education. Actually, in this instance it was an arbitrary decision. However, when individuals have had several important jobs over a period of, say, five to ten years, experience is mainly what they should emphasize; that is, it should be listed first.

Almost any job held for which payment was received is worth mentioning, whether it was a part-time job, a full-time job, or a job held during summer vacations. For example, Ludlum's brief experience in selling could give him a leg up on other applicants who lack any such experience (remember, the want ad said "Some sales experience helpful...."). In any event, the fact that an applicant has held one or more jobs—whether they relate to the position applied for or not—is an indication of that person's willingness to work. Ludlum even mentioned such jobs as street repairer, filling station worker, and car-wash attendant. There is nothing wrong with this; such jobs at least indicate a certain independence.

Observe that work experience is usually listed by year. An applicant should start with the most recent job and work backward.

6. *Organizations and hobbies*. Ludlum has used a single heading to describe the organizations he belonged to in college and the hobbies he enjoys. Eubank has used two. Either style is fine. The important thing is to reveal to an employer something that will provide clues as to the kind of person you are. For example, your membership in organizations says something about your liking to mix with people; the offices held, about your leadership ability; and special interests, about your general personality. Note that Ludlum has

mentioned short-story writing as a hobby. This is another example of adapting the résumé to fit a particular job; if he had applied for a position that did not require writing ability, he might not have included this hobby.

7. *Personal data.* Whether you include personal data is up to you. Including such information is not a requirement, and the tendency these days is to omit it. If you want to include personal data on your résumé, we suggest that you provide no more information than Eubank did. It is neither necessary nor wise to mention religious preference, ancestry, or marital status. Although this data may be important to you, it is not likely to interest an employer—indeed, it might even suggest bias.

8. *References.* We recommend that you list at least three references on the résumé. (The only exception is when you are already employed and don't want your references to be contacted until you're pretty certain the job you're applying for is in the bag. In this case you simply say on the résumé, "References supplied on request.")

   Since education will probably be your most marketable asset, make sure that at least one of your references is a dean, a professor, or some other college person who knows you well. If you've held a job or two (even a temporary or part-time job), you may want to list one of the employers as a reference. And many people include a person who can vouch for their general character—a priest, a minister, a rabbi, a prominent citizen, or a family friend who has achieved some local stature.

   It's a cardinal rule that you never use a person's name without first asking for permission. This can be done by means of a telephone call, a visit, or a letter. Stephen Ludlum's letter to one of his references follows.


```
Dear Judge Toffenetti:


Graduation is only a few weeks away, and if
everything goes right, I will receive my B.B.A.
degree from the University of Baltimore on
June 2.  I don't know who will be happier--me
or my dad!

Now I'm getting ready to look for a job.  My
interest is in marketing research, and I hope
to find perhaps a management trainee position
in a large company not too far away.  May I in-
clude your name as a reference on my applica-
tion?  If you are willing to vouch for me, just
write "OK" at the bottom of this letter and
return it to me in the enclosed stamped enve-
lope.

Best wishes to you and Mrs. Toffenetti.  I will
```

be in Randallstown about June 8, and I hope to
see both of you then.

                    Sincerely,

"YOUR JOB HUNT" PROJECT

Prepare résumés for any two of the following 20 positions, emphasizing in each one the skills or abilities you possess that match the employer's requirements.

1. PERSONNEL ASSISTANT (JOB EVALUATION). Excellent opportunity for college-trained person in personnel department of large advertising agency. Must have at least two years of college, preferably in personnel or business administration. We'll train you, and you earn as you learn. Write to Box M1465, Post. An equal opportunity employer.

2. PERSONNEL INTERVIEWER. We want people who are interested in a career in human resources administration, and interviewing prospective employees is an ideal place to start. Business training (some college) required. Must be able to speak well, present good appearance, write reports. In this job you will learn to interview, screen, and test applicants for jobs. Send résumé to Box 14, Times.

3. MANAGER TRAINEE. Publicly owned multimillion-dollar building company needs person to train for manager of new subdivision. Must have feeling for organization, marketing, sales/display, advertising, and public relations. Security, salary, and fringe benefits of major corporation. Excellent starting salary for the right person. Write Mrs. L. Jones, Suite 309, Bradley Building.

4. MANAGEMENT TRAINEE. Interested in finance? Our company has three openings for young college-educated persons who have good training in finance and are interested in managing a finance or budget department. Excellent starting salary and fringe benefits. Nationally known corporation, excellent chances for advancement. Address Box 98-C, Star-Ledger. E.O.E.

5. HOSPITAL ADMINISTRATION. Want young man or woman to train as hospital administrator. Degree preferred but not essential. Applicant should have general knowledge of accounting. This job requires an individual who can work well with people and who is strong in communication skills. Modest beginning salary but outstanding opportunities for frequent financial and career advancement. Send résumé to J. I. Trumble, 2401 Blueridge Avenue, Morristown, New Jersey 07960.

6. MANAGEMENT TRAINEES—AVIATION ACTIVITIES. Firm dealing in aviation activities (we have several government contracts) desires to interview people who have management aspirations. Good benefits, fine starting salary. Address Box 123, Inquirer.

7. SALES CAREER. Century-old international financial institution has opening for two counselors in investment and insurance. Complete two-year training program. Will consider those with no experience. For interview, send brief personal history to Box M1434, Chronicle.

8. SALES. Top opportunity for ambitious go-getter. Any good experience in

auto or route selling will help. Salary plus commission. Write Cynthia Olwell, 217 Mayfair Building.

9. SALES. We are a nationally recognized sales and marketing personnel agency, and we are seeking an intelligent, motivated, people- and sales-oriented individual capable of justifying and maintaining a five-figure income with consistency. Previous history of success in sales or personnel would be advantageous but will consider good college business administration background. Must be able to communicate effectively on all levels from recent college grad to executive. Ability to work successfully with a minimum of supervision a must. Candidate selected will take over currently productive desk. Call John Mulholland, Ajax Agency. Have résumé ready.

10. INFORMATION PROCESSING. Individual with a minimum of two years' college training in business required to operate information processing equipment. Exciting opportunity to learn automated communication methods. We teach you. Must be highly skillful typist, have strong background in English and communication, and be willing to adapt to new situations. Send résumé to Box 0072, Times.

11. MARKETING/PUBLIC RELATIONS. Rare opportunity in education field. We are interviewing for several openings in our marketing management training program. If you like people and are ambitious, hard-working, and college-trained, then you will be thoroughly trained in our successful marketing methods. Earn an excellent salary. Opportunity for advancement into management as fast as ability and performance warrant. Send résumé to Box 27, World Globe.

12. ACCOUNTANT—AUTOMOTIVE. Fast-growing auto dealership requires accountant to work closely with general manager in overall operations. Applicant must have strong background in accounting principles and be looking for a permanent position with a bright future. Some experience in automotive accounting preferred. Reply Box 2 (Mrs. Agnes Lawson), Examiner.

13. ACCOUNTING MANAGER. Growing firm has immediate need for fully qualified, aggressive accountant who can quickly develop to take full charge of general accounting and auditing functions. Knowledge of cost accounting and budgeting techniques desired. Excellent opportunity for the right person. Full package of employee benefits. Salary commensurate with education and experience. Submit résumé to Daily Blade, Box 47113.

14. COMPUTER SPECIALISTS. Well-known insurance company needs college-trained people with special interest in and knowledge of computer technology— programming, computer operation, word processing, EDP system design, and systems analysis. Excellent training program. $15,000 starting salary with opportunities for advancement. Write Box 1277, Courier-Journal, and include résumé.

15. JR. INTERNAL AUDITOR. Office of controller in large, expanding firm is seeking an individual for a full-time junior auditor's position. If you are a two- or four-year graduate or a student attending night school in accounting and want to earn while you learn, here is an excellent opportunity. No experience necessary. Salary commensurate with education. Write to Oscar Jesurun, Star Foods Inc., 6900 Landover Road. Equal opportunity employer.

16. ADMINISTRATIVE SECRETARY. No shorthand. For this spot you must be a thoroughly trained individual with emphasis in business administration, office procedures, and supervision. Lots of public contact, so you must enjoy working with all sorts of people. Can advance to department manager. Good typing ability, letter writing, routine reports. Pleasant private office. Assist president in public relations work. Résumé to Box 16, Clarion.

17. EXECUTIVE SECRETARY. Great opportunity for person with high level of stenographic skills. Work for V.P. of Marketing, assisting her in planning, research, contacts with sales representatives, advertising and promotion, and so on. General knowledge of accounting helpful but not necessary. Prefer some college. Good salary, with all benefits; sophisticated offices. Send résumé to J. T. Evans, Albert Gamble Building.

18. ADMINISTRATIVE ASSISTANT—INTERNATIONAL AND CRIMINAL LAW. Well-known lawyer seeks versatile person to be his right arm. You'll handle various administrative matters and may even attend court cases. Fast-paced and challenging opportunity, with typing and shorthand skills. No law experience needed. More of a management job than secretarial—managing the boss, supervising small clerical staff, etc. "Takeover" type desired! Write to Lawrence Applebaum, Box 4747, Centertown.

19. ADMINISTRATIVE AIDE—URBAN RENEWAL. As executive secretary to senior partner of firm dealing with urban renewal, you will be in a key administrative position where you can utilize your executive talents along with your shorthand and typing. Excellent future and benefits. Want to be "involved"? This is the place. Write to Betty Grayson, 1102 Riddell Building. An E.O.E.

20. MEDICAL SECRETARY. Medical secretary (work for Chief Medical Officer) with good skills and knowledge of medical terminology. Exciting opportunity. Write to Personnel Manager, Providence Hospital.

STYLE CHECKUP

Rewrite the following sentences to eliminate overwriting and stuffy language.

1. During the course of our conversation in my office on January 7, I mentioned the procedure for returning unsalable merchandise in which there was complete agreement between us.

2. When the Employee Suggestion Committee held its March meeting, it was decided to increase the minimum award from $15 to $25.

3. The human resources manager is engaged in making a study of local educational opportunities available to Holloway employees.

4. I suggest that we delay our decision until such time as we have more data.

5. In this day and age, it is very difficult to predict the need for workers for the period of more than a year ahead.

CASE 2

Writing the Application Letter

THE SETTING

Now that Roberta Eubank and Stephen Ludlum have completed their résumés for the positions they want, each is ready to prepare a letter of application.

Your Objective   To write letters of application that will be used to transmit their résumés to the prospective employers.

BACKGROUND

The résumé is essentially a personal history that concentrates on dates and events. But even though it is an individual presentation of one's qualifications, it is not intended to be a highly *personal* one. On the other hand, the letter of application is quite personal. Since it is accompanied by a résumé, the letter does not merely repeat the dates, events, and achievements listed in the résumé. Instead, it concentrates on why the applicant is interested in the position applied for and the applicant's special fitness for it. Its main purpose is to attract the employer's attention, create interest in the applicant, build a desire to look carefully at the résumé, and make it easy for the employer to take positive action. Thus, you see, the application letter has all the basic elements of a sales letter, which it is.

You won't need a long letter. If your résumé is complete, you should be able in less than a page to say all that needs to be said.

Guidelines

1. We mentioned earlier that you should not be overly modest in presenting your qualifications in a résumé. The same is true in writing a letter of application. However, some people think the letter should be considered as an opportunity to employ the hard sell, and they open their message something like this:

```
For the position you advertised in the May 14
Sun (management trainee in marketing research),
I'm confident that you want a person who has
outstanding training in marketing research
techniques and who is also dynamic, resource-
ful, imaginative, innovative, and intelligent.
I am such an individual!
```

Such a beginning is not likely to impress the personnel representative who screens applications for employment. The applicant will almost surely be labeled a smart aleck, and the letter will land in the wastebasket.

2. On the other hand, the application letter should have some life and reveal the applicant's self-confidence. Following is a letter that leans too far in the other direction.

```
I want to apply for the job as management
trainee in marketing research that you recently
advertised.  My resume is enclosed.

A job in your company is very appealing to me
because I want to work in Baltimore, where I
have many relatives and friends.  It is also
close to my home.  Although I have no experi-
ence, I believe I could learn the rudiments of
the job in a fairly short time.

May I hear from you at your earliest conven-
ience?
```

The letter illustrated is too apologetic. Surely, no employer will be flattered by the reason the applicant gives for wanting the job. Nor should one apologize for lacking experience, especially when the position doesn't require it. The old saying "Accentuate the positive and eliminate the negative" applies here.

3. In your letter of application, you will want to strike a chord somewhere between the boastful and modest.

SAMPLE APPLICATION LETTERS

Ludlum's Application Letter

```
                              518 Burnett Road
                              Randallstown, Maryland 21123
                              May 17, 19--

Mr. Wilson Goddard
Box 417
Baltimore Sun
Baltimore, Maryland 21215

Dear Mr. Goddard:

The position you advertised in the May 14 Sun for
a management trainee in marketing research is ex-
```

actly the opportunity I had hoped to find. As I read the ad, I felt that you were talking to me.

As you will see in the enclosed resume, I will be graduated from the University of Baltimore in early June with a major in marketing. I feel that I have an excellent marketing education (18 semester hours), supported by a broad program in general business. Of special interest to me was my work in marketing research. We not only studied modern data-gathering techniques (including interviewing and sampling methods) but were also required to read and report on significant books in the field. Two that I found especially interesting were <u>Marketing Strategies for the Computer Age</u> (E. B. Weiss) and <u>Markets and Media</u> (Martha C. Lanham), on which I wrote papers that received special honors awards.

I would like very much to meet you and tell you in person why I believe I can be useful to your organization. Certainly, I have an intense interest in and deep commitment to marketing research, and I will be most eager to learn from the specialists in your company the many facets of this exciting field.

If you prefer to telephone me, I am usually home by 4 p.m. (555-1234) each weekday except Wednesday, when I participate in a tennis meet or intramural competition.

                              Sincerely yours,

Analysis   There are several things to observe in Letter A.

1. *Heading.* Note that Ludlum shows his mailing address, even though it appears on the résumé, and, of course, the letter is dated. *Caution:* Never use a company letterhead or social stationery for a letter of application. White bond paper, 8½ by 11, is recommended.
2. *Inside address and salutation.* The ad Ludlum is answering included the name of the person to write to, so the inside address and salutation are no problem. Some ads simply say, "Send application to Box 257, News," in which case the salutation would be *To Whom It May Concern.* If a title is given but no name ("Write Personnel Director, Box 257, News"), use the salutation *Dear Sir or Madam.*

3. *Opening paragraph.* Ludlum's opening is quite effective. He refers to the specific position he is applying for and the source of his information. Then he indicates that the job is one he had hoped to find and says he feels that the ad was addressed personally to him. The latter is an advance indication that the job requirements and the applicant's qualifications are a good match.

Following are other possible openings Ludlum might have used:

a. The enclosed resume will, I believe, provide evidence that I am a logical candidate for the position of management trainee in marketing research that you advertised in the May 14 Sun.

b. Until I saw the ad, I didn't dare hope that such an opportunity existed, and I am eager to tell you why it has so much appeal for me. In the first place, . . .

c. My interest and specialized training in marketing make me an exceptionally qualified candidate for the position of management trainee in marketing research (May 14 Sun). Will you please consider me an enthusiastic applicant?

d. The enclosed resume contains my "vital statistics." What it doesn't show, however, is my dedication to the science of marketing research and my determination to. . . .

e. A genuine interest in the field of marketing, a strong desire to pursue a career in marketing research, energy and ambition, and a well-rounded college education--these are some of the things I can offer in response to your advertisement in the May 14 Sun.

If Ludlum had known the name of the company where the job exists, he might have used the following opening effectively:

Marcal Associates is a name that I am quite familiar with because of your excellent reputation in the field of marketing research. My professors at the University of Baltimore referred frequently to your brand-recognition studies and your innovations in packaging and design. I would consider it a privilege to work as a management trainee in marketing research in your organization.

4. *Second paragraph.* You will have to think long and hard about what to say in your second paragraph. The opening introduces you and attracts the employer's attention. The second paragraph should attempt to convince the reader that you have the education, talents, and interest necessary for the position.

   Stephen Ludlum concentrated on the breadth of his marketing education, with special emphasis on marketing research. Ludlum assumes that the executive who is in a position to hire him will be familiar with the work of E. B. Weiss and Martha C. Lanham. Even if he or she isn't, the statement shows that Ludlum is up to date on the current literature in the field. Note the reference to written reports; since the ability to write well is a requirement, this skill can hardly be overemphasized.

5. *Third paragraph.* In the third paragraph, Ludlum reemphasizes his deep interest in marketing research and states that he would be eager to "sit at the feet of the experts" to learn more about the field.

6. *Final paragraph.* Here Ludlum supplies specific information about how to telephone him if that is the employer's preference.

B Eubank's Application Letter

```
                              17 Cayuga Lane
                              Redwood City, California
                              94064
                              May 27, 19—


Miss Carolyn Mayheu
Vice President and Controller
Western Container Corporation
1820 Telegraph Avenue
Oakland, California 94612

Dear Miss Mayheu:

Mr. Ralph Meadows, the placement director of the
College of San Mateo, has suggested that I apply
for the position as your executive assistant,
which you spoke to him about earlier this week.
The job sounds very interesting and challenging,
and I would like to be considered for it.

As you will see in the resume enclosed, I have
been the administrative assistant to the Dean of
Faculties, College of San Mateo, for the past
year while completing my degree.  This gave me
many opportunities to apply my secretarial skills
and also to do some independent writing.  Cer-
```

tainly, I enjoyed my secretarial duties enormously, but I was equally interested in and I think adept at assisting the dean in various accounting activities. The truth is that I don't know whether I'm an executive secretary with a special interest in accounting or an accountant with a special talent for secretarial work! I like both fields, and I consider the position as your assistant the "best of both worlds."

I hope I may have the privilege of meeting you so that I can discuss my qualifications. I can come to Oakland at your convenience. You may write me either at the college (Dean of Faculties office) or at my home. If you wish to telephone me, I can be reached at 555-2788; it's the college number--I am rarely at home on weekdays.

Sincerely yours,

Analysis   The best entrée you can have to a job is when you are recommended by a person whom the employer has called on for suggestions.

1. Note that Roberta Eubank has opened her letter with a reference to the placement director's recommendation that she apply for the position. This will, of course, attract Mayheu's immediate and favorable attention.
2. Eubank makes the most of her experience in both secretarial and accounting work; there is little doubt left that she considers herself competent in both fields.
3. Note, however, that she does not belabor the point; she leaves the details to the résumé.
4. Eubank is also specific about where she can be reached, both by mail and by telephone.

THE SALARY QUESTION

Some advertisements ask applicants to state the salary expected, although most do not. Never bring up the subject of money on your own unless you have a critical financial problem and a few extra dollars will make a big difference. If you must state your salary requirements, then the following is appropriate:

As to salary, I feel that the minimum I could accept is $14,000.

UNSOLICITED APPLICATION LETTERS

Sometimes you may have your heart set on a job in a particular section of the country but do not have any leads. One way to get leads is to obtain newspapers from cities where you want to work and see if there are advertisements that appeal to you. Another way is to contact local firms that are likely to have a branch or main office in a particular city. In some cases you will simply have to choose the type of firm you want to work for, obtain the addresses of several leading firms in the city of your choice, and write to the personnel directors. (In many cities you can obtain the telephone directories of any city in the United States.)

Suppose that you live in Youngstown, Ohio, and want to work in Seattle. If you're like most people, you can't afford to make the long trip unless there is some definite hope that you will have a job when you get there.

Let's say that you are interested in petroleum accounting and that you have selected five major oil companies with offices in or near Seattle to which you will direct your inquiries about job opportunities. Assume in each case that you have learned the name of the controller. Following is an example of the letter you might write to each of the five controllers.

Dear Mr. Otagami:

Do you have a place in the Accounting Department at Western Oil Company for a young college-trained person who:

1. Hopes to make a career in accounting, specifically in the petroleum industry?
2. Has a broad educational background in accounting, including special courses in petroleum accounting?
3. Is eager to learn and not afraid to dig in?

On June 10 I will graduate from Ohio University, and I am eager to find a challenging position in the Seattle area.

A complete description of my qualifications is enclosed. Would you let me know, please, whether you have a place in your organization for me? Thank you!

Cordially yours,

"YOUR JOB HUNT" PROJECTS

1. Write application letters to accompany the résumés you prepared in Case 1.
2. Carlton J. Sibley, assistant human resources manager of the Jason Products Corporation, has informed your major professor of an opening in a certain department. (Choose the type of position in which you have an interest and the necessary qualifications.) Your professor has suggested that you apply. Write an application letter to Sibley, assuming that you will accompany it with a résumé.
3. Select an area of the United States in which you would like to work (or a company with overseas operations). Write an unsolicited letter of application that you could send to several firms.

STYLE CHECKUP

Rewrite the following sentences, each of which contains unnecessary or incorrect terms.

1. Attached hereto is our latest discount schedule.
2. Please rest assured that the installation of the computer will be made to suit your convenience.
3. Your new price list is at hand, and I want to thank you for your kind attention to this matter.
4. I request that you advise me of your plans at an early date.
5. In appreciation of your kind indulgence, I remain.

CASE 3

Thanking the Interviewer

THE SETTING

Roberta Eubank has been called to Oakland to be interviewed for the position of executive assistant to the controller of Western Container Corporation, Carolyn Mayheu. Eubank's visit with Miss Mayheu and two of her accounting executives was very pleasant, and she (Eubank) believes she has a better-than-average chance of getting the job. However, Mayheu said that several other applicants were also being considered and that Eubank would be notified just as soon as a decision is reached.

Since there are several applicants for the position that Eubank was interviewed for, there is no guarantee that she will be hired. Mayheu did mention that she felt Eubank was a little "light" on statistics, but she did not indicate that this was really serious. Eubank decides to write a thank-you letter to Mayheu for the interview.

Your Objective   To retain the employer's interest in the applicant and do a bit of selling in the same message.

BACKGROUND

A thank-you letter following a job interview will give you an advantage over applicants who don't think of writing (most people don't). Even though the firm to which you are applying is local, it is better to write than to telephone and to do so no later than a day after the interview. (Of course, if you are actually hired during the interview, a thank-you letter is not necessary.)

Guidelines

1. The type of letter you write will depend on how things went at the interview.
2. If you are practically assured that the job is yours, even though there has been no actual offer, you might write a letter like this:

```
Dear Mr. Revere:

Thank you for allowing me to meet with you this
week and discuss the position of sales corre-
spondent at Halliburton's Inc.

The job is most attractive to me and offers the
kind of opportunity that I have been looking
for.  I know I would find the work challenging
and interesting.

                          Sincerely yours,
```

SAMPLE LETTER

```
Dear Miss Mayheu:

Thank you for a very pleasant meeting this week
to discuss the position as your executive assis-
tant.  I really enjoyed getting acquainted with
you.

The job is most attractive to me;  I know I would
find the work challenging and satisfying.

After learning more about the duties required, I
realize that my knowledge of advanced statistical
```

methods may be somewhat light. The subject intrigues me, however (I did well in the one course I completed at the College of San Mateo), and I really want to learn more about it. I notice that Meritt College, in Oakland, offers advanced programs in statistics, and I would plan to enroll for this training in the evening division.

Would you please express my appreciation to Mr. Conrad and Mrs. Kibbey for giving me so much of their time.

Sincerely yours,

Analysis   Eubank has used this letter to her advantage.

1. She points out her desire to become more expert in statistics, since she felt this was the only thing about which Miss Mayheu was even slightly concerned.
2. Although admitting one's weakness may appear to be negative, we think Eubank did the right thing.
3. Her plans for further training will certainly show her willingness and intention to correct this deficiency.

"YOUR JOB HUNT" PROJECTS

1. Assume that one of the application letters you wrote in Project 1 on page 290 resulted in an invitation to appear for an interview. (The company is located 50 miles from where you live.)

    You felt that the interview went very well, and you are optimistic about getting the job—a position that would give you an opportunity to make decisions, which especially pleases you. The interviewer, Mrs. Verna Elliott, told you that there are several other applicants whom she must talk to before a final decision is reached, but she made you feel that you meet the job requirements nicely, and she seemed to like you. Just before you left, Mrs. Elliott asked you to submit a statement of your expenses so that you could be reimbursed. (The amount was $16.80.) Write a letter to Mrs. Elliott.

2. Carlton J. Sibley (see project 2, page 290) called you for an interview. Everything went very smoothly, and you really want the job. It pays well and is only a short distance from your home. Sibley discussed the need for excellent typing skills and mentioned that there are opportunities in the company for additional training. Let's say that you are a typist but that your skills do not fall in the "excellent" category. Write an appropriate letter to Sibley.

Rewrite each of the following sentences, using simpler words and better construction.

1. Your communication of April 3 is hereby gratefully acknowledged.
2. Kindly return the postcard at an early date.
3. I trust the suggestion offered will meet with your approval.
4. This is to advise you that we have received your check in the amount of $672.75.
5. With regard to your request for a refund, I wish to state that a check will be forwarded to you as soon as conveniently possible—two or three days at the outside.

C A S E 4

Accepting a Job Offer

THE SETTING

It has been two weeks since Stephen Ludlum applied for the position of management trainee in marketing research. He received a postcard from Mr. Goddard (see Case 2) on May 22 that said that the application had been received and was being considered along with many others, but Ludlum has heard nothing since.

In the meantime, Ludlum has been told by the university placement director that a good job in marketing research is open and that she has been asked to recommend someone for it. She recommended that Ludlum apply. He did so, and within four days after the interview, he received a letter saying that he had been selected. The job appears to be better than the one advertised in the *Sun*, and Ludlum plans to accept the position.

Your Objective To write three letters: (1) an acceptance of the position offered, (2) a thank you to those who permitted him to use their name as references, and (3) a notification to Mr. Goddard that Ludlum is no longer a candidate for the job originally applied for.

BACKGROUND

Accepting a job offer involves three activities: accepting the job offered, thanking your references, and notifying other employers that you are no longer a candidate for the other jobs for which you applied. Because these three situations involve different guidelines, sample letters, and analyses, each is discussed separately in the pages that follow.

Guidelines—Accepting a Job Offer

1. The person who writes offering you a job will expect you to respond immediately. Be sure to do so.
2. Although you could telephone your acceptance, it is usually a good idea to respond in writing.

SAMPLE LETTER

Dear Mr. Jacobi:

I am delighted to accept the position in the Marketing Research Department of Cantrell Corporation. As you suggested, I will report to the medical office at 8:30 a.m. on June 16 for a physical examination and will come directly to your office afterward.

The prospect of joining your team is immensely exciting, and I really look forward to getting started. You may be sure that I will read the booklet you sent me, <u>The Cantrell Commitment--A Guide to New Employees</u>, with much interest.

Cordially yours,

Analysis   Ludlum's letter was a good one for three reasons:

1. Ludlum accepted the job offer.
2. He confirmed the date and hour of reporting to work.
3. He expressed his enthusiasm for the job opportunity.

Guidelines—Thanking Your References

1. Once you have obtained a position it is important that you inform those whom you listed as references in your résumé and thank them for their help.
2. In some cases a telephone call or a personal visit will be satisfactory.
3. You usually have no way of knowing whether your prospective employer actually sought information from your references, but it is wise to assume that this was done, so a thank-you letter should be written.
    Stephen Ludlum listed Judge R. N. Toffenetti, a family friend and neighbor, as a reference on the résumé.

Dear Judge Toffenetti:

I'm mighty happy to tell you that I have obtained a position in the Marketing Research Department of Cantrell Corporation, in Silver Spring. It looks like a great opportunity, and I couldn't be more pleased.

Since the commute is too long from Randallstown, I expect to leave shortly to find an apartment in the Silver Spring area.

Thank you for letting me use your name as a reference in my job applications. You must have said the right thing! I'll be seeing you and Mrs. Toffenetti before I leave Randallstown for good. In the meantime, best wishes to you both.

Yours,

Analysis   This is an effective letter to Judge Toffenetti.

1. It is obviously a very personal letter to an old family friend, and the tone is quite appropriate.
2. Chances are that Toffenetti won't be interested in the details about the job; if he is, Ludlum can convey this information in person at a later date.
3. Ludlum's letter to Dr. Christine Hale, professor of marketing at the University of Baltimore, will be somewhat different from that to Toffenetti.

Dear Professor Hale:

I think you'll be pleased that I have been hired by Cantrell Corporation, in Silver Spring, for a position in the Marketing Research Department. The company manufactures computer components, and I've been told that my first assignment will be to research computer applications in the agricultural industry.

Please be assured that I appreciate your allowing me to use your name as a reference. I'm certain your recommendation carried a lot of weight in Cantrell's decision to hire me, and I'll do my best to prove that I deserve your confidence.

I hope to see you from time to time to let you
know what (and how) I'm doing. When you are next
in Silver Spring, I hope you'll visit my office.
The company is located at 2300 Viers Mill Road.

Sincerely,

Analysis . Ludlum's letter to Dr. Christine Hale, professor of marketing at the University of Baltimore, is necessarily different from that to Toffennetti. After all, Ludlum's relationship with each reference is different.

1. Since Hale seems to be Ludlum's former professor and not a family friend, he wrote a letter expressing gratitude but in a formal way.
2. We think Ludlum's plan to keep Hale apprised of his progress at Cantrell Corporation is a nice touch. It shows his respect for his professor and acknowledges that they will both now be working in the same professional area.

Guidelines—Notifying Other Firms   Each individual must decide independently whether to write a letter to a company where application was made but no position was offered. For example, Ludlum owes nothing to the company that Goddard represents; it would appear that that organization has ruled Ludlum out as a candidate and failed to notify him of the decision. Yet we don't know. Our opinion is that it will do no harm if Ludlum notifies Goddard of his new position. After all, he may still be a candidate for the job Goddard advertised.

SAMPLE LETTERS

 Dear Mr. Goddard:

This is to let you know that I have accepted a
marketing research position with another company
and am no longer a candidate for the job I applied for in your organization.

I appreciate whatever consideration you gave my
application.

Sincerely yours,

Analysis   Ludlum has said all that needs to be said.

1. Although the letter is not particularly friendly (Ludlum had no good reason for making it so), it is courteous (last paragraph).
2. Suppose, on the other hand, that Stephen Ludlum was notified by Goddard that he had been selected as a management trainee in marketing research and should report to work on such and such a date. (The letter arrived, say,

a couple of days after Ludlum accepted the Cantrell position.) In this case Ludlum does owe Goddard a letter, which might be as follows.

Dear Mr. Goddard:

Thank you very much for offering me the position of management trainee in marketing research at Northeast Research Associates.

Shortly after I made application to your organization, Mr. Goddard, I was encouraged by a member of the university staff to apply for a vacancy in marketing research in a large company near Washington, D.C. I did so and was notified two days ago that I had been selected, and I immediately accepted the offer.

I am grateful for the opportunity you have given me and appreciate especially your confidence in me.

Sincerely yours,

Analysis   Letter B would be an appropriate response to Goddard if he, as sometimes happens, offered a job to Ludlum after Ludlum had accepted another one. Ludlum owes Goddard a letter for expressing enough confidence in him to offer him a job.

1. Ludlum begins his letter, quite appropriately we think, by thanking Goddard for the job offer.
2. Nothing in Ludlum's letter implies that his job with Cantrell corporation is superior to the one offered at Northeast Research Associates. This ensures that Goddard will not feel slighted by Ludlum's choice and informs him that it was timing that determined his choice. This is tactful and leaves the door open to future employment at Northeast Research Associates, should Ludlum desire to apply.

"YOUR JOB HUNT" PROJECTS

1. You have received a letter from Mrs. Verna Elliott (Project 1, page 290) telling you that the job is yours. You are to report to work at 9 a.m. on Monday, June 27. You will go first to the medical department for a physical examination and then proceed to Mrs. Elliott's office immediately afterward. Respond to the job offer, indicating your pleasure in accepting it.
2. Select one of the references given when you applied for the position in Project 1 above, and write an appropriate letter of thanks.

3. When you applied for the position in the company that Mrs. Elliott represents, you also made application for a similar job with Dilworth Corporation (Randall Bouton, assistant human resources manager). Bouton was very encouraging at the interview, but you have not yet received a job offer. In the meantime, you have accepted the position in Project 1 above. Write Bouton a letter asking that your name be withdrawn from consideration as a candidate for the opening he discussed with you.

STYLE CHECKUP

Rewrite the following sentences to remove excess words and trite expressions.

1. I would appreciate receiving this information by return mail.
2. I hope you will avail yourself of the opportunity to save on your July purchases.
3. Our retail outlet nearest you is in the city of Kensington, and I would advise you to patronize that establishment.
4. Enclosed please find a copy of your invoice under the date of May 16.
5. Concerning your order for Widgets, please be advised that this product is manufactured not by the above-named company but by another enterprise by the name of Gossett's Inc., and I suggest that you communicate with Gossett's to obtain the appropriate information.

C A S E 5 Resigning From a Position—Better Opportunity

THE SETTING

Peter Famularo has been employed at Walden Steel Company for three years. He started out as a junior accountant and after two promotions became the budget director of the company. He has been happy in his job and feels that management has been extremely good to him. Recently, however, a friend at Corwin Industries told Famularo that the assistant to the controller is retiring and that the company is searching for a replacement. Famularo made application, was interviewed, and received notice that the job is his. The new salary is one-third more than Famularo now earns, and the opportunities for advancement seem excellent (the controller is nearing retirement age).

Famularo discussed the offer with his immediate supervisor, Sibil VanHorst, who said that Walden Steel could not match the salary or opportunity and encouraged Famularo, with regret, to accept the job.

Your Objective To submit a letter of resignation, expressing regret at leaving and appreciation for opportunities and favors given.

BACKGROUND

When you resign from a job, there is no rule that you must do so in writing. Many people simply tell their supervisor that they're leaving, give the reason, and propose a date of departure. (Ordinarily, you will give at least two weeks' notice, although in some positions a month's notice in not uncommon.)

A good reason for putting the resignation in writing is simply to have on record in your personnel files the circumstances that led to your decision. You may need to make reference to a former employer many years after your resignation, and the staff members currently on board may have never heard of you. For all they know, you may have been fired.

A letter of resignation serves another purpose—if your departure is an amicable one: to express your appreciation for the opportunities given you, for training, and for special favors.

Guidelines

1. Make a record of the reason for the resignation and its effective date for your personnel files.
2. Express appreciation, if appropriate, for the opportunities and growth in the job.

SAMPLE LETTERS

 A

Dear Sibil:

As we discussed in your office yesterday, I have made the decision to submit my resignation, effective three weeks hence--August 16.

The reasons, as I told you, are that I have had an offer to take a much bigger job at a substantially greater salary than I am earning at Walden Steel. And the opportunity for advancement cannot be matched in this company.

I will continue, as in the past, to perform my duties as budget director in a responsible manner, and I stand ready to do whatever I can to break in my replacement.

Sincerely,

Analysis Letter A is not a bad letter, but we think it has three basic flaws:

1. It's a bit pompous; the second paragraph downgrades the present job ("much bigger job"), the reference to salary is blunt, and the mention of opportunity ("cannot be matched in this company") is coarse.

2. It lacks personal warmth. Surely, after three years in a satisfying job, Famularo might have mentioned his regret at severing relationships.
3. There are no kudos or expressions of appreciation. Indeed, the writer sounds smug, and we have reason to believe that this is not a suitable label for him.

 B

Dear Sibil:

As we discussed in your office yesterday, I have decided to submit my resignation as budget director, effective three weeks hence--August 16.

It was a hard decision for me because I have liked so much working at Walden Steel. You and the members of our staff could not have been more helpful, friendlier, and more cooperative. You created a perfect environment for me for learning and growing. And, of course, I would not feel competent to accept the new job if I had not had the rich experience here. I will always be grateful for your confidence in me.

Reluctant though I am to leave Walden, I'm sure you understand. I felt that I simply could not turn down a position that appears to offer such promise. The additional income is a factor, of course, but a relatively minor one. What I am most excited about is the chance to assume broad accounting responsibilities that could lead to exciting new opportunities in financial management.

I am, of course, determined to get my unit in the best possible shape in the three weeks I have left. If you can think of anything I can do to help my replacement take over the duties of budget director, I'll be glad to have your suggestions.

Sincerely,

Analysis Assuming that Famularo is honest in his statements about the environment and people at Walden Steel, this is an appropriate letter of resignation.

1. The writer speaks first about his three years at Walden and what they have meant to him.
2. Then he briefly and without bombast describes the reasons why he feels he must accept the new position.

3. Finally, Famularo expresses determination to wind up his work as budget director in the best possible manner.

"YOUR JOB CHANGE" PROJECT

You have held your first job for two years. You found the work very enjoyable and learned a great deal from your supervisor and others with whom you associated. However, you have been invited to accept a job that offers greater responsibility, a more convenient location for commuting, a higher salary, and better promotion opportunities. You are quite excited about it—you don't think you can afford to turn down the offer. You discussed the situation with your supervisor, Harlan Cosgrove, who expressed his disappointment at your leaving but admitted that the company could not match the advantages offered. You agreed to remain at your present job for two weeks—three, if necessary— although you had hoped for a week's vacation before reporting to your new assignment.

Write an appropriate letter to Cosgrove. Be sure to supply the appropriate details: dates, the name of the new employer, the position to which you have been appointed, and so on.

STYLE CHECKUP

Rewrite the following to eliminate excess words and trite expressions.

1. Thanking you in advance for your early attention to this matter, I remain.
2. Your order is being held pending receipt of satisfactory financial data by the writer.
3. In reply to your letter under the date of October 17, I would say that 10,000 bumper stickers will arrive in Newark in due time.
4. The party to whom you addressed your esteemed favor will respond during the course of the coming week.
5. I would like to acknowledge receipt of the signed contract with appreciation of same.

CASE 6 Resigning From a Position— Dissatisfaction

THE SETTING

Emily Nash has been the administrative assistant to Ralph Seagraves, manufacturing manager at Riegelwood Paper Company, for one year. She had previously been the secretary to the purchasing director, and when the opportunity arose to become an administrative assistant at a higher salary, she quickly took advantage of it.

Although Seagraves is likable and easygoing, he has one fault: he cannot delegate responsibility. Nash's new job turned out to be even less challenging than the previous one. Seagraves likes to do everything himself, even when he is so busy with manufacturing problems that he really should turn over routine matters to Nash. Although the salary is good and the working atmosphere pleasant, Nash is unhappy being merely a clerk-typist and telephone answerer. When she spoke to Seagraves several times about taking certain burdens off his shoulders, he simply shrugged and said, "Why change things? We're a good team."

Finally, Nash decides to resign.

Your Objective   To write an appropriate letter of resignation.

BACKGROUND

Emily Nash, in the situation described, could simply announce to Seagraves that she is quitting, state frankly the reasons why, and walk out. Many people do that.

We think, however, that a person who resigns should leave some record of the event in her or his personnel files. The question here is what kind of record.

When an employee is dissatisfied with working conditions, treatment, opportunities for growth, and so on, the temptation is great to write a stinging letter of rebuke to the supervisor just to get even. It's especially hard not to be bitter when a supervisor has been downright mean, abusive, and unfair. When this is the employee's attitude, we think it best not to write a letter; a letter written in anger is always dangerous. It could come back to haunt the writer.

Nash's supervisor may have difficulty delegating responsibility, but this is not an uncommon problem. Indeed, he seems to be a decent sort of man. If Emily Nash decides to write a letter of resignation in this situation, she can handle it in two ways, as described in the following guidelines.

Guidelines

1. Fabricate a reason for leaving without facing the issue. This is often done in order to avoid hard feelings.
2. Announce the resignation and then tactfully explain why this decision was reached.
3. In either case, express appreciation for whatever privileges and opportunities she enjoyed.

SAMPLE LETTERS

Dear Mr. Seagraves:

Please consider this my resignation from the position as your administrative assistant, effective November 10.

As I mentioned to you, I have decided to take a position in another company, although I have not yet made a definite commitment to any particular one. I do think I would be happier and more productive in publishing or advertising, and I expect to concentrate on firms that can offer me this opportunity.

Thank you for the help you have given me. I have learned a great deal from my work at Riegelwood that should prove useful in my new work.

Sincerely yours,

Analysis This is a fabricated letter; it eliminates the negatives.

1. The writer hedges in the statement of her plans ("although I have not yet made a definite commitment").
2. It may be true that she hopes to find a job in publishing or advertising, but even if this has never occurred to her before, it seems to be a reasonable out if she does not want to reveal the reason for leaving.
3. Note that the writer expresses appreciation for the help given.
4. She does not say that she learned a great deal from Seagraves (she mentions the company), and he may infer from the statement whatever he wishes.

B Dear Mr. Seagraves:

This will confirm my resignation as your administrative assistant, effective November 10.

I have found Riegelwood a very congenial place to work, and my decision to leave was not an easy one to make. However, as I have discussed with you on a number of occasions, I do not feel that my present position allows me freedom to make decisions and to operate independently in situations where I feel perfectly competent to do so. I'm sure you know that I have aspirations in management, and I can see no way to advance toward that goal in my present job.

In the past several weeks, I have talked with a number of placement specialists in the Boston area, and I have been assured that the opportuni-

ties for women in management are the best they
have ever been. I received a great deal of encouragement concerning vacancies, and I expect to
pursue some of the leads given me.

Thank you very much for the many kindnesses you
have shown me. I have learned a great deal at
Riegelwood, and I'm especially indebted to you
for giving me the title of administrative assistant. I'm confident this will enhance my stature
in the eyes of prospective new employers.

                              Sincerely yours,

Analysis   Letter B effectively accomplishes the writer's intention.

1. Nash first announces her resignation and the effective date.
2. She begins the second paragraph with a positive statement and then proceeds to present in a straightforward manner the precise reasons for making the decision. Although the reasons given are tactfully stated, Seagraves may still read between the lines that he was a poor excuse for a leader. This is the risk one takes in being explicit, which is why some people would choose Letter A.
3. The third paragraph is optional, but assuming that it is true, there is no harm it telling Seagraves that the future looks bright.
4. Nash expresses her appreciation for "kindnesses" in the final paragraph, stopping short of saying how much she learned from Seagraves. However, he is the person who bestowed the title of administrative assistant, and this fact should be gratefully acknowledged.

"YOUR JOB CHANGE" PROJECT

Margaret Kinkaid has decided to resign from her position as assistant training director. Her reason is that she has no freedom—her supervisor, Howard Frankenthaler, refuses to give her any real responsibility, hovers over her constantly, complains about the quality of her work without offering constructive suggestions, and goes out of his way to belittle her efforts. Although Kinkaid tried to be a conscientious worker, she couldn't seem to resolve the personality clash with Frankenthaler. When she discussed with him her desire to be more independent, he gave her the brush-off, saying, "If you learn to do your work right, your chance for responsibility will come."

Kinkaid has given up. She knows she is competent—she has received many compliments from groups for which she has set up and operated training programs. She thinks that Frankenthaler happens to be one of those people who think that nobody else can rise to their standard of performance. Actually, he has given Kinkaid several salary increases, so he must think privately that she is valuable.

Kinkaid has looked around for other opportunities and has been offered a job as supervisor of education and training at Metropolitan Computer Services. The salary is about the same as she is now receiving, but at Metropolitan she will have full responsibility for education and training. Her new supervisor, the personnel vice president, has assured her of that.

Write a letter of resignation that you would prepare if you were faced with Kinkaid's situation.

STYLE CHECKUP

Rewrite each of the following sentences to eliminate the redundancy or unnecessary word.

1. I was mystified and puzzled by Vanniver's letter.
2. The members of the planning committee join with me in expressing appreciation.
3. I think you will be pleased to see the results of these new innovations.
4. Johnston repeated back the instructions so that everyone would understand them.
5. Judy feels that there is no other alternative than to place Damon on probation.

PART TWO

WRITING EFFECTIVE MEMORANDUMS

THE ROLE OF MEMORANDUMS IN BUSINESS

Depending on your job title and responsibilities, you are likely to write far more business memorandums than business letters. Memorandums are often referred to as *interoffice letters*. It is through the memorandum that you learn what is going on in the company and in turn contribute your own share of information in memo form for others to read and act on or learn from. So there is a lot of business transacted by business memorandums.

The memorandum is used for such topics as:

- Why are overtime costs increasing so much?
- Congratulations, Erlene, on your promotion to assistant purchasing manager!
- May I have permission to hire an additional job placement specialist?
- I have an idea that we might call on local colleges and universities to train computer programmers rather than do our own instruction.
- Please let me have your opinion of the revised performance rating, attached.
- Can we meet competitors' price and still maintian our profit margin?
- Before you order new furniture, be sure to examine our used furniture in storage.
- I appreciate your filling in for me while I was on a business trip.

But memorandums are not confined to personal exchanges between employees. They are also used to report investigations, results of ambitious research and progress, and to analyze these findings and offer recommendations. For example:

- How can we get a bigger share of the auto parts market?
- Should we lease automobiles for our sales representatives rather than purchase them outright?

- What is your prediction for growth in sales and profits for five and ten years hence?
- We are considering adding three new distribution centers during the coming year. Where should they be located and why?
- Acquisitions are taking place constantly in other large companies—the "hottest" method of immediate growth. Should we diversify by purchasing available companies?

In this chapter we focus on the simpler (though not unimportant) memos. In a later chapter we will deal with memorandums as business reports.

BUSINESS MEMORANDUMS IN YOUR FUTURE

If you write only letters that go outside the company, chances are that relatively few people within the company will see copies of these letters and thus may not be fully aware of your expertise in communicating. Memos often provide much greater "visibility" for the writer since they may be seen by many people, including top-ranking executives. So the memo writer may be constantly on display. If you can write clear, concise, and persuasive business memos, your chances of enhancing your value to the company will be greatly increased.

FORM OF THE MEMORANDUM

Parts of the Memorandum

The stationery on which memos are written contains printed headings that eliminate the need for formal inside addresses, salutations, and closings. Although memo forms differ, most of them contain at least four headings: "TO," FROM," "SUBJECT," and "DATE." Other headings are often added to expedite delivery and establish identification: "DEPARTMENT," "LO-CATION" (e.g., branch office), "FLOOR," "TELEPHONE EXTENSION," "ROOM," and so on.

The "TO" line.   The addressee is not usually given a courtesy title, such as Mr., Miss, and Dr. It is common, however, to use a title when the person addressed is of much higher rank than the writer. The job title—Vice President, Operations, for example—may be used in very formal circumstances. If there is no provision in the form for "Department," this may be indicated alongside the addressee's name; for instance, Bryan Sawyer, Accounting Department. Such an identification may be important in a very large company.

When the memo is addressed to more than one person, the "TO" line may appear as follows:

TO: Publications Committee

TO: See Below (At the end of the memo, the names or initials addressed are listed; thus: Distribution: ST, MMc, LRB, RJH, FMS, TRR.)

Copy Notation. The name of the person receiving a copy of the memorandum may be placed below the addresse's name but more often appears at the bottom left margin. If several people are to receive copies, the notation is placed at the bottom:

cc: C. J. Moore, Albert J. Elliot, Grace Hotchkiss, Amelia Post, Anthony Finletter, Allene H. Locke

The "FROM" Line. Neither a courtesy title nor a job title is given to the writer of the memo. However, when the memo form does not provide for an identification of the department from which the message is sent, the writer should include this information beside or below; for example, "FROM: Paula C. SaSalle, Customer Relations." This is especially important when the writer is a new employee in a larger company or an employee who is not likely to be widely known in the firm.

The "SUBJECT" Line. Stating the subject enables the reader to know at a glance the topic or subject of the memo. The wording should be as brief and concise as possible but long enough to tell the reader what you're going to talk about; thus,

SUBJECT: Request for a Leave of Absence
SUBJECT: Overpayment to Jefferson Associates
SUBJECT: Reducing Costs in Product Packaging

The Body. The body of the memo, like the body of a letter is usually single-spaced. If the message is very short, double spacing may be appropriate.

The Signature. Many memo writers feel that their name on the "FROM" line renders a signature unnecessary, either typewritten or handwritten. Again, whether you initial or sign your memorandum is up to you. If you want to personalize the memorandums, initial or sign them. The best place for a signature is at the bottom of the memo, although some people prefer to write their initials above or alongside their name on the "FROM" line; thus,

FROM: Stanley F. Shapiro *SFS*

SAMPLE MEMORANDUMS

Following are two typical interoffice memorandums. Note that in the first example, Frances Malloy chose to use a salutation ("Dear Ed:"), a closing ("Sincerely"), and a signature ("Fran"). In the second example there is no salutation and no signature.

Centennial Products Company

MEMORANDUM

TO: Edwin Rosenberg   **FROM:** Frances Malloy

LOCATION: Colorado Springs   **LOCATION:** Denver

SUBJECT: Blank Desk Calendars for Tyndall's Pharmacy   **DATE:** June 19, 19--

Dear Ed:

I'm enclosing a letter from Tyndall's Pharmacy in Colorado Springs in which the owner requests fifty blank desk calendars for her customers (she has her own address labels).

Our inventory of blanks in Denver is getting very low, and I wonder if you have an ample supply to handle this request. If so, I'd appreciate it if you could get in touch with Tyndall and personally deliver the calendars to her.

If you can't spare the entire fifty, Ed, let me know how many you can supply. Perhaps we can make up the remainder from here.

Sincerely,

Fran

NATIONAL CAREER
INSTITUTE

INTEROFFICE MEMORANDUM

TO: Adele Shipman

FROM: Perry Glasser

SUBJECT: Automatic Shrink-Wrapping Machine

DATE: March 6, 19—

When I attended the Des Moines Industrial Show last week, I saw a demonstration of an automated shrink-wrapping machine that has just been introduced by Kelflex Inc. I was much impressed with its efficiency and economy; I think it may be the answer to our problem in packaging very small parts for our automotive kits.

An illustrated brochure is attached. Note the reference to the film that is available for loan without cost. If you think it would be useful, I'd be glad to order it.

CHAPTER 16

EVERYDAY MEMORANDUMS

YOUR JOB

You are special assistant to the director of marketing sevices at Taylor, Aaron, and Bache, a pharmaceutical manufacturer. In this position you write some letters to the firm's customers such as hospitals, physicians in private practice, and pharmacists. Most of your writing, however, consists of memorandums to those employed at Taylor, Aaron, and Bache. The marketing director, to whom you report, is David Chan, whom you address by his first name.

CASE 1

Writing a Transmittal Memorandum

THE SETTING

David Chan has been working with the advertising staff to develop a full-page advertisement to be published in various medical journals. No particular product of Taylor, Aaron, and Bache will be featured. Instead, the ad is to be an "institutional" type—that is, designed to build goodwill and confidence in Taylor, Aaron, and Bache products. Chan is ready to send each branch office manager the rough layout and copy for their reaction and comments. You are to write the transmittal memorandum.

Your Objective   To write the transmittal memorandum in as simple a form as possible.

SAMPLE MEMORANDUM

TO:	All Branch Managers	**FROM:**	Your Name
SUBJECT:	Advertising Layout and Copy	**DATE:**	June 1, 19--

Attached is a rough layout with copy of an advertisement which we are planning to publish in a number of medical periodicals, including the <u>New England Journal of Medicine</u>, in December.

As you will see, the ad is strictly "institutional"--no products are mentioned by name.

Please let me have your comments and suggestions, if any.

Analysis   This is an excellent example of a simple transmittal of materials by memorandum. There is no need to go into detail about the enclosure. (It speaks for itself.) You do, however, ask for comments and suggestions.

"YOUR JOB" PROJECTS

1. David Chan has asked you to obtain budgeted sales figures and actual sales figures for the 24 regional offices of Taylor, Aaron, and Bache for the first quarter of the year. The report itself will break down like this:

Regional Office	Budgeted Sales	Actual Sales	+ or − Amount
Ada, Oklahoma	$536,000	$394,000	− $42,000
Boise, Idaho	396,000	402,000	* 8,000
etc.	etc.	etc.	etc.

   The total budgeted sales figures for the 24 regional offices came to $7,300,000; the actual sales for these regions amounted to $6,814,000. Write a memorandum to David Chan transmitting the information requested. The transmittal memo, however, gives only the total budget and actual sales and the difference between the two for the first quarter.

2. The president of Taylor, Aaron, and Bache has asked David Chan to find out from each regional manager the turnover of sales representatives during the first six months of this year. The specific information wanted: name of the representative, regional office, employment dates (years), and reason for leaving. You are to write a memorandum transmitting the categories of data to the regional office managers along with a form on which to place the information.

3. You serve as chairperson of the Sales Orientation Committee, made up of seven members of the marketing staff. At a meeting on May 17 the format of the orientation program for new representatives was changed substantially. You write up the minutes of the meeting and are ready to transmit it to the other six members of the committee, pointing out especially the changes that were approved at the May 17 meeting. These changes include the use of a greater variety of visual aids; more participation of top marketing people in the company, including regional office managers; periodic use of pharmacists and physicians; and a tour of the headquarters office.

Write the memorandum to the members of the Sales Orientation Committee, including the details given. Add whatever comments you think are appropriate.

SUPPLEMENTARY PROJECT

4. The Fairchild Aluminum Corporation is getting ready to revise its employee handbook, and you, as an assistant in the employee relations department, are asked to obtain cost figures for producing the handbook from three different suppliers: Polazzi, Cowart, and Seagraves. Here are the specifications:
   a. 24 pages, 6 by 9 inches
   b. Line drawings on each page
   c. 50-pound offset paper, printed in two colors
   d. Saddle-wire binding, 50-pound Triumph antique beige
   e. Quantity of printing: 4,000
   The individual costs per booklet are as follows:

Cowart	Polazzi	Seagraves
$0.741	$0.807	$0.728

Write a memorandum transmitting this information to the employee relations manager, P. R. Trevino, saying that the cost breakdown for composition, paper, printing, and binding is attached.

STYLE CHECKUP

From each pair of words in parentheses, circle the one that correctly completes the sentence.

1. We have looked at the property and have (appraised, apprised) the owner of its value.
2. For the (balance, remainder) of the test, we will use weekly newspapers.
3. (Most, The bulk) of the applicants are college graduates.
4. In your (advanced, advance) planning, please consider space needs.
5. Our promotion people are (eager, anxious) to help you with your displays.

C A S E
2

Writing a Request Memorandum

THE SETTING

You are responsible for sending out various documents to personnel in the company headquarters office, in the branch offices, and to the 200 or more sales representatives throughout the country. The photocopier in your department is old and inefficient. You would like to replace it with a computerized copier-printer, which is much faster than a photocopier. The one you have in mind costs $5,250. You have discussed this with David Chan, and he has asked you to put your request in writing, since he will need to get the approval of a company vice president.

Your Objective   To present to David Chan the most convincing case possible for investing in the new equipment.

BACKGROUND

You've already seen examples of memorandums, but let's look at the setup more closely and then talk about content. When you write to a supervisor to request something—the purchase of equipment or services, authority to employ additional personnel, permission to make important changes in your department, and so on—you are actually preparing a sales message. That is, you want to sell your idea to the person who must give approval. Many executives are very cautious when it comes to making changes (especially when money must be spent!), and often your chance of getting what you want is best if you put your request in writing. Follow these guidelines.

Guidelines

1. State your request clearly, recalling earlier discussions concerning it, if appropriate. However, ask tactfully—don't demand.
2. Describe in detail the reason or reasons for your request.
3. Estimate the cost involved, show how you obtained the figures, and say why you think the investment is sound.
4. Indicate the steps you have taken, if any, to avoid making the request.
5. Make whatever recommendations you think are appropriate.

SAMPLE MEMOS

Dear David:

We need a new photocopier desperately. May I have your permission to purchase one?

Analysis   Memo A violates the guidelines above. Obviously, this is not a convincing sales message.

1. The recipient needs the answer to these questions: What? Why? How much? When? These elements are obviously missing.

2. You will need to describe what steps you took to avoid making the request if Chan must sell the idea "upstairs."

Dear David:

As I mentioned last week, our Tru-Copy photo-copier is no longer adequate for our needs, and I'd like your authorization to buy a new one.

The Tru-Copy is now four years old and very slow. The copies we get from it are faint (see the samples attached). What's more, the machine breaks down constantly, and while we're waiting for it to be repaired, we have to use the machine on the fifth floor. This puts us behind in getting out new-product information announcements, price changes, and various policy bulletins to the regional offices, sales representatives, and customers. Delays are just one problem; the appearance of the copies gives our customers a low opinion of Taylor, Aaron, and Bache.

Last week representatives from UltraFax demonstrated their F87 computerized copier-printer, and we were quite impressed. I am convinced that this machine would pay for itself (it costs $4,150) within a few years. In 1987 we spent $587 for repairing the Tru-Copy, and the wasted time and paper would probably double that figure.

The UltraFax would do more than replace the Tru-Copy; it would significantly enhance our information processing system and speed the duplication of documents. As you can see from the attached circular, it can help diagnose its own problems, and this should cut down on service calls. It also has a memory that gives it many more capabilities than those of a conventional photocopier. UltraFax, by the way, will allow us a $150 trade-in allowance on the Tru-Copy.

Analysis Memorandum B provides all the information Chan will need to make a decision about whether to recommend the purchase. Note the following:

1. Reference is made to the conversation that took place between the reader and the writer. This provides the purpose for writing the memorandum.

2. The inadequacies of the old machine are described thoroughly, with emphasis on delays and the appearance of the copies. (The reference to customer opinion should be an especially compelling argument.)
3. The proposal of the UltraFax F87 is then presented in terms of cost. To soften the blow of the expenditure of $4,150, mention is made of the repair bills for the old machine and wasted time and paper.
4. The emphasis on the advantages of the UltraFax F87 and the reference to the trade-in allowance for the old machine are additional convincing arguments.

"YOUR JOB" PROJECT

Four months ago you hired a new advertising copywriter, Melita Caponi, to replace an unproductive employee. At the time you hired Caponi, you felt that you really needed two copywriters, but budget restrictions would not permit you to hire two.

Caponi is highly imaginative and skillful, and by arriving early and working late and on weekends, she has cleared out the huge backlog of copy left by her predecessor, much of which you had planned to assign to free-lance writers.

It is the policy of Taylor, Aaron, and Bache to put each new employee on six months' probation and to offer no increases in pay during that period. The maximum raise after probation is 10 percent of the employee's salary. However, Melita Caponi, after only four months, has proved to be so outstanding that you want to give her a 20 percent increase in salary (she was hired at $16,500 a year). You figure that her many extra hours on the job have already saved you nearly $2,000 in free-lance costs, and at her present rate of productivity, there will be no need to hire the additional copywriter you had previously envisioned.

Write a memorandum to David Chan requesting the pay increase. Assume that you have commented to him many times on the excellent work being done by Melita Caponi.

STYLE CHECKUP

Rewrite each of the following sentences to eliminate the redundancy or unnecessary words.

1. I cannot accept your alibi as an excuse for postponing shipment.
2. Katz could find no answers or solutions to the pilferage question.
3. Claybaugh reiterated again and again the dangers of flexible pricing.
4. I will expect to receive your payment by certified check by December 3.
5. We plan to meet in the city of Philadelphia.

C A S E 3

Writing a Confirmation Memorandum

THE SETTING

Among the departments in Taylor, Aaron, and Bache is the sales training department, which is supervised by Carolyn Masters. Yesterday you met with Masters to discuss several changes in her department. You are now to summarize in writing the meeting that took place.

Your Objective   To confirm the agreements reached.

BACKGROUND

When company meetings take place in which very important matters are discussed, the agreements reached should be put in writing so that there will be no question about what was decided. This is usually done by memorandum and is generally the responsibility of the individual in a position to make decisions—in this case, you.

Guidelines

1. As in writing confirmation letters, you should be very specific about the major points discussed orally and agreed on.
2. When more than one topic is covered, it is a good idea to number them so that they stand out and can be easily referred to if further discussions take place.

SAMPLE MEMO

TO: Carolyn Masters   **FROM:** Your Name

SUBJECT: Changes in the   **DATE:** November 14, 19--
Sales Training
Department

Dear Carolyn:

This will confirm our discussion in my office yesterday in which we agreed on the following:

1. You are authorized to hire two additional people: an instructor and an audiovisual specialist, effective December 1, at a total annual salary not to

exceed $42,000. You may allocate this amount as you see fit, depending on the qualifications of the people you hire.

2. Two additional modular office units are to be installed on the fourth floor, and you are authorized to order these units and the equipment that will be required by the two new employees. We agreed on a total expenditure of $6,200 for these units and equipment, and you are to prepare the appropriate purchase orders for my signature.

3. Shari Gibson is to be promoted to the position of Coordinator of Training Materials, also effective December 1, at a 15 percent increase over her present salary. You will prepare a memorandum announcing Gibson's promotion, which will be sent to Distribution Lists A and B.

If you have any questions or reservations about the points covered above, please let me know. Otherwise, I will assume that we are in agreement on everything mentioned in this memorandum.

Analysis   This is a good memorandum for these three reasons.

1. In the first paragraph the writer expresses confirmation of the oral discussion. This serves as the purpose of the memorandum.
2. The writer enumerates the three major changes agreed on, being very specific about authorized expenditures and the procedures Masters is to follow.
3. In the final paragraph the writer gives Masters an opportunity to ask questions or express any reservations she may have about the writer's summation of the discussion. This should eliminate future controversy.

"YOUR JOB" PROJECT

From January 17 to 22 five regional managers of Taylor, Aaron, and Bache (Dallas, San Francisco, Chicago, New York, and Boston) met in your office to discuss various matters, the most important of which were territory realignment, compensation for sales representatives, and training. The first major decision was to establish two new regional offices—one in Atlanta and one in Seattle—effective April 1. Byron Walthrup will be the regional manager in Atlanta, and Lorraine Berman will manage the new regional office in Seattle. The Atlanta office will have under its jurisdiction the states of Florida, Georgia, Alabama, South Carolina, and North Carolina (all previously part of the New York region). The Seattle office will include the states of Washington, Oregon, Montana, Utah, and Nevada (all formerly under the jurisdiction of the San Francisco office). Ten additional representatives are to be hired immediately: one each for eastern Pennsylvania, southern Illinois, northern Michigan, western Maryland, Hawaii, Los Angeles, Chicago, New York City, Houston, and Minneapolis-St. Paul. Each regional manager is to decide whether to transfer existing representatives to these new territories or place new people in them. Effective March 1, all sales representatives are to receive annual bonuses above their regular salaries as follows: For each percentage point above budget, the representative will be given a bonus of twice that percentage; thus, a representative whose regular annual salary is $18,000 exceeds the sales budget by 20 percent will receive a bonus of $7,200 ($18,000 × 40% = $7,200). Also effective March 1, the car-mileage allowance for sales representatives with large geographic territories will be increased from 35 to 40 cents a mile; the allowance for those assigned to large-city areas only will be increased from 40 to 55 cents a mile. (You will issue an announcement of the new compensation and car-mileage allowance plans in a few days.) A new director of sales training will be appointed on July 1. This individual (whom you will select) will visit each regional office at least four times a year to conduct sales training courses for new representatives and offer refresher training for those who, in the regional manager's opinion, can profit from this training. (Further details will be announced later from your office.)

Prepare a confirmation memorandum that sets forth the points covered at the January 17 to 22 meeting. Set up the memo with appropriate display headings so that the material is easy to read and refer to.

STYLE CHECKUP

Rewrite the following sentences to eliminate excess words.

1. I am enclosing for your information a copy of our standard lease.
2. As to your question about exchanging the Handyman tool kits for the Professional kits, I would say that this is acceptable to us.
3. I take great pleasure in announcing to all our dealers a clearance sale on all Star outboard motors.
4. Please return the postcard as soon as conveniently possible for you to do so.

C A S E 4

Writing an Informational Memorandum

THE SETTING

David Chan, your boss, has decided to reorganize the marketing services division, of which he is director. At present there is no clear-cut organization; everyone in the division reports directly to Chan. The marketing services division will be organized into four departments—customer services, market research, advertising, and field sales. Phyllis Knox will be manager of customer services, Lawrence Benson will be manager of market research, J. L. Barrow will be manager of advertising, and Harry Harson will be manager of field sales. You are to remain in the position of special assistant to the director of marketing services.

Objective   To announce by memo the new organization, addressing it to the Executive Committee and the Operations Committee.

BACKGROUND

Most larger organizations are constantly making changes—in job classifications, organization, procedures, promotions, transfers, new appointments, and so on. At the same time, special meetings, visitation by prominent guests, clarification of new policies, and other issues are announced by memorandum. Such memos may be addressed to those at the highest level (e.g., "Executive Committee," "Operations Committee," "Division Managers") or to "All Employees."

SAMPLE MEMOS

TO: Executive Committee   **FROM:** David Chan
Operations Committee

SUBJECT: Reorganization of the   **DATE:** April 25, 19--
Marketing Services
Division

Effective immediately, the marketing services division is to be reorganized as follows: There will be four separate departments--customer services, market research, advertising, and field sales.

Phyllis Knox is promoted to the position of Manager, Customer Services; Lawrence Benson is promoted to Manager, Market Research; J. L. Barrow is promoted to Manager, Advertising; and Harry Harson is promoted to General Manager, Field Sales.

The purpose of this new organization is to provide better guidance and supervision to the four areas indicated and to place responsibility where it belongs.

David Chan

Analysis This is an acceptable informational memorandum. There is a way, however, to make the memo even more readable.

B

TO: Executive Committee   **FROM:** David Chan
Operations Committee

                                         DATE: April 25, 19--

Effective immediately, the marketing services division has been reorganized as follows. There will be four separate departments--customer services, market research, advertising, and field sales.

Phyllis Knox is promoted to the position of Manager, Customer Services; Lawrence Benson is promoted to Manager, Market Research; J. L. Barrow is promoted to Manager, Advertising; and Harry Harson is promoted to General Manager, Field Sales.

The new organization looks like this:

MARKETING SERVICES DIVISION

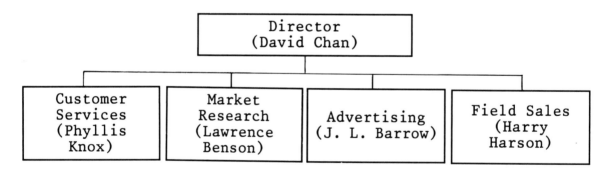

The purpose of this new organization is to provide better guidance and supervision to the four areas indicated and to place responsibility where it belongs.

David Chan

Analysis As you can see, Memorandums A and B are almost the same. However, the inclusion of an organization chart makes B a much more understandable memo.

"YOUR JOB" PROJECTS

1. The firm of Taylor, Aaron, and Bache has decided to build three new distribution centers in the western section of the country—Spokane, Washington; Helena, Montana; and Salem, Oregon. Mr. Bache and David Chan have met twice with Western Construction Company to discuss building these centers. Representatives of Western have been invited to visit Taylor, Aaron, and Bache the week of October 13 to discuss distribution center needs with those responsible for receiving, storing, and shipping pharmaceutical products. David Chan was asked by Bache to choose the people in the company who will meet with the Western Construction people and "chair" the various meetings and discussions. Chosen were Dwight Cowart, Melanie Percival, Floyd Rosen, and Josephine Raeford.

   Chan has roughed out the following memo describing the activities of October 13.

TO: Cowart, Percival, Raeford, and Rosen

FROM: David Chan

SUBJECT: Visit by Western Construction Company

DATE: September 18, 19--

To alleviate the shortage of space in our present distribution centers, Mr. Bache and I have initiated preliminary negotiations with Western Construction Company (there were two confrontations) for the construction of three new distribution centers--in Spokane, Washington; Salem, Oregon; and Helena, Montana--and it is mandatory that we know the requirements of space needs no later than September 26. The representatives of Western Construction Company plan to visit our premises during the entire week of October 13 to converse with each one who has responsibilities for receiving, storing, and shipping activities, and you must check your calendars now immediately, informing the writer of plans you may have arranged about being absent during that period.

Western Construction appears to be eminently qualified to undertake the design and construction of these facilities; our previous meetings with these people were encouraging.

cc: Mr. Bache   David Chan

After reading this rough draft, Chan realizes that it is poor. Chan's revision of the memorandum follows.

TO: Cowart, Percival, Raeford, and Rosen

FROM: David Chan

SUBJECT: Visit by Western Construction Company

DATE: September 18, 19--

Mr. Bache and I have met twice with representatives of Western Construction Company about our plans to build new distribution centers in Spokane, Washington; Helena, Montana; and Salem, Oregon. We like their proposal and think we may have found the right people to do the job for us.

Several of the Western representatives will be here the week of October 13 to learn more about our requirements. They are particularly interested in the procedures for receiving, storing, and shipping our products. To get ready for their visit, we'll need an updated estimate of our space needs in these three locations.

Will you reexamine your earlier reports and, as appropriate, revise your figures? I'll need these new estimates by September 26.

It is very important that you and your principal supervisors be available the week of October 13 for individual conferences with the Western Construction people. If for any reason you plan to be

away from your desk that week, please let
me know at once.

cc: Mr. Bache   David Chan

Read the two informational memorandums carefully. Tell specifically what is wrong with the first memorandum and give examples of how the revised memo is a vast improvement over the first.

2. A new regional sales office for Taylor, Aaron, and Bache will open in Columbia, South Carolina, on July 21. Sales activity in the Carolinas has increased substantially during the past year, and the decision was made to open a new regional office. All representatives who travel in North and South Carolina will now report to the new regional office manager in Columbia, South Carolina, rather than to Atlanta. These people are Melissa Cummings, Rudolph Winston, L. B. O'Rourke, Edward Amend, and Janice Kluzinski. They will report to the field office manager in Columbia, T. W. Korvette.

Write the memorandum to announce this development. Address it to "All Supervisors and Managers." For "FROM," use David Chan.

SUPPLEMENTARY PROJECT

3. In many larger companies the purchase of new furniture and equipment goes on constantly. When a new piece of furniture, say, a secretarial desk, is purchased to replace a desk that no longer serves its purpose, the old one is stored for a certain period of time and finally disposed of by selling it to a used-furniture and equipment dealer.

The purchasing director of Matlock Trucking Company, Tracy Rosetti, wants to inform all supervisors and managers who purchase office furniture and equipment that there is a sizable inventory of these items (used but usable) at Matlock Trucking Company. These include desks, chairs, electric typewriters, electronic calculators, tables, sofas, filing equipment, lamps, wall hangings, film projectors, and several other used items. Rosetti thinks a great deal of money can be saved on office furniture and equipment if people see what the company has on hand at virtually no cost. The inventory is in Warehouse B, and those interested should call Rosetti at Extension 2174. Write the memorandum.

STYLE CHECKUP

Insert hyphens where you think they are needed.

1. You don't need a high priced calculator for this job.
2. We consider this an all important decision.
3. Morgan Corporation issued 10 and 20 year bonds.
4. All these reports are to be sent by first class mail.
5. Our decision was based on long established practice.
6. Are you keeping up to date with the merchandising policies?

PART THREE

WRITING EFFECTIVE BUSINESS REPORTS

In Part 2 we discussed interoffice memorandums, stressing their importance as the most frequently used method of communicating with people within the same company—not only with those of lesser or equal rank but those of higher rank such as supervisors, managers, and top executives.

In Part 3 we continue our discussion of memos but this time as business reports. The distinction between an everyday memo and a memorandum report is not in form but in substance. An everyday memo can be considered as a somewhat brief communication concerning routine matters in the company, while a memorandum report is often somewhat longer and usually pertains to more weighty subjects than those treated in everyday memos.

In this part we also introduce you to another important business communication—the formal business report or, as they are sometimes called, the formally structured report. Following are some of the subjects that formally structured reports deal with.

- Reorganization of one or more larger departments in the company.
- Plans for acquiring one or two smaller companies and fitting them within the present organization.
- Establishment of new concepts and strategies that affect the entire company.
- Reexamination of the company's objectives that may represent a sweeping change in personnel, managerial responsibilities, and method of operating.
- An intensive study of current products being marketed and taking on new products.
- Studies of customer preferences as to product and method of distribution.
- An overhaul of the company's policy on retirement—age, retirement pay, life insurance and medical benefits.

Thus, where the memorandum is the jack-of-all-trades in interoffice communication, the formally structured report usually concentrates on the "big picture."

BUSINESS REPORTS AND COMPUTERS

Today information for various types of reports can easily be obtained from computers, for data can be stored in a computer's memory for quick retrieval. For example, if an executive asks the human services director the number of employees who have a good knowledge of electronic data processing, it is quite likely that the computer can deliver a printout of these figures in seconds. The same is true when the manufacturing director is asked about the amount spent during the third quarter on factory overtime or when the purchasing director is asked how many requisitions for new equipment were received in March. In these cases, the computer may easily supply everything that is needed. In other instances the computer may provide part of the data asked for; the rest—say, your interpretation of the data—must be created from your own brain.

Very frequently, however, reports are written without any help from a computer. Suppose, for example, that a top executive asks, "What effect do you think a change in office hours—say, 8:30 to 4:30 instead of 9 to 5—would have on employee morale?" Here you will have to do a lot of interviewing, both in person and by questionnaire, to obtain the answer. Once you have gathered the information you need and have written your report, you may decide to store the data in a computer for later retrieval. But the legwork and "brainwork" must be done by you.

<table>
<tr><td>

CHAPTER
17

</td><td>

BASIC GUIDELINES FOR WRITING REPORTS

</td></tr>
</table>

Report types, setup, content, and wording vary from one company to another, even by departments within the same organization. However, the following four basic guidelines pertain to all narrative business reports.

1. Have clearly in mind the reason for writing the report—the purpose—and identify it for the reader(s).
2. Know who your readers are, for on them depends the kind of presentation you make.
3. Make sure that your report are believable.
4. Use display to give the report a readable appearance, particularly in longer reports. By *display* we mean headings, enumerations, indentions, tables, and special illustrations. These displays may include *computer graphics*, which are charts, graphs, and pictures that a computer produces automatically from verbal or numerical information.

STATING THE PURPOSE OF THE REPORT

Every report should, of course, have a purpose. This seems to be an elementary piece of advice, but it is surprising how many business reports are received that trigger this question from the recipient: Why did I get this?

In some informal reports written as memos, the purpose may be implied rather than precisely stated. For example:

1. Here is the report you asked for last week explaining why the September expenses of the Mail Processing Unit exceeded the budget.
2. During my visit to the new Petersborough Distribution Center on May 14, the managerial staff discussed several problems that I think you should know about.
3. At the October meeting of the Systems Improvement Committee, I was asked to investigate the possibility of preparing our own microfilm and microfiche records rather than contracting the work to outsiders. This is my report of that study.
4. Executive Directive 46 asks for ways in which the company can persuade more employees to participate in the new suggestion plan. Following are my thoughts on the matter.

Formal reports, on the other hand, often require a fairly detailed statement of purpose. Thus:

PURPOSE

Requests from employees for a sabbatical to pursue further education have accelerated greatly during the past year, many citing the liberal policy of other companies in the industry. The Management Group appointed a fact-finding committee to undertake a survey of 50 selected companies on this subject, and the information has now been gathered. The purpose of this report is to present the committee's findings, along with recommendations for a standard policy at Forstner Inc.

KNOWING YOUR READER

The person or persons to whom your report is addressed will determine to a large extent the manner in which you write it. You must take into account the reader's preferences as to language and style, biases regarding the subject (if any), knowledge of the subject, and familiarity with the terms the report contains. Three factors must be taken into account in determining the style and language of your reports:

1. *The subject of the report.* The topic you are writing on may be so ponderous (a detailed proposal for the acquisition of a business or a recommendation that the company's retirement plan be completely overhauled, for example) that a conversational tone could take away the objective flavor that some top executives may expect.
2. *Your place in the organization.* A report addressed to the company president, who is several layers of management above you, is likely to be more formal in tone than one addressed to your supervisor, with whom you may have a warm, personal relationship.
3. *Your expertise in the subject of the report.* The company's top tax expert can express personal opinions on the subject of taxes with heavy emphasis on personal pronouns (*I believe, I recommend, My experience tells me*). One who knows very little about taxes would be wise to state one's opinions a little more formally—for example, *It would appear that* rather than *I'm convinced that.*

Reader Bias Sometimes bias on the part of the reader will influence your handling of the subject if not the language. If the addressee is known to be very conservative about experiments and innovations, then your suggestions about new designs for existing products and new packaging will concentrate mostly on hard facts rather than on personal opinions. Including some computer graphics in your report might make the advantages of your proposal more obvious and more persuasive. On the other hand, you can let yourself go when presenting the same ideas to the executive who is keenly interested in anything new. If you need new furnishings for your department but the executive to whom you must send a report hates to spend money, you will focus on increased efficiency and productivity. You would probably emphasize essentially the same things in a report to an innovator, but you would not be reluctant to mention beauty, company image, and morale.

Subject Knowledge   Before you sit down to put a report together, you should ask yourself, "How much do the people who will read this know about the subject?" If the accounting department frequently discusses the lack of a good system for cash control, you won't need to supply much background data when you deliver your suggestions to the controller. On the other hand, if you know that other people outside the accounting department will read the report, you'll need to describe the problem and state the need for a change before you launch into the report itself. People who aren't experts in a field (and even those who are) may be able to understand your information more easily if you supplement the text with graphics—an easy matter if you're using a microcomputer with graphics capability.

Definitions of Terms   Every profession has its own jargon. You don't have to define *debentures* for the company treasurer or *hard disk* for the computer-room manager, and you don't have to explain *PERT* to the head of manufacturing or *ultrafiche* to a records management supervisor. Yet anyone outside these specialities probably will not understand what you're talking about if you don't provide definitions.

Not only do writers frequently have to define technical terminology, they must also be prepared to explain what they may regard as everyday terms to some readers. Nowhere is this more apparent than in computer-related areas. For example, many people outside the administrative office are confused by such terms as *systems analysis* (the process of designing and developing information processing systems), *flowchart* (a chart showing the flow of work from start to finish with symbols representing operations and equipment), *interface* (an electrical connector that permits equipment such as printers to be attached to an information processing system), *input* (the transfer of text or data into an information processing system or the text or data itself), and *soft copy* (the text that is displayed on a video display terminal as opposed to text that is printed). A report on how to gain access to electronic files must define the term *file* (a document-storage area in the computer's memory) because it means something entirely different to someone using computers than to someone in an office which is not automated. So when you write your report, include clear definitions of terms that you know might give your readers trouble.

MAKING REPORTS BELIEVABLE

Everyone has biases—about clothing, cars, music, entertainers, art, and a hundred other things. Most of us bring some biases to work. Marketing people, manufacturing employees, personnel staff members, accountants, and so on, have pro biases concerning the importance of the work they do as compared with what others do. These biases are to be expected; indeed, they are sometimes encouraged by management in the interest of team spirit. And since we're all human, we develop biases about individuals.

These biases can be excused provided they're kept under wraps and are not allowed to affect our actions. But when biases rise to the surface and are used to score points, they can only be labeled as insidious. In business reports insidious bias is particularly dangerous—it destroys your credibility.

Insidious bias is present when we:

1. Attach labels to people or activities to prove a selfish point. The self-made executive indicates insidious bias when labeling college graduates (especially M.B.A.s) as "boy or girl wonders" or "gung-ho eggheads." Those who refer to others' motives as "ulterior" or "specious" do more harm to themselves than to the accused. And the use of such terms as *ilk* (to identify a group whose opinions are not respected), *spiel* (referring to a presentation), *elitist*, and so on, is a dead giveaway that insidious bias is present.

2. Fail to separate fact from opinion. Suppose that a department manager writes the following: "The Shipping Department employees work longer hours than any other group in the company and get the least recognition from management." Unless this statement can be proved, readers will be suspicious of it. This would have been an honest statement: "I'm proud of the willingness of the Shipping Department employees to work whatever hours are necessary to get orders out to customers, and I think that occasional recognition of their efforts by top management would do wonders for morale."

3. Slant our writing to prove a point. For example:

   a. "I'm losing my best customers," wrote a sales representative, "because of poor service from Order Fulfillment." The writer may be honest, but we raise an eyebrow when specific examples are missing. Perhaps the representative meant this: "Six of my good customers in Greater Louisville told me in July that they've had to wait as long as two weeks for an order."

   b. "Most of the employees in the company," wrote a department manager, "are disgusted with our so-called promotion-from-within policy." The term *so-called* gives away the writer's opinion of the policy, and it alone destroys credibility. Also, one wonders how this information was obtained. How many is "most"? Does the writer mean 51 percent? Or 97 percent? This is better: "Of the twelve people I talked with in various departments in the company, eight said they feel that our promotion-from-within policy is too often violated."

   c. "The reason we can't keep secretaries," wrote a human resources supervisor, "is that their supervisors treat them as second-class citizens." On what evidence is this assertion based? Also, the statement is so sweeping that we question its validity. Perhaps this is more to the point: "Of the six secretaries who resigned in February, four told me at the exit interview that they were unhappy with their clerical status (meaning that they were not allowed to show initiative). The other two said they had received offers that they couldn't afford to turn down."

4. Use fallacious reasoning.

   a. "A cutback of 20 percent in our staff will undoubtedly mean that at least one-fifth of our customers will receive inadequate service." More logical: "It's difficult to predict the results of a 20-percent cutback in our staff. Undoubtedly, it will be much harder to provide our current level of service with ten fewer people."

b. "The great majority of our administrative assistants are women; therefore, it is unlikely that we could attract men to jobs they consider women's work." More logical: "Of the 50 administrative assistants in the company, only 2 are men. This could mean that we simply haven't given enough publicity to the opportunities for men in these positions."

c. "Start-up costs for computerizing the stock control system are estimated at $450,000. We aren't spending nearly that much at present on our manual system, so I don't see how we can justify that kind of money." More logical: "Start-up costs for computerizing the stock control system are estimated at $450,000. This amount seems high compared with what we're spending now, yet in the long run, a computer system could mean substantial savings."

USING EFFECTIVE DISPLAY

If you've ever been lost while driving at night in a strange suburban area of a large city because the road signs were either nonexistent or confusing, then you know the importance of frequent markers. We can compare this situation with reading reports, particularly long ones. People like to know where they're being led, and they need signs to tell them. These signs are in the form of headings, enumerations, indentions, tables, and special illustrations.

In most short, informal reports, you may not need any display—reading them involves only a short "trip," and the route seems clear. To enhance clarity regardless of the length of your report, you nearly always have an opportunity to use some display.

Headings For longer reports, you are almost certain to need headings. Not only are they guides to easier reading, they also provide white space. Solid copy, no matter how well written, is tough going for readers.

The number of headings to use depends on the type of material you are presenting. Unless you're writing a very long and complicated report, you can usually get by with four or five headings. For example:

A PROFIT-SHARING PLAN FOR DETTMER AND COMPANY

```
This is the number one head--in this case, the
title of the report.  If your report contains,
say, four major and distinct sections, you may
want to center each section title and type it in
all caps.
```

TYPES OF PROFIT-SHARING PLANS

Three basic types of profit-sharing plans are
used in most. . . .

The head above is a number two head, written in all caps and flush with the left
margin.

Cash Profit Sharing

Under this type of plan, the share of profits is
paid the employee. . . .

Deferred Profit Sharing

The share of profits due employees under this
plan. . . .

Combination Profit Sharing

Combination profit sharing combines the elements
of the. . . .

The three heads shown are third in importance. They are written in uppercase
and lowercase—or ulc—and they are underlined and flush with the left margin.

**Features of the Combination Profit-Sharing
Plan.** Three special features of the combination
profit-sharing plan are worthy of special mention. They. . . .

The number four head is ulc and underlined. In addition, the copy runs in—that
is, it starts on the same line.

     Investment of the Employee's Share. The
company takes the responsibility for investing
for each employee the amount that is held in
trust. . . .

The number five head is indented five spaces, ulc, and underlined, and the copy
runs in.

    Usually, there is no reason for you to go beyond the five heads illustrated
(more likely than not, you can get by with only three or four). If you need more
than five, study your report to see whether it needs to be reorganized. Although
headings are important, they can be confusing if there are too many.

Enumerations   You can give emphasis to major points by numbering them.
For example:

THE INTERNAL REVENUE CODE IN PROFIT SHARING

Any profit-sharing plan should be set up in such a manner that it qualifies for special tax treatment under the Internal Revenue Code. Four basic criteria for a qualified plan follow:

1. The plan must be primarily a deferred compensation plan.
2. It must be part of a permanent arrangement and not a temporary expedient.
3. It must be for the exclusive use of the employees.
4. It must cover either a specified percentage of the employees or a nondiscriminatory class of employees.

If you prefer, you can provide heads for your enumerations. For example:

ADVANTAGES OF PROFIT SHARING

Two basic advantages of profit sharing that are mentioned most frequently by companies that have installed a plan are as follows:

1. _Incentive._ It has been proved over and over that the most attractive feature of profit sharing is the incentive it. . . .
2. _Retirement._ Profit sharing has been found to be an excellent way to provide a retirement trust for employees. This feature. . . .

Indentions   Another way to make important things stand out in your reports is to indent them. This is especially effective when you're listing names, titles, and figures. It is standard practice to indent when you are quoting people or printed sources.

Profit Sharing Defined
There are several definitions of profit sharing. Perhaps the most widely accepted definition is that given by the Council of Profit-Sharing Industries (a trade association that promotes the idea of profit sharing among businesses):

Any procedure under which an employer pays or makes available to all regular employees subject to reasonable eligibility rules, in addi-

tion to prevailing rates of pay, special current or deferred sums based upon the profits
of the business.

Note in this definition the reference to "all
regular employees." This would seem to indicate
that a. . . .

Tables If your report contains a good many figures, it is best, when you can,
to set them up in table form. Figures interspersed with narrative are hard to
follow, and for that reason readers often skip over them. While preparing tables
can be difficult and time-consuming if you are using a typewriter, word processors
have made this task much easier. A typical table follows.

The policy of paying overtime to supervisory personnel varies widely. Often the rate of overtime
pay is based on the salary range. A typical
overtime pay provision for supervisory personnel
is shown in the table below.

TABLE 14. OVERTIME PAY RATES FOR SUPERVISORS

Salary Range	Overtime Rate
$ 9,000-$12,000	1.50
$12,000-$15,000	1.25
$15,000-$18,000	1.00
$18,000-$20,000	0.75
$20,000-$22,000	0.50
$22,000-$25,000	0.25
Over $25,000	0.00

Note that the table shown is very simple and contains no rules. If you have
one that is fairly complicated, you may wish to separate the data with vertical
and horizontal rules as shown on page 337.

Graphs In some reports various types of graphs can be used effectively. The
three most popular graphs for business reports are the line graph, the bar graph,
and the circle graph.

The *line graph* is especially effective to show patterns, trends, and changes
(for example, company profits earned over a ten-year period). The *bar graph*
is best to show comparative data (for example, the net sales and profits of six
retail chain stores during the past year). The *circle graph*, often called a *pie
chart*, is best for showing the relationship of the parts of something to the whole
(for example, the percentage or amount spent for each employee benefit based
on 100 percent or $1).

PROJECTED WORK STOPPAGES IN AUTOMOTIVE AND
RELATED INDUSTRIES OVER A 10-YEAR PERIOD

Year	Number of stoppages	Number of workers involved (rounded off to nearest thousand)	Worker-days idle
1	2,968	840,000	4,183,000
2	3,752	1,981,000	13,501,000
3	4,956	2,116,000	8,721,000
4	4,750	3,470,000	38,000,000
5	4,985	4,600,000	116,000,000
6	3,693	2,170,000	34,600,000
7	3,419	1,960,000	34,100,000
8	3,606	3,030,000	50,500,000
9	4,843	2,410,000	38,800,000
10	7,112	3,276,000	22,580,000

If you have the right software, a microcomputer may be able to create graphs automatically on the basis of your data. It may even be able to produce them in several vivid colors. If you're preparing them without a computer, however, you should be acquainted with special techniques required to set up effective graphs. A good textbook on statistics, available in most business libraries, will include the illustrations you need.

"YOUR JOB" PROJECTS

1. Your supervisor, E. A. Haskell, has asked for a memorandum report on the number of physically disabled people employed in the company (Warner-Dennison) and how they are rated by their supervisors in terms of safety, attendance, and job performance.

   To get the information you need, you sent a questionnaire to all executives in the company asking them to give you the total number of disabled workers employed in five categories—professional and technical workers, supervisors and managers, clerks, artisans, and laborers—and to rate those in each category as above average, average, or below average.

   Following are two possible reports that could have been sent to your supervisor.

   a.

   TO: E. A. Haskell   **FROM:** G. C. Harmon

   SUBJECT: Physically Disabled Employees   **DATE:** Current date

   Following is information on the physically disabled.

Professional and technical workers: Total
employed: 82. In terms of safety, 40 of
these were rated above average, 41 average,
and 1 below average. In terms of attendance,
33 were rated above average, 40 as average,
and 9 below average. As to job performance,
32 were rated above average, 45 average, and
5 below average.

Supervisors and Managers: Total employed:
38. In terms of safety, 22 were rated as
above average, 16 as average, and 0 as below
average. In terms of attendance, 16 were
rated above average, 20 as average, and 2 below average.

Clerks: Total employed: 65. As to safety,
34 were rated as above average, 30 as average, and 1 as below average. In terms of attendance, 35 were above average, 25 average,
and 5 below average. In job performance, 27
were rated above average, 32 average, and 6
below average.

Artisans: Total employed: 110. In safety,
39 were rated above average, 67 as average,
and 4 below average. In attendance, 40 were
rated as above average, 52 as average, and 18
as below average. As to job performance, 30
were considered above average, 60 as average,
and 20 as below average.

Laborers: Total employed: 14. As to
safety, 3 were rated as above average, 10 as
average, and 1 as below average. In terms of
attendance, 4 were rated above average, 9 average, and 1 below average. Concerning job
performance, 2 were rated above average, 8
average, and 4 below average.

Many of those reporting made enthusiastic
comments about their disabled workers. The
most consistent reason given for the outstanding performance of these people is that
they have a higher degree of motivation, pre-

sumably because they appreciate the opportunity to work.

Included in the disabled category are people who are blind, partially sighted, and deaf, as well as amputees, paraplegics, and others crippled from various causes--polio, accidents, birth defects, and so on.

b.

TO:	E. A. Haskell	**FROM:**	G. C. Harmon
SUBJECT:	Performance Report on the Physically Disabled	**DATE:**	Current date

Following is the information you asked for concerning the performance of physically disabled employees at Warner-Dennison.

DEFINITION AND CLASSIFICATION

Warner-Dennison employs people with various kinds of physical disabilities--the blind, the partially sighted, and the deaf, as well as amputees, paraplegics, and others who are crippled (victims of polio, accidents, birth defects, and so on). For the purposes of this report, physically disabled employees were placed in five employment categories: professional and technical workers, supervisors and managers, clerks, artisans, and laborers. Each executive and department head was asked to rate his or her disabled workers as above average, average or below average in terms of safety, attendance, and job performance.

RATINGS GIVEN DISABLED WORKERS

The following table shows the ratings given disabled workers by their supervisors. AA indicates above average, A indicates average, and BA indicates below average.

Job Classification	Total	Safety			Attendance			Job Performance		
		AA	A	BA	AA	A	BA	AA	A	BA
Professional and technical workers	82	40	41	1	33	40	9	32	45	5
Supervisors and managers	38	22	16	0	16	20	2	15	21	2
Clerks	65	34	30	1	35	25	5	27	32	6
Artisans	110	39	67	4	40	52	18	30	60	20
Laborers	14	3	10	1	4	9	1	2	8	4
TOTALS	309	138	164	7	128	146	35	106	166	37

In terms of overall evaluation, the percentages shown below are significant.

Safety		Attendance		Job Performance	
Above Average	Below Average	Above Average	Below Average	Above Average	Below Average
44.6%	2.3%	41%	10.5%	34%	10.5%

Those rating disabled workers were enthusiastic about their competence and worth. The most consistent reason given for the outstanding performance of these people is that they have a higher degree of motivation, presumably because they appreciate the opportunity to work and are eager not to forfeit this opportunity.

Which of the two reports do you think is better? In what specific ways?

2. You are the director of new-product research for Nowata Electronics Corporation and have just completed a six-month study of fire alarm systems on the market. Your study includes a detailed analysis of the strengths and weaknesses of the systems. You are now ready to prepare a report of your findings. It will be addressed to the Executive Committee, of which the company president is chairperson.

In your job you also serve as the president of the Outdoor Club, a group of employees who devote their leisure time to skiing, backpacking, and other outdoor sports. You plan to write a short message to the members about the big Bear Mountain hike, which is coming up. You want to encourage them to sign up, and to find out who can help with transportation.

How will the two reports differ in wording and tone? Why?

3. Write the following in a more formal, impersonal tone.

   a. I think we should first find out why dealers are returning so many lawn mowers this spring.

   b. Of course, we will look only at people who have the experience these jobs call for.

   c. It's clear to me, on the basis of the interviews I've had with top people here, that we've got to find a better way to compensate our executives.

   d. I think the first step we should take is to interview our supervisors to find out what they think the needs are for a training program.

   e. I will continue my daily check on the efficiency of this new installation and report to you at the end of October—earlier if something important develops.

   f. Would you like a further breakdown on the inventory situation in Dayton and Chattanooga? I have the information and can get it to you quickly.

   g. When the figures arrive from Harrison, I'll be in a better position to make an accurate long-range forecast for you.

   h. This is about as far as I can go until our committee has a meeting in December, after which I will report in more detail.

4. Rewrite the following, using less formal (more personal) language.

```
Per person sales performance was substantially
improved during the last year.  Volume is signif-
icantly higher (40 percent) with fewer represen-
tatives, leading to the conclusion that the cali-
ber of sales personnel is superior to that in any
previous period in Cranston history.  This can no
doubt be attributed to improved training and su-
pervision.
```

STYLE CHECKUP

Rewrite each of the following sentences to eliminate the redundancy or unnecessary words.

1. This appears to be the same identical problem we had last year.
2. Some of our products, such as, for example, large appliances, are protected by a two-year warranty.
3. It is our policy to bear the cost and expense of shipping cash orders.
4. We decided to sell off the remaining stock at a 50 percent discount.
5. The receptionist greeted each visitor and called him or her by name.

MEMORANDUMS AS REPORTS

CHAPTER 18

YOUR JOB

You are the assistant marketing manager of Permatrax Corporation. In this position you write many letters to customers and others. Most of your writing, however, consists of memorandums and other informal reports. Some are self-initiated, and others are written at the request of the marketing manager, Harold C. Simank.

CASE 1

Writing a Periodic Memorandum Report

THE SETTING

H. C. Simank, the marketing manager of Permatrax, has asked you to prepare quarterly reports of bonuses earned by the seven regional managers during the year. At the end of every three months, therefore, you gather the information and submit a report. Simank wants figures for the current quarter and for the same quarter last year, the amount of increase or decrease, and any comments you feel are appropriate.

Your Objective   To set up the report in such a way that it is easy to prepare and to read.

BACKGROUND

Periodic reports are reports that are written according to a specified schedule—daily, weekly, monthly, quarterly, and so on. More often than not, such reports consist mainly of figures—monthly financial statements, weekly reports on overtime worked by employees in various departments, daily reports of articles produced in a factory, annual reports of employee turnover, and so on.
  In writing periodic reports, follow these guidelines.

Guidelines

1. When possible, set up the memorandum as a fill-in form that can be duplicated and used over and over again.
2. If narrative comments may be required in the periodic reports, leave space somewhere on the memorandum form for writing these comments.

SAMPLE MEMO REPORTS
....

PERMATRAX CORPORATION

INTEROFFICE MEMORANDUM

(A)

TO: H. C. Simank   **FROM:** Your Name

SUBJECT: Quarterly Report of   **DATE:** July 16, 19--
Bonuses Earned by
Regional Managers

Following is a report of the bonus earnings of the seven regional managers for the period April 1 through June 30 (second quarter).

This year, L. Berman earned $4,238 (her first full quarter as a regional manager). C. Burke earned $5,657 as compared with $5,046 last year, which is an increase of $611. L. Carey earned $6,617 this year and $6,958 last year, a decrease of $341. W. Dorr's second-quarter earnings this year were $3,986, and last year they amounted to $6,456. (Note: Dorr's territory was split off on April 1, which accounts in large measure for the decrease of $2,470). R. Espinoza earned $7,566 this year as compared with $6,437 last year, an increase of $1,129. B. Walthrup's earnings amounted to $3,320 (his first full quarter as a regional manager). T. Yerian had a bonus of $4,286 in the second quarter of this year and $7,706 last year. (Note: Yerian's territory was split off on April 1, which accounts in large measure for the decrease of $3,420.)

Analysis   As you will quickly notice, Memo A should have been better thought out before it was written.

1. Memo A will be difficult to read, and it will be hard to make comparisons.
2. The report will have to be constructed from scratch at the end of each quarter.

PERMATRAX CORPORATION

INTEROFFICE MEMORANDUM

TO: H. C. Simank   **FROM:** Your Name

SUBJECT: Quarterly Report of Bonuses Earned by Regional Managers   **DATE:** July 16, 19--

Quarter _2nd_ Year _19-_

Manager	This Year	Last Year	Increase	Decrease	Comments
Berman, L.	4,238	—	—	—	First quarter as regional manager
Burke, C.	5,657	5,046	611		
Carey, L.	6,617	6,958	659	341	
Dorr, W.	3,986	6,456		2,470	See below
Espinoza, R.	7,566	6,437	1,129		
Walthrop, B.	3,320	—	—	—	First quarter as regional manager
Yerian, T.	4,286	7,706		3,420	See below

Additional Comments: _Both Dorr's and Yerian's territories were split on April 1, which accounts in large measure for the decreases indicated._

Analysis Memo B's writer carefully took into account how the memo would be used and read.

1. The report is designed so that it can be duplicated and used over and over again; only the date and quarter, earnings figures, and comments need to be entered.
2. This form is ruled for handwritten insertions. If, however, the form is to be filled in on a typewriter, the horizontal rules may be omitted.
3. Vertical rules are optional in either case, but they are helpful in separating the data.
4. Note that dollar signs do not appear; they are usually not necessary in form reports dealing almost entirely with amounts of money.

"YOUR JOB" PROJECT

You have decided to ask the seven regional managers to keep a record of the expenses of each of their sales representatives and send you a report once a month. The information you want includes the name of the representative; car mileage, per-mile rate, and total cost; other transportation expenses (plane, bus, taxi); hotel and motel expenses; the cost of meals; expenditures for the entertainment of customers; and miscellaneous expenses (telephone calls, postage, and tips).

Design a report form that you will supply in quantity to the regional managers. Since the columns required will not fit vertically on a memorandum form, use a plain sheet of paper, turning it sideways. Give the report a title, and allow for other appropriate identification data.

STYLE CHECKUP

Rewrite each sentence below to eliminate the negative statements.

1. We are unable to send the wall coverings until May 12. (*Note*: The date of the letter in which the sentence appears is May 2.)
2. I am sorry to discourage you about employment opportunities in the near future at Sencland Corporation, but the prospects are dismal.
3. The only work experience I have to offer is in my family's real estate business for the past three years.
4. The reason you did not receive earlier the catalog you requested is that we couldn't read your handwriting in the address supplied.
5. A customer is not entitled to a discount unless the purchase is paid for within ten days of receipt of the merchandise.

C A S E 2 Reporting the Results of an Informal Study

THE SETTING

At a recent national sales conference, the marketing manager (H. C. Simank) heard a number of complaints from sales representatives about the letters that are being sent to their customers by the home office. You have been asked to read copies of all outgoing letters to customers for a month and to submit your findings along with your recommendations.

Your Objective To present your findings and recommendations in such a way that the information is easy to read and interpret.

BACKGROUND

Often you will write reports that are based on informal studies, investigations, and research. These reports may be self-initiated or prepared at the request of someone higher up in the organization. For many such reports, you may use a memorandum, depending on the preferences of those who are to read them. In the situation described above, a memorandum report would be acceptable.

In writing a memorandum report based on an informal study, follow these guidelines.

Guidelines

1. State the purpose of the report. The statement may be merely a reference to a request memorandum, a telephone call, or a personal visit.
2. Use suitable side headings to guide the reader. Among the most important are *Findings* and *Recommendations* (including *Procedure*).
3. Unless otherwise instructed, use informal language, including personal pronouns.
4. Describe the method you used to obtain the data for your report (often this is done under the heading *Method*).

SAMPLE REPORT

PERMATRAX CORPORATION

INTEROFFICE MEMORANDUM

TO: H. C. Simank **FROM:** Your Name

SUBJECT: Review of Customer Correspondence **DATE:** July 7, 19--

Dear Harold:

I have completed the review of customer correspondence (your memorandum of May 16) for the period May 21 through June 21. As you suggested, I read copies of all outgoing letters written by the four correspondents in the Customer Services Unit. (These were sent to me daily at your request.) During this period, 1,079 letters were written and mailed to customers.

METHOD

As I read each letter, I assigned a grade to it: A (excellent), B (good), C (passable), and D (poor). The elements considered in assigning these grades were tone (friendliness), helpfulness, accuracy of information, organization, and grammatical correctness.

Findings

The findings follow:

Number of Letters	Grade Assigned
146	A
212	B
527	C
194	D
1,079	

Although my evaluations were necessarily subjective, the grade distributions indicated above would appear to give credence to the sales representatives' criticism. As they mentioned to you at the conference, there are many examples of indifference, carelessness with facts, repetition and circumlocution, and negativsm. It seems apparent, based on the 1,079 letters examined, that the standard of customer letters in Permatrax is much lower than it should be.

As might be expected, most of the letters in the C and D categories were written by the same people, and the same is true of the A and B categories. Yet individuals predominantly in the C category, for example, frequently produced good to excellent letters and a few of those whose letters fell mostly in the A and B categories wrote some letters that were barely passable.

RECOMMENDATIONS

Based on this quick study, I recommend that we set up a special course for all sales correspondents, say, two hours a week for whatever period of time is required--perhaps twelve weeks or so. I believe the logical person in the company to teach the course is Dorothy Fasnacht in Human Resources Training. She is a communications specialist (last year she organized and taught a course for credit correspondents and, according to the credit manager, Clark Pinson, it was a great success).

Procedure

I recommend that whoever handles the assignment might proceed as follows:

1. Prepare photocopies of perhaps 100 letters representing all categories and distribute them to the participants. All names would be concealed so that it would not be readily apparent who wrote the letters.
2. These letters would, in effect, serve as the textbook for the course. Each letter would be examined critically by the class, and everyone

would be asked to contribute to a revision of those that contain flaws. In this way, we can get across all the basic elements of good letter writing in the most practical setting possible.

3. During the course the participants would continue to supply the instructor with copies of their outgoing letters to enable the instructor to measure the results being achieved in the course and perhaps schedule private sessions with those who continue to have difficulty.

I will be happy to assist in setting up the course and help the instructor in any way that I can if you think these ideas are feasible.

Analysis   Note the following about this report:

1. The opening paragraph indicates the purpose of the report (reference to Simank's written request) and provides a brief background that leads into the body of the report.
2. Four major heads are provided—*Method, Findings, Recommendations,* and *Procedure.* Even though the report is brief, these are excellent guides for the reader.
3. The writer has set up the results under *Findings* in tabular form for easy reference and briefly interprets those findings.
4. Simank asked the writer not only to evaluate the letters but also to make recommendations on the basis of findings. These recommendations are set up so that they are easy to read and understand.
5. Some writers would have sent a "rant-and-rave" report, expressing shock at the awful letters samples and naming names. The writer has not done this. If Simank wants this information, he will ask for it. (*Note:* We recommend that you refrain from making personal attacks in all the reports that you write unless you are specifically asked to evaluate individuals.)

"YOUR JOB" PROJECT

The Operations Committee of Permatrax Corporation, of which you are the chairperson, has discussed the feasibility of establishing an employee suggestion plan for the company. You asked a member of the committee, P C. Baffle, to study the matter and present a brief report, including specific recommendations concerning how the system might be operated.

Following is the report you received.

PERMATRAX CORPORATION

INTEROFFICE MEMORANDUM

TO: Your Name   **FROM:** P. C. Baffle

SUBJECT: Employee Suggestion   **DATE:** Current date
Plan

Suggestion plans of five different companies were studied, and the best features of all these were selected as most pertinent to Permatrax.

The five companies referred to maintain that they have benefited in three ways from having a suggestion system: Encourages workers to make improvements and eliminate waste. Provides an effective means whereby the worker can communicate with management. Improves morale--gives employees a sense of contributing.

Based on my study, I would recommend that the following procedures be established. A special form be designed (sample attached hereto) and printed in quantity and distributed to employees, along with an announcement of the general plan. Suggestion boxes should be placed on each floor of the building and employees encouraged to drop their suggestions in the boxes. A committee of six people, each representing a different department, should be named to administer the awards. (This might be called the Suggestion System Committee.)

Two types of awards would be presented--Class A and Class B. As to Class A, where savings can be computed, an award equal to 25% of the first year's savings would be paid. If the award is $100 or more, half of the amount (based on _esti-mated_ savings) would be paid as soon as possible after the suggestion is adopted. The remainder (based on _actual_ savings) would be paid within a year after the suggestion is adopted. If the award is less than $100, the entire amount would be paid as soon as possible after the suggestion is adopted.

As to Class B awards, where savings cannot be precisely computed (for example, safety suggestions) awards from $25 to $50 would be made. When exceptional circumstances warrant, the committee referred to above should be authorized to offer an award up to $100 for such suggestions.

In terms of operating rules, all suggestions, on submission, would become the property of the employer. Suggestions would be collected daily and date-stamped. This date would become the official date of the suggestion. (A separate sheet is attached on which are listed 20 additional operating rules that might be adapted for our purposes.)

I trust the information given will be helpful to you.

Assume that the information supplied is quite helpful. However, the report itself has several flaws in terms of organization and wording. Rewrite it, supplying whatever devices you think are appropriate to make it more readable.

STYLE CHECKUP

Rewrite the following sentences, each of which contains an example of bigwordism.

1. I will cogitate on the suggestion and let you know my decision soon.
2. Marvin could not comprehend the new pricing formula.
3. The panel was composed of six insurance experts.
4. Smith conjectures that sales will decline in the third quarter.
5. Whitman corroborated Foley's opinion about the Ackerson account.

C A S E
3

Presenting Ideas and Suggestions by Memorandum

THE SETTING

Permatrax Corporation publishes a monthly magazine (*Tabs*) for its employees. The editor, J. R. Sanchez, has written a memo to all department heads asking for suggestions on improving the publication. There has been widespread criticism of the magazine, and Sanchez would like to have recommendations for making it better.

Your Objective   To present your ideas and suggestions for improving *Tabs*.

BACKGROUND

Employees are often asked for their ideas and suggestions for making the company a better organization—ideas for improving personnel relations, saving time and effort, cutting costs, serving customers better, and building public goodwill.

In responding to such requests, follow these guidelines.

Guidelines

1. Don't be overly modest in offering your opinion; you would not have received an invitation to contribute your ideas if they were not considered valuable.
2. If appropriate, try to begin with positive remarks about the present situation, and then tactfully proceed with your suggestions for change.
3. Be specific; don't leave it to the reader's imagination to determine what you have in mind.
4. When appropriate, group your ideas according to subject, and display the subjects prominently.

SAMPLE SUGGESTION MEMOS

INTEROFFICE MEMORANDUM

TO: J. R. Sanchez   **FROM:** Your Name

SUBJECT: Suggestions for <u>Tabs</u>   **DATE:** Current date

Although I do not consider myself an authority in employee magazine publishing, I will offer a few suggestions for improving <u>Tabs</u> in response to your memorandum.

I would leave the title as it is, but there ought to be more photographs, a "Letter to the Editor" column, a new masthead, a better typeface, more stories about typical workers, and a gossip column. Also, I think you might consider an Employee of the Month Award.

I hope you won't think I have been too critical.

Analysis   Memo A is a poor memorandum for two reasons.

1. The writer is excessively modest, and the suggestions offered are too vague to be helpful.

2. The organization is very weak. None of the guidelines suggested has been followed.

INTEROFFICE MEMORANDUM

B

TO: J. R. Sanchez   **FROM:** Your Name

SUBJECT: Suggestions for <u>Tabs</u>   **DATE:** Current date

I am pleased to respond to your invitation to offer suggestions for <u>Tabs</u>.

First, let me say that there are many good things about <u>Tabs</u>. I like the informal style, the editorial quality, the "Shop and Swap" column, the "What's New?" feature, and many other things. But I know you want suggestions rather than praise, and mine follow.

TITLE

Although a new title for the magazine has been suggested, I believe it would be a mistake to change it. Everyone recognizes the publication by the name <u>Tabs</u>, and it still seems to me to be entirely appropriate.

DESIGN

A new masthead would help, and I would like to see us engage a professional designer to do one. Indeed, this designer might be asked to give a new look to the entire magazine.

PHOTOGRAPHS

More photographs would help--photographs of employees celebrating anniversaries, participating in athletics and hobbies, receiving special recognition, and so on.

FEATURES

1. A "Letters to the Editor" column would be especially popular. It would have good readership and, at the same time, give employees a chance to "sound off" on their pet likes and dislikes.

2. After studying the issues for the past year, I feel that we have too many management stories and too few stories about the typical worker. It seems to me that this should be principally a publication for and about employees--not a management PR magazine.
3. I recommend that the magazine establish an Employee of the Month Award. A committee of employees would select this person on the basis of recommendations of supervisors and department heads. You might run the employee's picture with a brief biographical sketch and story about that person's special recognition.
4. Finally, I suggest that a monthly gossip column be added. This column would be light and whimsical--nothing scandalous, of course, but fun to read and laugh about.

If you wish, I'd be glad to discuss these recommendations further with you. Certainly, <u>Tabs</u> is an excellent instrument for communicating with employees, and I'm all for experimenting with ideas that will help to make it even better.

Analysis   Memo B is excellent. How it will be read and used is clear from how it was written.

1. The opening paragraph clearly defines the purpose of the memorandum.
2. The writer points out several favorable things about *Tabs* and then quickly acknowledges that Sanchez wants ideas rather than praise.
3. The suggestions are grouped by subject; this setup makes them easier to read. Under each head the writer carefully explains what is meant by the suggestion given.
4. Under the *Features* head the suggestions are enumerated. Enumerations, where appropriate, always aid the reader, and the numbers make it easy to refer to a topic if a response is required.
5. In the final paragraph the writer offers to discuss the suggestions with Sanchez in person; then the memo ends on a positive, complimentary note.

"YOUR JOB" PROJECT

The human resources department of Permatrax Corporation runs a two-day orientation seminar for new office employees every other month. At this seminar various executives speak to the employees on such topics as company history, objectives, product lines, and company regulations. The purpose of the seminars is to familiarize the beginning workers with the organization and give them a sense of belonging. You have appeared on these programs many times as a representative of the marketing department.

The human resources director, Hannah Sebrell, is not satisfied with the orientation seminars; the feedback she has received from the employees who participated has been less than enthusiastic. In a memo to all company personnel who have spoken to these groups, Sebrell asks for suggestions for improving the seminars.

Although you believe that the idea behind the orientation seminars is excellent and that the programs are, in some respects, interesting and valuable, you have long felt that a better job could be done with them. Among your ideas are the following:

- A parade of speakers from the company is fine, but too many are ill prepared and simply read their presentations. You think that the listeners may find these talks dull and uninspiring.
- There is no opportunity for the new employees to actually meet the executives who appear on the programs. After giving their talk, most of them simply walk out; there is no opportunity for the new employees to ask questions.
- You think that the participants would find the programs much more interesting if more visual aids were used—flip charts, filmstrips, overhead transparencies, and even chalkboards.
- Less time should be spent on such topics as company history, objectives, and product innovation and more time on general employee policies—pay increases (based to some extent on merit ratings), vacations, time off the job due to illness and other emergencies, and various employee benefits (pensions, insurance, medical services, and so on).
- You would recommend that only two or three company executives be asked to speak (each not more than 15 to 20 minutes) and that several employees who have been on the job a short time be invited to appear on the program (perhaps 5 to 10 minutes each) to discuss their jobs and say a few words about their experience in getting adjusted at Permatrax.
- A brief question-and-answer period should follow each major presentation.
- At the end of the entire seminar, there might be a social hour where all speakers and the new employees share refreshments—soft drinks, snacks, coffee, and so on—and get a chance to mingle.
- The room used for the seminars is arranged like an auditorium and is not satisfactory, in your opinion. Might it be possible to use the company boardroom, which has comfortable chairs arranged around a large table? A meeting in the boardroom would be more informal, and the new employees would feel less like students at a school assembly.
- At the end of each hour, there should be a 15-minute break, with coffee and soft drinks available.
- At the beginning of the seminar (after the human resources director has made a few opening remarks), all new employees should be asked, in turn, to stand and give their names, departments, and job titles. This will help to create a feeling of camaraderie at the outset.

Present the foregoing suggestions in a memorandum to Hanna Sebrell.

Rewrite each of the following sentences to eliminate the redundancy or unnecessary words.

1. I am sending you a free sample with my compliments.
2. I would appreciate your suggestions and recommendations for a new office layout.
3. Bates was once a former employee in our company.
4. It is certainly permissible and acceptable for you to return the unsold copies of the handbook.
5. I have gathered all the facts and will assemble the data for your examination.

CASE 4

Reporting the Minutes of Meetings

THE SETTING

The marketing manager of Permatrax Corporation, H. C. Simank, has asked you to serve as a member of the Forms Standardization Committee, a group recently formed to study ways of saving time and money through the more intelligent design, use, and disposition of company forms. At the first meeting of the committee, you were appointed secretary. Your primary duty in this assignment is to prepare the minutes of each meeting and distribute copies to members. (The term *minutes* simply means a written summary of what took place at a meeting.)

Your Objective   To record the proceedings and digest your notes into a set of minutes that every member can understand and make easy reference to later.

BACKGROUND

Although meetings are often joked about as necessary evils—nearly all the people who attend them think there are too many—it would be difficult to operate a business without them. Often meetings provide the only opportunity for certain people in an organization to communicate on a face-to-face basis.

Committees are of two types: standing committees and as hoc committees. *Standing committees* are permanent; the membership changes from time to time, but the committee stands. *Ad hoc* committees are formed to do a specific job and are dissolved when that job is over. Typical of an ad hoc committee is one appointed to steer a company drive for, say, United Way funds. When the drive ends, the committee disbands.

The Agenda The person named to head a committee is usually responsible for planning each meeting and issuing in advance what is called an *agenda* (program) to all members. Following is the agenda for the fourth meeting of the Forms Standardization Committee on October 29.

FORMS STANDARDIZATION COMMITTEE
Agenda for October 29, 19—
Sixth-Floor Conference Room, 10 a.m.

1. Personnel Forms
   Sol Slater
2. Stock-Control Forms Simplification Study
   C. R. Wilkes
3. Filing Problems Created by New Forms
   Millie Fein
4. Snap-Out versus Padded Forms
   Arthur Hobbs
5. Visit to Computer Data Systems
   Eileen Metz

Eileen Metz
Chairperson

Recording the Proceedings The recorder must be a discriminating note-taker, listening for key ideas and writing just enough to get the main points the speaker is making. For example:

What the Speaker Said	What the Recorder Wrote
I see very little need to recommend a change in the policy that requires committee approval of all forms before they are printed. People have a natural tendency to develop a form for every purpose, and it isn't very long before we've got a stockroom full of forms that nobody uses. Just to let people know that any form they design for official use must be approved by a committee is a healthy thing and serves three basic purposes: it helps to cut down the number of forms	No need to change policy requiring committee approval of forms. Committee approval accomplishes three purposes: 1. Cuts down number of forms 2. Simplifies filing 3. Saves time and money

```
designed in the first
place, it simplifies the
filing problem, and it
saves time and money.
```

Preparing the Minutes   Generally, the minutes of meetings have three parts: the heading, the body, and the distribution designation.

The Heading   There are only two rigid rules about the heading of the minutes. It should contain the name of the committee, and it should include the date of the meeting. Some people like to show the time and place, but this is rare. Quite often, minutes of meetings are prepared on memorandum forms, in which case the heading will appear as follows:

PERMATRAX CORPORATION

INTEROFFICE MEMORANDUM

TO: Forms Standardization Committee   **FROM:** Your Name, Secretary

SUBJECT: Minutes of Meeting, October 29, 19--   **DATE:** October 31, 19--

Some recorders like to use plain paper for the minutes. In this case the heading might appear as follows:

```
FORMS STANDARDIZATION COMMITTEE
       Permatrax Corporation

 Minutes of Meeting, October 29, 19--
```

Actually, in the heading directly above, it is not necessary to include the company name, assuming that the minutes are distributed only to company employees.

The Body   The style of the minutes is also a matter of individual preference. In choosing a setup, the recorder should consider the form that will be most readable and useful for reference purposes.

   The topic discussed and the name of the person presenting it should be displayed in some way. (Usually, the topic is more important than the person and is therefore given greater emphasis.) It is also a good idea to number the topics so that they may be easily referred to. Some recorders identify the topic and presenter in the margin like this:

```
1. Personnel Forms        All personnel forms have
   (Slater)               been standardized--that is,
                          assigned official names and
                          numbers--and are being re-
                          viewed in terms of need and
                          efficiency.  So far, the
                          number of forms has been re-
                          duced by 12, by making one
                          form do the job of two or
                          three and eliminating others
                          entirely.  A problem that
                          Personnel constantly faces
                          is that of revisions and ad-
                          ditions arising from new
                          federal government regula-
                          tions.
```

Another way of displaying the topic and the name of the presenter follows:

```
1. PERSONNEL FORMS (Slater).  All personnel forms
   have been standardized--that is, assigned of-
   ficial names and numbers--and are being re-
   viewed in terms of need and. . . .
```

Although not quite as useful for reference, the latter example saves a great deal of space.

Even if there is no set agenda for a meeting and the proceedings are loosely structured, it is wise to give headings to the major topics discussed. Without headings, minutes of meetings can be difficult to read and refer to later.

When discussion follows a presentation, the highlights may follow the topic summary like this:

```
1. Personnel Forms        All personnel forms have
   (Slater)               been standardized--that is,
                          assigned official names and
                          numbers--and are being
                          reviewed in terms of need
                          and. . . .
   Discussion             TM asked whether the merit
                          rating form will be revised
                          (he says many people think
                          it is awkward and
                          imprecise).  SS said the
                          personnel manager has named
                          a task force to gather and
                          analyze. . . .
```

Distribution The names of the committee members and others who are to receive copies of the minutes are often listed at the bottom as follows:

```
Distribution
  Committee Members: Metz (chairperson), Fein,
                     Hobbs, Ruiz (absent), Slater,
                     Varnum, Wilkes
  Others: Mr. Ellis, Mrs. Katzenbach, Ms. Nugent,
          Mr. Weir
```

Before the copies of the minutes are distributed, the secretary can underline or circle in red on each member's copy that person's assignment. For example:

```
This study has been delayed because of department
reorganization.  CRW will give this report at the
November meeting.
```

Guidelines

1. Identify in the heading the group or committee, and indicate the date.
2. Display each major topic presented, and identify the person who made the presentation.
3. Condense the minutes to the barest essentials. Although everything that is really important should be written up, don't overwrite. A telegraphic style is best so long as your meaning is clear.
4. If there is a discussion following a presentation, identify the person or persons who participated, and briefly indicate the results of the discussion.
5. Avoid personal pronouns unless you are quoting someone's remarks verbatim.

SAMPLE MINUTES OF MEETING

PERMATRAX CORPORATION

INTEROFFICE MEMORANDUM

```
      TO: Forms Standardization   FROM: Your Name,
          Committee                      Secretary
 SUBJECT: Minutes of Meeting      DATE: October 31, 19--
          October 29, 19--

          1. Personnel Forms            All personnel forms have
             (Slater)                   been standardized--that is,
                                        assigned official names and
```

	numbers—and are being reviewed in terms of need and efficiency. So far, the number of forms has been reduced by 12, by making one form do the job of two or three and by eliminating others entirely. A problem that Personnel constantly faces is that of revisions and additions arising from new federal government regulations.
Discussion	TV asked whether the merit rating form will be revised (he says many people think it is awkward and imprecise). SS said the personnel manager has named a task force to gather and analyze the merit rating forms of about 20 similar companies for ideas on how ours might be improved. Results are expected in early January.
2. Stock-Control Form Simplification Study (Wilkes)	This study has been delayed because of department reorganization. CRW will give this report at the November meeting.
3. Filing Problems Created by New Forms (Fein)	Most people who design forms do not consider the problem created for Records Control when forms are improperly designed. Size of the form and layout of the top portion are special problems. MF suggested that Anna Roach (Records Control) be asked to inspect each new form before design is approved and printing authorized.

Discussion	EM suggested that Roach be invited to become a member of this Committee, and everyone agreed. EM will follow up.
4. Snap-Out vs. Padded Forms (Hobbs)	Recent studies have shown that snap-out packs have definite advantages over padded forms. Although the cost is higher, AH says the time-saving feature more than offsets the added expense of purchase; recommends that padded forms be dispensed with entirely.
Discussion	There were various objections to AH's recommendations, and it was agreed that this topic would be discussed further before final action is taken.
5. Visit to Computer Data Systems (Metz)	Computer Data Systems has invited the Committee to visit its plant to observe a new process of producing microfiche. The date is November 16 from 11 a.m. to 3 p.m., and a smorgasbord luncheon will be served. EM will issue further details next week, incuding transportation arrangements.
6. Other Business	EM announced that she will represent the Committee at a meeting of the Management Council on November 9 at which various committee heads will report on their activities during the past year.

NEXT MEETING	The next meeting will be held November 30 in the Board Room at 10 a.m. Charles A. Kiernan, of Steber Business Graphics, will speak on trends in form design.
	Y.N.

Distribution

Committee Members: Metz (chairperson), Fein, Hobbs, Ruiz, (absent), Slater, Varnum, Wilkes
Others: Mr. Ellis, Mrs. Katzenbach, Ms. Nugent, Mr. Weir

Analysis   Note the following points concerning the minutes illustrated.

1. The items that were listed on the agenda (page 357) are given the same number in the minutes. This may not always be feasible—for example, a topic that was scheduled on the agenda might be canceled before the meeting— but it's a good idea when possible.
2. First names are omitted under the topic headings, and only initials are given in the presentation notes. These are optional methods of identification; some people prefer that full names be given in all cases.
3. Note that item 2, although not discussed, is accounted for because it had not previously been canceled.
4. Describing plans for the next meeting is a good way of giving advance notice.
5. Note under *Distribution* the method of indicating that someone was absent. Some recorders prefer this:

Committee Members Present: Metz (chairperson), Fein, Hobbs, Slater, Varnum, Wilkes
Committee Members Absent: Ruiz

"YOUR JOB" PROJECT

You are the secretary of the Employee Activities Committee of Permatrax Corporation. This committee is made up of six people, and the chairperson is Mary Beth Rooney. The group was formed to deal with such matters as planning recreational activities, recognizing employee achievements and anniversaries, operating an employee suggestion system, and so on. The following notes were made during the meeting of April 3.

Catherine Vining recommended that the profits from vending machines in the building ($2,440.55 last year) be used to establish a scholarship fund for children of employees. The members of the committee participated in a full discussion of this suggestion. There was one dissenting voice. Bert Whelan raised the question as to how the recipient or recipients would be chosen for the scholarship, and he pointed out the difficulties of administering such a program. He wound up by saying that the program would create ill feelings among employees whose children were not selected--that it would not accomplish what it was designed to do. On the other hand, Paul Zackowitz felt that the suggestion was a worthy one. He said that an independent committee (outside the company) should be appointed and that candidates for the scholarship award should be recommended by their high school principal on the basis of scholarship, leadership, and need. Helen Chu agreed with Mr. Zackowitz and further suggested that two scholarships of $1,000 each be awarded each year rather than one. The group agreed on the two-scholarship idea and also endorsed Mr. Zackowitz's suggestion about administering the program through an outside committee. The general consensus was that the scholarship idea was good enough to be thoroughly explored. Paul Zackowitz and Amy Rhodes were asked by Chairperson Rooney to find out how other companies, particularly competitors, handle scholarship programs. She further recommended that committee members talk with local high school principals and perhaps some teachers to see what criteria might be set up for the scholarships and to get ideas for names of people who would make the final judgment on winners of the scholarships. A full report will be given by Zackowitz and Rhodes at the next meeting, on April 27.

Concerning the formation of a bowling league, Bert Whelan reported that 17 employees have signed up as interested in participating. He is having a meeting of these people on Monday, April 7, to organize the teams. He has made arrangements to purchase bowling shirts with the Permatrax emblem imprinted on the back (the employee is to pay half the cost of the shirt). The shirts will not be ordered until after the first organization meeting.

Chairperson Rooney announced that suggestion boxes have already been installed on each floor of the building and forms for making suggestions distributed to each department manager. The policies and procedures concerning employee suggestions will appear in the next printing of the employee handbook. She also reported that the balance in the treasury of the Employee Activities Committee now stands at $3,426.17.

Amy Rhodes reported that 300 copies of the anniversary brochure of the 25-Year Club will be published in June. The printing cost per copy is $1.85, and President Ellis has said that the cost can be assumed by the company.

The next meeting of the committee will be on April 27.

Prepare the minutes of the meeting. Condense the discussion in an appropriate way, and set up the minutes in a form of your own choosing. These are unedited notes, so watch out for poor grammar, word choice, and so forth.

STYLE CHECKUP

The following sentences contain unbalanced constructions. Correct them.

1. The new advertisements *reduced* inquiries rather than *increasing* them.
2. We expect to *exhibit* in Milwaukee as well as *exhibiting* in St. Paul.
3. They are eager *not only* to make these panels for us but *also in making the hardware as well.*
4. Thank you for *writing* so promptly and for your *agreement to* settle your account in full.

CHAPTER 19	# WRITING FORMALLY STRUCTURED REPORTS

YOUR JOB

You are the assistant director of human resources at Bowden Industries, Inc., a fast-growing company that manufactures plumbing fixtures and trim for the construction industry. Among your many responsibilities is the supervision of employee training and development. You report to Glen C. Eden, director of human resources.

CASE PROBLEM: WRITING A RESEARCH REPORT

THE SETTING

Bowden Industries, Inc., is having difficulty filling management positions. This problem has become increasingly serious as the company has grown. At a recent meeting of the President's Advisory Committee, this matter was discussed at great length, and the committee decided that a full study should be made of the problem and recommendations offered for solving it. You have been chosen to make the study and prepare the report.

Your Objective   To make the required study and present your findings and recommendations to the President's Advisory Committee.

BACKGROUND

Longer reports that deal with particularly important issues and require substantial research are often highly structured and are written on plain paper (or paper designed expressly for the purpose)—not as memorandums. Structured reports are usually a bit more formal in tone than memorandum reports, and their format gives them a scholarly appearance that sets them apart from routine communications. Often such reports are distributed widely, and for this reason they are frequently bound in special folders with a transparent cover.

Guidelines   The parts of a formally structured report vary according to the needs of the writer, but in general, there are at least five:

1. *The title page.* This shows the title of the report, the person or group for whom the report was written, the name of the author, the date, and sometimes other information such as the position of the author and the name and location of the company.

2. *An introduction.* This often covers the following, although not necessarily in the order given.

   a. The history or background—a description of the events leading up to the preparation of the report.

   b. The purpose—the reason why the report was written.

   c. The need, or justification, for the report. (This is often included with the purpose.)

   d. The method—an explanation of how the data for the report was gathered.

   e. The scope—a statement of what the report covers and, if necessary, of what it does not cover.

   f. The definition of terms that may present problems for certain readers.

3. *The body*—that is, the main part of the report.

4. *A summary.* In this part the main points covered in the body of the report are capsuled for the readers. Traditionally, the summary has been placed at the end of the report. However, there is a tendency to place it up front, just before or after the introduction, the assumption being that this is all that some people will want to read.

5. *Conclusions and recommendations.* These may be separate parts or combined, and these, too, often appear at the front of the report, immediately following the summary.

Analysis   Because the report (on pages 368 to 374) is long, let's look at each part of it separately.

1. The title page contains the title of the report, the name of the group for which the report was written, the name of the author, and the date. Note that the name of the company is a part of the title and thus does not have to be repeated.

2. The title appears again on the first page of the report itself.

3. The introduction contains a background statement that leads up to the purpose of the report, which is specifically stated in the third paragraph. Note the complimentary remarks concerning the company's past performance. This is not merely politics; it is simply a way of presenting the positive side before describing the weaknesses in the present situation. Some writers, when asked to undertake a critical analysis of something, begin immediately to condemn the present status of things. This is poor psychology, since those to whom the report is addressed are often the people who are responsible for the problem.

4. Under *History*, the writer provides information that may be important to review and then proceeds to suggest tactfully that present procedures are unlikely to satisfy future requirements.

5. Under *Scope* the writer defines the term *management* so that everyone can identify the group for which a new program should be designed. You also make clear the extent of the report by stating what it does *not* cover.

6. The writer clearly establishes the need for the report under the heading *Need* and supports the premise of need with data.

7. The body of the report is shown in outline form. Note the variety of major

<u>A MANAGEMENT DEVELOPMENT PROGRAM</u>
for
<u>BOWDEN INDUSTRIES INC.</u>

A Report to the President's Advisory Committee

by
Your Name

June 17, 19--

A MANAGEMENT DEVELOPMENT PROGRAM
for
BOWDEN INDUSTRIES INC.

INTRODUCTION

It has often been said that Bowden Industries Inc., like Topsy, "just growed." This implies that in the company's twelve years of existence there was little planning, innovation, and management leadership. This is simply not so. How else can one account for an over 500 percent increase in sales and staff increase from about 300 to nearly 2,500? Product diversification, innovative marketing and manufacturing, and sound financial management all attest to the effective leadership with which the company has been blessed.

But what of the future? The continual need to adapt management strategies to new technologies, and increasingly complex business environment, the proliferation of aggressive competition--indeed, the simple fact of company size--all will call for especially skilled and aggressive managerial talent in the years ahead.

At the May 9 meeting of the President's Advisory Committee, the question, Where will the managerial expertise needed for future growth and expansion come from? was asked. The purpose of this report is to provide possible answers to that vital question.

HISTORY

In the past, Bowden has depended largely on universities and executive placement agencies for sources of managerial talent--and, of course, on its own promotion-from-within policy. By and large these have been good sources and no doubt will continue to be used. However, training and developing the people the company puts into management positions has been hit-or-miss, largely unstructured on-the-job supervision. The results are mixed. Some people were well trained and quickly moved up when bigger jobs became available. Others languished and, seeing no opportunity for growth, left the company.

SCOPE

The term "management" in this report refers to all positions from first-line supervisors (classified as Levels 13 and 14 by the Human Resources Department) right on up to the top executive positions. No attention has been given to lower-level jobs in this report, although this is obviously a subject that deserves full exploration later.

NEED

During the past year, 44 vacancies occurred in management positions. Of that number, 22 were the result of retirement because of age or health; 13 resigned to accept better positions in other companies; and the remaining 35 were the result of newly created positions.

It is interesting to find that 27 of the 44 openings had to be filled from the outside. In other words, only 17 employees were considered ready to accept the greater responsibilities of management. Actually, few of the people recruited from the outside were actually ready either (the unknown often looks better than the known); many required a long break-in period. Besides having a negative effect on employees who were denied promotion, outside recruiting and on-the-job adjustment are very expensive.

The time seems right, then, for a thorough examination of the company's education posture, for it seems apparent that no matter how successful we are in attracting bright management talent, we will not obtain the leadership required for the future without an effective management development program.

(The body of the report follows, perhaps with the following heads.)

JOB REQUIREMENTS

LEVELS 13 AND 14 (FIRST-LINE SUPERVISORS)
LEVEL 15 (ASSISTANT DEPARTMENT MANAGERS)
LEVELS 16 AND 17 (DEPARTMENT MANAGERS)
LEVEL 18 (DIVISION MANAGERS)

ON-THE-JOB TRAINING

ESTABLISHING OBJECTIVES
ORGANIZATION PLANNING
DELEGATION OF AUTHORITY
JOB COUNSELING

JOB ROTATION

PRINCIPLES OF JOB ROTATION
ADVANTAGES
PROBLEMS

IN-COMPANY COURSES

BASIC MANAGEMENT TECHNIQUES

<u>Supervision</u>
<u>Psychology of Motivation</u>
<u>Internal Communications</u>
<u>External Communications</u>
<u>Interpersonal Relationships</u>
<u>Management Decision-Making</u>
<u>Organization Planning and Control</u>

JOB-RELATED TRAINING

<u>Company Structure and Objectives</u>
<u>Long-Range Planning</u>
<u>Refresher Technical Training</u>

OUTSIDE SOURCES

UNIVERSITIES AND COLLEGES

<u>Typical Programs Available</u>
<u>Cost</u>

MANAGEMENT EDUCATION GROUPS (THE SEMINAR CONCEPT)

<u>Types of Seminars Offered</u>
<u>Cost</u>

SABBATICAL LEAVES

PURPOSES
SOURCES
ADVANTAGES AND LIMITATIONS

RECOMMENDATIONS

On the basis of this study, there would appear to be a definite need for a well-rounded education program at Bowden Industries Inc. There are numerous possible methods of operating and conducting it. The following recommendations are offered:

1. Appoint a director of management development, preferably a person with sound academic credentials (possibly a Ph.D.), teaching experience in management at the undergraduate and graduate levels, and broad business experience in supervision and management. The person appointed would report directly to the executive vice president or to the president.
2. Appoint a Management Education Committee, consisting of the top executive of each of the six divisions in the company and the executive vice president (ex officio). This committee would advise the director of management development in planning and operating the program, utilizing as many of the sources described in this report as seem feasible.

3. **(Further recommendations follow.)**

headings and subheadings. (There are five levels, including the title.) Obviously, under these headings the writer will include all the information gathered that will be important to the President's Advisory Committee, including tables, charts, and perhaps other illustrations.

8. The writer offers no conclusions, since they are self-evident.
9. The recommendations for action are given in 1-2-3 order (there will be several more than have been provided).

BOWDEN INDUSTRIES INC.

B

INTEROFFICE MEMORANDUM

TO: President's Advisory Committee   **FROM:** Your Name

SUBJECT: A Management Development Program for Bowden Industries Inc.   **DATE:** June 17, 19--

Here is the report you asked for (President Eichhorn's memorandum of May 10) on executive development for the years ahead.

During the study I gathered a good deal of literature on outside sources of training. If you wish to see it, I will be glad to share it with you.

I will be very pleased to know of any other way I can be helpful.

<u>Distribution:</u> Eichhorn, Chaffey, Monohan, Stern, Romano, Diffenbach, Terrence

Analysis Note how this transmittal memo includes the same information any effective memo would.

1. The report will be transmitted to the President's Advisory Committee by means of a brief memorandum.
2. In the first paragraph, you refer to Eichhorn's memorandum—the authorization for the study.
3. You volunteer to share with the committee the literature you gathered while preparing the report.
4. The names of the people on the commitee appear at the bottom, alongside *Distribution*. Each person's name will be checked or circled on the copy that she or he receives.

There has been a bit of unrest among the sales representatives and their supervisors in the Atlantic Coast regional offices, and the director of marketing has asked your supervisor, Glen C. Eden, to send someone to the four regional offices—Boston, Norfolk, Charleston, and Jacksonville—to investigate the problem. "I want someone outside the Marketing Division—preferably Human Services—to investigate the problem and prepare a report on the findings from that investigation." You were selected to make this study.

Following is the first draft of your report. Organize the material so that it is easy to read, supplying appropriate headings. When you have done this (1) prepare a title page and (2) write a memorandum to Glen C. Eden transmitting the report. You have been instructed by Eden to show on the title page that the report was done at the request of Marianne F. Motley, director of human services.

At the suggestion of Glen C. Eden I recently spent a week in each of the four Atlantic Coast regional offices to talk with managers and field supervisors about the personnel turnover problems Bowden Industries is having. The following is a brief report of that visit.

1. Boston is short two sales representatives and has been since October, and the Gloucester and Brockton areas have been left virtually uncovered since that time. One of the representatives, Alvin Cooper (New Bedford) is on the verge of resigning. The reasons given for the resignation of Poulan (Framingham) and Devaney (Cambridge) are just about identical: Dissatisfaction with the basic salary, inequitable incentive arrangement, and low mileage allowance. I learned that both received a substantial increase from Compton Corporation, our major East Coast competitor.

   While Cooper does not emphasize money as the basis for his unrest, it is certainly a major factor. Cooper's problem seems to be his inability to accept supervision, at least from the present field supervisor.

   The Boston office has found no effective sources of recruitment, relying almost entirely on newspaper ads in the Sunday *Globe* and word-of-mouth recommendations of other representatives. There does not appear to be any likely candidate on the horizon.

2. Norfolk is fully staffed at the moment, although a couple of people are unsettled about their jobs (Faust in Norfolk and Gleason in Alexandria). The regional manager told me that neither is performing up to capacity and that their loss would not be a serious blow.

   Norfolk seems to have no difficulty obtaining highly qualified candidates for sales positions. As a matter of fact, several applicants look quite promising. This office has established exceptionally good relations with surrounding colleges and universities and obtains many candidates from these institutions.

3. Charleston is short one sales representative; however, there have been several promising interviews, and the manager feels the vacancy will be filled by the end of the month. The situation here, however, is not so rosy as might be imagined. While Charleston seems to have little trouble in filling its vacancies, the turnover rate is extremely high. Of the 15 representatives in this office,

7 have been with the company less than a year, 4 less than two years, and 1 more than five years. According to the exit interviews, most of those who leave the company do so because of dissatisfaction with salary and incentives. However, a number seem to have some difficulty getting along with their field supervisors.

4. The Jacksonville regional office has twelve sales representatives. When I was in Jacksonville, the regional manager, Beth Yeary, was holding a conference at which all twelve representatives were present. With Beth's permission I had a private talk with each of these people (nine men and three women) and invited them to speak frankly about their jobs. Seven had no complaints. Five, however, expressed disappointment in salaries and mileage allowance. All of these people also complained about feeling "left out" of things—communication with the regional manager and field supervisors as well as home-office management people.

5. All in all, I have the definite impression that we are in serious trouble in the matter of hiring and retaining an effective sales staff. Even among those people who choose to remain with the company, the morale is low. To solve this problem, I think we should make a study of salaries of our sales representatives as compared with those in the industry as a whole and with several similar firms within each geographic district be undertaken. I also feel that a how-to-supervise program be established for regional managers, field supervisors, and sales supervisors. Another thing I recommend is that a conference be held in each region under the supervision of our Human Resources Department to instruct managers and field supervisors on the techniques of recruiting, testing, interviewing, and hiring sales representatives. Another thing: there should be more frequent contacts with management for all representatives by scheduling more regional and national conferences. In other words, I think representatives should meet more "brass" in top management so they will feel that they work in a family of intelligent and sensitive people. Finally, I would like to see a "field memo" or some such news-inspiration piece to be distributed every month to all sales personnel.

After you have read the 15-page report that accompanies this summary, I would like to talk with you further about some of the problems I found and enlarge on the recommendations I have made.

STYLE CHECKUP

Rewrite the following sentences to remove excess words.

1. Bernardi asked the question concerning plans to enlarge the parking space.
2. I am eager to have a meeting with the purchasing manager to discuss my ideas with him.
3. Our past experience indicates that we cannot expect to win the complete and total approval of all the people in our employ.
4. May I take the liberty of asking you for a free sample at no cost to me?
5. The two carpets are of the same identical pattern, and the one I prefer is in the color of beige.

CHAPTER 20

WRITING AT THE COMPUTER

Throughout this book you have learned that writing is a creative process that involves planning your message, composing your message, and editing and rewriting your message. The message may, of course, be a business letter, a memorandum, or a business report. Many people do all their writing on the computer. A computer, as you know, is simply a piece of equipment (*hardware*) that manipulates information automatically by interpreting electrical impulses.

The computer (often called a *word processor* or a *microcomputer*) used for composing, editing, and rewriting is a small machine that fits easily on one's desk and is a great help to writers. The word processor, sometimes referred to as a *text editor*, includes a typewriterlike keyboard connected to a video display terminal (VDT), which is actually a television screen. Sometimes the keyboard and VDT are connected to a printer, which makes paper copies (called *hard copy* or *printout*) on command.

Using a word processor is similar to using a typewriter. When you type, or *keyboard*, your message, the words first appear on the VDT screen rather than on paper, and you can edit and rewrite the material electronically—before you make a hard copy. For example, suppose that you want to send the following message to the members of the Sales Management Committee, each of whom has a word processor that is linked to your system:

```
The meeting of the Sales Management Committee
scheduled for January 13 at 10 o'clock has been
postponed. It will take place on January 21, same
time and place as usual.
```

Immediately after you keyboard this message, which appears on your VDT, you get word that the place of the meeting must also be changed because of a conflict. Thus, you electronically delete the phrase *time and place as usual* and replace it by keyboarding the following: *in Conference Room 3 rather than in the Board Room. The time is still 10 o'clock.*

Thus, you see that you have not used paper to correct the two changes, thereby wasting time and effort; the entire transaction took place electronically.

In using the computer as a writing tool for planning your message, composing your message, and editing and rewriting your message, you have used a very simple procedure to "scratch out, edit, and recompose your message." You should know, however, that planning, composing, revising, and editing vary according to the stage at which they occur. Some writers edit as they compose, and as they have difficulty, stop and complete some prewriting activities, such as brainstorming or outlining. Others outline first, then engage in preplanning, and, last, composing. And so on.

WRITING "LONG DISTANCE"

The computer for some people enables one to communicate electronically with various people within and outside the company. We have just given you an example of an electronic communication (concerning the change in date and place of a committee meeting). The same procedure may be used for writing reports to individuals throughout the company. As long as the recipient has a computer that links to your own data processing system, you can communicate electronically with that individual. Some large companies have electronic hookups with major customers and suppliers long distances away. Thus, for example, a sales manager can keyboard a message to a major supplier in which a delay in shipping is questioned, requesting the earliest date when a new product will be available, or indicating that the supplier neglected to grant a discount for prompt payment. No paper required!

SOFTWARE WRITING TOOLS

The following chart will give you an idea of just how many computer software tools are now on the market for each of the writing stages.

Writing Stage	Computer Software Tools
Prewriting	Word processing—free-writing Prompting program Outlining program Idea processors
Composing	Word processing—full text editing Boiler plates Modeling effective styles Combining material: document merge Researching material: access to databases
Revising	Word processing—full text editing Text-analysis programs Reviewer program

Editing	Word processing programs
	Spelling checkers
	On-line dictionaries
	On-line thesauruses
	Style and grammar checkers
	Formatting processors
	    Indexing
	    Footnoting

Before we discuss each tool, however, let's focus on the technology that allowed these tools to develop. This technology is in the area of text editing and word processing software.

Text Editors and Word Processors

Text editors and word processors allow you to complete the following processes:

1. Open an electronic file
2. Key in text
3. Recopy text
4. Change and/or delete text
5. Save your text electronically (filed on a recording tape or a disk)
6. Retrieve that same file for review, modification, or merging with another document

Many writers who use word processing feel that they compose more freely because making changes or reorganizing the document is no longer a time-consuming recopying or retyping task. One of the stronget advantages of word processing is its electronic erasing feature. Since good writing demands many revisions, you can see why the electronic erasing feature alone is a writer's delight. Unlike manual erasing, where the text becomes permanently erased, electronic erasing is like putting text in a reserve—this reserve is called a *buffer*. Text stored in a buffer can be retrieved and reused any place in the document.

Editing "On Screen"   To appreciate the value of editing "on screen" before printing, consider for a moment what happens when you use a standard typewriter to correct errors or make changes. On those occasions when you must correct only two or three characters, you *may* be able to reinsert the page in the typewriter and correct the error so that it is hardly noticeable. In all other cases, however, there are so many changes to be made that you must retype the entire letter or report.

Assume, for instance, that you typed the following sentence as part of a two-page letter:

```
As we discussed at our May 20 meeting, Mr. Ste-
venson, I am to pay 10 percent immediately of the
total cost of a one-year lease of the Pheasant
Run Mall. Our check for $9,462 is enclosed.
```

When you proofread the finished letter, you discovered that *$9,462* should really be *$19,462*. Further, the correct spelling is *Stephenson*, not *Stevenson*, and you have used his name several times on each page. Without a word processor, in order for you to correct the errors, you would need to retype the entire letter, two pages or perhaps a few hundred words. Even if you can type rapidly, you will waste a lot of time!

Using a word processor, you would correct the same errors by using *just a few keystrokes*, because with this equipment almost any error is easy to correct and any change is easy to make. Let's follow the steps in making the above changes, using a word processor.

First of all, on the computer screen, *a cursor*—a small flashing square—indicates your position. Now, using special keys with arrows showing four directions—up and down and left and right—you simply move the cursor to the position you want and proceed to make your correction. Pressing any alphabet or number key inserts that character at the cursor position. Pressing the Delete key erases the character at the cursor position. In this way you use the arrow keys to move the cursor to *$9,462* and correct it to read *$19,462* in a few seconds. It's that simple!

You can change each occurrence of the name *Stevenson* to *Stephenson* following the same procedure:

1. Move the cursor over the "v" (in Ste*v*enson)
2. Press the Delete key.
3. Keyboard "ph" (in Ste*ph*enson)

However, if the name is misspelled several times in the document, the word processor offers you an even faster alternative way to make all the changes. Instead of correcting each error individually, you simply instruct or command the computer to change all occurrences of *Stevenson* to *Stephenson*. Depending on the equipment you are using, the instruction might be as simple as this:

CHANGE: Stevenson   TO: Stephenson

Repetitive changes—changes that must be made throughout a document—are called *global changes*, and they are simple to make on a word processor. On the other hand, using a standard typewriter in order to make repetitive changes, you would be forced to retype the entire document. Using a word processor, you can change any part of a long document instantly, then print out the corrected copy while you do something else.

Remember that each time you *avoid* retyping an entire letter, you are effectively doubling your keyboarding speed. Thus, as you can see, one major benefit of using a word processor is a *quantitative* advantage. You can make corrections and process documents in much less time. Word processing also offers a number of *qualitative* benefits, which will be discussed later.

Whether you are using a standard typewriter or a word processor, you must always correct *errors*, of course. But other changes may be optional. For example, assume that you wrote:

```
Dear Mr. Chaney:

The error in your October statement was ours.   No
doubt about it!   A corrected statement is en-
closed.   Your records and ours agree.   Thank you.
We appreciate your help.
```

You wrote this message rather quickly. Now that you reread it, you realize that it sounds "choppy." You can improve it as follows:

Dear Mr. Chaney:

You are right--the error in your October statement was indeed ours. A corrected statement is
enclosed. Now your records and ours agree.

Thank you for telling us about our error. We appreciate your help.

Storing and Retrieving Files   Another quantitative advantage of word
processing is that it allows you great flexibility in using and reusing any documents
(even parts of documents) that you keyboard. To do so, you must understand
the basics of *saving* and *storing* documents, as well as retrieving stored
documents from memory. The techniques and principles discussed below are
applicable not only to letters but to all documents.

Store Letters in Separate Files   Different computer systems may use
different terminology. The *principles*, however, are the same. For example,
when you keyboard a letter you must then *save* or *store* that letter. Think of
saving or storing the way you would file a paper copy of a letter. If you do not
file the paper copy correctly, you will not find it in the future. The same is true
of word processing. Unless you name a file properly, you may not find it readily
either.

To store a document in word processing, you must (1) instruct or command
the computer to save the document and (2) assign a name to that particular
file. When you are using a word processor, there will be a *command line* on
the computer screen—a line on which you key in your instructions or *commands*.
The command to save or store a document is a simple SAVE or STORE.

Name Files Distinctly   Of course, if you are to be able to *find* that stored
document when you want it, you must store it carefully—that is, you must store
it with a distinctive name, a name that you can identify easily. For example,
when you write a letter to Gladys Eckerly, you can store that letter under the
filename ECKERLY. When you write to Lawrence J. Silver, you can store that
letter under the filename SILVER. And so on. (The reason is simple: Months
later, you would not remember filing such letters under meaningless filenames
such as XDC105 or ABC5FLD.)

Group Files Into Directories   A word processor also allows you to group
smaller, individual letter files into one "superfile" such as LETTERS. Over a year
or two, you can easily amass hundreds and hundreds of different files for letters,
memos, reports, manuscripts, invoices, and so on. Finding a letter that you wrote,
say, three months ago would be rather tricky without a good filing system!

The newest computers allow you to group similar documents or related
materials into a broad superfile called a *directory*. For example, you can store
all individual letter files in a directory called *LETTERS*. Then, whenever you
must find a leter that you wrote, you simply instruct the computer to list the

contents of the LETTERS directory. Depending on the word processing you are using, the command might look like this:

```
DIR LETTERS\*.*
```

When you press the Enter key, the command takes effect. The contents—that is, the filenames of the individual letters stored in the LETTERS directory—would then be displayed on the screen, as follows.

DOHERTY	1198	9-22-89	11:20a
ECKERLY	2176	12-09-88	4:32p
FORD	1298	11-16-89	3:46p
GRANGER	2367	10-11-88	8:35a
MARSHALL	2287	4-24-88	12:14p
SILVER	1909	3-20-89	3:17p
TENNENT	2202	8-10-88	9:22a

The first column lists the filename, and the second gives the "size" of each file (in computer measurements, of course). The third and fourth columns give the date and the time the file was last stored. Note that files are listed in alphabetical order for ease of use.

Retrieve or "Call-Up" Files   Once you know the filename of a stored document, retrieving or calling up that file is easy. Think of *calling up* a file as "*displaying* a stored file on the screen." The command may be LOAD, RETRIEVE, or CALL. But you must obviously tell the computer which file to call. Usually, you identify the file by specifying both the directory name and the filename after the command, for example:

```
CALL LETTERS/ECKERLY
```

This command will immediately display on screen the letter to Gladys Eckerly. These are just a few of the advantages of using a word processor; there are many more. Obviously, word processing offers tremendous time savings and permits maximum efficiency in writing business communications.

Other Features of Word Processors   As mentioned, computer editors are called *text editors* and *word processors*. While text editors and word processors use the same technology to input, process, and edit text, word processors offer more capabilties and are typically easier to learn and to use. For example, word processors offer a wide variety of formatting and printing options, while text editors usually limit line length and printing options.

Electronic bulletin boards, networking systems, electronic mail systems, and computer conferencing systems all use a text editor or word processor to keyboard and manage text. In fact, you will find a text editor or word processor in all computers and data communications systems. Text editors and word processors are found in microcomputers, minicomputers, and mainframe computers. The writing tools discussed in this chapter, however, are available mainly for microcomputers or minicomputer workstations. These work stations are made up of a computer (the CPU), a monitor or video display terminal, and a printer.

Depending on the word processing software you are using, specific operations and procedures will vary. Such differences are not important here. What is important is that you understand that all word processors allow you to:

- Create an electronic file.
- Create a document (letter, memo, or report).
- Revise a document (delete, insert, move, copy, highlight, etc.).
- Save a document on disk.
- Store a document.
- Print a document.
- Index and view all files available on disk.
- Delete files on the disk.
- Retrieve a document and reuse without keyboarding.
- Merge two documents together (into one).

In this context, the word *processing* makes this valuable tool sound mechanical and impersonal, and the letters you write can, indeed, be mechanical and impersonal if you lose sight of your goal. Your goal is not to use word processing simply to write more communications or longer communications or faster communications. With or without a word processor, your goal is always to write messages that are (1) goodwill builders, (2) personalized, (3) easy and interesting to read, and (4) persuasive in tone and helpful to the reader

WORD PROCESSING AND QUALITATIVE WRITING

Word processing can certainly help you achieve your broad goal in more than just quantitative ways. It also can help you improve your writing *qualitatively*. Let's see how.

Prewriting: Getting Started and Being Creative

In the introduction to this chapter, we identified four stages critical to effective writing: prewriting, composing, revising, and editing. Let's examine each of these processes separately.

Prewriting (also referred to as *preplanning*) activities include deciding what to say, making notes, outlining, and refining your topic. Prewriting is a way of sorting through and organizing ideas before beginning to compose. Here are some of the computer aids that help you with the prewriting process.

Free-writing *Free-writing* is virtually the opposite of composing. It is unrestrained and unrevised writing and is used to discover the subject or topic for composition or to expand on a selected topic. The goal is to encourage writers to "get ideas down" as quickly as possible without worrying about writing style or mechanics. Some of the prewriting software programs permit no editing at all. The cursor moves forward, and nothing can be erased. Some of the programs suggest that you turn off the monitor during free-writing to discourage editing or review.

Prompted Writing   *Prompted writing* software provides a series of questions or suggestions that help the writer to explore topics. The goal is to evaluate aspects of an idea that might not have been considered. Some software packages prompt the user with specific questions while others use the "5 Ws" (who, what, when, where, and why). Still others use a set of questions for each type of writing: descriptions, explanatory essays, persuasive essays, letters, and stories. Some of the word processors make it easy for writers to design and save their own sets of questions or "prompts," receiving electronic files with a "guided" set of questions to help in developing the writing assignment.

Idea Processors   *Idea processors* make outlining easier and more efficient on the computer. Some idea processors are stand-alone software products while others are part of a word processing program. Many idea processors allow you to create outlines with four or more levels of subtopics, while others allow you to "visually" organize your ideas by using *icons* (symbols) to mark and link ideas. The goal of the idea processor is to let you narrow, refine, and organize your topic for composition.

Composing

Composing takes place when you take the plans and notes you prepared in the prewriting process and translate them into a structured first draft of the document.

The composing part of the process requires flexibility, creativity, and organizational ability. The word processor is the main tool of the computer for composing because it offers the potential to work quickly and flexibly. In addition to the keyboarding features discussed earlier (delete, insert, move, copy, etc.), here are some techniques for composing on a computer.

Boiler Plates   *Boiler plates* are documents which are used again and again with minor, but important, changes. For example, you can create boiler plates of travel itinerary memos, product announcement letters, or monthly status reports. Master copies can be stored in the computer and specific information can be inserted or changed when the document is called into the word processor. The original or master copy is unaltered while the changed version is saved or printed as a separate or distinct copy of the master.

Mail Merging   Word processing programs designed for business writing include special features such as *document merge. Mail merging* is a computerized version of filling in the blanks of a form letter.

Cosmotron Computers developed a shell letter to send an authorized warrant card to each person who purchases a Cosmotron computer. This shell letter is stored in one computer file—let's call it File A. But this file is incomplete. To "fill in the blanks," this file must be *merged with* another file, File B, which contains the fill-in information. When these two files are *merged*, the computer prints out separate, individual, personalized letters.

Question: How does the computer know what to insert and where?

Answer: By the computer codes in the shell letter.

As the computer prints out each letter, it reads the codes in File B and follows the instructions of each code. Here are the functions of some codes in a shell document:

- To instruct the computer to print in today's date.

- To tell the computer to print a standard three-line name and address; for example:

```
Mrs. Andrea Horvath
12 Sun View Drive
Peru, Nebraska 68421
```

- To command the computer to print only the personal title and last name from the name and address.

- To tell the computer to print the name of the computer model the customer purchased (for example, *System X500*, *System X700*, or any of the other models that Cosmotron manufactures).

- To instruct the computer to print out the name of the specific dealer who sold the computer to this customer.

In this way, mail merge allows the sender of the form letter to personalize the response to each person who purchases a Cosmotron computer without needing to write a different letter each time.

Researching and Combining Material

The computer's capacities to store and access information are extremely valuable to the writer who uses a computer to compose. While some writers conduct computer-based research during the prewriting stage, many writers need information from other people, libraries, and other sources as they compose their material.

Computer-based material may be obtained from electronic mail systems (interviewing an expert by electronic mail), computer conferencing systems (a more structured dialog of three or more persons on the computer), or electronic databases.

Computer databases and search programs are becoming essential research systems. Such commercial database systems as *The Source, ComputerServe,* or the *New York Times Information Service* include news, financial data, and services. Special-purpose databases such as *Lexis* (legal case summaries) or *Eric* (educational research summaries) provide information of interest to people in specific careers.

Doing research from a database is more efficient than gathering information from individual magazines, books, journals, and news sources. With a computer, a modem is used to connect the computer via a phone line, and with access to several databases, a writer can browse through a large number of resources.

Modeling Effective Styles   Writers become better writers by modeling master or effective writers. Starting with formatted text copy and expanding the copy by "copying" the writer's technique and structure helps writers to gain a sense of what it feels like to write effectively.

Merging Graphics and Financial Data   Most word processors have the capacity to merge financial data from a spreadsheet or a graphic from a graphics or charting file into a word processed document. In these cases, the writer marks the place in the text they wish the *spreadsheet* or *graphics file* to be positioned, gives the commands to load in the file, and within two or three keystrokes the writer has a report that contains an annual budget or a pie chart without keying in the financial or graphic data.

Whenever the text of your letter (or of any other document, for that matter) is becoming too long or too complicated, consider the possibility of developing a visual aid. If you're developing a schedule, consider a tablular format. If you're comparing expenses of two departments, consider a simple two-column chart.

Here, for example, is a simple chart of second-quarter expenses.

Second-Quarter Expenses			
	April	**May**	**June**
Postage	1,234	1,765	1,565
Duplicating	2,765	2,987	3,011
Travel	5,876	2,899	4,761
Entertainment	980	1,321	1,782
Office supplies	1,900	1,941	1,450
TOTALS:	12,755	10,913	12,569

Imagine delivering the same information in *word format*: "For the month of April, postage expense totaled $1,234, duplicating was $2,765, travel totaled...."

Revising

Revising documents involves making changes in ideas, organization, tone, and expression. Revising documents on the computer can easily be done in stages. Unlike the manual cut-and-paste method of revision, the writer using a word processor does not have to recopy the entire text after each change. The ability to produce a neat copy after each revision helps the writer to focus on additional problems without interference from the revision marks.

Besides the computer's ability to delete, insert, move, and copy text, word processors offer these revision aids: search-replace option, electronic file sharing and reviews, and text analysis and prompt programs.

Search and Replace Almost all word processors allow you to search and replace any word, phrase, or number in your document. Say, for example, that you have a form letter that is sent to 300 customers. Recently, one of the products was renamed. Word processing allows you to search for all instances of the old name and automatically insert the new name.

Electronic File Sharing By sending document files electronically through the use of the computer, networks, computer mail, and computer conferencing, writers can receive immediate reactions to their compositions. They can interact with the reviewers to clarify comments and to ask questions about specific aspects of the composition. Special software programs permit a number of reviewers to review the same file while the program manages each set of comments separately. The original writer can review the comments from all the reviewers on each section of the document.

Text Analysis Programs Text analysis programs help writers to critique and revise their compositions by analyzing long or awkward sentences, creating postcomposition outlines which point the writer to structural or organizational problems (if they exist), and pointing to areas where word use and overall conciseness may be a problem. Text analysis programs scan the completed document for aspects such as repeated words, unnecessary words, and readability. These programs offer specific ways to improve the composition.

Editing

Editing is the process of refining wording, spelling, usage, and punctuation. Once your composition is well organized, you can begin to "polish" the document with a variety of computer-based editing tools.

Spelling Checker Spell-check programs compare all the words in the document to words in a dictionary list which reside on the disk. Words that either do not match or are not included in the list are identified as possible misspellings. Not all spelling errors are caught by the spell checker. For example, the word *they* instead of *the* would not be noted as an error because both words can be found in the dictionary.

Electronic Dictionaries and Thesauruses If your word processing software program offers a dictionary, you can type in the word you want and the program will display on screen: part of speech, meanings, and sample sentences—the same information found in an ordinary dictionary. Similarly, if your software offers a *thesaurus* (a book of synonyms and antonyms), you type a word into the computer and the program will list word synonyms and antonyms. You can then select the word you wish to use.

Style and Grammar Rule Books   Select word processors have chosen to support style and grammar checkers. Writers can view grammar rules on line and evaluate them in the context of a specific grammatical problem they are experiencing.

Formatting Aids   Sophisticated text and word processors include features for outlining the text after it is completed and for automatically numbering or printing different headings for each level of the document. Other products offer a text indexing feature and/or footnoting capability.

As you can see, the word processors available now offer a variety of writing aids designed to help you organize, write, and revise more efficiently. Word processors of the future will respond to voice command; others will "speak" the words as they are keyed into the computer.

Desktop publishing will become commonplace in the future. Secretaries, sales and marketing people, and supervisors will have access to systems that allow them to create documents using a variety of typefaces, two-column (newspaper) formats, as well as illustrations and graphics.

This chapter shows how the computer can be used to facilitate both the quality and the quantity of the writing process. Remember that the goal of the writing process—prewriting, composing, revising, and editing—is to create business documents that are clear, concise, persuasive, personalized, and interesting to read. Word processing and writing aids can help you become a more creative and confident writer.

PROJECTS

1. Review the four stages of writing and think about how you handle each stage Answer these questions:
   a. Which stage causes you the most difficulty?
   b. Which stage comes easiest for you?
   c. Which stage do you tend to neglect or minimize?
   d. What sequence do you tend to follow?
   e. Does this sequence work well for your final compositions?
2. Assume that you are the sales manager's assistant and have been asked to write a paper comparing your company's marketing strategies over the past three years with your three main competitors' strategies. But you are struggling to come up with a well-defined approach to handling this topic. What computer aids might help you with this stage of writing?
3. Assume that you have access to a computer database which contains sales history and marketing information on the competitive products. How could you use the database to help you write your paper?
4. You have drafted your paper but are concerned that you may have long or awkward sentences, and that you switch between passive and active voice. What computer aids would help you to revise your composition?
5. Your paper is complete and now exceeds ten pages. On a final read-through you decide all references to product sales should be changed to unit sales.

What words processing feature would help you make this change?

6. Name the two most important *quantitative* benefits of word processing.

7. Name three ways computer aids can help improve the quality of your writing.

8. Assume you used all the computer writing aids available. Can you be guaranteed that your writing is clear, concise, persuasive, and interesting to read? Why or why not?

9. Your supervisor has asked you to write a paper that summarizes *your* perceptions of *your* abilities, interests, and career plans. Draft a two-page paper that concludes with an assessment of *which careers* fit with your abilities and interests and which careers do not fit with your abilities and interests. Explain why or why not in each case. If prewriting software is available, use it to help you explore and outline this topic. If available, compose and revise your topic using word processing or text editing software. Edit your paper with the spell-check program and writing analysis software if it is available to you.

ELECTRONIC OFFICE GLOSSARY

Access The ability to retrieve information from a computer system. *Access* is sometimes used as a verb in computerese, as in "To prepare the report, she had to *access* the salary files."

Anti-glare Screen A device placed over a VDT to reduce eyestrain.

Aperture Card A paper or plastic card with an opening, or *aperture*, that holds a small piece of microfilm. *Aperture cards* are often used to store engineers' drawings.

Applications Specific purposes for which computers are used, such as word processing or accounts receivable.

Automated Office See *Electronic Office*.

Boiler Plate Paragraphs that can be retrieved from storage in a word processing system so they can be reused without being keyboarded again. Boiler plate is usually used in combination with variable information that is newly keyboarded, but some documents are assembled entirely of boiler plate.

Byte A unit of measurement in computer storage, roughly equivalent to one printed character.

Calendar Program *Software* used for keeping track of schedules. Some calendar *programs* can flash a reminder onto a *VDT* as the time for an appointment approaches.

Computer A machine that performs calculations or otherwise manipulates information automatically by interpreting electrical impulses.

Computer Graphics The automated creation of charts, graphs, or pictures by a computer program from verbal or numerical information.

Computer Security The control of access to the information in a computer system, usually to prevent unauthorized persons from obtaining confidential information. *Computer security* also refers to the protection of hardware.

Continuous-form Paper Connected sheets of paper that have strips of sprocket holes along their sides to permit automatic feeding through a printer. The edges of the sheets are perforated so they can be separated easily from each other and from the sprockethold strips.

Daisy Wheel A type element for a word processing printer, serving the same function as the type ball of a Selectric typewriter. A *daisy wheel* is so named because it resembles a daisy, with the characters at the ends of the "petals."

Data, Data Processing Although *data* is just another word for facts, in the electronic office it generally means numerical information. *Data processing* refers to the use of computers to perform calculations or other numerical operations (as opposed to word processing, which refers to the manipulation of verbal text).

Data Bank A collection of verbal or numerical information in a computer system to which businesses and individuals can gain access, usually for a fee. Some of the data banks now in operation offer magazine indexes and copies of articles, stock market prices, court decisions, and medical information.

Data Base A collection of related data that are organized so they can be used for more than one application. A *data base* that included information about New York City government's electric bills, for example, could be used in preparing a citywide budget as well as in determining what it costs a single department to maintain a particular building.

Disk, Diskette A circular piece of magnetic material that retains documents by recording the electrical impulses generated by a computer or word processor. *Disks*, which are about as big as long-playing phonograph records, can store hundreds of pages of text or numbers and are usually used with big computer systems. Independent personal computers generally use *diskettes*, which are smaller and can store as much as one hundred pages of information. See also *Optical Disk* and *Storage.*

Electronic Copier/Printer A copying machine that is faster than conventional photocopiers and can be linked with other electronic equipment.

Electronic Files, Electronic Filing Documents that are stored in an information processing system are called *electronic files. Electronic filing* refers to recording these documents on storage disks or retrieving them from the disks for viewing, editing, or printing.

Electronic Mail The transmission of correspondence between *VDTs* rather than through the use of paper.

Electronic Office An office equipped with word processors and other sophisticated electronic equipment that automatically performs some tasks involved in communication.

Electronic Scheduling The use of a computer to arrange a meeting by electronically checking and adjusting the electronic calendars of the participants.

Executive Workstation The information processing equipment, such as a personal computer, in a manager's office.

Facsimile, Facsimile Transmission A *facsimile* is a copy of a printed document. *Facsimile transmission* is the use of electronic equipment to transmit copies between distant points. *Facsimile transmission* involves the use of one device to scan the original electronically and another device to print the copy. These devices are connected over telephone lines or by other electronic means.

File A document storage area in a computer's memory.

Flow Chart A chart showing the flow of work from start to finish, with symbols that represent operations and pieces of equipment.

Global Search A word processor function that electronically finds a word (or any string of characters) wherever it appears in a document.

Hard Copy A printed copy of a document stored in an information processing system.

Hardware The physical components of an information processing system: the computer, the keyboards, and so on.

Information Processing A term that includes both word processing and data processing and refers to all operations that can be performed by a computer.

Input The transfer of text or data into an information processing system. *Input* can also refer to the text or data itself.

Interface An electrical connector that permits a piece of equipment, such as a printer, to be attached to an information processing system.

Keyboarding Using the keyboard of a computer or word processor to put information into the system. Since a word processing keyboard closely resembles a typewriter keyboard, *keyboarding* is the computer-age counterpart of typing.

Laser A device that transmits an extremely narrow beam of light. Laser technology is increasingly being used to store, transmit, and print documents in information processing systems. The word *laser* is actually an acronym for *L*ight *A*pplication by *S*imulated *E*mission of *R*adiation.

Log-On, Log-Off The process of keying in the code that tells a computer or word processor when you are using the system or when you have finished. *Logging on* may require that you use a password identifying yourself as an authorized user.

Microfiche A sheet of microfilm about the size of an index card, on which dozens of documents may be stored photographically.

Microwaves Electronic signals that can be beamed in straight lines through open air for distances as great as 30 miles.

Modem A device that enables personal computers to communicate over long distances. A *modem* converts electrical impulses from the computers into signals that can be transmitted over telephone wires, then converts them back to electrical impulses for the receiving computer.

Network, Networking The use of cables, telephone lines, satellites, and other technologies to allow communication among pieces of electronic equipment, sometimes over long distances.

Optical Character Reader (OCR) A device that scans printed pages and converts them into electrical signals for input into an information processing system, so they do not have to be keyboarded.

Optical Disk A computer storage medium,

about the size of a large phonograph record, that can retain thousands of pages of words and photographs through the use of laser technology.

Optical Fiber A microscopic strand of glasslike material that can be used with lasers to transmit data from between pieces of electronic equipment.

Personal Computer A computer, used independently or as part of a larger computer system, that fits on a desk and can be used by people who are not data processing specialists.

Photocomposition, Photocompositor *Photocomposition* is the use of computers and photographic film, rather than metal type, for printing. A *photocompositor* is a person or business specializing in this process.

Printer The component of an information processing system that electronically prints copies of text that is stored in the system. The printer is operated through the use of the word processor's keyboard to input commands to the system's computer.

Printout A paper copy, or hard copy, of information that is stored in an information processing system.

Program A set of instructions, also called software, that tells a computer how to perform a task. Some programs are mass produced and sold for use with personal computers, while others are written for specific systems.

Random Access Memory (RAM) A feature that enables a computer to find a document in its storage unit without requiring the user to view other documents that are stored there.

Reprographics The reproduction of printed documents.

Retrieve, Retrieval This is the process of taking a document out of storage. In word processing, *retrieval* usually means calling a document from a storage disk onto a *VDT* so it can be read, edited, or printed.

Soft Copy The text that is displayed on a *VDT*, as opposed to text that is printed.

Software Instructions that tell a computer how to perform a task. See also *Program.*

Storage The electronic recording of documents so they can be read, edited, or printed later. See also *Disk/Diskette.*

Systems Analysis, Systems Analyst The process of designing and developing information processing systems is known as *systems analysis,* and the people who do this are called *systems analysts.*

Systems Integration The linking of electronic equipment and procedures into a unified system for information processing. See also *Information Processing* and *Network*

Systems Manager The person who oversees the design and operation of an information processing system.

Telecommunications The transmission and reception of information over long distances, usually by way of telephone lines.

Telecommuting Working at home or at a site other than at the traditional workplace on a personal computer that is connected with a company's information processing system.

Teleconference A "meeting" in which several participants at distant locations use telecommunications equipment to exchange documents, converse, and perhaps see each other on television screens.

Ultrafiche A sheet of microfilm containing images that have been reduced to one-ninetieth of their original size. See also *Microfiche.*

Video Display Terminal (VDT) A television-like screen on which information being keyed into an information processing system, or already stored there, is displayed for reading or editing.

Voice Recognition Technology that allows electronic equipment to accept spoken commands as well as input from a keyboard or OCR.

Voice Verification The use of voiceprints, which are as individual as fingerprints, to control access to buildings, equipment, or information. The security system contains voiceprints of all authorized users and grants access only to people whose voices match the prints.

Word Processing The use of electronic equipment to create, edit, store, print, or transmit documents electronically.

Word Processing Center, Word Processing Operator An organization's *word processing center* is responsible for preparing finished documents from rough drafts or dictation dictated by authors throughout the organization. The people who work in the center are called *word processing operators.*

Word Processor   A computer terminal, either independent or part of a larger system, that performs word processing. A *word processor* consists of a keyboard, a VDT, a storage unit, an internal processor (or computer), and a printer.

Work Station   A computer terminal used for information processing. A *work station* consists of a VDT and a keyboard. The storage unit, processor, and printer may be located at the work station or elsewhere.

WORD USAGE

Refer to this section for help when completing the "Style Checkup" Exercises at the end of the textbook cases.

accede, exceed   *Accede* means to comply with; *exceed* means to surpass. • Not only do I think you will meet your budget, I think you will *exceed* it. / I *accede* to your request for more time to settle your account.

accept, except   *Accept* means to take with consent; *except* means to exclude. • We're happy to *accept* your invitation to tour your new building. / Everything in the report, *except* the cost analysis, is satisfactory.

accidentally, accidently   There is no such word as *accidently*. • Joe *accidentally* (not *accidently*) left the motor running.

adapt, adopt   *Adapt* means to adjust; *adopt* means to choose. • We can *adapt* this form letter to fit varying situations. / Your system of filing is so efficient that I plan to *adopt it.*

adverse, averse   *Adverse* means hostile or unfavorable; *averse* means disinclined to accept. • We've had many *adverse* reactions to the change in cafeteria hours. / The sales representative is *averse* to an expansion of her territory.

advice, advise   *Advice* means recommendation regarding a decision or course of conduct; *advise* means to give advice or counsel. • My *advice* is to stay in your present job until you have mastered it. / We *advise* you to investigate time-sharing rather than buy your own computers.

affect, effect   *Affect* means to influence or change; *effect* is a result or outcome. • How will the price change *affect* profits? / What *effect* will the price change have on profits?

aggravate, annoy   *Aggravate* means to make worse; *annoy* means to disturb or bother. • You will only *aggravate* the situation by criticizing the employee publicly.   Two reminders in the same week are like to *annoy* Mrs. Hadrian.

alike, both alike   Do not use *both* with *alike*. • The two brands of desk computers are *alike* in many respects. (Not *both alike.*)

all, all of   Do not use *of* after *all* unless the following word is a pronoun. • *All* the applications received were impressive. / *All of* us are grateful for the three-day weekend.

all right, alright   There is no such word as "alright." *All right* is always two words. • It is *all right* to part here? (Not *alright* or *allright.*)

all-round, all-around   Do not use *all-around* for *all-round*. • Cindy is an all-round athlete.

and etc.   Never use *and* with *etc.* • We ordered new letterheads, envelopes, memorandum forms, *etc.* (Not *and etc.*)

anxious, eager   It is often important to distinguish between *anxious* and *eager. Anxious* means uneasy or worried; *eager* means enthusiastic about, looking forward to. • I am *eager* to have my own office. / Karl is *anxious* to learn the results of his physical examination.

any, any other, anyone, anyone else's   Beware of comparing a person or thing with itself. • Wrong: Alaska is larger than any state. (Alaska cannot be larger than itself.) / Right: Alaska is larger than any *other* state. / Wrong: Martha's bowling score was higher than anyone's on the team. / Right: Martha's bowling score was higher than *anyone else's* on the team.

anywhere, anywheres Do not use *anywheres* for *anywhere*. • I can't locate the Kimball contract *anywhere*. (Not *anywheres*.)

appraise, apprise *Appraise* means to set a value on; *apprise* means to inform. • Norton Realty will *appraise* the property this week. / I want to *apprise* you of the danger of overbuying during this period.

around (for *about*) Use *about* instead of *around* to indicate approximate time. • I hope you will be able to see me *about* 10:30. (Not *around* 10:30.)

at about Omit *at* before *about*. • Can you have the work completed *about* May 1? (Not *at about* May 1.)

balance, remainder It's best not to use *balance* for *remainder*. • The *remainder* (not *balance*) of your order will be sent July 14.

between, among Use *between* when referring to two persons or things; use *among* when referring to more than two persons or things. • The workload is divided evenly *between* Don and Louise. / There is considerable rivalry *among* the six teams in the league.

between you and me (I) Do not use *between you and I*. • Remember, this conversation is just between *you and me*. (Not *you and I*.)

but what, but that Do not use *but what* for *that*. • I do not doubt *that* the merchandise can be sold quickly. (Not *but what*.)

can't (couldn't hardly) Do not use *can't* or *couldn't* with *hardly*. • I *can* hardly wait until the year-end results are published. (Not *can't* hardly.) / Kreitzer *could* hardly believe the amount of her pay increase. (Not *couldn't* hardly.)

canvas, canvass *Canvas* is a coarse cloth; *canvass* means to solicit support or opinions. • The room divider has *canvas* panels. / Let's *canvass* our dealers for their recommendations.

Capital means a seat of government; *capitol* refers to a government building. • The former *capital* of Oklahoma was Guthrie; today it is Oklahoma City. / The state insurance commissioner's office is in the capitol building in Raleigh. (But: The U.S. Congress meets in the Capitol.)

coarse, course *Coarse* means rough, unrefined; *course* refers to direction. • The speaker stunned the audience with his *coarse* language. / What is the best *course* to take—rent a warehouse or build our own?

complementary, complimentary *Complementary* means in agreement with; *complimentary* means bestowing praise. • The colors of the drapes and carpeting are *complementary*. / I genuinely appreciate your *complimentary* remarks about our service.

confidant, confident A *confidant* is a friend or trusted adviser (feminine form: *confidante*); *confident* means certain or self-reliant. • Meg is a valued *confidante* with whom I can share my true feelings. / Morris is *confident* that he can meet the October deadline.

credible, creditable *Credible* means believable; *creditable* means deserving of praise. • The reason Walston gave for his absence sounds *credible* to me. / The Longview store made a *creditable* showing in spite of labor problems.

deduce, deduct *Deduce* means to infer; *deduct* means to subtract. • From your remarks, I *deduce* that you are not in favor of changing agencies. / Please *deduct* payment of my credit union loan from my biweekly check.

deprecate, depreciate *Deprecate* means to express disapproval; *depreciation* means loss in value. • I don't *deprecate* her motive, but I do question her method. / The equipment will *depreciate* rapidly through hard use.

disapprove, disproved *Disapprove* means to withhold approval; *disprove* means to prove the falsity of. • Fischer felt that she had to *disapprove* Ray's request for a month's leave of absence. / I believe I can *disprove* your statement that you were overcharged.

disburse, disperse *Disburse* means to pay out; *disperse* means to scatter. • Only the cashier may *disburse* funds from the petty cash box. / Let's *disperse* these fire extinguishers throughout the factory.

discreet, discrete You must be *discreet* in answering questions about our new product plans. / Please arrange the data in *discrete* families for easy sorting.

different than Do not use *different than* for *different from*. • The turnover problem this year is entirely *different from* that of last year. (Not *different than.*)

elicit, illicit *Elicit* means to draw forth; *illicit* means unlawful. • I tried to *elicit* from Peabody his reason for ignoring company policy. / *Illicit* claims in advertising our product will get us in trouble with the Federal Trade Commission.

eminent, imminent *Eminent* means well known or prominent; *imminent* means ready to take place or threatening. • The *eminent* economist, Dr. Paul C. Hargreaves, will address our May meeting. / A work slowdown at the Hartford plant appears to be *imminent.*

envelop, envelope *Envelop* means to cover or wrap; an *envelope* is a wrapper for a written message. • Our survey will *envelop* all of Blaine County. / Please use an interoffice *envelope* to send messages to employees.

equally as good Use either *equally good* or *just as good.* • The Whiz calculator costs much less than the Rapidex but it is *equally good* (or *just as good*).

farther, further *Farther* means at a greater distance (refers to space); *further* means in addition (refers to time, quantity, or degree). • The new distribution center is *farther* from town than the old one was. / If you have *further* suggestions, please let me have them immediately.

fewer, less Do not use *less* for *fewer.* • There were *fewer* breakdowns in factory machines this month than last. / We have had *fewer* returns in merchandise in the first quarter, so our net profit should not be *less* than expected.

Fewer people are buying expensive cuts of meat this year. (Not *less* people.)

finish, finish up Omit *up* after *finish.* • The carpenters expect to *finish* framing the house today. (Not *finish up.*)

forward, foreword *Forward* means to send, advance; *foreword* is the preface in a book. • Now that our staff is complete, let's go *forward* with our plans. / Julie wrote an excellent *foreword* for the employee handbook.

healthy, healthful Do not use *healthy* for *healthful.* People are healthy; foods and climate are healthful. • John appears to be very *healthy* since recovering from surgery. / In planning the family menu, you should include such *healthful* foods as fresh fruit and vegetables. / A high priority for many retirees is a *healthful* climate.

imply, infer *Imply* means to suggest (you imply something by your own words or actions); *infer* means to arrive at a conclusion (you *infer* something from another person's words or actions). • I do not mean to *imply* that Rossiter was wilfully negligent. / I *infer* from your remarks that my department is overstaffed.

inside of (for *within*) Do not use *inside of* for *within.* • Ellen says she will have the figures *within* an hour. (Not *inside of* an hour.)

irregardless There is no such word as "irregardless." • I intend to finish the inventory by Thursday, *regardless* of the overtime hours required. (Not "irregardless.")

kind of, sort of Use *somewhat* or *rather* instead of *kind of* or *sort of.* • The dealers were *rather* pleased with the display material we sent them. / The speaker appeared *somewhat* annoyed by Digby's questions.

kind, kinds *Kind* is singular; *kinds,* plural. • I prefer this *kind* of chair to the one I have been using. / These *kinds* of mistakes can be very costly.

last, latest *Last* means after all others or final; *latest* means most recent. • This is the *last* copy available of the annual report. (There are no others.) / The information you need will be found in our *latest* catalog. (The most recent; there will be others.)

later, latter *Later* means after a time or more late; *latter* means second in a series of two. • In the beginning of your report, you objected to the use of performance tests; *later,* however, you said they were excellent screening devices. / Of the two layouts you sent me, I prefer the *latter.* (The second one.)

like, as Don't use *like* for *as.* • The kerosene heater saves fuel cost, *as* the dealer said it would. (Not *like* the dealer said it would.)

loath, loathe *Loath* means reluctant; *loathe,* to detest. • We are *loath* to move from this fine old building, but we need more space. / I *loathe* the drab wall covering in the foyer.

more, most Use *more* when two things are being compared and *most* when more than two things are being compared. • Of the two restaurants recommended, I believe the Toucan has a *more* cheerful atmosphere. / All seven sketches are good, but the one with the skiing scene has the *most* sales appeal.

myself (for *me* and *I*) Do not use *myself* for *me* or *I*. • You were very helpful to Ms. Thornton and *me*. (Not *myself*.) / Harry and *I* will attend the Phoenix Antique Show. (Not *myself*.)

nothing like Do not use *nothing like* when you mean *not nearly*. • Our production costs are *not nearly* as high as they were last year. (Not *nothing like* as high.)

notorious (for *noted* or *famed*) Do not use *notorious* when you mean *noted* or *famed*. The word *notorious* means bad repute, as a notorious swindler. • Wilhelms is a *noted* (or *famous*) psychologist. (Not *notorious* psychologist.)

off of Omit *of* after *off*. • The ball bounced *off* the rim. / I took the figures *off* the computer printout.

ordinance, ordnance An *ordinance* is a local law; *ordnance* refers to arms, munitions. • The city *ordinance* requires a set-back of 25 feet from the curb. / Vehicles for hauling *ordnance* must be easily identifiable as such.

outside of Do not use *of* after *outside*. • The accident occurred *outside* the city limits. (Not *outside of*.)

partition, petition A *partition* is a division; a *petition* is a formal written request. • We plan to build a *partition* to separate the two mailing functions. / The Citizens Tax Committee sent a *petition* to the mayor protesting the reassessment of private property.

party (for *person*) Don't use *party* when referring to an individual (expect in legal work). • Will you ask the *person* who called to telephone me Monday morning. OR Will you ask the *caller* to telephone me Monday morning. (Not ask the *party*.)

per (for *a* or *an*) Do not use *per* for *a* or *an*. • Beverly's shorthand speed is 100 words a minute. (Not *per* minute.) / We averaged 50 miles *an* hour on our trip to Georgetown. (Not *per* hour.)

perquisite, prerequisite A *perquisite* is an added privilege and is usually plural; *prerequisite* means a preliminary requirement. • Members of the embassy staff receive many *perquisites*, such as a housing allowance, over-seas pay, and free transportation. / A *prerequisite* for admission to law school is a bachelor's degree.

precede, proceed *Precede* means to go before; *proceed* means to advance. • A movie will *precede* the general meeting. / The conclusions you made in your report are excellent, and I hope you will *proceed* with your recommendations.

principal, principle *Principal* means chief or main; *principle* means a general truth or rule. • The president's *principal* concern is the effect of this change on morale. / Our compensation policy is based on the *principle* of equal pay for equal performance.

provided, providing *Provided* means on condition that; *providing* means supplying. • The class will be held, *provided* there are at least twenty students. / Thank you for *providing* the refreshments for our get-together.

real, really Do not use *real* for *really* and vice versa. Also avoid *real* as a synonym for *very*. • We're *really* pleased to welcome you as a Zenith dealer. / This coat collar is *real* wool—not a synthetic fiber. / It was *very* thoughtful of you to write. (Not *real* thoughtful.)

reason is because or due to Do not say *reason is because* or *due to*; instead, say *that*. • The reason I was late for the meeting is *that* I had a dental appointment. OR My reason for being late is *that* I had a dental appointment. (Not *due to*.)

same (for *it*) Do not use *same* for *it*. • The new catalog is beautiful, and I thank you for sending *it*. / (Not thank you for sending *same*.)

seldom ever Do not use *ever* to follow *seldom*. • We *seldom* (or *hardly ever*) get requests for that model. (Not *seldom ever*.)

stationary, stationery *Stationary* means fixed or unmovable; *stationery* refers to writing materials. • Although the smaller factory machines are movable, the larger ones are *stationary*. / Have you ordered letterheads and other *stationery* for the new vice president?

suspicion, suspect Do not use *suspicion* as a verb. • We did not *suspect* that Grange was so heavily in debt. (Not *suspicion*.) / Allender is under *suspicion* as an embezzler.

through (for *finished*) Do not use *through*

when you mean *finished.* • I hope to be *finished* with my dictation by noon. (Not *through* with my dictation.)

try and (for *try to*)   Don't say *try and* when you mean *try to.* • Please *try to* visit our showroom when you are in Akron. (Not *try and* visit.)

unique   *Unique* means only one of a kind; therefore, you need not qualify it. • Ogden Nash's poems, as well as James Thurber's drawings, are *unique.* (Not *very unique* or *most unique.*)

who, that   *Who* is preferred when an individual person is meant; *that,* when a class is meant. • Among those *who* commented favorably were the president and the controller. / Carruthers is the type of supervisor *that* employees respect.

FORMS OF ADDRESS

Refer to the following list whenever you need the correct forms of address for government, military, religious, or education officials. In addition to forms of address, the list includes appropriate salutations, listed in order of decreasing formality.

The forms of address and salutations given include (for the sake of simplicity) only the masculine forms. Of course, change *Mr.* to *Miss, Mrs.,* or *Ms.,* and change *Sir* to *Madam,* as appropriate.

Government Officials

PRESIDENT OF THE UNITED STATES
   The President
   The White House
   Washington, DC 20500

   Mr. President:
   Dear Mr. President:

VICE PRESIDENT OF THE UNITED STATES
   The Vice President
   United States Senate
   Washington, DC 20510
Or: The Honorable ... (*full name*)
   Vice President of the United States
   Washington, DC 20501

   Sir:
   Dear Mr. Vice President:

CHIEF JUSTICE OF THE UNITED STATES
   The Chief Justice of the United States
   Washington, DC 20543

Or: The Chief Justice
   The Supreme Court
   Washington, DC 20543

   Sir:
   Dear Mr. Chief Justice:

CABINET MEMBER
   The Honorable ... (*full name*)
   Secretary ... (*department*)
   Washington, DC   ZIP Code

Or: The Secretary of ... (*department*)
   Washington, DC   ZIP Code

   Sir:
   Dear Mr. Secretary:

UNITED STATES SENATOR
   The Honorable ... (*full name*)
   United States Senate
   Washington, DC 20510
Or: The Honorable ... (full name)
   United States Senator
   (*local address and ZIP Code*)

   Sir:
   Dear Senator ... :

UNITED STATES REPRESENTATIVE
   The Honorable ... (*full name*)
   House of Representatives
   Washington, DC 20515
Or: The Honorable ... (*full name*)
   Representative in Congress
   (*local address and ZIP Code*)

   Sir:
   Dear Mr. ... :

GOVERNOR
In Massachusetts, New Hampshire, and by courtesy in some other states:

   His Excellency the Governor of ...
   State Capital, State   ZIP Code
In other states:
   The Honorable ... (*full name*)

Governor of ...
State Capital, State   ZIP
    Code
Sir:
Dear Governor ...:

STATE SENATOR
    The Honorable ... (*full
        name*)
    The State Senate
    State Capital, State   ZIP
        Code

    Sir
    Dear Senator ...:

STATE REPRESENTATIVE
OR ASSEMBLY MEMBER
    The Honorable ... (*full
        name*)
    House of Representatives
        (**or** The State
        Assembly)
    State Capital, State   ZIP
        Code

    Sir:
    Dear Mr. ...:

MAYOR
    The Honorable ... (*full
        name*)
    Mayor of ... (*city*)
    City, State   ZIP Code
Or: The Mayor of the City
    of ...
    City, State   ZIP Code

    Sir:
    Dear Mr. Mayor:
    Dear Mayor ...:

**Members of the Armed
Services**

The addresses of both officers
and enlisted men in the armed
services should include title of
rank, full name followed by a
comma and the initials USA, USN,
USAF, USMC, or USCG. Below
are some specific examples together with the appropriate salutations.

ARMY, AIR FORCE, AND
MARINE CORPS OFFICERS
    Lieutenant General ... (*full
        name*), USA
    Address

    Sir:
    Dear General ...:
    (**not** Dear Lieutenant
        General ...:

For first and second lieutenants,
use:

    Dear Lieutenant ...:

NAVY AND COAST GUARD
OFFICERS
    Rear Admiral ... (*full
        name*), USN
    Address

    Sir:
    Dear Admiral ...:

For officers below the rank of
Commander, use:

    Dear Mr. ...:

ENLISTED MEN
    Sergeant ... (*full name*), USA
    Address

    Seaman ... (*full name*) USN
    Address

    Dear Sergeant (**or**
        Seaman) ...:

Roman Catholic Dignitaries

CARDINAL
    His Eminence ... (*given
        name*)
        Cardinal ... (*surname*)
    Archbishop of ... (*place*)
    Address

    Your Eminence:
    Dear Cardinal ...:

ARCHBISHOP AND BISHOP
    The Most Reverend ... (*full
        name*)
    Archbishop (**or** Bishop) of ...
        (*place*)
    Address

Your Excellency:
Dear Archbishop (**or** Bishop)
    ...

MONSIGNOR
    The Right Reverend Monsi-
        gnor ... (*full name*)
    Address

    Right Reverend Monsignor:
    Dear Monsignor ...:

PRIEST
    The Reverend ... (*full name,
        followed by comma and
        initials of order*)
    Address

    Reverend Father:
    Dear Father ...:

MOTHER SUPERIOR
    The Reverend Mother Supe-
        rior
    Address
Or: Reverend Mother ... (*name,
        followed by comma and
        initials of order*)
    Address

    Reverend Mother:
    Dear Reverend Mother:
    Dear Mother ...:

SISTER
    Sister ... (*name, followed by
        comma and initials of
        order*)
    Address

    Dear Sister:
    Dear Sister ...:

Protestant Dignitaries

PROTESTANT EPISCOPAL
BISHOP
    The Right Reverend ...
        (*full name*)
    Bishop of ... (*place*)
    Address

    Right Reverend Sir:
    Dear Bishop ...:

PROTESTANT EPISCOPAL
DEAN

The Very Reverend ... (*full name*)
Dean of ...
Address

Very Reverend Sir:
Dear Dean ...:

METHODIST BISHOP
The Reverend ... (*full name*)
Bishop of ...
Address

Reverend Sir:
Dear Bishop ...:

CLERGYMAN WITH
DOCTOR'S DEGREE
The Reverend Dr. ... (*full name*)
Address
Or: The Reverend ... (*full name*), D.D.
Address

Reverend Sir:
Dear Dr. ...:

CLERGYMAN WITHOUT
DOCTOR'S DEGREE
The Reverend ... (*full name*)
Address

Reverend Sir:
Dear Mr. ...:

Jewish Dignitaries

RABBI WITH DOCTOR'S DE-
GREE
Rabbi ... (*full name*), D.D.
Address

Or: Dr. ... (*full name*)
Address

Dear Rabbi (**or** Dr.) ...:

RABBI WITHOUT DOCTOR'S
DEGREE
Rabbi ... (*full name*)
Address

Dear Rabbi ...:

Education Officials

PRESIDENT OF A COLLEGE
OR UNIVERSITY
... (*full name, followed by comma and highest degree*)
President, ... (*name of college*)
Address
Or: Dr. ... (*full name*)
President, ... (*name of college*)
Address

Dear President ...:
Dear Dr. ...:

PROFESSOR
Professor ... (*full name*)
Department of ...
... (*name of college*)
Address
Or: ... (*full name, followed by comma and highest degree*)

Department of ...
... (*name of college*)
Address
Or: Dr. ... (*full name*)
Professor of ... (*subject*) ...
(*name of college*)
Address

Dear Professor (**or** Dr.) ...:
Dear Mr. ...:

SUPERINTENDENT OF
SCHOOLS
Mr. (**or** Dr.) ... (*full name*)
Superintendent of ... Schools
Address

Dear Mr. (**or** Dr.) ...:

MEMBER OF BOARD OF
EDUCATION
Mr. ... (*full name*)
Member, ... (*name of city*)
Board of Education
Address

Dear Mr. ...:

PRINCIPAL
Mr. (**or** Dr.) ... (*full name*)
Principal, ... (*name of school*)
Address

Dear Mr. (**or** Dr.) ...:

TEACHER
Mr. (or Dr.) ... (*full name*)
... (*name of school*)
Address

Dear Mr. (**or** Dr.) ...:

INDEX

Acceptance of job offer, letters involved, in **293–298**

Accusations, avoiding, **68**

Acknowledgment, letters of
for compliments and suggestions, **17, 19, 215–218**
for first orders, **33–34, 147–151, 173–175**

Active versus passive voice, **38–39**

Ad hoc committees, defined, **356**

Administrative communications, **197–214**
absence of executive, handling, **197–202**
discretion in, **203–206**
for versus on behalf of executive, **211–214**
referred to others, **206–210**

Advertising purchases, answering requests for, **22, 23, 226–227**

Agendas for meetings, **357**

Anecdotes, opening sales letters with, **139**

Apology, letters of, **17, 18, 219**

Applications, job
letters of, **283–290**
responding to, **37–38, 241–248**
résumés for, **273–282**

Appointments, requesting, **89–92**

Appreciation, expressing (see also Thank-you letters)
to employees, **20–21, 254–257**

Bar graphs, **336**

Biases, **331–332**
gender, avoiding, **48–49, 69–71**
insidious, in reports, **332–333**
of report readers, **330–331**

Boiler plates, **384**

Business hours, announcement of, **74–75**

Business letters (see Letters)

Calling up computer files, **382**

Charts and tables
computer use for, **386**
in reports, **336, 337**

Checks, transmitting, **126–127**

Circle graphs, **336**

Clichés, **49**

Closings, complimentary, **33**

Clutter words and phrases, **43–45**

Collection letters, **10–11, 190–195**
requests for copies of, denying, **230–233**

Committees, types of, **356**

Company policy letters, **230–234**

Complaint letters, customer
about delays, **169–172**
about merchandise, **165–168**

Complimentary closings, **33**

Compliments
acknowledging, **17, 19, 215–218**
to employees, **20–21, 254–257**

Composing on computers, **384–386**

Computer directories, **381–382**

Computers, **377–389**
capabilities, range of, **378, 383**
commands, punctuation marks versus, **71–72**
composing on, **384—386**
editing with, **379–381, 387–388**
files, operations with (see Files, computer)
for long-distance communication, **378**
prewriting with, **383–384**
reports and, **328**
revising on, **386–387**
terminology of, defining, **331**

Condolence letters, **262–264**

Confirmations, **130–135**
of job offers, **249–253**
in memorandums, **318–320**
of oral agreements, **131–132, 318–320**
of receipts, **132–133**
of telegrams, **133**
of time and sequence, **134**

Congratulations
to employees, **20–21, 254–256**
to promoted coworkers, **258–262**

Contracts, transmitting, **127–128**

Contribution requests, answering, **224–226**

Copy notations in memorandums, **309**

Coworker promotions, congratulations on, **258–262**

Credit, granting and refusing, to customers, **186–189**

Critics, responding to, **235–239**

Customer-to-supplier letters, **156–172**
delays, complaining about, **169–172**
discount not given, arguing for, **162–164**
dissatisfaction, expressing, **165–168**
orders, placing, **156–158**
of thanks, **159–161**

Customers, supplier letters to (see Supplier-to-customer letters)

Data sheets (résumés), **273–282**

Databases, **385–386**

Definitions of terms in reports, **331**

Delays to customers
complaining about, **169–172**
explaining, **22, 24, 59–60**

Dictionaries, electronic, **387**

Dignifying reader, **67–68**

Directories, computer, **381–382**

Discounts
not earned, asking customers for, **178–181**
not given, arguing for, **162–164**

Discretion in writing for executives, **203–206**

Display, use of
computer for, **386**
in minutes, **358–359**
in reports, **333–337**

Distribution of minutes, **360**

Document merging on computer
financial data or graphics, **386**
mail merging, **384–385**

Donation requests, answering, **224–226**

Editing, **42–58**
with computers, **379–381, 387–388**

Education, listing, on résumé, **278**

Electronic equipment (see Computers)

Elliptical expressions, **51–52**

Employment and employees (*see* Job-related letters)
Enumerations
    in memorandums, **318–319**
    for paragraph breaks, **53**
    in reports, **334–335**
Errors, apologizing for, **17, 18**
Exaggeration, avoiding, **65–67**
Executives, answering letters for, **197–214**
Experience, listing, on résumé, **278**

Favors
    routine, requesting, **93–96**
    special
        requesting, **97–100**
        thanking suppliers for, **159–161**
Files, computer
    calling up, **382**
    grouping, **381–382**
    merging, **385** (*see also* Merging of computer documents)
    naming, **381**
    retrieving, **382**
    revising, **386–387**
    sharing, **387**
    storing, **381**
Financial data, merging, with word processor, **386**
Flattery, overdone, avoiding, **66–67**
Follow-up letters, **144–147**
    to former customers, **151–154**
Formally structured reports, **366–376**
    analysis of example, **367, 374**
    example, **368–373**
    parts of, **366–367**
    statement of purpose, example of, **330**
    subjects of, **327**
    transmittal of, **374**
Formatting aids, computer, **388**
Former customers, winning back, **151–154**
Formulas for writing, **5**
Free materials, requesting, **7–9, 82–85**
Free-writing with computer, **383–384**
FROM line of memorandums, **309**

Gender bias, avoiding, **48–49, 69–71**
Goodwill building (*see* Public relations [PR, goodwill])
Grammar, correct, **71**
    computer checkers for, **388**
Graphics, merging, with word processor, **386**
Graphs for reports, **336–337**

Headings
    in body of minutes, **359**

Headings (*cont.*)
    of minutes, **358**
    for paragraph subtopics, **54**
    in reports, **333–335**
Human resources (*see* Job-related letters)

Idea processors, **384**
Ideas and suggestions, memorandum reports for, **351–355**
Indentions in reports, **335–336**
Informal reports (*see* Memorandum reports)
Informal studies, reporting results of, **346–351**
Information, product, requests for, **86–89**
    answering, **6–7, 15–16, 106–110**
Informational memorandums, **320–325**
Inquiries (*see also* Requests)
    difficult situations, responding in, **114–124**
    following up, **144–147**
    price, responding to, **34–35, 110–114**
Insinuations, avoiding, **68**
Interoffice communication (*see* Memorandums; Reports)
Interviews, job, thank-you letters for, **290–292**
Introductions to reports, items in, **367**

Jargon, **49**
    defining, in reports, **331**
Job-related letters, **241–305**
    of application, **283–290**
    applications, responding to, **37–38, 241–248**
    of congratulations and appreciation to employees, **20–21, 254–257**
    of congratulations to promoted coworkers, **258–262**
    getting job, techniques for, **271–298**
    to interviewers, **290–292**
    offer acceptance, **293–298**
    offer confirmation, **249–253**
    of reference, **265–269**
    to references, **279–280, 294–296**
    of resignation, **298–305**
    résumés with, **273–282**
    of sympathy, **262–264**
    of thanks
        to interviewers, **290–292**
        to references, **294–296**

Lecturing, avoiding, **68**
Letters, **1–3**
    of apology, **17, 18, 219**
    in computer files, **381–382**

Letters (*cont.*)
    of confirmation, **130–135, 249–253**
    between customers and suppliers (*see* Customer-to-supplier letters; Supplier-to-customer letters)
    effectiveness in, **4–13** (*see also* Personalization of letters; Persuasiveness in letters; Public relations [PR, goodwill]; Review and revision of letters)
    employment and employee (*see* Job-related letters)
    for executives, **197–214**
    interoffice (*see* Memorandums)
    modified block style for, example of, **73**
    sales-opportunity (*see* Requests; Response letters)
    sales and sales-promotion, **136–155**
    of transmittal, **125–129**
Line graphs, **336**
Logic in communications, **72–75, 332–333**

Mail merging, **384–385**
Meetings
    agendas for, **357**
    confirmation memorandums following, **318–320**
    minutes of, **356–365**
Memorandum reports, **307–308, 327, 342–365**
    for ideas and suggestions, **351–355**
    informal studies, results of, **346–351**
    minutes of meetings, **356–365**
    periodic, **342–345**
    purpose of, implied, **329**
Memorandums, **1–2, 307–325**
    announcement of business hours, **74–75**
    confirmation, **318–320**
    gender bias in, avoiding, **69–71**
    informational, **320–325**
    parts of, **308–309**
    as reports (*see* Memorandum reports)
    request, **314–317**
    topics, examples of, **307**
    transmittal, **312–314, 374**
Merchandise
    discontinued, responding to order for, **62–64**
    dissatisfaction with, expressing, **165–168**
    substitute, suggesting, **61**
    unknown, responding to order for, **64–65**

Merchandise (*cont.*)
    unsalable, customer's return of, **181–185**
Merging of computer documents
    financial data or graphics, **386**
    mail merging, **384–385**
Minutes of meetings, **356–365**
    body of, **358–359**
    distribution of, **360**
    heading of, **358**
    recording proceedings for, **357–358**
    sample, **360–363**
Modified block style, example of, **73**

Names, using
    in letters, **29–30**
    in memorandums, **308–309**
    minutes, distribution designation in, **360**
Negative situations, responding in, **110–124**
    delays, explaining, **22, 24, 59–60**
    goodwill, maintaining, **22–24, 221–239**
    to job applicants, **37–38, 243–246**
    postponement of, **75–76**
    in reference letters, **266–269**
    requests, turning down, **22, 23, 36–37, 221–234**
New customers, welcoming, **33–34, 147–151, 173–175**

Offers
    job
        accepting, **293–298**
        confirming, **249–253**
    special, opening sales letters with, **138–139**
Office letters (*see* Memorandums)
Openings for letters
    job application, **286**
    sales, **138–139**
Oral agreements, confirming
    by letter, **131–132**
    by memorandum, **318–320**
Orders
    for discontinued merchandise, responding to, **62–64**
    first, acknowledging, **33–34, 147–151, 173–175**
    placing, **156–158**
    for unknown merchandise, responding to, **64–65**
Overstatement, avoiding, **67**

Paragraphs
    of job application letters, **286–287**
    reviewing, **52–54**

Passive versus active voice, **38–39**
Periodic memorandum reports, **342–345**
Personal profiles (résumés), **273–282**
Personal pronouns, using, **32**
Personalization of letters, **29–41**
    active versus passive voice, **38–39**
    examples, **31, 33–38**
    formality, level of, **32–33**
    name of reader, using, **29–30**
    pronoun use, **32**
Persuasiveness in letters, **59–81**
    appearance of page, **72, 73**
    dignifying reader, **67–68**
    exaggeration, avoiding, **65–67**
    gender bias, avoiding, **69–71**
    going beyond requirements, **64–65**
    grammar and punctuation, **71–72**
    logic, **72–75**
    positiveness, **59–61**
    promptness of answers, **75–76**
    reader satisfaction, **62–64**
Phrases and words, reviewing (*see* Words and phrases, reviewing and revising)
Pie charts, **336**
Pompous words and phrases, **45–47**
Positiveness in letters, **59–61**
Prewriting, computer-aided, **383–384**
Price inquiries, responding to, **34–35, 110–114**
Product information, requests for, **86–89**
    answering, **6–7, 15–16, 106–110**
Promotions, congratulating coworkers on, **258–262**
Prompted writing software, **384**
Pronouns, personal, using, **32**
Provocative statements, opening sales letters with, **139**
Public relations (PR, goodwill), **14–28, 215–240**
    advertising purchases, answering requests for, **22, 23, 226–227**
    apologies, **17, 18, 219**
    company policy letters, **230–234**
    compliments to employees, **20–21, 254–257**
    compliments and suggestions, acknowledging, **17, 19, 215–218**
    critics, responding to, **235–239**
    delays, explaining, **22, 24, 59–60**
    donation requests, answering, **224–226**
    extra effort, **64–65**
    information requests and, **15–16**
    in refusal of requests, **22, 23, 36–37, 221–234**
    thank-you letters, **17, 19–20**
Punctuation marks, use of, **71–72**

Purpose, statement of, in reports, **329–330**

Qualifications summaries (résumés), **273–282**
Quotations, opening sales letters with, **139**

Readers
    dignifying, **67–68**
    of reports, knowing, **330–331**
    satisfying, **62–64**
    writer's relationship with, influence of, **7–9, 32–33**
Receipts, confirming, **132–133**
Redundancies, **44**
Reference letters, **265–269**
References
    listing, on résumé, **279**
    thanking, **294–296**
Referral of communications to others, **206–210**
Refusals (*see also* Negative situations, responding in)
    of credit, **187–189**
Reports, **327–376**
    bias in, insidious, **332–333**
    and computers, **328**
    display in, effective, **333–337**
    formal (*see* Formally structured reports)
    memorandums as (*see* Memorandum reports)
    purpose of, stating, **329–330**
    readers of, knowing, **330–331**
    style and language of, factors in, **330**
    term in, definitions of, **331**
Requests, **82–105**
    for advertising purchases, answering, **22, 23, 226–227**
    for appointments, **89–92**
    for donations, answering, **224–226**
    for favors
        routine, **93–96**
        special, **97–100**
    for free materials, **7–9, 82–85**
    memorandums for, **314–317**
    for product information, **86–89**
        answering, **6–7, 15–16, 106–110**
    for speakers, **101–105**
    turning down, **22, 23, 36–37, 221–234**
    in violation of company policy, answering, **230–234**
Research, computer-based, **385–386**
Resignation, letters of
    better opportunity and, **298–301**
    dissatisfaction and, **301–305**

Response letters, **106–124**
    to advertising-purchase requests, **22, 23, 226–227**
    company policy, upholding, **230–234**
    to compliments and suggestions, **17, 19, 215–218**
    to critics, **235–239**
    to donation requests, **224–226**
    for executive, **197–214**
    to job applications, **37–38, 241–248**
    to job offers, **294**
    in negative situations (*see* Negative situations, responding in)
    to price inquiries, **34–35, 110–114**
    to problem letters, **114–119**
    to product inquiries, **6–7, 15–16, 106–110**
    about terms not granted, **72–74**
Résumés, **273–282**
    parts of, **277–279**
    sample, **273–277**
Retrieval of computer documents, **382**
Returned merchandise, unsalable, **181–185**
Review and revision of letters, **42–58**
    paragraphs, **52–54**
    sentence length, **50–52**
    total message, **54–55**
    words and phrases, **42–50**
Revising on computers, **386–387**

Salary, statement of, in job application, **288**
Sales-opportunity letters (*see* Requests; Response letters)
Sales and sales-promotion letters, **136–155**
    former customers, winning back, **151–154**
    inquiries, following up, **144–147**
    new customers, welcoming, **147–151**
    openings for, **138–139**
    sales message in, **139–140**
    salutation in, **138**
Salutations, **32**
    in job application letters, **285**
    in sales letters, **138**
Sample materials, requesting, **7–9**
Search-replace option in word processing, **387**
Sentence length, **50–52**
Sexist language, avoiding, **48–49, 69–71**

Signatures, use of, in memorandums, **309**
Slanted writing, **332**
Software writing tools, **378**
    composing, **384–386**
    editing, **387–388**
    prewriting, **383–384**
    revising, **386–387**
Speakers
    requesting sample materials from, **7–9**
    requesting services of, **101–105**
    thanking, **9–10**
Spell-check programs, **387**
Spelling of reader's name, **30**
Spreadsheet data, merging, with word processor, **386**
Standing committees, defined, **356**
Stevenson, Robert Louis, quoted, **42**
Storage of computer documents, **381**
Studies, informal, reporting results of, **346–351**
Style, writing
    computer checkers for, **388**
    individual, **5–7**
    of reports, factors in, **330**
SUBJECT line of memorandums, **309**
Substitute merchandise, suggesting, **61**
Suggestions
    acknowledging, **17, 19, 215–217**
    memorandum reports for, **351–355**
Supplier-to-customer letters, **173–196** (*see also* Sales and sales-promotion letters)
    collection, **10–11, 190–195**
    credit, granting and refusing, **186–189**
    delays, explaining, **22, 24, 59–60**
    discount not earned, asking for, **178–181**
    first order, acknowledging, **33–34, 147–151, 173–175**
    price inquiries, responding to, **34–35, 110–114**
    in problem situations, **114–119**
    product information, providing, **6–7, 15–16, 106–110**
    substitute merchandise, suggesting, **61**
    about terms not granted, **72–74**
    of thanks, **17, 19–20, 173–177**
    about unsalable merchandise returned, **181–185**
Suppliers, customer letters to (*see* Customer-to-supplier letters)
Sympathy letters, **262–264**

Tables
    computer use for, **386**
    in reports, **336, 337**
Talking down, avoiding, **67–68**
Telegrams
    confirming, **133**
    as follow-ups, **145**
Text analysis programs, **387**
Text editors (*see* Computers)
Thank-you letters
    for compliments, **17, 19, 215–218**
    to customers, **17, 19–20, 173–177**
    for job interviews, **290–292**
    to references, **294–296**
    to speakers, **9–10**
    to suppliers, **159–161**
Thesauruses, electronic, **387**
Time and sequence, confirming, **134**
Titles of addressees
    in letters, **30**
    in memorandums, **308**
TO line of memorandums, **308–309**
Transmittal letters, **125–129**
    for checks, **126–127**
    for contracts, **127–128**
    for materials sent separately, **128–129**
Transmittal memorandums, **312–314, 374**

Unsolicited job applications
    letters for, **289**
    responding to, **37–38**

Vogue words, **49–50**
Voice of verbs, **38–39**

Welcome, letters of, to new customers, **33–34, 147–151, 173–175**
Word processors (*see* Computers)
Words and phrases, reviewing and revising, **42–50**
    biased, **48–49**
    clichés, **49**
    clutter, **43–45**
    jargon, **49**
    pompous, **45–47**
    vogue, **49–50**
Writer-reader relationship, **7–9**
    and formality, **32–33**